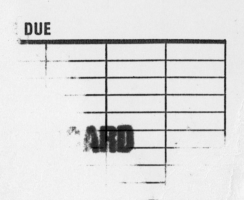

THE TRIUMPH
OF NATIONALISM

THE TRIUMPH OF NATIONALISM

State Sovereignty, the Founding Fathers, and the Making of the Constitution

by

William P. Murphy

CHICAGO

Quadrangle Books

Library of Congress Catalog Card Number: 67-21644

PREFACE

IN 1953, when I became a professor of law at the University of Mississippi and inherited the course in Constitutional Law, the University was still offering an annual prize for the best student essay on the right of the southern states to secede. In May 1954 the United States Supreme Court handed down its historic decision in the School Segregation cases. One month later I supported the Court's decision publicly in a letter to the newspapers in Memphis, Tennessee, and Jackson, Mississippi. A vigorous reply was published by William J. Simmons, who later became executive director of the Citizens Council and chief adviser to Governor Ross Barnett.

The aftermath in the South of the Court's decision is well known and need not be summarized here. The best account of events in Mississippi itself is Professor James W. Silver's *Mississippi: The Closed Society.* The lowest level of criticism advanced in the state against the Court's decision was based on the supposed racial inferiority of Negroes to whites. Although I am a native southerner, having been born and reared in Memphis, nothing in my experience had prepared me for the virulent racism of the most vocal Mississippians. On a somewhat more sophisticated level, politicians and press throughout the state denounced the Court for having violated various alleged fundamental principles of constitutional law and government. The Court, said these sources, had flouted state sovereignty, states rights, the Tenth Amendment, and the federal system created by the Constitution. Nevertheless, as Governor J. P. Coleman told the state, Mississippi could not secede again—the state constitution prohibited it.

In 1957, however, a prominent newspaper editor in Virginia, James J. Kilpatrick of the *Richmond News-Leader,* published *The Sovereign States,* an attempted resurrection of the long-buried doctrine of state interposition. At least ten southern legislatures were thus encouraged to resort to a device repudiated both by law and history since the days of Andrew Jackson. Kilpatrick's thesis, drawn from the Virginia and Kentucky Resolutions of 1798, was that the Constitution of the United States was a compact among sovereign states, and that the government of the United States was therefore an agent exercising powers delegated to it by sovereign states which retained the prerogative of determining when these delegated powers had been exceeded. When Kilpatrick's book appeared I had been engaged for some time in research on the formation of the Constitution, particularly with reference to the question of national supremacy as opposed to state sovereignty. The December 1957 issue of the *Mississippi Law Journal,* a law school publication, carried my highly critical review of Kilpatrick's book, which prompted in the next issue a review of my review by a lawyer prominent in the Citizens Council.

In the naive hope that the educational process might result in some intellectual conversion among the lawyers of the state, I published as an article in the March 1958 issue of the *Mississippi Law Journal* the first part of my research, "State Sovereignty Prior to the Constitution." This was followed by several succeeding articles. The result was that the *Law Journal,* which is subsidized by the Mississippi Bar Association, received numerous protests. In the summer of 1960 I was informed that the *Law Journal* would publish no more of my articles on this subject. I appealed this decision to Dr. Robert J. Farley, the principled and courageous dean of the Law School, who reversed the edict of censorship. Shortly thereafter Dean Farley received a letter from the late Judge Ben Cameron, a Mississippian who was a member of the United States Court of Appeals for the Fifth Circuit. Judge Cameron was disturbed and saddened by the fact that an Ole Miss professor would write and that the *Law Journal* would publish material so destructive of state sovereignty and constitutional government. He suggested that the least Dean Farley could do was to solicit a refutation from some well-known scholarly authority.

I had become *persona non grata* not only for my publications but because of my failure to support the state's official condemnation of the Supreme Court in my Constitutional Law classes. Most of Mississippi's lawyers, judges, and legislators receive their legal education at the University law school, and from the point of view of the state sovereignty and segregation devotees, it was highly undesirable, even suicidal, to have such a "dangerous man" (as they put it) in such an influential position. In 1959 a group of alumni, all Citizens Council leaders, demanded that the Board of Trustees dismiss some twelve members of the University faculty, including Dean Farley and me, for subversion of the Mississippi way of life. University Chancellor J. D. Williams publicly proclaimed his dedication to state sovereignty and segregation, and the Board of Trustees announced with straight face that, although some professors had been "indiscreet," there was no evidence of a communist cell at Ole Miss.

Failing in its ambition to achieve a mass purge, the Citizens Council decided to concentrate its efforts upon eliminating me. In the spring of 1960 a resolution in the State Senate called upon the trustees to dismiss me from the law faculty, and a rider to the higher education appropriation bill would have prevented paying me any salary. That same year the Senate adopted a resolution calling upon the trustees, to dismiss me from the law faculty. A year later the trustees, dominated by Governor Ross Barnett, refused to permit me to teach in the summer session (although they did pay my salary) or to renew my contract for the next academic year. A resolution by the law faculty asking the trustees to rescind these decisions was rejected. Only after Dean Farley personally intervened with Governor Barnett were the trustees willing to grant me leave of absence, which implied continuing faculty status, to accept a one-year visiting professorship at the University of Missouri. The leave was intended to be terminal, and Chancellor Williams advised me that, although I was qualified for tenure status, he would not approve it for me. The Academic Freedom Committee of the Association of American Law Schools investigated the matter and determined that the principles of academic freedom and tenure had been violated. Two respected southern law deans were sent to Mississippi to confer with the trustees and the administration. No action was ever taken, since the temporary appointment at Missouri developed into a permanent position. I resigned from Ole Miss in 1962.

During the entire period, Dean Farley and I received no aid or support (aside from a few private assurances of sympathy) from either the University faculty or the Mississippi bar. In fact, in the spring of 1961 a committee of leading lawyers had sought to have Dean Farley solicit my resignation, and that summer the lawyer members of the Board of Trustees made the same attempt. Being the man he is, Dean Farley refused to cooperate and at all times gave me his fullest confidence and support.

Although this book is based upon the dissertation I wrote for the Yale Law School in the 1950's, and has its further origin in a bizarre personal situation, it is my hope that it may have some permanent value of a wider nature. Mississippians are not the only persons who have believed in or still embrace the sovereignty of the states in the American system of government. As Woodrow Wilson noted in 1908, "The question of the relation of the states to the federal government is the cardinal question of our constitutional system. At every turn of our national development we have been brought face to face with it, and no definition either of statesmen or of judges has ever quieted or decided it." Many persons who today are willing to justify national power as a matter of necessity nevertheless regretfully assert that the states are more and more becoming appendages of the federal government. Diehards will never be reconciled to the modern extensions of national power, but even among those who accept such power as desirable or at least inevitable, there are doubtless many who feel that the constitutional status of the states has been radically altered from what was originally intended. It is my hope that such persons will draw some comfort from the following inquiry into the dialectics of original intent.

I take this occasion to express appreciation to the Research Council and the Law School of the University of Missouri for the financial assistance which made possible the revision of the manuscript.

W.P.M.

Washington, D.C., 1967

CONTENTS

THE TRIUMPH
OF NATIONALISM

Introduction

ANYONE who undertakes a serious study of the formation of the United States Constitution quickly discovers that he cannot begin and end with the year 1787, when the document was drafted. Inevitably he is driven to a study of the preceding years under the Articles of Confederation; it was precisely dissatisfaction with the political system of the Articles which led to their replacement. But the Articles of Confederation, like the Declaration of Independence, were the product of the American Revolution, which was in turn the result of forces and decisions involving British-American relations in the 1760's and early 1770's. The changes which occurred in America between the Stamp Act Congress of 1765 and the inauguration of the new government in 1789 were in turn determined largely by conditions and institutions that had developed over generations of colonial life. Thus, as Robert E. Brown has stated, "The Constitution did not spring full-blown from the pens of the Founding Fathers as something completely new in government. Since it was not a document that was imposed upon the American people by force, we must consider it as the product of a long evolutionary process."

All of these historic events and forces—the Constitution, the Articles of Confederation, the Revolution, the occurrences which produced it, the nature of colonial society—and their relationship to each other have been the subjects of intensive inquiry and analysis. It is not surprising that differing interpretations have been advanced as the correct ones. The present time is one of renewed interest and research in our national origins, and recent years have seen the publication of important and exciting studies which re-evaluate and reinterpret the American past and the period of our beginnings.

Throughout most of the nineteenth century the prevailing image of the Revolutionary leaders and Constitution drafters was drawn in nationalistic, patriotic, and largely uncritical terms. One can say, with only slight exaggeration, that the Declaration of Independence and the

Constitution were viewed as a triumph of liberty over tyranny and order over anarchy, achieved by a band of Homeric heroes whose selfless idealism and noble wisdom were no doubt being directed by the hand of God. The outstanding examples of this school are George Bancroft's *History of the United States* (10 vols., 1834-1874) and *History of the Formation of the Constitution of the United States of America* (1882); and George Ticknor Curtis' *History of the Origin, Formation and Adoption of the Constitution* (1854). The foremost source for the view of the Constitution as having saved America from the chaos and catastrophe which prevailed under the Articles is John Fiske's *The Critical Period of American History, 1783-1789* (1888).

During the first half of the twentieth century, new economic, social, and political interpretations were advanced. Charles A. Beard's *An Economic Interpretation of the Constitution of the United States* (1912) portrayed the Constitution as an instrument drafted by representatives of a privileged minority of property holders, and especially owners of personal securities, to protect their own particular interests against the leveling tendencies of state legislatures. Largely through the influence of Carl Becker's *History of Political Parties in the Province of New York, 1760-1776* (1909) and John Franklin Jameson's *The American Revolution Considered as a Social Movement* (1926), the view became accepted that colonial society was sharply divided between a privileged minority of aristocrats and men of property and a politically powerless majority of the dispossessed. The American Revolution was thus seen in a dual capacity—as a war for independence and as a domestic struggle by the common man for democracy and economic opportunity.

Under this view, the new state constitutions and the Articles of Confederation were the political expression of the Revolution and the ascendant forces of democratic reform. Having been repressed for so long by the apparatus of a central government personified by the Crown, the lower classes believed their aspirations could best be realized under a system in which the new states were dominant and the central authority weak. Leading expositions of this political interpretation are Merrill Jensen's *The Articles of Confederation* (1940) and Elisha P. Douglass' *Rebels and Democrats* (1955). The logical conclusion was that the Constitution was a counterrevolution engineered by the upper classes to restore their political dominance and protect their property interests. The new economic, social, and political interpretations thus reinforced each other, with the result that the Constitution was seen almost as a *coup d'état* resulting from a conspiracy by the few against the many.

In the past twelve years all of the above views have been sharply challenged. Part of Beard's argument was refuted by Douglass Adair in "The Tenth Federalist Revisited" (1951). Robert E. Brown's *Middle-Class Democracy and the Revolution in Massachusetts, 1691-1780* (1955) advanced the proposition that colonial society was largely middle class, with widespread economic opportunity and political participation. The economic interpretation was seriously undermined by Robert E. Brown's devastating analysis in *Charles Beard and the Constitution* (1956). The economic approach was further challenged by Benjamin F. Wright in *Consensus and Continuity, 1776-1787* (1958). The painstaking research of Forrest McDonald's *We The People* (1958) demonstrated that Beard's principal thesis was not supported by, but was in fact contrary to, the available evidence. In a recent work, *E Pluribus Unum: The Formation of the American Republic, 1776-1790* (1965), McDonald has offered his own economic analysis.

The motivations and methods of the framers of the Constitution are likewise being re-examined, although it seems unlikely there will be a return to the view that they were demigods. In "The Founding Fathers: Young Men of the Revolution" (1961), by Stanley Elkins and Eric McKitrick, the nationalism of the framers is depicted as a result of combined patriotic ambition for a stronger country and personal ambition seeking a larger stage on which to operate. The conspiracy-*coup d'état* allegation has been effectively answered by John P. Roche in "The Founding Fathers: A Reform Caucus in Action" (1961), which portrays the adoption of the Constitution as a masterpiece of political skill achieved in an open but largely hostile society by legitimate democratic methods. Current reinterpretations of colonial society, the Revolution, and the Constitution are effectively summarized in Robert E. Brown's *Reinterpretation of the Formation of the American Constitution* (1963). In *1787: The Grand Convention* (1966), Clinton Rossiter pictures the framers as embodying a judicious blend of patriotism and class interest, of idealism and practical experience, and the Constitution as a compromise product representing the best framework of government politically possible of adoption.

To minimize the extent and influence of economic and social divisions in the formative period in effect re-emphasizes the Revolution, the Confederation period, and the Constitution as constitutional and political phenomena. Thus the Revolution is seen as having occurred primarily because of a failure by Britain and the colonies to achieve a successful political relationship: when it became clear that the claimed rights and prerogatives of the colonies could not be assured within the Empire, separation followed. The Articles of Confederation and the Constitution grappled with the ensuing problem of political relations between the new states and the Union. When independence was declared, the question immediately arose whether American aspirations could best be realized through sovereign and independent states or through a strong central authority to which the states were subordinate. State sovereignty prevailed over nationalism in 1776, but nationalists never accepted the result as final. Continuing their efforts and capitalizing on events, they finally achieved their goal in 1789.

Whatever the differences of opinion as to social and economic divisions during the period, there is no controversy at all concerning the existence of a division between nationalists and anti-nationalists. For whatever reasons satisfactory to them, men aligned themselves behind the quest for greater national power or opposed it in the name of state sovereignty. Some individuals changed their position, but the line itself remained clearly drawn.

The purpose of this book is to ascertain to what extent considerations of state sovereignty influenced the adoption of the Constitution. I have not sought to determine the overall political philosophy of the framers but merely one aspect of it: their view on the question of national supremacy as distinguished from state sovereignty. Nor have I tried to analyze—even when these are obvious—the various forces and factors which brought any particular delegate to the Convention to the view he held on the question of state sovereignty. I have sought simply to ascertain what that view was. Frequently, a delegate was more nationalist on some issues than on others. I have examined the many issues dealt with during the Convention solely for the light they may shed upon the question under inquiry; no effort has been made here to explore the many other political ideas which went into the Constitution.

Since I am a constitutional lawyer and not a historian of early America, I feel that the limited inquiry made in this study renders it unnecessary for me to espouse any of the various competing interpretations which have been summarized. The evidence indicates that many persons in the upper or propertied classes were anti-nationalists who consistently opposed strengthening central authority, and that many other persons of less advantaged status were nationalist in sympathy. This would seem to indicate that while economic and social factors may and do influence men's thoughts and actions, they are by no means exclusive, perhaps not even dominant in a given case. Modern psychology supports what common sense would indicate—that human motivations and beliefs were as multiple and complex in the 1780's as they are today.

Since under our system the final interpretation of the Constitution rests with judges, it is rather curious that most of the research into the Constitution's origins has been done not by lawyers but by historians. Since I have presumed to enter the field, I should say that, as I read the record of the period 1776-1789, the Founding Fathers and the Constitution they produced emerge with substantially more nationalism, as a matter of original intent, than most historians have recognized. The difference between me and the historians, I hasten to add, is one of degree and not of principle: knowledgeable and responsible historians do not plump for state sovereignty and the compact theory of the Constitution. And yet they have, I think, attributed to the dominant figures and triumphant forces of 1787-1789 more solicitude and consideration for state prerogatives than actually existed. They have to some extent attributed to the winners the beliefs and attitudes of the losers. They have, in my judgment, been too much influenced by the development of federalism since 1789 and have concluded that its many aspects were original intentions of the framers. Judges have done the same thing, as have statesmen and politicians, and by and large American public opinion has supported if not actually required such an approach.

But what has happened since 1789 is one thing. What the Founding Fathers said and did before 1789 is a separate inquiry. Professor W. W. Crosskey, in his *Politics and the Constitution* (1953), argued that the framers actually intended to create a unitary state, and that our whole constitutional history has been a departure from the original design. Although most scholars have disagreed, Crosskey has not been without some support. The position I have taken in this book does not go so far, but is still, I think, more in the nationalist direction than most historians would go.

Since my analysis of the Convention and ratification debates is primarily a legal one, historians may consider me as a poacher in their own preserve and feel that, as a lawyer, I am inclined more to advocacy than to objectivity. My defenses are that even impartial judges write opinions in the form of argument and that even impartial historians, once they form an opinion, seek to marshal their evidence and argument as persuasively as possible.

The Constitutional Convention and the state ratification conventions occurred, to borrow Edmund S. Morgan's perceptive phrase, "during that brief period when America's intellectual leaders were her political leaders." These leaders had their say in the federal convention which drafted the Constitution and in the state conventions which ratified it. Daniel J. Boorstin has noted that "In that age men were inclined to take their opponents at their word; the Revolutionary debate seems to have been carried on in the belief that men meant what they said." The same may surely be said of the constitutional debates. For that reason, my discussion of the views of the framers, the drafting of the Constitution, and the ratification campaigns is based almost entirely upon the words which were spoken on convention floors. Spelling and punctuation have been regularized to modern forms. All facts and quotations may be found in the sources set forth in the Bibliographical Notes at the end of the book.

Part One:
State Sovereignty
Before the
Constitution

I

Early Conflict Between
State and Nation

INDEPENDENCE from Britain was declared in 1776 by a Continental Congress composed of delegates from the thirteen colonies. This Congress in 1777 adopted and submitted to the new states for ratification Articles of Confederation. Pending state approval, the Continental Congress remained in session to prosecute the war, by and large governing itself by the Articles as though they had been ratified. The Articles became officially operative in 1781, persisting until 1789 when they were replaced by the Constitution.

Almost immediately after the adoption of the Constitution, sharply conflicting conceptions were advanced concerning the nature of the political system under the Constitution—what it was intended to be or ought to be. One position, broadly speaking, was that the Constitution was a compact of sovereign states, that the states retained their sovereignty except to the extent that sovereignty had been expressly surrendered, and that the powers of the central government should be strictly and narrowly construed. The nationalist position, on the other hand, was that the Constitution had been ordained not by the states as entities but by the people of the United States and that it created a supreme central government whose powers should be broadly and liberally construed so as best to effect the objects and purposes expressed in the Constitution itself.

Each position sought to bolster itself by resorting to the experience and history of the period which preceded the Constitution. The one side argued that the states had been sovereign upon separation from Britain, that they had been sovereign under the Articles of Confederation, and that this sovereignty was to continue under the Constitution unless expressly surrendered. Of course, if the states had *not* been sovereign

on separation from Britain or under the Articles, then it would be difficult, if not impossible, to support their sovereignty under the Constitution. Nationalists therefore argued in favor of a national existence and
an exercise of national sovereignty continually since 1776.

Throughout American constitutional history there has been unending
disagreement and contest over the distribution of power between the
central government and the states. The first conflict occurred between
the drafting of the Articles of Confederation in 1776 and the drafting of
the Constitution in 1787.

The Articles of Confederation

THE FIRST Continental Congress, which met in September 1774, went no
further than to advocate what today we would call a dominion conception of colonial status. But by the spring of 1776, Lexington, Concord,
and Bunker Hill were history, *de facto* revolutionary governments had
been organized in the colonies, and the movement toward independence
was sweeping with irresistible momentum to its inevitable end. The delegations to the Second Continental Congress from several of the colonies
had been authorized to declare independence. On June 7, 1776, therefore,
Richard Henry Lee, in accordance with such instructions from the
revolutionary government of Virginia, rose in Congress and moved
"that these United Colonies are, and of right ought to be, free and independent states, and that they are absolved from all allegiance to the
British crown, and that all connection between them and the state of
Great Britain is, and ought to be, totally dissolved." In the same motion
Lee also proposed that "a plan of confederation be prepared and transmitted to the respective colonies for their consideration and approbation."

The drafting and promulgation of the Declaration of Independence
have tended to overshadow what resulted from the second part of Lee's
motion: the drafting and ratification of the Articles of Confederation.
On June 12, 1776, a committee was appointed to draft articles; exactly
a month later it submitted a proposed draft. The Continental Congress
debated the matter during July and August of that year, then dropped it
until April 1777, when it was taken up again and debated more or less
regularly until November. At that time the Articles were finally approved and sent to the states for ratification.

The confederacy created by the Articles was styled "The United
States of America." The nature of the union was described as a "league

of friendship" between the states "for their common defense, the security of their liberties, and their mutual and general welfare." The central government consisted of a single representative body called the Congress, the members of which were chosen by the states in such manner as the legislature of each state might determine. No state was to be represented by less than two or more than seven members, and no person could be a delegate for more than three years in any period of six. Each state was to maintain its own delegates, reserving the right to recall them. Voting in the Congress was by states, and each state had one vote.

Congress was granted the "sole and exclusive right and power" of determining war and peace; sending and receiving ambassadors; entering into treaties and alliances (but no treaty could curtail the power of the states over imports or exports); establishing rules for deciding captures on land and sea; appointing courts for piracies and felonies and determining appeals in prize cases; regulating the value of all coinage, its own and that of the states (but there was no control over state issuance of paper money); fixing a uniform standard of weights and measures; regulating trade with the Indians (except within the territory of any state); establishing post offices; and appointing officers and making rules and regulations for the government of land and naval forces (except that each state reserved the power to make all appointments under the rank of colonel). Congress was to be the last resort on appeal in disputes between states concerning boundaries, jurisdiction, or any other cause. Congress had authority to appoint a "Committee of the States" to consist of one delegate from each state, the committee to sit when Congress was not in session and execute such powers as Congress might vest it with. For the execution of Congress' most important powers, the consent of nine states was necessary; in all other situations a majority of the states was required. All expenses were to be defrayed out of a common treasury, to which each state would contribute in proportion to the value of its land.

Individual states were not to send or receive ambassadors; enter into treaties or confederations with each other without the consent of Congress; lay any imposts or duties which were in conflict with treaties; or, unless they were invaded, engage in war without the consent of Congress. The free inhabitants of each state were to be entitled to all the privileges of free citizens in the several states; traffic into and out of all states was to be free for purposes of trade and commerce; fugitives from justice from one state to another were to be delivered up; and each state was to give "full faith and credit" to the records, acts, and judicial proceedings of all other states. The most important provision of all was Article II which stated that "Each state retains its sovereignty, freedom, and independence, and every power, jurisdiction, and right, which is not by this confederation expressly delegated to the United States, in Congress assembled." Each state agreed to abide by the determination of Congress on all questions delegated to it by the Articles, and all the Articles were to be inviolably observed by every state. The union was declared to be perpetual, and no alteration could be made in the Articles unless by agreement in Congress, and approval by the legislature of every state.

The Dickinson Draft

INDEPENDENCE from Britain confronted the new states with the question of what sort of union they would have. The exigencies of war dictated that some kind was essential, but the nature of the union, particularly the power of the central authority and its relation to the states, provoked sharp disagreement. From 1776 to 1779, Americans divided themselves broadly into two groups over this question. One group consistently advocated a strong central government created along "national" lines and possessed of authority and power paramount to the states. The other group just as persistently espoused a "federal" government in which the central authority was limited and distinctly subordinate to the political sovereignty of the states.

It has been noted that historians disagree over the extent to which this political alignment resulted from and reflected economic and social class distinctions. On one crucial question, however, nationalists and anti-nationalists always differed: whether it was possible for a republican government to exist in a large, far-flung, and diverse community such as the United States. Many persons believed that "republican" or "democratic" principles could survive only in relatively small and compact communities where government would be more directly responsive and responsible to the people. Such persons therefore favored state sovereignty and, within the state, legislative rather than executive or judicial power. Nationalists, on the other hand, thought that centralized power, including strong executive and judicial authority, was essential in order for the United States to compete with foreign nations and to preserve domestic peace and individual liberties, neither of which, nationalists thought, could safely be left to the states.

The contest in the Continental Congress over the Articles of Confederation revealed sharply the division between nationalists and antinationalists. The fact is that the Articles as finally adopted, and as summarized above, were substantially different in their essential provisions from the proposed document which the drafting committee had submitted to Congress in July 1776. The chairman of the drafting committee was John Dickinson, who, after a legal education in London, returned to a successful practice in Philadelphia. He had been a delegate to the Stamp Act Congress in 1765, and in 1767-1768 won great fame for his "Letters from a Farmer in Pennsylvania," in which he argued against Parliament's power to tax the colonies. Although he defended the right of the colonies to self-government, he was as much of a monarchist as a republican. As a delegate from Pennsylvania, he refused to vote in favor of independence. His personal contribution to the original draft of the Articles was so great that the committee's product has forever since been known as the Dickinson draft.

The Dickinson draft would have created a national government with substantial and independent power, and at the same time would have placed severe restrictions on the powers of the states. Most important of all, in the vast area of powers not specifically enumerated or specifically denied, the balance clearly was struck in favor of the nation and against the states. In this original draft, the "sole and exclusive" powers of Congress were not limited by those restrictions which later found expression in the Articles as adopted. Provision was made for a permanent executive, with strong powers and capacity for centralization of authority. The numerous restrictions on the states did not contain those exceptions which diluted their strength in the final form. (All of these provisions will be more fully considered later.) Important as they were, however, they were not the most significant parts of the Dickinson draft. The essential provisions were those which related to the distribution of power between the central and state governments.

Article III provided that: "Each colony shall retain and enjoy as much of its present laws, rights, and customs, as it may think fit, and reserves to itself the sole and exclusive regulation and government of its internal policy, *in all matters that shall not interfere with the Articles of this Confederation.*" And in Article XVIII, which granted power to Congress, it was provided that the United States should not "interfere in the internal policy of any colony, *any further than such policy may be affected by the Articles of this Confederation.*" The significant portions have been italicized. On its surface, Article III appeared to be a recognition and guarantee of state sovereignty. Actually, state sovereignty was limited by the provision that state control over its "internal policy" should not "interfere with" the Articles, including their grants of power to Congress. Similarly, in Section XVIII, the disclaimer of interference by the United States in "internal policy" was to a large and indefinite extent negated by the modifying clause "any further than such policy may be affected" by the Articles. In substance, the powers of the national government were to be the standard by which the internal police powers of the states were to be determined. To put it the other way around, the internal police powers of the states were not to be considered as a limitation on the powers of the United States.

This, of course, was directly opposed to the intent and purpose of the states that had formed revolutionary governments in which the anti-nationalists were ascendant. The state constitutions which were prepared and put into effect by the anti-nationalists endowed state governments with all those powers which attend political sovereignty, including control of war and peace. Members of the Continental Congress recognized that independence could not be declared unless the congressional delegates were authorized by their respective states to declare it, and that "if the delegates of any particular colony had no power to declare such colony independent, . . . others could not declare it for them, the colonies being as yet perfectly independent of each other." As a matter of fact, even after Congress had declared independence, seven states supplemented the action in concert by declarations of their own. If declaring independence was considered within the province and control of the states, it is not surprising that the states which authorized their delegates to the Second Continental Congress to unite with the other colonies did so only on the condition that a state's sovereignty over its internal affairs would be recognized in any such union.

Thus Pennsylvania reserved "to the people of this colony the sole and exclusive right of regulating the internal government and police of the same." North Carolina authorized its delegates to unite "in declaring independency and forming foreign alliances, reserving to this colony the sole and exclusive right of forming a constitution and laws for this colony." Rhode Island delegates were cautioned in their instructions to secure "in the strongest and most perfect manner, its present established form and all the powers of government, so far as relates to its internal police and conduct of our own affairs, civil and religious." Maryland likewise authorized its delegates to join the other colonies in declaring independence and forming a confederation, providing that the "sole and exclusive right of regulating the internal government and police of this colony be reserved to the people thereof." And Virginia, under whose authority Richard Henry Lee had moved for independence and a plan of confederation, included in its instructions to its delegates provision that "the power of forming government for, and the regulations of the internal concerns of each colony, be left to the respective colonial legislatures."

Obviously, such instructions were completely consistent with the beliefs and program of the anti-nationalists, who felt that the kind of democracy they were seeking was incompatible with a strong central government and could only be realized in states which were sovereign in their internal affairs. The Dickinson draft, on the other hand, was equally consistent with the beliefs and program of the nationalists, who disliked and feared democratic rule, and who felt that their best protection lay in a strong central government with broad powers over the states. To achieve this goal in the face of the limiting instructions which the states had imposed upon their delegates required an oblique approach and a certain subtlety of language on the nationalists' part. Hence the apparently unambiguous recognition of state sovereignty in Articles III and XVIII, without which approval of the Articles would have been politically impossible. The true nature of the proposal, however, lay in the phrases italicized above, the latent potential of which was not obvious to most eighteenth-century minds unaccustomed to written constitutions and to their interpretation. After adoption of the draft, the phrases would be available for use to establish whatever degree of national supremacy might be necessary to curb democratic excesses in the states. The language of the draft, then, although it might convey one meaning to the lay mind, was readily adapted by a skilled and trained legal ability to the support of entirely different purposes.

Edward Rutledge of South Carolina, another member of the drafting committee, immediately perceived the essence of the Dickinson draft: it could be used against state sovereignty and hence would be opposed in the Congress. Writing to John Jay in late June, Rutledge said: "I have been much engaged lately upon a plan of a confederation which Dickinson has drawn. It has the vice of all his productions to a considerable degree, I mean the vice of refining too much. Unless it's greatly curtailed it never can pass, as it is to be submitted to men in the respective provinces who will not be led or rather driven into measures which may lay the foundation of their ruin. . . . The idea of destroying all provincial distinctions and making every thing of the most minute kind bend to what they call the good of the whole, is in other terms to say that these colonies must be subject to the government of the Eastern provinces. . . . I am resolved to vest the Congress with no more power than that is absolutely necessary."

Early Debates

ONE OF the principles advanced to justify independence generally was that ultimate political authority resided in the people. When independence was declared, nationalists were quick to turn this theory to their own use in advocating centralized authority. Thus it was argued that the people of the thirteen states constituted one collective people whose representative was Congress, from which it followed that Congress was superior to any state government which represented only a portion of the sovereign people. In the debate on the Dickinson draft during the summer of 1776, James Wilson thus expressed the nationalist position: "It has been said that Congress is a representation of states; not of individuals. I say that the objects of its care are all the individuals of the states. . . . As to those matters which are referred to Congress, we are not so many states, we are one large state. We lay aside our individuality whenever we come here." And Benjamin Rush asserted that Congress represented the people, declaring that we were now a new nation and assuring the delegates that when he sat in Congress he considered himself not a citizen of Pennsylvania but of America. John Adams declared that the purpose of confederation was to "form us, like separate parcels of metal, into one common mass. We shall no longer retain our separate individuality."

Anti-nationalists responded by urging that what the doctrine of the sovereignty of the people really meant was sovereignty of the people organized into states, not a collective people organized into one nation known as the "United States." Members of Congress, therefore, were the representatives of the states from which they came. Roger Sherman of Connecticut specifically asserted that the delegates in Congress were "representatives of states, not individuals." And John Witherspoon of New Jersey at this time made the distinction, later recognized in the Convention of 1787, between a national government which operated on individuals and a federal union of sovereign states. He emphasized that it was the latter which Congress was engaged in creating, a system in which "Every colony is a distinct person."

The Dickinson draft was debated less than a month, in July and August of 1776. Although conflicting views on sovereignty emerged at this time, these early debates centered largely on the questions of representation in Congress, apportionment of expenses among the states, and the disposition of the western lands. The Dickinson draft debates first revealed what was to be repeatedly demonstrated in subsequent American constitutional history: how highly expedient the "national-versus-state sovereignty" arguments were. On the representation question, for example, the large states desired representation in accordance with population and supported their position by "national" arguments. This was true even of those large states which, like Virginia, were on other issues quite emphatic about state sovereignty. And on the question of the disposition of the western lands, the states that had charter claims "to the South Seas" insisted on retaining their state sovereignty, whereas those states with definite boundaries advanced the argument that the lands were the common property of all, and that the Continental Congress had succeeded to British sovereignty in disposing of them. Again, the argument was not necessarily consistent with the position boundaried states might take on other questions. In both situations the "state sovereignty" position prevailed. As to representation, the practice of the Continental Congress—that each colony should have one vote in the determination of questions—was retained in the draft of the Articles, with no consideration being given to population. Where the western lands were concerned, certain clauses in the Dickinson draft would have given Congress powers of "limiting the bounds of those colonies" claiming land "to the South Sea"; of "assigning territories for new colonies" out of lands thus separated from the old colonies; and of "disposing of all such lands for the general benefit of all the United Colonies." These clauses were now eliminated.

Thomas Burke—The First States Righter

IN THESE early stages of the debates over the Articles of Confederation, however, it is generally true that the anti-nationalists do not seem to have realized how latently ambiguous Sections III and XVIII of the Dickinson draft were, or how this uncertainty of language might be construed later on the side of centralization. The nationalists, however, were not content to wait for the adoption of the Articles, an event which might be long delayed or possibly never occur. Instead, they immediately sought to create precedents which would establish the superiority of Congress over the states. In the process they revealed their purpose and brought the attention of the anti-nationalists directly to the question of ultimate sovereignty. The eventual result, once the issue materialized clearly, was that the Dickinson draft was drastically amended, the powers of Congress being curtailed to those which were expressly granted and state sovereignty being asserted unequivocally. The national government contemplated by the Dickinson draft was cast aside in favor of a compact among thirteen independent sovereignties. That such a complete turnabout occurred was due largely to the efforts and energies of a single delegate. A brilliant and tough-minded man, he led the fight against centralized authority so zealously that he may be appropriately called, without historical inaccuracy, the first states righter: Thomas Burke, who came to Congress in 1777 as a delegate from North Carolina.

Burke deserves more attention in American history. He was born in Ireland about 1747, studied at the University of Dublin, and migrated to North Carolina in 1771, where, after a brief career in medicine, he began the practice of law in 1772. Burke represented Orange County in the North Carolina provincial congress, where he was a member of the committee that drafted the resolution authorizing North Carolina's delegates to the Continental Congress to declare independence. As a member of another committee, established to draft a constitution for North Carolina, he was a strong advocate of popular sovereignty, annual elections, separation of the organs of government, separation of church and state, and ratification by the people.

He was elected to the Continental Congress in December 1776, appeared in February 1777, and served until June 1781, with the exception of the period from April to August 1778. His losing his seat in early April 1778 may be traced to his having approved the appointment of a Pennsylvania officer as brigadier over some North Carolina troops. Almost immediately an incident occurred, or more probably was engineered, by means of which he was able to recoup his political fortunes. On the night of April 10, in the course of a debate in Congress, Burke left the meeting hall, thereby destroying the necessary quorum. He refused to return even though Congress summoned him. The next day, when Congress sought to discipline him, Burke stoutly maintained that for his actions in Congress he was accountable only to the people of North Carolina. Thereupon he left the Congress, returned home, and put his case before the North Carolina assembly, which promptly exonerated him. He was re-elected to Congress in August, after having established a strategy which Southern politicians follow to this day. In April 1781, upon being elected governor of North Carolina, Burke immediately began the mobilization of troops and materials with great vigor. He was captured by the Tories in September 1781, escaped in January 1782, returned and resumed his duties as governor. Accounts vary as to whether he refused to run for re-election or whether he ran and was defeated. He died the next year at the age of about thirty-seven. But during his approximately ten years in public life he altered, even though temporarily, the main course of American history.

Burke had barely arrived in Congress in February 1777 when an occasion arose which revealed his extreme sensitivity to any suggestion of encroachment upon what he considered to be state prerogatives. In an effort to bolster lagging attendance in Congress, one of the delegates made a motion which, as amended, would have authorized the presiding officer to make a written request for a fuller delegation from any state whenever the number of its representatives fell below three. Burke, with courtesy but firmness, objected. He stated that he considered it "a matter which each state had an exclusive right to judge of," and he "could not agree that Congress should at all interfere with it." Furthermore, since Burke at the time was the only delegate present from North Carolina, he said he "considered the amendment relative to three as implying a censure on his country and he must therefore protest against it." In the face of this stout defense, the "intention to censure was disclaimed" and the motion defeated. Burke was the man, then, who became alerted to the purpose and design of the nationalists in the Dickinson draft and who, sounding the alarum, more than any other man frustrated it.

II

Failure of a System

IMMEDIATELY upon his arriving in Congress, Burke's suspicions were excited by a debate following a motion presented on February 4, 1777. In December 1776 the New England states, faced with invasion, had held a meeting at Providence for the purpose of discussing the war and developing plans to support it by their collective action. A report of this meeting was sent to Congress, where James Wilson promptly moved to consider whether the Rhode Island meeting had been a proper one and whether it needed the approval of Congress to make it valid. Burke saw clearly the purpose of the motion, for he reported that both Maryland and Pennsylvania were eager to have Congress vote approval precisely because this action would imply Congress' right to disapprove as well. In support of the motion, Wilson argued that the committee of the New England states had sent the report to Congress *for* approval and that "the business the committee transacted was wholly *continental* and of course required the approbation of Congress." John Adams asserted that "the four New England states bore the same relation to the Congress that four counties bore to a single state." Although the states had the right to deal with local matters such as roads and poor laws, he said, "they have no right to touch upon continental subjects." And Benjamin Rush thought that the New England meeting "should be regarded with a serious and jealous eye. Their business was chiefly continental, and therefore they usurped the powers of Congress."

The anti-nationalists, of course, opposed Wilson's motion. Samuel Adams maintained that "a right to assemble upon all occasions to consult measures for promoting liberty and happiness was the privilege to freemen"—a liberty that was "dreaded only by tyrants." Arguing more legalistically, Richard Henry Lee pointed out that the states "were not yet confederated—therefore no law of the Union infringed." Thomas Burke refused to say what his state could not do, declaring he thought she could do everything which she had not precluded herself from by plain and express declaration; to yield up any of her rights was not in his power, and very far from his inclination. The result of the "long metaphysical debate" is not exactly clear. Congress' approval was denied, and Burke reported that he voted against it because it might have set precedent for future disputes. The general opinion, according to Burke, was that "Congress had no right to prohibit meetings, or censure them if the transactions in them were not injurious to others," but that Congress did have "a right to inquire into the causes of any meeting" and "to know what was transacted." William Ellery of Rhode Island, on the other hand, reported to his governor that "Congress were equally divided. All the members agreed that the meeting was right considering the circumstances . . . but split upon the question of right hinted at."

On February 25, 1777, another incident occurred in which the nationalists sought to aggrandize the powers of Congress. Congress had before it a report on desertion, which in its original form recommended that the individual states enact laws empowering constables and others to take into custody suspected deserters and carry them before a justice of the peace. To this report the nationalists offered a significant amendment, as Burke recorded it, that "the power should go immediately from Congress—without the intervention of the states." The amendment passed, Burke said, because many gentlemen were "inattentive." Burke thereupon demanded that his dissent be entered upon the journal. As he interpreted the amendment, "Congress was herein assuming a power to give authority from themselves to persons within the states to seize and imprison the persons of the citizens." To Burke, this was "thereby to endanger the personal liberty of every man in America." He stated that he was not apprehensive of any injury from it in the state which he represented because "it would never there be observed," but that as it was as much as his life was worth to consent to the Congress exercising such a power, he desired that he might be able "to prove from the Journal that he did not." A motion was then made to reconsider, and a debate followed in which the chief protagonists were Burke and James Wilson. Wilson argued that congressional authority extended to all matters of continental concern, which the army certainly was, that preventing desertion from the army was as necessary as raising it, and that Congress had power to authorize persons to execute congressional measures for prevention of the evil.

Burke's lengthy reply reflected the anti-nationalists' philosophical distrust of centralized power. Although he admitted that continental objects were the proper subjects of congressional concern, Burke denied that measures of Congress were to be enforced by congressional authority. Such enforcement "would be giving Congress a power to prostrate all the laws and constitutions of the states because they might create a power within each that must act independently of them, and might act directly contrary to them. . . . This built-in power might render ineffectual all the barriers provided in the states for the security of the rights of the citizens, for if they gave a power to act coercively it must be against the subject of some state, and the subject of every state was entitled to the protection of that particular state, and subject to the laws of that alone." Since only the states were empowered to "act coercively against their citizens," Burke maintained, only the states were "competent to carry into execution any provisions whether continental or municipal." Burke felt that the amendment went beyond giving Congress the right to authorize apprehension of deserters. Congress would also have power to appoint persons to determine who *were* deserters. "If the Congress has the power to appoint any person to decide this question, the Congress has power unlimited over the lives and liberties of all men in America." Furthermore, Burke said, the North Carolina constitution provided that no man should be proceeded against except "under the authority of the laws of the state." The proposed authority for Congress could therefore never be exercised in North Carolina, Burke declared, unless that state's own bill of rights and constitution were no longer operative. Burke further insisted that "civil authority must be derived from the state and not the Congress, and the rules and limits whereby it was to be exercised must be expressly laid down by the states and could not be altered or extended by the Congress unless they had a power over the internal laws of the states which power never would be given." Confronted by such a vigorous defense of state authority, with which a majority of the delegates unquestionably agreed, Wilson was forced to back down.

The very next day a "peevish altercation" occurred over the question of an adjournment by Congress from Baltimore to Philadelphia. Burke moved, on behalf of North Carolina, to put off the question. The rule of the Congress was that voting was by states, with each state having one vote. James Wilson, John Adams, and others now asserted that a majority of Congress, rather than a majority of the states, should decide whether the rule should apply in the instance of adjournment, and whether North Carolina could move for postponement. Burke noted that "a fierce debate ensued." Richard Henry Lee "urged the violent impropriety of putting such a question at a time when a state attempted to avail itself of a privilege reserved to each by the original rules of the

Congress which certainly formed its Constitution." Haywood of South Carolina thought it "a very extraordinary kind of proposition to submit to a majority whether that majority should be checked by a power absolutely reserved for that purpose."

As for Burke, he flatly declared that he would not debate a right which the original Constitution of the Congress specifically reserved to every state. "If a majority of the Congress could vote away the rules of the Congress," Burke said, "then they were a body governed by no rule at all but only by arbitrary discretion, [and] if this was the case, no state was secure, since a majority might vote that two or three states could form a Congress, although the rule required nine," or even that voting "should not be by states but by voice individually." Even to proceed to a vote on the question Burke would consider "a most violent invasion of the right of his state." If the question were put at all, he would know what to do. He said that he hoped he should always have firmness enough to maintain even the smallest privilege of the state he represented; that gentlemen were exceedingly mistaken if they deemed him a man who would tamely suffer an invasion or encroachment on its rights; that if the assembly proceeded to so arbitrary and tyrannical an exertion of power he would consider it as no longer that which ought to be trusted with the liberties of their fellow citizens, and he would shape his conduct accordingly. Other states joined with Burke and North Carolina. The question of adjournment was withdrawn.

These experiences during his first month in Congress made a profound impression upon Burke, who expressed his feelings in a letter to his governor, Caswell, on March 11, 1777. "The more experience I acquire," he wrote, "the stronger is my conviction, that *unlimited power can not be safely trusted* to any man or set of men on earth." Members of the Congress had tried to be "generous and disinterested" in exercising their authority, yet they seemed intent upon increasing the power vested in them. Burke believed this could be explained only by "a plain declaration that power of all kinds has an irresistible propensity to increase a desire for itself." He was disturbed by the time-consuming debates over whether the power of Congress should be increased or restrained. "These and many other considerations make me earnestly wish that the power of Congress was accurately defined and that there were adequate check provided to prevent any excess." And, referring to the adjournment controversy, Burke added, "The last matter in the abstract will show you that even thus early, men so eminent as members of Congress are willing to explain away any power that stands in the way of their particular purposes. What may we not expect some time hence, when the seat of power shall become firm by habit, and men will be accustomed to obedience, and perhaps forgetful of the original principles which gave rise thereto."

State Sovereignty Prevails

THUS when Congress, in April 1777, resumed its consideration of the Articles, Burke was acutely aware of the potential danger the Dickinson draft held for the sovereignty and independence of the states. The third article, he said, "expressed only a reservation of the power of regulating the internal police, and consequently resigned away every other power." To Burke this meant that "it left it in the power of the future Congress or general council to explain away every right belonging to the states and to make their own power as unlimited as they please." Burke added that this did not seem to be what the states expected.

Having evaluated the situation, he moved boldly to deal with it by proposing an amendment which utterly transformed the character of the Articles and completely reversed the contemplated power relationship between the central authority and the states. His amendment, he said, "held up the principle, that all sovereign power was in the states separately, and that particular acts of it, which should be expressly enumerated, would be exercised in conjunction, and not otherwise; but that in all things else each state would exercise all the rights and power of sovereignty, uncontrolled."

In these terms, Burke put the fundamental issue squarely before the Congress. What was to be the distribution of power between Congress and the states? More specifically, was ultimate political sovereignty to reside in the central or in the state governments?

The tremendous import of Burke's proposal was not immediately realized since he had gone so far beyond other delegates in penetrating the matter. He reports that his amendment "was at first so little understood that it was some time before it was seconded, and South Carolina first took it up." Opposition to the amendment came principally from James Wilson. With the issue thus nakedly drawn and clarified by Burke, the result was not unexpected in a Congress in which the antinationalists were a numerical majority: the vote was 11 to 1 in favor of the amendment, with one divided. (Strangely, the one state which opposed it was Virginia.) In its final form, the Burke amendment appeared as Article II of the Articles of Confederation: "Each state retains its sovereignty, freedom, and independence, and every power, jurisdiction, and right which is not by this confederation expressly delegated to the United States in Congress assembled."

Other modifications of the Dickinson draft then followed in the same direction, favoring state rather than national supremacy. The language of Article XVIII previously referred to disappeared completely. Article II of the Dickinson draft had begun by stating, "The said Colonies unite themselves so as never to be divided by any act whatever." This clause, emphasizing a permanent nationality, was now struck by the anti-nationalists. The provision relating to regulation of trade was significantly altered. The Dickinson draft expressly prohibited the states from levying duties or imposts which would interfere with treaties made by Congress. In the amended version, Congress' sole and exclusive power to enter into treaties and alliances was modified by adding provisos that no commercial treaty should restrict any state from prohibiting exports and imports, or from imposing such imposts and duties on foreigners as those to which the state's own citizens were subject. The practical effect of the amendment was that congressional power to make commercial treaties was distinctly subordinate to trade regulation by the states.

The Dickinson draft would have created central authority to settle disputes between individual states by granting to Congress "sole and exclusive right and power" of "settling all disputes and differences now subsisting, or that hereafter may arise between two or more colonies concerning boundaries, jurisdictions, or any other cause whatever." This central power to settle disputes as of right was amended to provide merely that Congress should be the "last resort on appeal" only when petition was made to it by a state. A cumbersome procedure was set forth by which a decision could be reached, but there was no method provided for enforcing any decision. Rather than issuing the binding judgments which the Dickinson draft had contemplated, Congress became an arbitrator whose awards were not necessarily binding upon the states. And for the benefit of those states with land claims, a proviso was added that no state should be deprived of any territory for the benefit of the United States. This refuted the nationalist theory that Congress had inherited from the English Parliament sovereign power over the western lands.

The Dickinson provision that would have created what might be called an executive branch underwent almost complete transformation. Under the early draft, Congress was to create a "Council of States, and such committees and civil officers as may be necessary for managing the general affairs of the United States, under their direction while assembled, and in their recess, of the Council of States." The Council's powers, set forth in a separate article, were to have charge of military and naval operations while Congress was not in session, make contracts, draw upon the money in the treasury, superintend and control civil and military officers of the United States, prepare matters for the consideration of Congress, and even summon Congress into session earlier than the appointed time if deemed necessary. It seems clear that the Dickinson version contemplated the creation of a permanent executive body; and the listing of its powers amply indicates its potential capacity for centralization. In the amended provision, the "Council of States" became the "Committee of the States," the very title indicating the change in emphasis. Instead of having the power to control committees, it became one itself. Instead of being a permanent body, it became one which sat only when Congress was not in session. Instead of having numerous expressly granted powers, it emerged with no powers specifically delegated. It was only to have such power as nine states in Congress might agree to grant it, but Congress was prohibited from vesting it with any of the really important powers—those which could not be exercised without the assent of nine states. All of these emasculating amendments, of course, were accurate reflections of the anti-nationalists' distrust of any strong executive authority.

And so the crucial issue before the Congress was resolved. The Articles as originally drafted would have created a central government of great and potentially vast power to which the states were distinctly subordinate. What finally emerged, after amendment by the anti-nationalists, was a compact among sovereign states which created a central agency with expressly delegated and strictly limited powers but with no independent means of enforcing them. It was a compact in which ultimate power, including the vast area of unenumerated and undefined powers, was retained by the states themselves. As James Wilson said in 1787, comparing the Dickinson draft with the final form of the Articles, "How different!" On May 2, 1777, Burke could write with high satisfaction to his governor reporting an incident in which Congress suspended a captain of a continental ship from his command for having insulted the governor of Maryland. "Every gentlemen (a few only excepted) seem to feel his own state injured in this insult, and they are determined that nothing less should do, than what would satisfy Maryland, and convince officers that they were very inferior to the magistrates of the states, and must treat them with the most profound respect. I never had more hopes of Congress than I have now."

State Sovereignty During the Revolution

WHILE the Articles were before the states awaiting ratification, the war continued under the direction of the Continental Congress. Anyone who studies the actual conduct of military operations can have little doubt that the states were *de facto* sovereign during the period prior to the adoption of the Articles in 1781.

The War for Independence, as a matter of fact, almost foundered due to the lack of centralized power and an excessive attachment to state sovereignty. Congress appointed Washington as commander-in-chief of the Continental Army on June 15, 1775. Throughout the war, the existence of his army depended upon voluntary enlistments and troops supplied by the states. Enlistments were limited and of short duration, and the quotas assigned to the states by Congress were almost never met. The states feared the existence of a strong army operating under a central authority, so they drained available manpower to maintain their own militias. Congress in 1775 had set the size of the Continental Army at twenty thousand, but the peak strength ever attained under a single commander during the entire war was in the summer of 1776 when, in the first bloom of patriotic ardor, Washington had fourteen thousand troops fit for duty. Before the year was out the number had dwindled to fewer than five thousand. And less than six months before Yorktown, Washington noted in his diary that scarcely a single state had one-eighth of its quota in the field.

From Washington's point of view, what the Army desperately needed was that "every matter which relates to it should be under the immediate direction and providence of Congress." Sometimes, he said, he did not know whether he was commanding one army or thirteen. But the necessary power—to draft men into the Continental Army—was one which Congress did not have; largely anti-nationalist, it was not disposed to seek the power since its members considered the power to draft an attribute of state sovereignty. Congress, as a matter of fact, had little sympathy with Washington's efforts to destroy state distinctions in the Continental Army, and a committee which returned to Congress in 1780 from a visit with Washington and sought to impress Congress with his views was charged with being "too strongly tinctured with the army principles."

On one occasion Washington wrote bitterly that if he had possessed a permanent national army from the beginning, "we should not have been for the greater part of the war inferior to the enemy, indebted for our safety to their inactivity, enduring frequently the mortification of seeing inviting opportunities to ruin them pass unimproved for want of a force which the country was completely able to afford, and of seeing the country ravaged, our towns burnt, the inhabitants plundered, abused, murdered, from the same cause." Allan Nevins has written that if "we were to take from Washington's writings those letters in which he complains of the evil results of the compromises between Congress and the states in military affairs, we should reduce his correspondence during the Revolution by almost a fourth; and beyond doubt, if he had possessed a Continental Line of twenty thousand men, well trained, well officered, and serving for the whole conflict, the war would have ended years before it did."

The almost disastrous effects which ensued from the necessary dependence on the states were also manifest in the supplies situation. In this, too, the states were forever delinquent in their quotas, and again there was no adequate central power to expedite matters. Volumes of correspondence flowed back and forth between congressional supply officers and the states. But there was never a period of three months in which Washington did not have to complain of supply shortages, and it was his common plight not to have more than a day's provisions in camp. Many "patriotic" farmers sold their provisions to the British for gold, rather than to the Army for Continental paper money. Congress could not, and the states would not, prevent it. In 1779 Congress summarized its frustration in a circular prepared for transmission to the states: "The inattention in the states has almost endangered our very existence as a people." Feelings of state sovereignty were so deep, however, that the circular was never approved or transmitted.

Throughout the war, the nationalists repeatedly warned that victory could never be attained unless Congress were granted more power. In this they were eventually proved wrong, but there is no doubt that the independence of the states and the weakness of central authority did in fact prolong the war.

State Sovereignty Under the Articles

THE INADEQUACY of the Articles of Confederation in meeting the needs of their time has always been a commonplace in discussions of American history. The years between 1781 and 1789 have traditionally been depicted as a period of increasing political ineptitude and weakness at home and steady deterioration of our status and prestige abroad. The wonder probably is that things were not worse, when the root of the trouble was obvious enough to provide historians with a point of general agreement. The central government was not powerful enough, and it lacked means of enforcing even the limited powers it had been given by the Articles.

The nationalists, of course, had been dissatisfied from the beginning with the lack of centralized power. As the minority in Congress in 1776 and 1777, they had been defeated by various means in their efforts to increase central authority over the states. Although independence had been won through colony-wide cooperation, delegates who were primarily anti-nationalists were interested in the politics of their own state and local governments. Consequently, once they had won the day for state sovereignty, generally speaking they devoted their energies to local matters rather than to Congress and failed to maintain the organization which had brought about their triumph. The effect of defeat on the nationalists was just the opposite. Their ambitions continued, and they redoubled their efforts to realize them. Throughout the period 1776-1789, they kept up a steady drumfire of criticism of the debility of the government and laid responsibility for all political, social, and economic ills on the lack of sufficient central authority. In 1781, when the Articles were ratified, the influence of the nationalists was ascendant in Congress. A campaign to expand congressional power began immediately.

The Articles, it will be recalled, required that for the most important actions of Congress the assent of nine states was required. This meant that even with nine states present, one state could outvote eight, and that if fewer than nine were on hand, Congress could not vote at all. This provision, furthermore, was clear and unambiguous and not susceptible to being avoided by interpretation. On all questions other than those requiring nine votes, however, the Articles provided for determination "by the votes of a majority of the United States, in Congress assembled." If this could be interpreted to mean a majority of the states *who were present at a particular time* rather than a majority of all the states, then Congress might function more effectively. James Madison had just come to Congress as a delegate from Virginia, and it was he who, four days after the official ratification of the Articles, led a group which advanced the construction that only a majority of a quorum was necessary under this clause.

The opposition to this argument was led, naturally enough, by the war horse of state sovereignty, Thomas Burke. Burke recalled the debates during the drafting of the Articles, when Congress had clearly indicated its intent to require seven votes in all cases that did not require nine. In typical fashion, Burke warned that if Congress "attempted so early to claim powers that were not expressly given by that charter, or began to pervert it to increase their power, they would give a dreadful alarm to their constituents who are so jealous of their liberty." After a two-day debate, Burke's view again prevailed. As a result, minority rule was fastened on all congressional action, and the requirement of seven affirmative votes made absenteeism a negative weapon. Irving Brant states that "as an effective lawmaking and executive body, the United States in Congress assembled died right there and then, at the age of six days." Burke, who was to leave Congress a month later to become governor of North Carolina, had stayed long enough to strike one last telling blow against centralized power.

The essential nature of the Articles was best revealed in Burke's brainchild, Article II, which reserved to the states every power, jurisdiction, and right that was not "expressly delegated" to the United States. Article XIII, however, provided that "Every state shall abide by the determination of the United States in Congress assembled, on all questions which by this confederation are submitted to them." By this provision, Madison argued, "a general and implied power is vested in the United States in Congress assembled to enforce and carry into effect all the articles of the said confederation against any of the states which shall refuse or neglect to abide by such their determinations, or shall otherwise violate any of the said articles." No specific provision existed, however, to enforce this implied power. Because it was "most consonant to the spirit of a free constitution" and, more practically, because he realized it was futile to proceed any other way, Madison sought an amendment to the Articles.

In May 1781 a committee which Madison headed, recognizing that the principal defect in the Articles was the lack of an enforcement power in Congress, reported a scheme with a bold and drastic remedy. This was that whenever one or more states refused to abide by the decisions of Congress or to observe all the Articles, Congress should then be authorized to "employ the force of the United States as well by sea as by land" to compel such states to fulfill their federal obligations, and also to seize and hold the property of the states or its citizens, and to cut off its trade with the rest of the United States and the world. The report alarmed the state-sovereignty delegates, and a second committee to which it was referred shelved it and came up in July with a timid plan of its own. This in turn was referred to still a third committee which in August proposed a well-considered plan for patching up the Articles by adding seven new articles to increase the powers of Congress. But no action was ever taken. One final effort was made in October by still a fourth committee to obtain a temporary increase in congressional power, but the surrender of Cornwallis relieved any sense of emergency, and again the matter was dropped.

The problems of peace, however, no less than the problems of war, provided nationalists with ample evidence that a compact of independent states, not subject to any coercive central authority, was a fundamentally defective governmental system. The deficiency was most apparent in the three areas of revenue and finance, regulation of trade, and foreign relations.

During the war Congress had operated financially on a precarious hand-to-mouth basis, obtaining its funds principally through loans obtained in France and Holland, private loans in America, requisitions from the states, and the issuance of paper money. The army was disbanded with a commutation of payment for which certificates were issued. In 1783, therefore, the public debt amounted to roughly $42 million, with annual interest of around $2.4 million.

Obviously, if Congress was to maintain its credit—indeed if the Confederacy was to operate at all—it had to have money. In February 1781, even before the Articles were ratified, Congress asked the states for the power to levy a 5 per cent duty on all foreign imports, the income to be used to pay existing debts, interests, and accruing obligations. This proposal was approved by some states as requested, and approved by others with conditions. But it eventually foundered on the unanimous consent requirement for amendment of the Articles. Rhode Island would not consent on the ground that such a levying power in Congress would be a threat to her liberties as a sovereign state. And Virginia, which had earlier consented, now reneged.

Pending the action of the states on the impost request, Congress in October 1781 made a requisition upon the states for $8 million for the coming year. In January 1783, a year and three months later, less than half a million had been paid. Robert Morris, nationalist leader and superintendent of finance, depicted his plight: "Imagine the situation of a man who is to direct the finances of a country almost without revenue (for such you will perceive this to be) surrounded by creditors whose distresses, while they increase their clamors, render it more difficult to appease them; an army ready to disband or mutiny; a government whose sole authority consists in the power of framing recommendations." Writing to Washington in February 1783, Morris conceded that Congress wanted to do the right thing but that its members were "afraid of offending their states."

In April 1783, with the situation becoming increasingly desperate, Congress tried again. The plan this time requested the states to vest in Congress the power, for a limited period of twenty-five years, to levy a duty on foreign imports, the money to be used exclusively to discharge the public debt and interest, the duties to be collected by agents appointed by the states but acting under orders of Congress. In addition, the states were requested to establish for twenty-five years a substantial and effectual revenue, by whatever means each state desired, out of which each state would pay its proportionate share of $1.5 million to Congress annually. But this proposal fared no better than its predecessor. The truth was that the public debt was another issue involving the politics of national as opposed to state power. Nationalization of the debt would be a step toward a strong central government, since it would require an independent source of national income and at the same time would consolidate the creditor class behind the central government rather than the states. Anti-nationalists saw it as the opening wedge in the ultimate destruction of state sovereignty and local democracy. Their plan was to divide the public debt among the states and let the states pay their own shares. The result was that three years after the proposal was submitted by Congress, only two states had accepted it as offered, seven states had accepted it with varying conditions, qualifications, and reservations, and four states had never approved any part of the plan.

In 1786, when Congress again appealed helplessly to the states to approve the plan, the country was virtually bankrupt. The foreign debt had increased by almost $3 million, and the unpaid interest was rapidly rolling up on the domestic debt. Between October 1781 and the beginning of 1786, Congress had requisitioned from the states a total of $15,670,000. Of this amount the states had paid only $2,419,000—and two states had paid not a penny. In February 1786 a committee of Congress reported that "The crisis has arrived when the people of these United States, by whose will, and for whose benefit the federal government was instituted, must decide whether they will support their rank as a nation."

Similar problems developed in the regulation of trade and in Congress' efforts to obtain sufficient power for protection of commercial interests against competition and discrimination. With the war over, British-made goods poured into the former colony, competing with infant home industries and draining the country of specie. While this trade was being carried on in British ships, American ships were at the same time prohibited by Britain from engaging in the West Indies trade. The first defensive reaction to this commercial warfare was the enactment of legislation by states, but it quickly became apparent that state jealousies and the lack of uniformity in state laws made this a frail and unsuccessful remedy. Again, effective national action was needed, but the Congress had no power under the Articles. Accordingly, in April 1784 Congress asked the states for power to pass navigation acts which would prohibit importation or exportation of any goods in or out of any American port in vessels owned or operated by the subjects of any power with whom the United States did not have a treaty of commerce. Congress also asked for power to prohibit foreigners in this country from importing goods other than those from their native land. This grant of power was to be for the limited period of fifteen years.

While this request for sorely needed authority was pending before the states, Congress, late in 1784, received from James Monroe a committee report which made a far-reaching recommendation for an amendment to the Articles. The proposed amendment would have granted to Congress perpetual power to regulate trade with foreign nations and between the states and to lay duties on imports and exports. Even though the amendment was studded with concessions to state sovereignty, fear of a strong central government was too strong, and the amendment was not even approved by Congress for submission to the states. This quick death did not matter much, for in March 1786 the 1784 congressional request for a fifteen-year power had met the usual fate in the states. Only four states had consented to the request as framed by Congress, six states had conditioned their consent upon amendments and restrictions which they had added to Congress' proposal, and three states had taken no action whatever. In October 1786 Congress issued another futile appeal to the states for favorable action, which was still pending when the Confederation came to an end.

Though the Articles did not confer upon Congress either the power of taxation or the power to regulate trade and commerce, they did specifically provide that Congress should have "sole and exclusive" power of determining peace and war, and of entering into treaties. And each state had bound itself to abide by Congress' determination on all questions submitted to Congress by the Articles. Thus, even though the states were unwilling to grant new taxation and commercial powers to Congress no matter how urgently these were needed, it might have been reasonably expected, when Congress acted within its expressly delegated powers, that the states would fulfill their solemn pledges. As it turned out, sovereignty meant more to the states than the fulfillment of their commitments under the Articles.

By the treaty of 1783, England recognized the independence of the former colonies and agreed to a prompt withdrawal of British troops from within stipulated boundary lines. The fourth article provided that creditors on either side should meet with no lawful impediment to the recovery of their debts at full sterling value. The fifth article required Congress to recommend to the states restoration of all property confiscated from British subjects who had not borne arms against the United States. Persons of any other description—this would include loyalists who had not borne arms—were to have full liberty to go anywhere in the United States and remain unmolested for a year for the purpose of recovering their property. The sixth article declared that no further confiscation of British or loyalist property, or any further prosecution of loyalists, should take place. In 1786 John Jay, nationalist leader and Secretary of Foreign Affairs since 1783, made a succinct summary of the ensuing situation. According to Jay, there had not been a single day since the ratification of the treaty on which it had "not been violated by one or other of the states." In many southern states, laws preventing British creditors from collecting debts, or from recovering other property, were continued in force after the treaty and even amplified. The Governor of Virginia ordered all British subjects and loyalists to leave the state. In many places, riots against the loyalists took place. New York enacted a Trespass Act under which British subjects who relied upon the treaty of 1783 and remained after the peace were faced with trespass actions and confronted with heavy verdicts for damages. Meanwhile, Great Britain refused to withdraw from the lake and western posts as the treaty required, maintaining that she would fulfill her treaty obligations when the United States fulfilled hers.

In the midst of these flagrant violations of the treaty, committed under the aegis of state sovereignty, nationalists assumed the role of defenders of Congress' constitutional prerogatives. In 1784 Hamilton argued in New York, in the case of *Rutgers v. Waddington,* that the Trespass Act was invalid on the ground that it violated a treaty which was superior to state law since it was made under a constitutional power of

Congress "not controllable by any state." In 1786 Jay sought to persuade the states that they were bound by the treaty. "Your secretary considers the thirteen independent sovereign states as having, by express delegation of power, formed and vested in Congress a perfect though limited sovereignty for the general and national purposes specified in the Confederation. In this sovereignty they cannot severally participate (except by their delegates) or have concurrent jurisdiction. . . . When therefore a treaty is constitutionally made, ratified and published by Congress, it immediately becomes binding on the whole nation, and superadded to the laws of the land, without the intervention, consent or fiat of state legislatures." And in the spring of 1787 Congress resolved in emphatic language "that the legislatures of the several States cannot of right pass any act or acts for interpreting, explaining, or construing a national treaty, or any part or clause of it; nor for restraining, limiting, or in any manner impeding, retarding, or counteracting the operation and execution of the same; for that on being constitutionally made, ratified, and published, they become in virtue of the Confederation, part of the law of the land, and are not only independent of the will and power of such Legislatures, but also binding and obligatory on them."

But such brave resolves amounted to no more than a combination of political propaganda and hopeful optimism in the absence of any power to make them effective. The actual respect accorded to the treaty was revealed not only by the repeated infractions of it by the states but also by a resolution of the New York legislature which stated "That while this legislature entertain the highest sense of national honor, of the sanction of treaties, and of the deference which is due the advice of the United States in Congress assembled, they find it inconsistent with their duty to comply with the recommendation of the said United States, on the subject matter of the fifth article of the said definitive treaty of peace." The "sole and exclusive power" of Congress of entering into treaties was thus reduced to mere "advice" and "recommendation" which sovereign states were free to ignore contemptuously and with complete impunity.

The need for more centralized power in foreign relations was further revealed in embarrassing fashion by the depredations which the Barbary powers made upon American shipping in the Mediterranean. As a condition for the operation of American ships in what these piratical states considered their lake, the Barbary powers extorted payments under the guise of treaties and backed up their demands by repeated seizures of American vessels and imprisonment of American seamen. Negotiations with hardbitten rulers who respected only wealth and power were unsuccessful. Too poor to pay and too weak to fight, America could only suffer the continued humiliation. The nationalists were given still another reason for insisting upon greater centralized power.

In ways other than those already discussed, the states manifested sovereign indifference to their obligations to the Congress, even within its own legitimate area of authority. Contrary to the specific prohibitions of the Articles, individual states engaged in war with the Indians, concluded treaties, carried on diplomatic negotiations with foreign nations, organized their own navies, fitted out their own armies, and formed compacts with each other. In the Constitutional Convention in 1787 James Madison, at that time a nationalist, was to ask: "Has not Georgia, in direct violation of the Constitution, made war with the Indians and concluded treaties? Have not Virginia and Maryland entered into a partial compact? Have not Pennsylvania and New Jersey regulated the bounds of the Delaware? Has not the state of Massachusetts at this time a considerable body of troops in pay?"

Congress had to deal with yet another problem under the Articles: it had no permanent seat. Leaving Philadelphia in overnight haste to escape the threat of outraged, unpaid soldiers, it moved to Princeton, to Annapolis, to Trenton, and finally in 1785 to New York, where it sat until its dissolution in 1789. The states were continually lax in maintaining their delegations in Congress. Because the Articles required two delegates for a state to vote at all, a concurrence of nine states for most important actions, and a majority of seven for all others, the Congress was frequently unable to function at all. Between October 1785 and April 1786, for example, there were only three days when as many as nine states were represented in Congress. Further, the declining respect for Congress was reflected in the declining quality of delegates. Whereas the Continental Congress before and during the Revolution had functioned through the elite of colonial leadership, the Congresses under the Articles, with some notable individual exceptions, were composed of mediocre men. Outstanding leaders preferred to exercise their talents where the centers of real power existed—in the states. Congress repeatedly urged and prodded the states to improve their representation in Congress, but in this, as in all other matters, to use Robert Morris' phrase, "talking to the states [was] like preaching to the dead."

Unwilling to grant additional power to Congress or even to respect the powers which the Articles actually gave it, and refusing to observe the limitations expressly placed upon them by the Articles, the states went their own disparate ways, each legislating in its own self-interest. The states in which the ports of entry were located laid duties upon foreign imports for their own enrichment and to protect domestic commerce. In retaliation, the states thus disadvantaged laid taxes of their own upon interstate commerce. The result, as depicted by the nationalists (and therefore probably exaggerated), was a series of retaliatory trade wars and a mass of state legislation which hampered and restricted the free flow of commerce throughout the country. As James Madison said, "New Jersey, placed between Philadelphia and New York, was likened to a cask tapped at both ends; and North Carolina, between Virginia and South Carolina, to a patient bleeding at both arms." Lack of a uniform currency created a monetary confusion which made things even worse. The specie of many nations was in circulation, but the exchange fluctuated sharply from state to state. Voluminous tables of exchange rates encumbered all business transactions and made calculation of value an arithmetical problem of real dimension. Furthermore, counterfeiting was widely practiced, and the clipping of coin was so prevalent that Washington complained that, unless something were done, a man would be forced to travel with a pair of money scales in his pocket. The difficulty was increased by the unreliability and fluctuating value of the paper currencies of the various states.

Many states enacted statutes which favored debtors against creditors; the demand for such legislation was increased when the postwar boom was followed by an economic depression in 1784. This legislation was of various kinds. There were laws which required creditors to settle obligations by accepting property instead of money; which granted such liberal extension of time for the payment of debts as to amount virtually to indefinite moratoria; which prohibited the foreclosure of mortgages; and which closed the courts of the state to suits by creditors against debtors. All of these laws, of course, were in derogation of contracts entered into before their passage and limited the enforcement of all contracts, past and future.

Men of property probably considered the paper money laws to be most subversive of their interests and, indeed, the interests of society at large. Throughout the states there was a constant demand by debtors for the issuance of paper money which would be legal tender for debts. Seven states at one time or another succumbed to the agitation for paper currency. Each additional issue, of course, further depreciated the value and exposed creditors to complete or partial losses on their loans or commodities. The pressures of the debtor classes for remedial legislation were manifested not only by the favorable responsive action in many states but also by the willingness of indebted groups to act directly when legislatures under conservative control failed to move against the interests of creditors. Thus, the armed outbreak in Massachusetts known as Shays Rebellion was a conflict in which bands of farmers, debtors, and malcontents sought to coerce the passage of radical legislation by forcibly closing the courts in much of the interior of the state and even threatening to lay siege to Boston. Congress was powerless to respond to a request by Massachusetts for assistance in quelling the disorder. The uprising was finally put down, but not without causing consternation and alarm in the minds of many persons at what seemed to be a shaking of the very foundations of society.

Six years, then, after the Articles had been ratified, and four years after the treaty of peace had been signed, nationalists were able to describe a scene in which national finances were in a state of practical bankruptcy; national honor was flaunted by treaty violations, and foreign commerce was prey to discrimination and piracy; national government was no government at all, but a debating society of inferior men; Congress was constantly humiliated and degraded and ignored by the states, who would not grant it the powers it needed nor respect the powers which it had; states violated with impunity restrictions placed upon them in a constitution they themselves had created and sworn to obey; commerce and trade were restricted and hampered by conflicting and retaliatory state laws; property values were diminished by fluctuating currencies and subjected to discriminatory legislation; and society itself was threatened by civil violence and insurrection.

No one could doubt that, politically, the Articles of Confederation were a failure. But the view that social and economic chaos and catastrophe prevailed during the period is obviously an *ex parte* presentation of the situation. Too often historians either have not recognized or have not emphasized the fact that "most of the interpretations or evaluations of the Articles were made by nationalists seeking to point out defects and aiming to secure either radical revisions or replacement of the form of government thereby established."

A recent study of the Confederation period by Merrill Jensen presents quite a different picture—of a new nation fairly bursting with energetic activity and making progress in many directions. Jensen emphasizes many social and economic facts not usually found in the traditional literature on the period. Thus, the rapid increase in population, resulting from a large birth rate and a renewal of immigration after the war, brought about a growth in towns and cities and stimulated the migration which pushed settlements ever farther west. The new state constitutions encouraged a far wider and more democratic participation of citizens in government than ever obtained before. The church was disestablished. The concepts of entail and primogeniture were abolished in property law. Criminal codes and prison conditions were improved. The distribution of great loyalist estates confiscated during the revolution resulted in a more democratic pattern of land ownership. Companies were organized to build roads, canals, and bridges. Newspapers and magazines began publication. Medical, social, and humanitarian societies were formed. Banks were founded. Artisans became small manufacturers, with the result that more and more goods were produced democratically. British legal restrictions on American shipping were widely ignored, and trade with France, Holland, and the Orient expanded so that shipping tonnages increased everywhere throughout the states. The discriminatory trade laws between states were actually few; reciprocity and trade between states was the rule rather than the exception. Agricultural production increased, despite the fact that many farmers suffered because of the scarcity of specie and because of the farmer's perennial predicament—selling in a buyer's market and buying in a seller's. Boundary disputes between states were settled amicably, and by 1787 all states but Virginia had repealed those laws which conflicted with the treaty of 1783.

This catalog of achievements certainly does not seem to reflect a "critical period" of social chaos and economic stagnation. On the contrary, it conveys a picture of what must have seemed to many men to be an evolution of the good society. This more favorable appraisal of economic and social conditions does not of course gainsay the basic criticism of the nationalists—that politically the central government was weak to the point of virtual impotence.

From the nationalists' point of view, the lack of a strong central authority independent of and superior to the states was the great flaw and inadequacy of the Articles. This is what they were out to change. They set about accomplishing their nationalist ends like the able politicians they were. Organizing and maintaining a vigorous campaign throughout the states, nationalists and their partisan lawyers and newspapers emphasized the actual and imagined ills of the times and linked these ills directly to a faulty political system. Most of the published writings of the Confederation period, as a matter of fact, emanate from nationalist sources. The success of the campaign is demonstrated by the fact that nationalist *ex parte* writings—an inseparable blend of factual reporting and political propaganda—have been widely accepted by succeeding generations of Americans as good and true history.

The National Sovereignty Argument

The political system created by the Articles has been described as a compact of independent and sovereign states. It should be noted, in all fairness, that this description has not been unanimously accepted by constitutional historians. A debate over the nature of the government during the Confederation period began almost immediately after the adoption of the Constitution and has been going on ever since. In the early days of the Constitution as well as in the present, many historians have taken the position that national sovereignty existed from the moment independence was declared. They have denied that the states were ever sovereign in the period prior to the Constitution. It is therefore necessary to examine the case they present for the existence and exercise of national sovereignty during the Confederation period.

Emphasis is placed, first of all, on the fact that, prior to the adoption of the Articles, the Continental Congress exercised national functions for national purposes. The strongest case for the existence of a clearly recognized and exercised national sovereignty is therefore found in the fields of war, peace, and foreign relations. And in support of this position an unexpected witness is summoned forth.

Even before the adoption of the Articles, which expressly authorized the practice, Congress had created a procedure for hearing appeals from the states in cases of captures and prizes. In one such case the decision of a Pennsylvania court of admiralty was reversed by the congressional Commissioners of Appeal. Pennsylvania refused to execute the award of the Commissioners on the ground that the state law was supreme. To consider the matter, Congress appointed a committee of which Thomas Burke, the champion of state sovereignty, was chairman. The report of Burke's committee unpredictably asserted that disputes concerning captures "must be determined by the law of nations," that "the power of executing the law of nations is essential to the sovereign supreme power of war and peace," that Congress "is by these United States invested with the supreme sovereign power of war and peace," and that therefore the right of appeal to Congress in prize cases could not be destroyed by the "act of any one state." This report was adopted unanimously by all the states except Pennsylvania.

The question, of course, is: How can the committee's position be reconciled with the Confederation? One possible answer is that, although Burke certainly intended to retain the bulk of governmental power for the states and to deny any extension by implication of powers expressly granted to Congress, he nevertheless recognized that certain powers were rightfully national and that, as to these, sovereignty rested not with the states but with the Congress. Even before this incident occurred, Burke had written to Governor Caswell that "it was the proper policy of America to maintain that the American states stand in no other relation to Britain than as an independent empire at War with her."

Burke's view later received judicial recognition. The case of *Penhallow v. Doane,* decided by the Supreme Court in 1795, raised the same question considered by Burke's committee. A congressional commission of appeal had reversed a prize decision of a New Hampshire admiralty court. New Hampshire argued that upon casting off allegiance to the crown, the colonies had become distinct, independent states, and that Congress was a convention of ambassadors from sovereign states. New Hampshire denied that Congress had the exclusive power of war. The Court was unanimous in upholding congressional authority. Under the custom of that time, each of the four justices who decided the case delivered a separate opinion; all four opinions recognized the supremacy of Congress in the field of foreign relations. In discussing the situation before the ratification of the Articles, Justice Paterson stated:

> The powers of Congress were revolutionary in their nature, arising out of events, adequate to every national emergency, and co-extensive with the object to be attained. Congress was the general, supreme, and controlling council of the nation, the center of the union, the center of force, and the sun of the political system. To determine what their powers were we must inquire what powers they exercised. Congress raised armies, fitted out a navy, and prescribed rules for their government. Congress conducted all military operations both by land and sea. Congress emitted bills of credit, received and sent ambassadors, and made treaties. Congress commissioned privateers to cruise against the enemy, directed what vessels should be liable to capture, and prescribed rules for the distribution of prizes. These high acts of sovereignty were submitted to, acquiesced in, and approved of, by the people of America. In Congress were vested, because by Congress were exercised with the approbation of the people, the rights and powers of war and peace. In every government, whether it consists of many states or of a few, or whether it be of a federal or consolidated nature, there must be a supreme power or will; the rights of war and peace are component parts of this supremacy, and

incidental thereto is the question of prize. If it be asked, by whom, during our revolutionary war, was lodged, and by whom was exercised this supreme authority, no one will hesitate for an answer. It was lodged in, and exercised by Congress; it was there, or nowhere; the states individually did not, and, with safety, could not exercise it. Disastrous would have been the issue of the contest, if the states, separately, had exercised the powers of war. For, in such case, there would have been as many supreme wills as there were states, and as many wars as there were wills. Happily, however, for America, this was not the case, there was but one war, and one sovereign will to conduct it. The danger being imminent, and common, it became necessary for the people or colonies to coalesce and act in concert, in order to divert, or break, the violence of the gathering storm; they accordingly grew into union, and formed one great political body, of which Congress was the directing principle and soul. As to war and peace, and their necessary incidents, Congress, by the unanimous voice of the people, exercised exclusive jurisdiction, and stood, like Jove, amidst the deities of old, paramount, and supreme. The truth is, that the states, individually, were not known nor recognized as sovereign by foreign nations, nor are they now; the states collectively, under Congress, as the connecting point, or head, were acknowledged by foreign powers as sovereign, particularly in that acceptation of the term, which is applicable to all great national concerns, and in the exercise of which other sovereigns would be more immediately interested; such, for instance, as the rights of war and peace, of making treaties, and sending and receiving ambassadors.

The next year, 1796, Justice Chase expressed his view on the matter in the case of *Ware v. Hylton*. Referring to the Declaration of Independence, Chase stated:

> I consider this as a declaration, not that the United Colonies jointly, in a collective capacity, were independent states, etc., but that each of them had a right to govern itself by its own authority, and its own laws, without any control from any other power on earth. . . . From the 4th of July, 1776, the American states were *de facto* as well as *de jure*, in the possession and actual exercise of all the rights of independent governments . . . all laws made by the legislatures of the several states, after the declaration of independence, were the laws of sovereign and independent governments.

But this apparently unequivocal assertion was later in his opinion substantially qualified.

> It has been enquired what powers Congress possessed from the first meeting, in September, 1774, until the ratification of the articles of confederation, on the 1st of March, 1781? It appears to me, that the powers of Congress, during that whole period, were derived from the people they represented, expressly given, through the medium of their state conventions, or state legislatures;

or that after they were exercised they were impliedly ratified by the acquiescence and obedience of the people. After the confederacy was completed, the powers of Congress rested on the authority of the state legislatures, and the implied ratifications of the people; and was a government over governments. The powers of Congress originated from necessity, and arose out of and were only limited by, events; or, in other words, they were revolutionary in their very nature. Their extent depended on the exigencies and necessities of public affairs. It was absolutely and indispensably necessary that Congress should possess the power of conducting the war against Great Britain, and therefore if not expressly given by all (as it was by some of the states), I do not hesitate to say, that Congress did rightfully possess such power. I entertain this general idea, that the several states retained all internal sovereignty; and that Congress properly possessed the great rights of external sovereignty.

Each of the justices in these two cases based his opinion that Congress possessed an external sovereignty over foreign affairs on a finding that there was either an implied or an express grant of the power to Congress by the states, or an acquiescence in the exercise of such power, arising out of the necessity for united action against the common enemy.

The external area of foreign affairs is not the only one, it has been argued, in which a national sovereignty existed prior to the Constitution. Historians point out that Article I of the Articles recognized the existence of a political body entitled "The United States of America." To the Congress created by the Articles was granted by that document certain "sole and exclusive" powers, many of which dealt with matters of internal and domestic concern. The Articles also laid express prohibitions upon the states to prevent their interference with the Congress in the area of its delegated powers. It is therefore maintained that the Articles clearly recognized a national authority which was to have national sovereignty over certain matters of national concern.

There is also the matter of the western lands. By their royal charters many of the colonies were entitled to lands west of the Appalachians. When independence was declared, the newly formed states asserted title claims. The states which did not have land claims advanced the theory that sovereignty over the western territory had devolved from the Parliament to the Congress, but the language in the Dickinson draft providing for congressional power over such lands was scrapped in favor of a proviso recognizing state sovereignty. The landless states were dissatisfied and felt that the western lands should be surrendered to the central government; Maryland delayed the adoption of the Articles until 1781 for this very reason. Between 1781 and 1786 most of the landed states successively ceded their western claims to Congress, which thus came into possession of millions and millions of acres in the name of "The United States of America." To provide for the government of this territory and its eventual organization into states, Congress enacted in 1787 the Northwest Ordinance. These events subsequent to the adoption of the Articles, it is maintained, constitute specific evidence of a national unity recognized by all of the states and the exercise of a national sovereignty over nationally owned territory.

Finally, the writings and utterances of the leaders of the period are also adduced in support of the position that there was national existence and national sovereignty. The rhetoric of the time was rich in words and phrases which mirrored the users' recognition of the United States as a free, sovereign, independent nation. This "diction of sovereign nationhood" is present not only in diplomatic correspondence and treaties but also in personal correspondence and writing from 1776 on.

That Americans in later years, and even today, have been unable to agree upon the essential nature of the government which existed before the Constitution is not so surprising if we remember that the political leaders themselves during and after the Revolution were in fundamental dispute about it. But the disagreement has another and more revealing explanation. Adherents of conflicting positions have examined the history of the period between 1776 and 1789 in search of evidence to support their own particular interpretation of the Constitution which replaced the Articles. In the process, both sides have operated under a logical fallacy. The nationalists thought that in order to disprove state sovereignty *after* the Constitution, they had to show that it did not exist during the Confederation. And the states righters thought that they could prove state sovereignty under the Constitution by proving it before the Constitution. Since all historical research and writing requires both the selection and the interpretation of facts, it should come as no surprise that each side was able to "prove" its case by historical evidence.

A prime example of the equivocal use of the facts of history occurred in the Constitutional Convention in a debate over the effect of the Declaration of Independence. In its opening sentence the Declaration referred to "one people" assuming "among the powers of the earth" a "separate and equal station." In the last paragraph the Declaration stated that "these united colonies are, and of right ought to be, free and independent states." In the convention, Luther Martin and James Wilson clashed over what the true effect of the Declaration was. To Martin it was clear that the separation from Great Britain "placed the thirteen states in a state of nature toward each other," that "the people of America preferred the establishment of themselves into thirteen separate sovereignties instead of incorporating themselves into one." Wilson, on the other hand, "could not admit the doctrine that when the colonies became independent of Great Britain, they became independent also of each other." He read the Declaration of Independence, observing that "the United Colonies were declared to be free and independent states," and inferring that "they were independent, not individually but unitedly."

III

Prelude to Nationhood

IN THE context of such sustained historical disagreement, one can only state his own view without any hope of settling the question. It seems clear that state sovereignty prevailed in the period under discussion. But since there is no single definition or concept of "sovereignty" which is universally accepted, an additional word of explanation should be offered of the sense in which the term is used here. To say that the states were sovereign before the adoption of the Constitution means that there was no superior authority, either in law or in fact, to which the states were required to yield. Certainly it is true that the states were incompetent separately to accomplish many of the purposes which the times and the needs of the people demanded; for the realization of certain objectives, centralized, coordinated, and unified action was essential. It is also true that the central government was authorized to exercise, and did exercise, national power for national purposes. But when these things are admitted, certain irrefutable practical facts remain. The central government had no national existence or authority independent of its creators. It was the subservient creature of the states, operating, with minor exceptions, through the states rather than directly on the people. It had only narrow powers resulting from express grant, with no room for powers by implication. And even within the area of express power, it had no power of enforcement against the states. Both before and during the Articles of Confederation, central authority existed and was exercised just so far as the states were willing to recognize and accept it, and no further. It is doubtless true that, in the consciousness of many people, there was an American nationality. But there was no national government; there was only a central common agency. In the final analysis, the states were *de jure* and *de facto* supreme. For this reason, so far as the system of government before the Constitution may be described in words, it is most accurately referred to as a compact among sovereign states.

The Articles of Confederation, short-lived though they were, nevertheless constituted a necessary transitional step between the Declaration of Independence and the adoption of the Constitution. In 1776 the American people revolted against a foreign government which exercised strong central authority. At that time they were simply unwilling to replace it with another strong central government, even of domestic origin. Hence the fate of the Dickinson draft and the triumph of Thomas Burke. But the victory of 1777 for the forces of state sovereignty was destined to be only temporary. It lasted, as a matter of fact, only ten years, and, ironically, the very principle for which Burke fought proved in practice to contain the seed of its own destruction. For the practical consequences of state sovereignty during the revolution were almost disastrous to the cause of independence. Once independence was achieved, the Articles of Confederation offered convincing evidence that a system based on state sovereignty was inadequate to the needs and aspirations of the American people.

From an economic and social point of view, the "chaos and catastrophe" version of the Confederation period is largely discredited. Through strong personal initiative the people moved ahead, especially after the economic depression of 1784. But progress was achieved in spite of the political system, rather than as a result of being stimulated by it. Without strong central authority herself, America found it steadily more difficult to compete in a world of powerful national states. Domestically, with the increasing debility of Congress, the dissolution of the union loomed more and more as a serious danger. There was much talk of three confederacies, and with Britain and France waiting in the wings, dissolution of the union was likely to destroy the magnificent achievement and splendid promise of independence. In the minds of many men, republican government hung precariously in the balance. By 1787, even anti-nationalist leaders recognized and admitted that there were national problems which demanded national solutions and that the central government needed more power. This might have been accomplished by amending the Articles to confer the necessary power upon Congress. That events did not unfold in this manner may be attributed to a cohesive group of nationalist leaders—men of rare intelligence and ability—who knew what they wanted and moved with great political skill to achieve it.

Having been defeated in the drafting of the Articles, the nationalists immediately upon their adoption sought to strengthen the central government, first by construction and then by amendment. But while they wanted additional power for Congress so long as the Articles were in effect, the nationalists never accepted the Articles and the type of government created by them as permanent institutions for the United States. The Articles provided for a confederation type of government in which the central authority was the creature of the states, acting through the states, and hence, in final analysis, no matter how many additional powers it might be granted, subordinate to the states. What the nationalists wanted was a central government independent of the states and paramount to them both in law and in fact. Like the anti-nationalists in 1776, the nationalists ten years later shrewdly and boldly seized the historic opportunity afforded by a climate of opinion favorable to political change.

During the Confederation period, nationalist leaders regularly and vigorously wrote and spoke in favor of a strong central government. Giving action to their words, by a series of shrewdly timed maneuvers they brought about the series of events which finally culminated in the Constitutional Convention. The idea of providing for an adequate government through a convention had been advanced by Alexander Hamilton in 1780, even before the Articles had been ratified. In 1783 he tried without success to persuade Congress to pass resolutions declaring the inadequacy of the Confederation and calling for a convention drawn from all the states to remedy its defects. In 1785 Massachusetts nationalists had elected their leader, James Bowdoin, as governor and were temporarily in control. Under Bowdoin's leadership they seized the opportunity to put through the legislature a resolution calling for a convention to recommend enlargements of the power of the central government. In 1786, having consulted with Washington and others at Mount Vernon, Madison was instrumental in bringing about the adoption by the Virginia legislature of a resolution calling on all the states to send commissioners to a meeting which would consider the whole subject of the trade and commerce of the United States. This resolution led to the Annapolis convention which met in September 1786.

The moving spirits at the Annapolis Convention were Alexander Hamilton and James Madison. The meeting was attended by other well-known nationalists interested in commercial reform, and although it did not realize its immediate purpose, because most of the states sent no delegates, it nevertheless afforded an opportunity to send out the call for a general convention. The Annapolis delegates therefore unanimously adopted a report drafted by Hamilton which proposed that a convention of delegates from all the states meet at Philadelphia on the second Monday in May 1787, "to take into consideration the situation of the United States, to devise such further provisions as shall appear to them necessary to render the constitution of the federal government adequate to the exigencies of the Union; and to report such an act for that purpose to the United States in Congress assembled, as, when agreed by them, and afterwards confirmed by the legislatures of every state, will effectually provide for the same."

Congress, led by the adherents of state sovereignty, opposed the idea as being an encroachment on its own prerogatives; it is of course true that the Articles provided that amendments should be proposed by Congress and made no mention of a convention. Moving against this opposition, the nationalists sought to bring sufficient pressure for favorable action by Congress. Without waiting for congressional sanction, the Virginia legislature, led by Madison, approved the recommendation of the Annapolis convention and appointed its delegates to the convention; they were headed by Washington and included Madison, Governor Edmund Randolph, and George Mason. New Jersey and Pennsylvania acted before the year was out, adding to the list of delegates other names which were illustrious throughout the states. Early in 1787 North Carolina and Delaware appointed delegates. In New York, Hamilton, despite opposition from Governor Clinton, managed by masterful political maneuvering to carry a resolution in which the legislature called upon the state delegation in Congress to press for a convention. Massachusetts, under the leadership of Bowdoin, was next in appointing delegates, with Rufus King, who had originally opposed the idea, now approving and becoming a delegate himself.

Under the pressures of this campaign, Congress yielded. To save face, however, it issued a recommendation that made no reference to the Annapolis Convention but made its own convention proposal correspond in terms of time and place with the proposal recommended by the Annapolis delegates. The resolution furthermore was careful to limit the purpose of the convention to a revision of the Articles of Confederation, and it expressly provided that amendments and new provisions were to be reported to Congress for its approval and for subsequent unanimous state ratification as required by the Articles.

A consideration of the events which culminated in the calling of the Philadelphia meeting, and of the men who brought these events to pass, leaves no room for doubt on one very important point. The Constitutional Convention of 1787 was the result of a carefully executed plan and program which was carried out under the leadership of those individuals who, throughout the Confederation period, had consistently adhered to the view of national supremacy over the states. Thus the two dominant facts of the period from 1776 to 1789 were the failure of a political system based on state sovereignty and the existence of an able nationalist leadership to capitalize on that failure. The result of the conjunction of these two facts was that the Articles of Confederation, instead of being amended, were completely abandoned. They were replaced by a new and fundamentally different document, the Constitution of the United States, in the creation of which the nationalists in large measure realized their desires and in the process assured themselves immortal roles as Founding Fathers.

Part Two:
The Founding
Fathers

IV

Summer in Philadelphia, 1787

To THE Constitutional Convention which met in Philadelphia in 1787 came delegates from twelve states, Rhode Island being the exception. Seventy-four delegates altogether had been chosen by the state legislatures, but nineteen of these men either declined their appointments or failed to attend the convention. Notable absentees were Thomas Jefferson and John Adams, who were on diplomatic assignments to France and England. Of the fifty-five who did attend, many were present only part of the time, some of them very briefly or sporadically. The average daily attendance was about thirty, and no more than eleven states were represented at any one time.

If the delegates to the convention were not, as Jefferson referred to them, "an assembly of demigods," then certainly by any relevant standard they were a remarkable collection of political leaders. Collectively they possessed credentials of ability and experience which amply qualified them for their undertaking. Three men had attended the Stamp Act Congress and seven the First Continental Congress. Eight of them had signed the Declaration of Independence. At least thirty had rendered military service during the Revolution, over forty had served in Congress under the Articles, and five had attended the Annapolis Convention. About twenty had participated in the drafting of their own state constitutions, and all but a few had been officials in state governments. Seven delegates were governors. As Clinton Rossiter has said, "No gathering of the leaders of a newly independent nation at any time in history has had more cumulative political experience than the Convention of 1787." The Convention was to contribute to the future government under the Constitution two Presidents, over twenty-five senators and congressmen, five Supreme Court justices, and four ministers to foreign countries.

Sociologically and economically, the majority of the delegates came from middle-class backgrounds; fifteen of them, however, were born aristocrats and a few had worked their way up from the lower levels. Eight had been born outside America, and sixteen represented states other than those in which they had been born. Educationally, their qualifications were impressive. About thirty were college graduates; many had studied abroad. About three dozen had studied law, although only a dozen or so were in active practice. Thirteen were planters or large-scale farmers, and about the same number were men of commerce and business. Many were state office-holders, and there was a smattering of small farmers and doctors. The majority were men of substantial means; about ten were wealthy, and the same number were in modest circumstances. Sixteen were slaveholders.

Only twelve of the delegates were older than fifty-four; six were under thirty-one. The average age was about forty-two; many of those who played leading roles were in their thirties. They knew that the future of America and consequently their own and their posterity's fortunes would be intimately affected by what the convention did or failed to do. There is no doubt that they were conscious that they met at an important moment in history. They were not motivated by selfish motives alone, but being men, they were not completely selfless. Private and public fortune were inextricably interwoven; personal and patriotic ambition coincided.

The convention began on May 25 and adjourned on September 17; in the end, thirty-nine delegates signed the Constitution. During this period of almost four months, the convention met in private sessions with all members sworn against disclosure of the proceedings. Secrecy was imposed to free the delegates from any sense of political restraint in the expression of their views and thus to encourage the maximum possible freedom of discussion and deliberation. The rule achieved its purpose, for the delegates debated the issues before them with a candor and frankness extremely rare in popular assemblies. This is revealed by the records which, fortunately for succeeding generations, many of the delegates kept. Although in terms of volume these records do not begin to approximate everything which must have been said over the four-month span of debates and proceedings, there is no historical doubt that they give an accurate summary of the views of the delegates. The most frequent speakers were, in order, Gouverneur Morris, 173 speeches; James Wilson, 168; James Madison, 161; Roger Sherman, 138; George Mason, 136; and Elbridge Gerry, 119. The purpose of this part is to ascertain, wherever possible from their own words in the convention, the attitudes of the framers of the Constitution on the fundamental proposition of state sovereignty versus national supremacy. Delegations are discussed in the order of their appointment by states.

V

Delegates from Virginia

George Washington

MORE than any other person at the convention, Washington as commander-in-chief of the Continental Army had personally experienced the consequences of the impotence of the central government and the sovereignty of the states. His correspondence during the years before the convention clearly reveals the strong opinions he had formed on the subject. A letter to Dr. William Gordon in July 1783 set forth Washington's view of the basic difficulty: ". . . certain I am that, unless adequate powers are given to Congress for the general purposes of the federal union, we shall soon moulder into dust, and become contemptible in the eyes of Europe, if we are not made the sport of their politics. To suppose that the general concerns of this country can be directed by thirteen heads, or one head without competent powers, is a solecism, the bad effects of which every man who has had the practical knowledge to judge from, that I have, is fully convinced of though none perhaps has felt them in so forcible and distressing a degree."

In a letter to John Jay in August 1786, Washington stated the remedy succinctly: "I do not conceive we can exist long as a nation without having lodged somewhere a power, which will pervade the whole Union in as energetic a manner as the authority of the State governments extends over the several States." In his letter to Dr. Gordon, Washington elaborated his conception of the proper relationship which should prevail between nation and state. Other nations, he said, think of us as a union of states. Foreign powers care as little about the entities of Massachusetts and Virginia as those states care about the counties in other states. Counties, like states, Washington continued, have local policies and interests which should be attended to by the states. But when the policies and interests of counties and states run counter to the general interests of state and nation respectively, said Washington, the voices of county and state "should be heard no more." Otherwise why do the states pretend to be united, and why does the Congress work so hard on plans which embody the provisions of the Constitution? The members of the Congress are "creatures of the people" and must answer to the people, he wrote, so what danger can there be in giving the Congress its proper powers? It is clear that Washington considered some matters too local in their nature to be of national importance, but what concerned the union at large was a determination to be made by the central authority and not by the states, since it was a question which turned on considerations not local in their nature. Washington made his position perfectly clear in a letter to James McHenry in August 1785:

We are either a united people under one head, and for federal purposes, or we are thirteen independent sovereignties eternally counteracting each other. If the former, whatever such a majority of the states as the Constitution points out conceives to be for the benefit of the whole, should, in my humble opinion, be submitted to the minority. . . . I confess to you, candidly, that I can foresee no evil greater than disunion; than those unreasonable jealousies (I say unreasonable, because I would have a proper jealousy always awake, and the United States on the watch to prevent individual states from infracting the Constitution with impunity) which are continually poisoning our minds and filling them with imaginary evils for the prevention of real ones.

It is also clear from Washington's correspondence that he recognized the necessary reforms could not be effected without a drastic overhaul in the governmental structure. Writing to Madison in November 1786, Washington said, "Without an alteration in our political creed, the superstructure we have been seven years in raising, at the expense of so much treasure and blood, must fall. . . . Thirteen sovereignties pulling against each other, and all tugging at the federal head, will soon bring ruin on the whole; whereas a liberal and energetic Constitution, well guarded and closely watched to prevent encroachments, might restore us to that degree of respectability and consequences, to which we had a fair claim and the brightest prospect of attaining." And on the eve of the Convention, in March 1787, Washington again wrote to Madison, expressing his concern about public virtue. To provide the sovereign central power with "the means of coercion," Washington told Madison, members of the convention ought to "probe the defects of the Constitution to the bottom, and provide a radical cure, whether they are agreed to or not." Washington was afraid, however, that the public mind was too immature for such an important change. Writing to Jay in March 1787 he said: "My opinion is, that this country has yet to *feel* and *see* a little more before it can be accomplished. A thirst for power, and the bantling—I had like to have said MONSTER—sovereignty, which have taken such fast hold of the states individually, will, when joined by the many whose personal consequence in the line of state politics will in a manner be annihilated, form a strong phalanx against it."

At first reluctant to become a delegate for reasons of personal health and finances, Washington was finally persuaded, chiefly by Madison and Randolph, that his prestige would be instrumental in the success of the effort. He was unanimously chosen as presiding officer, and therefore, with one exception, did not enter into the debates. It is clear that throughout the convention he maintained his earlier views.

The records define Washington's position as a member of the Virginia delegation on seven specific matters. Significantly, in the three which dealt with the executive, Washington favored an increased power and independence in the executive—an article of the nationalist faith. Thus, he preferred a single rather than a plural executive, he opposed a plan providing for election of the executive by Congress and prohibiting re-eligibility, and he was against reducing from three-quarters to two-thirds the congressional majority necessary to override a veto. It may safely be assumed that Washington's nationalist views were generally known to the other members of the convention. Between May 30 and June 19, when the Convention sat as a committee of the whole, Nathaniel Gorham of Massachusetts presided and Washington sat on the floor. In these three weeks the convention took its most advanced nationalist positions. Luther Martin later reported to the Maryland legislature: "The honorable Mr. Washington was then on the floor, in the same situation with the other members of the convention at large, to oppose any system he thought injurious, or to propose any alterations or amendments he thought beneficial. To these propositions, so reported by the committee, no opposition was given by that illustrious personage, or by the President of the State of Pennsylvania. They both appeared cordially to approve them, and to give them their hearty concurrence . . ."

In short, there is no room for doubt that in Washington's view the primary evil in the governmental system was the sovereignty of states, and that the cure necessary was to create a national government which had increased powers and was armed with some means of enforcing its supremacy.

James Madison

BORN in 1750, a descendant of one of Virginia's old landed families, Madison was a graduate of Princeton. He studied but did not practice law, was a profound student of history and government, and engaged actively in politics and public affairs throughout his life. His efforts to increase national power as a delegate to Congress under the Articles have already been discussed. His role in the political maneuvering which led to the calling of the convention has also been noted. Madison's views of the deficiencies in the government and the measures necessary to remedy them were set forth in the months preceding the convention in letters to Washington, Randolph, and Jefferson, as well as in a tract, "Vices of the Political System of the United States."

In the first place, Madison urged, it was essential that the central government have greater power. "I would propose next," he said in a letter to Washington, April 1787, "that in addition to the present federal powers, the national government should be armed with positive and complete authority in all cases which require uniformity." Second, as a means of enforcing national supremacy in the exercise of these powers, there were to be a national executive, a national judiciary, and an express declaration of the right of coercion. A third goal should be some method of protecting the national government against state interferences. Here Madison's views of state sovereignty are clearly revealed. For his remedy was, as set forth in the same letter to Washington, that "over and above this positive power, a negative *in all cases whatsoever* on the legislative acts of the states, as heretofore exercised by the kingly prerogative, appears to me to be absolutely necessary, and to be the least possible encroachment on the state jurisdictions. Without this defense power, every positive power that can be given on paper will be evaded and defeated. The states will continue to invade the national jurisdiction, to violate treaties and the law of nations and to harass each other with rival and spiteful measures dictated by mistaken views of interest." Finally, such a radical transformation in the system of government dictated the necessary method of obtaining it: ratification must be sought from the people "and not merely from the ordinary authority of the legislatures."

Madison's role in the convention was so pre-eminent that his most secure niche in history is as "the father of the Constitution." In that role he was the recognized and acknowledged leader of the group which went farthest in its advocacy of a strong national government and in its derogation of the sovereignty of the states.

> Let it be supposed for a moment [said Madison] that indefinite power should be given to the general legislature, and the states reduced to corporations dependent on the general legislature; why should it follow that the general government would take from the states any branch of their power so far as its operation was beneficial, and its continuance desirable to the people? In some of the states, particularly in Connecticut, all the townships are incorporated, and have a certain limited jurisdiction. Have the representatives of the people of the townships in the legislature of the state ever endeavored to despoil the townships of any part of their local authority? As far as this local authority is convenient to the people they are attached to it; and their representatives chosen by and amenable to them naturally respect their attachment to this, as much as their attachment to any other right or interest. The relation of a general government to state governments is parallel. . . . The great objection made against an abolition of the state governments was that the general government could not extend its care to all the minute objects which fall under the cognizance of the local jurisdictions. The objection as stated lay not against the probable abuse of the general power but against the imperfect use that could be made of it throughout so great an extent of country, and over so great a variety of objects. As far as its operation would be practicable it could not in this view be improper; as far as it could be impracticable, the conveniency of the general government itself would concur with that of the people in the maintenance of subordinate governments. . . . Under the proposed government the powers of the states will be much farther reduced. According to the views of every member, the general government will have powers far beyond those exercised by the British parliament when the states were part of the British Empire.

It is obvious that nothing could be more destructive of state sovereignty than Madison's proposed congressional negative on state laws. Initially adopted by the convention, it was eventually dropped in favor of the supremacy clause, but Madison himself never ceased to cherish it and urge its adoption. He had come to regard the negative as a substitute for coercion and force in maintaining national supremacy.

On July 17, 1787, Madison urged the convention to retain the negative, nothing short of which, he felt, could effectually curb the states' natural propensity to advance their own interests even in opposition to the general good. Madison foresaw the difficulties which would attend the states' sending all laws up to the national legislature. One remedy would be "some emanation of the power into the states, so far at least, as to give a temporary effect to laws of immediate necessity." On August 28 Madison doggedly persisted, admitting "that inconveniences might arise from such a prohibition but thought on the whole it would be over-balanced by the utility of it. He conceived however that a negative on the state laws could alone secure the effect. Evasions might and would be devised by the ingenuity of the legislatures." And on September 12, just five days before the convention adjourned, Madison was still true to his conviction. "There will be the same security as in other cases. The jurisdiction of the Supreme Court must be the source of redress. So far only had provisions been made by the plan against injurious acts of the states. . . . This was insufficient—a negative on the state laws, alone, could meet all the shapes which these could assume. But this had been overruled."

Like Washington, Madison recognized that, although stripped of their sovereignty, the states would still play a needful and useful role in the new system. To Washington he distilled the essence of his proposals: "Conceiving that an individual independence of the states is utterly ir-reconcilable with their aggregate sovereignty, and that a consolidation of the whole into one simple republic would be as inexpedient as it is unattainable, I have sought for some middle ground, which may at once support a due supremacy of the national authority, and not exclude the local authorities wherever they can be subordinately useful."

Madison was instrumental in bringing about the ratification of the Constitution, both in his participation in the authorship of the *Federalist Papers* and in the Virginia convention, where he led the fight and bested the opposition of Patrick Henry and George Mason. In later years Madison became a Jeffersonian and, as the author of the Virginia Reso-lutions and subsequently as President, espoused the states-rights, strict-construction approach to the Constitution. But at the time of the convention, he was undoubtedly an ardent nationalist.

Edmund Randolph

A SELF-STYLED "child of the revolution," Randolph cast his lot with Vir-ginia when his loyalist father returned to England in 1775. A graduate of William and Mary, he helped draft the 1776 Virginia constitution, then served as attorney general of the state until he was elected gover-nor in 1786 at the age of thirty-three. A member of Congress between 1779 and 1782, Randolph had been chairman of a committee which re-ported on the inadequacies of the Confederation and the increased powers which were necessary. Having taken the lead in calling the convention, Virginia seemed the obvious state to submit some proposal to commence the deliberations. It was also natural that the proposal should be presented to the convention by the governor.

Randolph's role in the drafting and adoption of the Constitution was inconsistent from the beginning. In March 1787 he wrote to Madison that he had turned his attention "somewhat to the business of May next. . . . At present, I conceive . . . that the alterations should be grafted on the old Confederation." Subsequently he changed his attitude, explaining, after the Convention was over: "Before my departure for the convention, I believed, that the Confederation was not so eminently defective, as it had been supposed. But after I had entered into a free communication with those who were best informed of the condition and interest of each state; after I had compared the intelligence derived from them with the properties which ought to characterize the government of our union, I became persuaded, that the Confederation was destitute of every energy, which a Constitution of the United States ought to possess."

Historians generally agree that the Randolph (or Virginia) plan which was submitted to the convention on May 29 was largely the work of Madison. Specific proposals included in this plan will be discussed later. It is enough to say at this point that the Virginia plan provided for a national government with virtually unlimited power over the states. Of Randolph's proposals, Yates recorded: "He candidly confessed that they were not intended for a federal government—he meant a strong consolidated union, in which the idea of states should be nearly annihilated." The next day Randolph offered three motions for the purpose of establishing basic principles before considering the plan in detail. These motions were: "1. that a Union of the States merely federal will not accomplish the objects proposed by the Articles of Confederation, namely common defence, security of liberty, and general welfare. 2. that no treaty or treaties among the whole or part of the states, as individual sovereignties, would be sufficient. 3. that a *national* government ought to be established consisting of a *supreme* legislative, executive and judiciary."

At the very time he was thus proposing to destroy state sovereignty, Randolph was disclaiming any such intention. On May 30 McHenry noted: "Mr. Randolph explains the intention of the 3rd resolution. Repeats the substance of his yesterdays observations. It is only meant to give the national government a power to defend and protect itself. To take therefore from the respective legislatures or states, no more sovereignty than is competent to this end." Next day, McHenry observed further that Randolph "disclaimed any intention to give indefinite powers to the national legislature, declaring that he was entirely opposed to such an inroad on the state jurisdictions, and that he did not think any considerations whatever could ever change his determination. His opinion was fixed on this point." Meanwhile, on the same day, according to McHenry, "Mr. Randolph was of opinion that it would be impossible to define the powers and the length to which the federal legislature ought to extend just at this time." But on June 16, McHenry wrote:

> Mr. Randolph was not scrupulous on the point of power. When the salvation of the Republic was at stake, it would be treason to our trust, not to propose what we found necessary. He painted in strong colors, the imbecility of the existing Confederacy, and the danger of delaying a substantial reform. . . . The true question is whether we shall adhere to the federal plan, or introduce the national plan. The insufficiency of the former has been fully displayed by the trial already made. . . . They have therefore no will of their own, they are a mere diplomatic body, but are always obsequious to the views of the states, who are always encroaching on the authority of the United States. A provision for harmony among the states, as in trade, naturalization, etc.—for crushing rebellion whenever it may rear its crest—and for certain other general benefits, must be made. . . . A national government alone, properly constituted, will answer the purpose; and he begged it to be considered that the present is the last moment for establishing one. After this select experiment, the people will yield to despair.

On July 10, when differences between large states and small ones had stalled the convention, Randolph offered certain suggestions for conciliating the small states, including the following:

> 3. that the people of each state ought to retain the perfect right of adopting from time to time such forms of republican government as to them may seem best, and of making all laws not contrary to the articles of Union; subject to the supremacy of the general government in those instances only in which that supremacy shall be expressly declared by the articles of the Union. 4. that although every negative given to the law of a particular state shall prevent its operation, any state may appeal to the national judiciary against a negative; and that such negative if adjudged to be contrary to the power granted by the articles of the Union, shall be void. 5. that any individual conceiving himself injured or oppressed by the partiality or injustice of a law of any particular state may resort to the national judiciary, who may adjudge such law to be void, if found contrary to the principles of equity and justice.

Just how the supremacy of the central government could be limited to express instances while at the same time there was to be a national legislative and judicial authority over all state laws was not explained.

By July 17 Randolph's doubts had increased. Of a motion that Congress should be empowered to legislate in all cases for the general interests of the union, as well as in those to which the states were separately incompetent, Randolph stated: "This is a formidable idea indeed. It involves the power of violating all the laws and constitutions of the states, and of intermeddling with their police." Objection to the motion, Randolph felt, was strengthened by the plan's defining Congress' powers so loosely as to give Congress opportunities for usurping all state powers. And finally, when the convention had finished its labors, Randolph refused to sign the Constitution. Although "convinced that radical changes in the system of the Union were necessary," he felt that the "republican propositions" he had submitted had been "irreconcilably departed from." He specified many particulars in which he disagreed with the Constitution and urged that the plan go to the states for proposed amendments, after which a second general convention would be held. But, "animadverting on the indefinite and dangerous power given by the Constitution to Congress," Randolph felt he could not sign and thus promote the establishment of a plan which he verily believed would "end in tyranny." Madison, writing to Jefferson after the convention was over, said that the "objections of the governor turn principally on the latitude of the general powers."

Reporting to the Virginia House of Delegates on his objections to the Constitution, Randolph set forth various corrections which he considered necessary. Two of these which are relevant here were that all "ambiguities of expression" should be "precisely explained" and that the jurisdictions of Congress and individual states should be specifically distinguished and defined, not made ambiguous by "general words and implication." But in the same report Randolph stated that "the last, and perhaps only refuge in our difficulties, [is] a consolidation of the Union, as far as circumstances will permit. To fulfill this desirable object, the Constitution was framed by the federal convention." Inconsistent to the last, Randolph, after having refused to sign the Constitution, finally supported its ratification in the Virginia convention. He was later Attorney General and Secretary of State under Washington and served as chief counsel for Aaron Burr when the latter was tried for treason.

George Mason

A VIRGINIA planter who owned 75,000 acres at his death, a speculator in western lands who married into a merchant's family, Mason was a Revolutionary statesman and constitutionalist who believed strongly in the rights of the states. He framed the Declaration of Rights in the Virginia constitutional convention of 1776, this document later being used by Madison in drafting the Bill of Rights. Although he was throughout his life a defender of individual liberty and spoke against slavery in the convention, Mason himself owned three hundred slaves. He was interested in public affairs but valued his private life too much to make a career of public service.

Shortly after he arrived in Philadelphia, a week before the convention started, Mason wrote to his son that the major states seemed intent upon altering the federal system totally and "substituting a great national council or parliament, consisting of two branches of the legislature, founded upon the principles of equal proportionate representation, with full legislative powers upon all the subjects of the Union; and an executive; and to make the several State legislatures subordinate to the national, by giving the latter the power of a negative upon all such laws as they shall judge contrary to the interest of the federal Union." Mason foresaw that it would be difficult to organize a government on this scale without infringing upon state powers, but he felt that with "coolness, liberality, and candor" the convention might solve the problems.

Mason's interest in preserving the position of the states was revealed during the debate on how the Senate should be selected. He was very much in favor of the Senate's being chosen by the respective state legislatures, and on June 7 he gave the following reasons:

> Whatever power may be necessary for the national government, a certain portion must necessarily be left in the states. It is impossible for one power to pervade the extreme parts of the United States so as to carry equal justice to them. The state legislatures also ought to have some means of defending themselves against encroachments of the national government. In every other department we have studiously endeavored to provide for its self-defense. Shall we leave the states alone unprovided with the means for this purpose? And what better means can we provide than the giving them some share in, or rather to make them a constituent part of, the national establisment? There is danger on both sides no doubt; but we have only seen the evils arising on the side of the state government. Those on the other side re-

main to be displayed. The example of Congress does not apply. Congress had no power to carry their acts into execution as the national government will have.

Speaking on the same subject June 25, Mason noted that, to be efficient, both the central government and its branches ought to have the "faculty of self-defense." If the states were to be preserved, Mason said, they must "have this power, and the only mode left of giving it to them was by allowing them to appoint the second branch of the national legislature."

On June 8 Mason had voted against the congressional negative on state laws, but it is doubtful that he was firmly committed against it. On August 23 he asked to know how the negative power would be exercised. "Are all laws whatever to be brought up? Is no road nor bridge to be established without the sanction of the general legislature? Is this to sit constantly in order to receive and revise the state laws?" He posed these questions not to condemn the plan but to suggest the strong objections which would be raised against it. Madison, at least, did not think Mason was opposed to the negative, as will be seen. That Mason had some idea of divided sovereignty is shown by his remark on August 20, when the question of treason was before the convention. The United States, he said, "will have a qualified sovereignty only," individual states retaining a part of the power. "An act may be treason against a particular state which is not so against the United States," Mason said, citing the rebellion of Bacon in Virginia. And that he thought the convention was going too far in the subordination of the states is indicated by his remark on August 21 that if he favored "reducing the states to mere corporations, as seemed to be the tendency of some arguments," he should be for "subjecting their exports as well as imports to a power of general taxation."

On the other hand, Mason was strong for national power in two very controversial areas. He hoped that there would be no standing army in times of peace; therefore he felt that the militia would be better prepared for the public defense if they were controlled by the central government. "Thirteen states will never concur in any one system," he said, "if the disciplining of the militia be left in their hands. If they will not give up the power over the whole, they probably will over a part as a select militia." Mason also believed that the general government should have the power to prevent the "increase" of slavery. He himself continued to own slaves, but he consistently opposed slavery as an institution. This position, of course, set him at odds with adherents of state sovereignty, who later took their stand on slavery. Madison, writing to Jefferson after the convention was over, spoke of Mason thus: "He did not object in general to the powers vested in the national government, so much as to the modification. In some respects he admitted that some further powers would have improved the system. He acknowledged in particular that a negative on the state laws, and the appointment of the state executive ought to be ingredients; but supposed that the public mind would not now bear them, and that experience would hereafter produce these amendments."

Mason's position in the convention may stand as an illustration of how far even the anti-nationalists had come by 1787 in recognizing the inadequacy of the Articles. Although he was clearly attached to what he considered states rights, it is equally clear that Mason was no defender of state sovereignty as it existed in his time, and that he recognized the necessity for a national government with increased powers. This being so, it is significant that Mason refused to sign the Constitution and opposed its ratification in Virginia. On August 31 Mason stated that "he would sooner chop off his right hand than put it to the Constitution as it now stands." On September 15 Mason "seconded and followed Mr. Randolph in animadversions on the dangerous power and structure of the Government, concluding that it would end either in monarchy, or a tyrannical aristocracy; which, he was in doubt, but one or other, he was sure." Mason thought it would be improper to force upon the people a constitution which, he felt, had been formed without their knowledge or recommendations. A second convention might draw up a system that reflected and was more consonant with "the sense of the people." Then, presumably, he could sign. Specifically, Mason's objections were:

There is no Declaration of Rights, and the laws of the general government being paramount to the laws and constitution of the several states, the declaration of rights in the separate states are no security. . . . The judiciary of the United States is so constructed and extended, as to absorb and destroy the judiciaries of the several states. . . . Under their own construction of the general clause, at the end of the enumerated powers, the Congress may grant monopolies in trade and commerce, constitute new crimes, inflict unusual and severe punishments, and extend their powers as far as they shall think proper; so that the state legislatures have no security for the powers now presumed to remain to them, or the people for their rights. . . . This government will set out a moderate aristocracy: it is at present impossible to foresee whether

it will, in its operation, produce a monarchy, or a corrupt, tyrannical aristocracy; it will most probably vibrate some years between the two, and then
terminate in the one or the other.

Like Randolph, Mason wanted another convention.

John Blair

A LAWYER who had studied in London, Blair had been a member of the
House of Burgesses, clerk to the council, a delegate to the Virginia constitutional convention of 1776, and a member of the privy council. He
went on to become a judge of the general court, from which he was elevated to judge of the first court of appeals of Virginia, the court of last
resort. While on this court Blair, in the case of *Commonwealth v. Caton,*
one of the earliest cases on the issue, upheld the power of the judiciary
to declare a legislative act unconstitutional. This was of course contrary at the time to the doctrine of legislative supremacy espoused by
anti-nationalists. It is significant when one recalls that the defenders
of state sovereignty later launched bitter attacks against the doctrine
and practice of judicial review.

Blair did not make a single speech during the convention, and no correspondence of his during the period has been preserved. The only recorded action which reveals his attitude on the question of state sovereignty took place on June 8, when he voted in favor of the congressional
negative over all state laws. After the convention was over, Blair became
a delegate to the Virginia convention, where he supported ratification.
A Federalist, he was one of Washington's original appointments to the
Supreme Court, on which he served for seven years, resigning in 1796.

During his tenure on the Court, Blair participated in two cases which
involved the question of state sovereignty. One was the previously mentioned *Penhallow v. Doane,* in which the Court held that even before the
Articles of Confederation the power of Congress in war and foreign relations was paramount to that of the states. The other case was *Chisholm v. Georgia,* which raised the question whether the Supreme Court
could assert jurisdiction over a suit against a state by citizens of other
states. The Court's answer was "Yes," even in the face of Georgia's
argument that the exercise of jurisdiction by the federal courts "would
effectually destroy the retained sovereignty of the states." In both of
these cases Blair wrote a separate opinion upholding the result.

James McClurg

McClurg, a physician, had been a surgeon in the Virginia militia during the Revolution. Later he was director of hospitals and professor of anatomy and medicine at William and Mary, eventually being named president of the state medical society. It is ironic that McClurg became a delegate by appointment to fill the vacancy created by Patrick Henry's refusal to attend. For, although he did not stay for the entire duration of the convention, McClurg took nationalist positions while he was there. He was one of the early advocates of a single executive and later moved that the term of the executive be "during good behavior" so as to render him independent of Congress. McClurg voted in favor of the congressional negative over all state laws and evidently felt quite strongly on the subject, for after leaving the convention he wrote to Madison on August 22: "I have still some hope that I shall hear from you of the reinstatement of the negative, as it is certainly the only means by which the several legislatures can be restrained from disturbing the order and harmony of the whole, and the government rendered properly national and one. I should suppose that some of its former opponents must by this time have seen the necessity of advocating it, if they wish to support their own principles."

George Wythe

Wythe was active in colonial affairs of Virginia, and sat in the Continental Congress during 1775-76. He achieved his greatest renown as a judge on the Virginia high court of chancery and as a professor of law at William and Mary. While on the bench he enunciated the doctrine of judicial review in the case of *Commonwealth v. Caton*. Wythe attended the convention for only a few days, returning to Virginia due to the illness of his wife. No comments or correspondence of his concerning the convention have been recorded. He later became a delegate to the Virginia convention where he supported ratification.

VI

Delegates from New Jersey

William Paterson

BORN in Ireland, a graduate of Princeton, and a successful practicing lawyer, Paterson had been a member of the New Jersey constitutional convention in 1776 and attorney general of the state from 1776 to 1783. His principal role at the Convention in Philadelphia was as proponent of the New Jersey plan. The Virginia plan, as submitted by Randolph, would have utilized population as the basis of representation in both houses of Congress, and the larger states would therefore have had a dominant voice in the new government. This plan was opposed by Paterson and others who wanted the small states to have equal representation and influence in the new Congress. Paterson's opposition was couched in terms of the convention's lacking power to depart from a system of equal representation.

On June 9 Paterson reminded the convention that it and the commissions of several states had been called together by an act of Congress which limited the power of the convention to amending the Articles. "The idea of a national government as contra-distinguished from a federal one, never entered into the mind of any of them [the states], and to the public mind we must accommodate ourselves. We have no power to go beyond the federal scheme, and if we had, the people are not ripe for any other. We must follow the people; the people will not follow us." Yates on the same day recorded Paterson as having said: "We are met here as the deputies of thirteen independent, sovereign states, for federal purposes. Can we consolidate their sovereignty and form one nation, and annihilate the sovereignties of our states who have sent us here for other purposes?" On June 14, therefore, Paterson informed the convention that several delegations, particularly New Jersey's, wished to study the Virginia plan and evolve a "purely federal" scheme instead of the one proposed.

The New Jersey plan which Paterson submitted to the convention will be considered more fully later. It should be noted here that Paterson's scheme provided for a "federal" government which, although tripartite, called for a unicameral legislature which was to represent states rather than individuals. Speaking in support of his plan, Paterson said, "If we argue the matter on the supposition that no confederacy at present exists," or "If we argue on the fact that a federal compact actually exists," in either case "it cannot be denied that all the states stand on the footing of equal sovereignty." Therefore, representatives must be drawn not from the people but directly from the states, Paterson said, if state sovereignty is to be maintained. The convention, he added, has "no power to vary the idea of equal sovereignty."

Statements of this sort do not, of course, make Paterson a defender of state sovereignty. For the New Jersey plan itself contained a national supremacy section which, taken with its provisions for increased powers in Congress and for a separate executive and judiciary, would have gone a long way toward remedying the most serious inadequacies of the Articles which flowed from state sovereignty. This proposition was:

> Resolved that all acts of the United States in Congress made by virtue and in pursuance of the powers hereby and by the articles of confederation vested in them, and all treaties made and ratified under the authority of the United States shall be the supreme law of the respective states so far forth as those acts or treaties shall relate to the said states or their citizens, and that the judiciary of the several states shall be bound thereby in their decisions, anything in the respective laws of the individual states to the contrary notwithstanding; and that if any state, or any body of men in any state, shall oppose or prevent the carrying into execution such acts or treaties, the federal executive shall be authorized to call forth the power of the confederated states, or so much thereof as may be necessary to enforce and compel an obedience to such acts, or an observance of such treaties.

That state sovereignty was not a sacred cow with Paterson is also indicated by his considering the possibility of completely obliterating the existing states. On June 9 he argued that proportional representation "could not be maintained whether considered in reference to us as a nation, or as a confederacy. A confederacy supposes sovereignty in the members composing it and sovereignty supposes equality. If we are to be considered as a nation, all state distinctions must be abolished, the whole must be thrown into hotchpot, and when an equal division is made, then there may be fairly an equality of representation." And again, on June 16, Paterson declared that the only expedient was to throw the states into a "hotchpot." The "hotchpot" ought to be tried, he said, to see whether citizens of the larger states will "accede to it." Would the "coercion" of the "hotchpot" scheme be any more impractical, he asked, than the coercion incorporated in any other plan?

It is rather clear that these were not merely hortatory statements, made for purposes of argumentation. For one of the preliminary drafts of the New Jersey plan contains, in Paterson's own handwriting, the following remarkable provision:

> Whereas it is necessary in order to form the people of the United States of America into a nation, that the states should be consolidated, by which means all the citizens thereof will become equally entitled to and will equally participate in the same privileges and rights, and in all waste, uncultivated, and back territory and lands; it is therefore resolved, that all the lands contained within the limits of each state individually, and of the United States generally be considered as constituting one body or mass, and be divided into thirteen or more integral parts. —Resolved, That such divisions or integral parts shall be styled districts.

Paterson's position thus is clearly not a defense of state sovereignty against national supremacy but rather an insistence upon equality of state representation in whatever central government might be fashioned. He was concerned not with state sovereignty in its relationship to the central government, but with the equality of states among themselves. This is evidenced by the fact that he never opposed any of the extensive grants of power to the national government. As a matter of fact, he left the convention after the compromise which assured equal state representation in the Senate, and he did not return until the end to sign the Constitution. Writing to Ellsworh on August 23 he inquired:

> What are the convention about, When will they rise? Will they agree upon a system energetic and effectual, or will they break up without doing anything to the purpose? Full of disputation and noisy as the wind, it is said that you are afraid of the very windows, and have a man planted under them to prevent the secrets and doings from flying out. The business, however, is detailed. I hope you will not have as much altercation upon the detail, as there was in getting the principles of the system.

Bancroft confirms the foregoing assessment of Paterson's position. "A few days later (July 23) the number of senators for each state was fixed at two, and each of these, as had been proposed by Gerry and seconded by Sherman, was personally to have one vote. From the day when every doubt of the right of the smaller states to an equal vote in the senate was quieted, they—so I received it from the lips of Madison, and so it appears from the records—exceeded all others in zeal for granting powers to the general government. Ellsworth became one of its strongest pillars. Paterson of New Jersey was for the rest of his life a federalist of federalists." Paterson's biographer says: "Nothing could be more erroneous than the assumption that Paterson was a quondam Anti-federalist who later heard the call and joined the Federalist ranks. Throughout his entire political career he advocated new powers for the government."

Paterson's subsequent career supports these evaluations. After the ratification of the Constitution, he became one of New Jersey's first senators, and as such he was a member of the Senate Judiciary Committee which reported the Judiciary Act of 1789. Section 25 of this act, providing for Supreme Court appellate review of state court decisions on federal questions, later became a principal target of the state sovereignty advocates, who tried unsuccessfully several times to repeal it. Paterson resigned in 1790 to become Governor of New Jersey. He was appointed to the Supreme Court in 1795 as a Federalist, serving until his death in 1806.

David Brearly

A LAWYER, Brearly had been outspoken in favor of independence. He was a member of the New Jersey constitutional convention of 1776 and an officer in the New Jersey militia until 1779, when he became chief justice of the state supreme court. In this role he decided the case of *Holmes v. Walton*, one of the early instances of judicial review over legislative enactments. During the Philadelphia convention Brearly was closely associated with Paterson, supporting the New Jersey plan's principle of equal state representation. Like Paterson, however, he indicated a willingness to erase existing state boundaries and make a new division in order that the problem of representation might be fairly solved.

His position on these matters was set forth in a statement of June 9. Brearly felt that each sovereign state should have an equal vote. He admitted that a ratio basis might appear, on the face of things, to be a fair one, but he concluded that such a scheme would ultimately be "unfair and unjust." Virginia, with sixteen votes, would be a "formidable phalanx," whereas Georgia, with one vote, would not be able to make its weight felt except by throwing itself "into the scale" of a large state. "When the proposition for destroying the equality of votes came forward, he was astonished, he was alarmed. Is it fair, then, it will be asked, that Georgia should have an equal vote with Virginia? He would not say it was. What remedy then? One only, that a map of the United States be spread out, that all the existing boundaries be erased, and that a new partition of the whole be made into thirteen equal parts."

Brearly signed the Constitution, supported its ratification in New Jersey, and presided over the state convention which approved it. Appointed by Washington as a United States district judge in 1789, he died a year later.

William Livingston

A YALE graduate and a lawyer who, like John Blair of Virginia, had studied in London, Livingston had two political careers. As a liberal Whig he became a successful practitioner with considerable political influence in New York. In 1770 he moved to New Jersey, where he became a delegate to both the First and Second Continental Congresses. Elected the first governor of the state in 1776, he served until his death in 1790. As governor, he opposed paper money, urged moderate treatment of loyalists and their property, and advocated revision of the Articles of Confederation. During the convention he supported the New Jersey plan but made no speeches. He signed the Constitution and was largely responsible for its speedy ratification by New Jersey.

Jonathan Dayton

AT TWENTY-SIX, Dayton was the youngest delegate to the Convention. Son of a wealthy merchant and a graduate of Princeton, Dayton had served under his father during the Revolution and was a member of the New Jersey assembly during 1786-1787. He did not arrive at the convention until June 21; once there he supported the principle of equal state representation in Congress. On June 30 he said that it "should have been shown that the evils we have experienced have proceeded from the equality now objected to, and that the seeds of dissolution for the state governments are not sown in the general government." On July 14 Dayton stated that "The smaller states can never give up their equality." For himself he would "in no event yield that security for their rights."

These statements confirm that the dispute between proponents of the Virginia and New Jersey plans was essentially between large and small states over proportional or equal representation, and that the issue of national supremacy or state sovereignty was only peripherally involved. Dayton held no strong brief for state sovereignty, for on August 30 he supported John Dickinson's proposal to authorize suppression by the national government of domestic violence within a state, even without invitation from the state. "Mr. Dayton mentioned the conduct of Rhode Island as showing the necessity of giving latitude to the power of the United States on this subject."

A signer and supporter of the Constitution, Dayton went to Congress as a Federalist in 1791 and served four terms, the last as Speaker of the House. During this time he consistently supported Hamilton's financial policies. Representing New Jersey as Senator from 1799 to 1805, he voted against the attempt of the Jeffersonians to repeal the Judiciary Act of 1801.

William Churchill Houston

HOUSTON was graduated from the College of New Jersey, where he was later a professor of mathematics for five years. He had served two terms in the Continental Congress, had been a delegate to the Annapolis convention, and was at the time of the convention clerk to the supreme court of New Jersey. He was absent from the convention most of the time because of illness and made no contribution of recorded consequence while he was in attendance.

VII

Delegates from
New Hampshire

John Langdon

A WEALTHY merchant and shipper, Langdon had also been active in politics as a delegate to the Continental Congress in 1775, agent for continental prizes in New Hampshire throughout the war, member and twice speaker of the state legislature, and governor of the state. Langdon paid his own convention expenses and those of the other New Hampshire delegate, Nicholas Gilman. Langdon's attitude was typical of the merchant class on the question of the necessity for national rather than state authority in the regulation of commerce. Writing to some business associates in April 1784, Langdon despaired of better prospects for commerce until the several states relinquished their claims upon its regulation. For, Langdon said, "While thirteen different states, in thirteen different parts of the continent, undertake to regulate trade, it will not only destroy that social intercourse that ought to be cultivated between the states, but bring on the utmost confusion." He hoped that delegates would soon recognize that Congress alone could and ought to govern commerce.

Langdon was consistently in favor of a strong central government. He supported the right of the national government to subdue rebellion in the states without necessity of a state request for intervention, stating on August 17 that the "apprehension of the national force will have a salutary effect in preventing insurrections." He advocated the regulation and discipline of the state militias by the national government. He saw no more reason to fear the general government than the governments of the states. On August 23 he said he "could not understand the jealousy expressed by some gentlemen. The general and state governments were not enemies to each other, but different institutions for the good of the people of America." As one of the people he could say, "The national government is mine, the state government is mine. In transferring power from one to the other, I only take out of my left hand what it cannot so well use, and put it into my right hand where it can be better used." Langdon also favored the congressional negative over state laws and made it clear that he did not consider state sovereignty a limitation on national power. "He considered [the issue] as resolvable into the question whether the extent of the national constitution was to be judged of by the general or the state governments." In addition, Langdon believed that representatives to Congress should be paid by the United States rather than by the states, as under the Articles; he favored prohibiting state power to levy tonnage duties; he advocated giving the national government power to prohibit the slave trade; and he wished to reserve the power to admit new states on terms less than equality. Langdon signed the Constitution and supported its ratification in New Hampshire as a delegate to the state convention.

He was a U.S. Senator from 1789 to 1801. At first a Federalist, he supported Hamilton's funding system and the creation of the United States bank. He subsequently became a Republican, and when Jefferson came to power in 1801, Langdon became Republican leader in New Hampshire until his retirement in 1812.

Nicholas Gilman

THE OTHER delegate from New Hampshire, Gilman, was an officeholder and associate of important people throughout his life. Gilman never made any personal contribution of importance, however. An officer during the war, he was a delegate to Congress in 1786-1788. Although he later urged ratification of the Constitution, he took no part in the debates in the convention. He was a Federalist Congressman from 1789 to 1797 but is not recorded as having been active in affairs. After the election of Jefferson, he became a Republican and served as a U.S. Senator from 1804 until his death in 1814.

VIII

Delegates from Pennsylvania

Benjamin Franklin

PRINTER, author, inventor, scientist, philanthropist, diplomat, and statesman—this remarkable man was, at eighty-one, the oldest delegate present in Philadelphia. A true cosmopolitan, Franklin had been for almost twenty years before the Revolution, as resident agent in England for Pennsylvania and several other states, a diligent advocate of colonial interests. Returning in 1775, he had been a delegate to the Second Continental Congress and a signer of the Declaration of Independence. He was then sent to France where he represented Congress from 1776 to 1781. Franklin was one of the commissioners who negotiated the peace treaty with Britain. Returning again to America in 1785, he was elected president of the executive council of Pennsylvania.

Franklin was the first American to offer a plan of union for the colonies. In 1754, at the Albany conference of delegates of the northern colonies called by the Board of Trade to negotiate with the Indians, he had suggested a largely self-governing confederation. This plan would have created a representative assembly with powers to govern war and peace, to regulate trade, and to levy and collect taxes, with a single executive appointed by the Crown. Franklin's plan was much too far ahead of the times. Neither the Crown nor the colonies approved his proposal, the one because it was too democratic, the other because it was too centralized. Later, in the Continental Congress, Franklin again anticipated his contemporaries, offering a plan of union in 1775, a full year before Congress was ready to consider such a project.

It is clear that considerations of state sovereignty weighed not at all with Franklin. He had even less regard for the importance of the states than delegates who advocated representation based on population. Thus on June 11 he stated:

I must own that I was originally of opinion it would be better if every member of Congress, or our national council, were to consider himself rather as a representative of the whole, than as an agent for the interest of a particular state; in which case the proportion of members for each state would be of less consequences, and it would not be very material whether they voted by states or individually. But as I find this is not to be expected, I now think the number of representatives should bear some proportion to the number of the represented; and that the decisions should be by the majority of members, not by the majority of states. This is objected to from an apprehension that the greater states would then swallow up the smaller. I do not at present clearly see what advantage the greater states could propose to themselves by swallowing the smaller, and therefore do not apprehend they would attempt it.

Franklin approved of one means of preventing such "swallowing up." He would, he said, "not be against such a measure" if "equalizing the states" could be proved practicable. He also supported the congressional negative over state laws: his motion of May 31 expanded the negative by inserting a qualifying phrase concerning treaties. And Franklin's concurrence in the nationalist positions taken by the convention in its early weeks is evidenced by Luther Martin's report to the Maryland legislature, previously cited in the discussion of Washington.

Franklin's primary role in the convention, however, was not the contribution of substantive provisions or the formulation of particular language. Most of his specific suggestions, in fact, were rejected. His value and service derived rather from the veneration and respect with which he was regarded, and the wisdom, detachment, and humor with which he counseled the necessity for a spirit of accommodation, harmony, and compromise. More than once a conciliatory speech by Franklin, sometimes read for him by James Wilson, assisted the convention in reconciling divergent opinions. A prime example of Franklin's ability to engender compromise was in the very area of dispute over proportional or equal state representation. His proposal again revealed that he felt that men's attachment to their states was something which had to be lived with rather than valued.

On June 30 he made this proposition: "That the legislatures of the several states shall choose and send an equal number of delegates, namely who are to compose the second branch of the general legislature. That in all cases or questions wherein the sovereignty of individual states may be affected, or whereby their authority over their own citizens may be diminished, or the authority of the general government within the several states augmented, each state shall have equal suffrage." When the compromise was reported back to the convention, recommending proportional representation in the lower house and equal representation in the upper, Madison recorded that the report based on Franklin's motion was "barely acquiesced in by the members from the states opposed to an equality of votes in the second branch and was evidently considered by the members on the other side, as a gaining of their point." That Franklin regarded this merely as the best possible bargain under the circumstances is indicated again by Luther Martin who later stated that "the Honorable President of Pennsylvania was a member of the committee of compromise, and there advocated the right of the large states to an inequality in both branches, and only ultimately conceded it in the second branch on the principle of conciliation, when it was found no other terms would be accepted."

Although not agreeing completely with all the provisions of the final document, Franklin signed the Constitution and in a speech which exemplified his whole philosophy of accepting the best that was practically possible, advocated its unanimous acceptance by the other delegates.

James Wilson

BORN in 1742 in Scotland, where he attended the universities of St. Andrews and Edinburgh, Wilson came to America in 1763, studied law under John Dickinson, and became a successful practicing lawyer in Philadelphia and a profound student of history and political philosophy. As a member of the Continental Congress, he signed the Declaration of Independence. (His role in connection with the drafting of the Articles of Confederation has already been noted.) Both then and in subsequent terms in Congress he consistently sought to increase the powers of the central government.

In the convention Wilson's contribution was probably second only to Madison's. Like Madison, Wilson was an ardent nationalist. He believed that the national sentiments originally engendered by independence had been stifled by local interests that arose quickly when the states were formed. On June 8 he remarked that early in the First Congress much was said to the effect that individual states had lost their identities and were now one nation of brethren. But local interests were not buried for long, Wilson said: "No sooner were the state governments formed than their jealousy and ambition began to display themselves. Each endeavoured to cut a slice from the common loaf, to add to its own morsel, till at length the Confederation became frittered down to the impotent condition in which it now stands." The business of the convention, Wilson said, was to correct the "vices" which successive drafts had incorporated into the Articles. The chief flaw in the Articles was "the want of an effectual control in the whole over its parts."

Wilson's conception of what the new government should be like incorporated a necessary and useful role for the states. The states should therefore be preserved as entities for the accomplishment of subordinate purposes. Early in the convention, on June 6, the record states: "Mr. Wilson would not have spoken again, but for what had fallen from Mr. Read; namely, that the idea of preserving the state governments ought to be abandoned. [Wilson] saw no incompatibility between the national and state governments provided the latter were restrained to certain local purposes; nor any probability of their being devoured by the former. In all confederated systems ancient and modern the reverse had happened; the generality being destroyed gradually by the usurpations of the parts composing it." The next day, June 7, Wilson described the states as satellites of a national sun. The real danger, as he saw it, lay in the possibility that the states might "devour" the national government. On June 19 Wilson explained that he did not envision a national government that would swallow up the states, which should be preserved. The states, indeed, might subsist "on friendly terms" with the national government. "They were absolutely necessary for certain purposes which the former could not reach. All large governments must be subdivided into lesser jurisdictions." As examples he mentioned Persia, Rome, and particularly the divisions and subdivisions of England by Alfred.

Wilson was vehemently opposed, however, to the states' having equal representation in the national legislature, viewing this as inconsistent with a truly national government. Thus on May 31 he stated that he opposed increasing "the weight of the state legislatures by making them the electors of the national legislature. All interference between the general and local governments should be obviated as much as possible. On examination it would be found that the opposition of states to federal measures had proceeded much more from the officers of the states, than from the people at large." Continuing his opposition to an election by the state legislatures, Wilson said on June 25 that it was necessary to observe "the twofold relation in which the people would stand. 1. as citizens of the general government. 2. as citizens of their particular state. The general government was meant for them in the first capacity; the state governments in the second. Both governments were derived from the people—both meant for the people—both there-fore ought to be regulated on the same principles. . . . The election of the second branch by the legislatures, will introduce and cherish local in-terests and local prejudices. The general government is not an assem-blage of states but of individuals for certain political purposes. It is not meant for the states, but for the individuals composing them. The *indi-viduals* therefore, not the *states,* ought to be represented in it."

Nor did Wilson consider equal representation necessary as any polit-ical protection to the states. On June 21, he admitted that "a jealousy and rivalship would be felt between the general and particular govern-ments." Appointment of the Senate by state legislatures would give states an opportunity to defend *their* rights, Wilson continued, so the general government ought to have a "reciprocal opportunity" to ap-point "some one constituent branch" of the state governments. "If a security be necessary on one side," Wilson said, "it would seem rea-sonable to demand it on the other." But taking the matter in a more general view, he saw no danger to the states from the general govern-ment. In case a combination should be made by the large ones it would produce a general alarm among the rest; and the project would be frustrated. But there was no temptation to such a project. The states having in general a similar interest, in case of any proposition in the national legislature to encroach on the state legislatures, he thought a general alarm would take place in the national legislature itself, that it would communicate itself to the state legislatures and would finally spread among the people at large. The only real danger, he concluded, was "that in spite of every precaution the general government would be in perpetual danger of encroachments from the state governments."

Wilson elaborated upon this view on July 14. No real argument has been advanced to contradict the general principle of proportional rep-resentation, he said, yet some men feel that the states cannot be pre-served unless each has an equal vote in one branch of the legislature. But, Wilson asked, is "there any reason to suppose that if their preser-vation should depend more on the large than on the small states, the security of the states against the general government would be di-minished? Are the large states less attached to their existence, more likely to commit suicide, than the small?" Far from being necessary, according to Wilson, an equal vote would foster the kind of inaction which afflicted the Congress. By virtue of such equality, small states "may control the government as they have done in Congress." "This very measure is here prosecuted by a minority of the people of America.

Is then the object of the convention likely to be accomplished in this way? Will not our constituents say we sent you to form an efficient government and you have given us one more complex indeed, but having all the weakness of the former government?"

Wilson foresaw that state officers and state interests would feel a sense of rivalry against the national government. No opposition would be forthcoming from citizens of the states, who had parted with all necessary powers. It was immaterial to them by whom they were exercised, if well exercised. Wilson supposed that the people would be rather more attached to the national government than to the state governments, as being "more important in itself, and more flattering to their pride." On June 20, Wilson added that a "private citizen of a state is indifferent whether power be exercised by the general or state legislatures, provided it be exercised most for his happiness. His representative has an interest in its being exercised by the body to which he belongs. He will therefore view the national legislature with the eye of a jealous rival."

In such circumstances, national supremacy was essential. On June 7 Wilson had hoped that "the national government would be independent of state governments, in order to make it vigorous, and therefore [he] moved that the above resolution be postponed, and that the convention in its room adopt the following resolve: *That the second branch of the national legislature be chosen by districts, to be formed for that purpose.*" And on June 9 he stated that men "have been told that each state being sovereign, all are equal. So each man is naturally a sovereign over himself, and all men are therefore naturally equal. Can he retain this equality when he becomes a member of civil government? He cannot. As little can a sovereign state, when it becomes a member of a federal government. If New Jersey will not part with her sovereignty, it is in vain to talk of government. A new partition of the states is desirable, but evidently and totally impracticable." On June 21 he declared that in a clash of interests, the state should yield to preserve the general interest. "But let us try to designate the powers of each, and then no danger can be apprehended nor can the general government be possessed of any ambitious views to encroach on the state rights." Wilson realized that the allocation of power ought to be flexible, to shift with events, but the members of the national government should always be left "as independent as possible of the state governments in all respects."

The line of demarcation between national power and states rights was to be determined by the national government, and Wilson was therefore in favor of the congressional negative. Thus on June 8 he "would not say what modifications of the proposed power might be practicable or expedient. But however novel it might appear, the principle of it when viewed with close and steady eye, is right. There is no instance in which the laws say that the individual should be bound in one case, and at liberty to judge whether he will obey or disobey in another. The cases are parallel, abuses of the power over the individual person may happen as well as over the individual states. Federal liberty is to states, what civil liberty, is to private individuals. And states are not more unwilling to purchase it, by the necessary concession of their political sovereignty, than the savage is to purchase civil liberty by the surrender of the personal sovereignty, which he enjoys in a state of nature. A definition of the cases in which the negative should be exercised, is impracticable. A discretion must be left on one side or the other. Will it not be most safely lodged on the side of the national government?" And on August 23, Wilson alluded to the negative as the "keystone" needed to complete the "wide arch of government" the convention was raising. "The firmness of judges is not of itself sufficient" as the general government's self-defense. "Something further is requisite. It will be better to prevent the passage of an improper law, than to declare it void when passed."

More than most of the delegates, probably, Wilson had a vision of the America which was to be. On June 25 he said that when "he considered the amazing extent of country, the immense population which is to fill it, the influence which the government we are to form will have, not only on the present generation of our people and their multiplied posterity, but on the whole globe, he was lost in the magnitude of the object." And, in terms of this great future, he could not believe "that the state governments and sovereignties were so much the idols of the people, nor a national government so obnoxious to them, as some supposed." Wilson was confident that the people would accept the concept of a national government, and he thought it was proper that the Constitution was to be submitted not to the state legislatures but to the people for ratification. Not only an apostle of nationalism, Wilson was also far in advance of most of his contemporaries in his confidence in democracy. He thought that not only the members of both houses of Congress, but also the President, should be elected by popular vote.

After the convention was over, Wilson was the foremost advocate of ratification in Pennsylvania. In 1789 he was appointed an associate justice of the Supreme Court, a post which he held until his death in 1798. His opinion in *Chisholm v. Georgia* in 1793 was a ringing affirmation of the Constitution as an ordinance of the American people creating a national government in which the sovereignty of the states had been subordinated.

Gouverneur Morris

BORN to the landed aristocracy of New York, Morris was graduated from Columbia College, then became a lawyer and politician. He sought to preserve the union with Britain but supported independence when the break came. He was a member of the New York provincial congress and of the New York constitutional convention. Later he was a delegate to Congress in 1778-1779. Defeated for re-election, Morris moved to Philadelphia, where he quickly became prominent. From 1781 to 1785 he served as chief assistant to Robert Morris, to whom he was not related. Thirty-five years old, he was, even with a withered arm and a wooden leg, a charming, party-loving ladies' man.

In the convention Morris was one of the strongest nationalists. Brilliant, witty, suave, eloquent, and of unfailing self-assurance, he was also the most frequent speaker in the debates. He strongly favored representation based on population. Thus on May 28, with the support of Robert Morris and others from Pennsylvania, he argued that "the large states should unite in firmly refusing to the small states an equal vote, as unreasonable, and as enabling the small states to negative every good system of government, which must in the nature of things, be founded on a violation of that equality." Two days later he said that this principle was "so fundamental an article in a national government that it could not be dispensed with." Consequently, he was against any compromise on the question.

Morris felt that the state legislatures' control over the Senate would result in government by the states. "This," he said, was "going back to mere treaty. It is no government at all. It is altogether dependent on the states, and will act over again the part which Congress has acted. A firm government alone can protect our liberties." On the same day Yates' notes recorded Morris as stating that a "government by compact is no government at all. You may as well go back to your congressional federal government, where, in the character of ambassadors, they may form treaties for each state."

When the compromise committee made its report, Morris was still adamant, and in expressing his opposition he uttered some of the strongest language against the states used in the convention. On July 5 he declared:

> He came here as a representative of America. He flattered himself he came here in some degree as a representative of the whole human race, for the whole human race will be affected by the proceedings of this convention. He wished gentlemen to extend their views beyond the present moment of time; beyond the narrow limits of place from which they derive their political origin. If he were to believe some things which he had heard, he should suppose that we were assembled to truck and bargain for our particular states. He [could not] descend to think that any gentlemen are really actuated by these views. . . . As the second branch is now constituted, there will be constant disputes and appeals to the states which will undermine the general government and control and annihilate the first branch. What results? [Senators] will immediately declare that their state will not abide by the decision, and make such representations as will produce that effect. . . . Of what avail then will be what is on paper? State attachments, and state importance have been the bane of this country. We cannot annihilate; but we may perhaps take out the teeth of the serpents.

On July 7 he took a stand "against the report because it maintained the improper constitution of the second branch. It made it another congress, a mere whisp of straw. It had been said by Mr. Gerry," Morris maintained, "that the new government would be partly national, partly federal; that it ought in the first quality to protect individuals; in the second, the states. But in what quality was it to protect the aggregate interest of the whole?" he asked. None of the many provisions advanced in the convention supported the "dignity and splendor of the American empire," Morris said.

> It had been one of our greatest misfortunes that the great objects of the nation had been sacrificed constantly to local views; in like manner as the general interests of states had been sacrificed to those of the counties. What is to be the check in the Senate? None; unless it be to keep the majority of the people from injuring particular states. But particular states ought to be injured for the sake of a majority of the people, in case their conduct should deserve it. Suppose they should insist on claims evidently unjust, and pursue them in a manner detrimental to the whole body. Suppose they should give themselves up to foreign influence. Ought they to be protected in such cases? They were originally nothing more than colonial corporations. On the declaration of independence, a government was to be formed. The small states, aware of the necessity of preventing anarchy and taking advantage of the moment, extorted from the large ones an equality of votes. Standing now on that ground,

they demand under the new system greater rights as men, than their fellow citizens of the large states. The proper answer to them is that the same necessity of which they formerly took advantage does not now exist, and that the large states are at liberty now to consider what is right, rather than what may be expedient. We must have an efficient government and if there be an efficiency in the local governments the former is impossible.

Noting that Germany's weakness was a result of more energy in the local authorities than in the general government, Morris continued: "Do gentlemen wish this to be the case here? Good God, sir, is it possible they can so delude themselves? What if all the charters and constitutions of the states were thrown into the fire, and all their demagogues into the ocean? What would it be to the happiness of America?"

Morris' nationalism expressed itself in other ways. On July 17 he opposed a motion intended to protect the power of the states over their internal police, stating that "The internal police, as it would be called and understood by the state, ought to be infringed in many cases, as in the case of paper money and other tricks by which citizens of other states may be affected." He was also opposed to a motion to require invitation by a governor before the national government could intervene to subdue rebellion in a state, arguing that "the executive may possibly be at the head of the rebellion. The general government should enforce obedience in all cases where it may be necessary."

Morris had contempt for democracy, believing in property qualifications for voting and advocating life tenure for the President and for Senators. He foresaw that a strong national government would be opposed by state interests. "When it [the Constitution] first appears, with the sanction of this convention, the people will be favorable to it. By degrees the state officers and those interests in the state governments will intrigue and turn the popular current against it."

On July 2 he stated that it "should be considered too how the scheme could be carried through the states. He hoped there was strength of mind enough in this house to look truth in the face. He did not hesitate therefore to say that loaves and fishes must bribe the demagogues. They must be made to expect higher offices under the general than the state governments. A Senator for life will be a noble bait. Without such captivating prospects, the popular leaders will oppose and defeat the plan."

This anxiety lest the Constitution not become operative led Morris to take apparently inconsistent positions. Thus on July 17 he opposed the congressional negative on state laws, but on grounds that it would create too much opposition in the states and unnecessarily so. Later the same day he was even more opposed to the negative. "The proposal of it would disgust all the states. A law that ought to be negatived will be set aside in the judiciary department and, if that security should fail; may be repealed by a national law." Likewise, on September 15, he moved to annex a further proviso that "no state without its consent shall be deprived of its equal suffrage in the Senate." Madison's notes add at this point, "This motion being dictated by the circulating murmurs of the small states."

Morris was a member of the Committee on Style to which was delegated the task of putting the decisions of the convention in final form. According to Madison and his own statements, Morris was the author of the language of the Constitution as we now have it. Writing to Timothy Pickering in 1814, Morris in referring to the Constitution stated: "That instrument was written by the fingers which write this letter." And Madison, in 1831, wrote to Jared Sparks: "The finish given to the style and arrangement of the Constitution fairly belongs to the pen of Mr. Morris; the task having been probably handed over to him by the chairman of the committee, himself a highly respectable member, with the ready concurrence of the others. A better choice could not have been made, as the performance of the task proved."

After the convention Morris went to France on business in 1789 and while there was named by Washington as minister in 1792, serving until recalled at the request of France in 1794. Later he filled an unexpired Senate term between 1800 and 1812. He regarded the ascendancy of Jefferson and Republicanism with abhorrence, denounced the embargo, and condemned the War of 1812. Eventually, his hatred of what he regarded as a departure from the principles of the Constitution induced him to approve of the Hartford Convention.

Robert Morris

BORN in England, the other Morris from Pennsylvania was, by the time of the Revolution and for twenty years thereafter, the foremost merchant, financier, speculator, and broker in America. His far-flung economic interests reached into every section of the country and connected him closely with the most important men of the time. His enormous financial acumen was utilized in the cause of independence both in Pennsylvania and in Congress. When economic affairs reached their most critical point early in 1781, Morris was appointed by Congress as superintendent of finance and given virtually dictatorial economic powers. By almost miraculous manipulation, he managed to keep the armies in the field supplied (as well as enriching himself in the process), and he has forever since been known as "the financier of the Revolution."

Morris' efforts during the war to obtain money and supplies from sovereign states, and his natural conservatism, made him forever after a confirmed advocate of a strong central government, which, as a delegate to the Annapolis convention, he endeavored to achieve. Morris was host to George Washington during the Philadelphia convention, nominating him for presiding officer, but Morris did not participate in the debates. He declined the position of Secretary of the Treasury in Washington's cabinet. Instead, he became one of Pennsylvania's first Senators and a dedicated Federalist who worked closely with Hamilton in formulating and effectuating his financial program.

Thomas Mifflin

MIFFLIN was a prosperous merchant, son-in-law of Robert Morris, and a graduate of the College of Philadelphia (now the University of Pennsylvania). A delegate to both the First and Second Continental Congresses, he was quartermaster-general of the Continental Army for almost three years and subsequently a member of the cabal which sought to elevate General Gates above Washington. He served briefly as president of Congress in 1783-1784. During the convention Mifflin made no speeches that were recorded, but he did sign and support the Constitution. Governor of Pennsylvania between 1790 and 1799, he supported national intervention in the Whiskey Rebellion in western Pennsylvania in 1793 but managed also during his tenure to accommodate himself with the increasing influence of Republicanism. His career was marked more by success in bending with the wind than by any fixed principles of government.

Thomas Fitzsimmons

ANOTHER wealthy Philadelphia merchant who married a merchant's daughter, Fitzsimmons served in Congress in 1782 and later in the Pennsylvania legislature. In the convention he went along with the delegation, favored restricting the suffrage to freeholders, and spoke but little, on such matters as harbor improvements and aid to manufacturing. He signed the Constitution and was a Federalist member of the House of Representatives from 1789 to 1795, supporting the entire Federalist program, especially the Hamilton financial measures. In 1810 he was on a committee of Philadelphia businessmen seeking to recharter the Bank of the United States.

George Clymer

A WEALTHY Philadelphia merchant who married the daughter of another wealthy merchant, Clymer was nevertheless among the first to advocate complete independence and was immensely proud of having signed the Declaration. He was in Congress three times during the war, where his knowledge of business affairs made him useful on committees dealing with matters of finance and commerce, and where he strongly supported efforts to increase national power. He spoke little during the convention but supported the consistent nationalist positions of the Pennsylvania delegation. A signer of the Constitution, Clymer served in the First Congress as a Federalist.

Jared Ingersoll

A GRADUATE of Yale who studied law in London, Ingersoll was probably the ablest jury lawyer in Philadelphia. He was elected to Congress in 1780 and from then on urged the revision or replacement of the Articles. Inexplicably, he took no active part in the convention, so far as the records show. He regarded the principles of Republicanism as a betrayal of the Constitution, and in politics was a confirmed Federalist, even after Jeffersonianism had triumphed in Pennsylvania. Although he was put forward for Vice-President by Pennsylvania Federalists in 1812, Ingersoll's principal interest was always the practice of law rather than politics.

IX

Delegates from
North Carolina

Hugh Williamson

AFTER graduation from the College of Philadelphia, Williamson was successively a minister, a mathematics professor, a doctor, a merchant, and a politician. During the 1780's he served two terms both in the state legislature and in Congress, where he became a strong nationalist, and was a delegate to the Annapolis convention. At Philadelphia he was the most active of the North Carolina delegates. He advocated proportional representation and thought the small states had nothing to fear from it. Thus on June 9 Williamson "illustrated the cases by a comparison of the different states to counties of different sizes within the same state, observing that proportional representation was admitted to be just in the latter case, and could not therefore be fairly contested in the former." And on June 29 he said "that if any political truth could be grounded on mathematical demonstration, it was that if the states were equally sovereign now, and parted with equal proportions of sovereignty, that they would remain equally sovereign. He could not comprehend how the smaller states would be injured in the case, and wished some gentleman would vouchsafe a solution of it."

Although he advocated a stronger government, Williamson "professed himself a friend to such a system as would secure the existence of the state governments. The happiness of the people depended on it." He also thought that "the state legislatures ought to possess independent powers in cases purely local, and applying to their internal policy." Consequently, on the congressional negative Williamson took the position that the "national legislature ought to possess the power of negativing such laws only as will encroach on the national government." But he was against giving Congress an unlimited negative on all laws it thought improper, since "that might restrain the states from regulating their internal police." Apparently he was in favor of judicial review, for he stated with reference to the proposal to include an *ex-post facto* clause: "Such a prohibitory clause is in the Constitution of North Carolina, and though it had been violated, it has done good there and may do good here, because the judges can take hold of it." Williamson signed the Constitution and worked for its ratification in North Carolina. After serving in Congress from 1789 to 1793, he retired to New York to devote himself to literary and scientific pursuits until his death in 1819.

William Richardson Davie

BORN in England, graduated from Princeton, Davie saw continuous military service during the Revolution. He then went into law and politics, building a lucrative practice, serving in the state legislature from 1786 to 1798 and as Governor of North Carolina in 1798. In the convention Davie took only a slight role in the debates. On the question of representation in Congress, he stated on June 30 that local prejudices and interests would become issues in "the national councils whether the representatives should be chosen by the legislatures or by the people themselves. On the other hand, if a proportional representation was attended with insuperable difficulties, the making the Senate the representative of the states looked like bringing us back to Congress again, and shutting out all the advantages expected from it." Davie thought that in general there were extremes on both sides; he could not vote for any plan for the Senate yet proposed. Since, in our union, we were "partly federal, partly national," he "did not see why the government might not in some respects operate on the states, in others on the people." As for his own idea as to the proper basis of representation, "he seemed to think that wealth or property ought to be represented in the second branch, and numbers in the first branch."

Although Davie left the convention in August and was not present for the signing, he favored the Constitution and very actively fought for its ratification in North Carolina. A confirmed Federalist in a Republican state, as governor he denounced the Virginia and Kentucky Resolutions, and his strong opposition to Jeffersonianism eventually eliminated him from politics.

Richard Dobbs Spaight

SON OF a wealthy planter, Spaight was educated in Ireland and completed his studies at the University of Glasgow. Returning to North Carolina in 1778, he went to the state legislature, had a brief military career, served in Congress, and became speaker of the state legislature. He regarded the assumption of judicial review by the Carolina courts as a usurpation. In the convention he spoke seldom but believed in strengthening the government. Writing to James Iredell during the convention, Spaight said it was improbable "that the United States will in future be so ideal as to risk their happiness upon the unanimity of the whole, and thereby put it in the power of one or two states to defeat the most salutary propositions, and prevent the Union from rising out of that contemptible situation to which it is at present reduced." Having signed the Constitution, Spaight later was a member of the state convention where he actively urged ratification. Subsequently he became a Republican, serving as governor and Congressman.

Alexander Martin

A GRADUATE of Princeton, a planter, merchant, and politician, Martin resigned from the Continental Army after being acquitted of cowardice. He was elected governor in 1782 and served three terms. Although the titular head of his delegation, he was inconspicuous during the convention. He was defeated for election as a delegate to the ratification convention, but was re-elected governor. A sometime moderate Federalist, Martin changed with the political winds in North Carolina and became a Republican. Elected to the Senate in 1792, he voted for the Alien and Sedition laws. This stand contributed to his failure of re-election, but he continued his office-holding career in the state legislature.

William Blount

BLOUNT, a former paymaster during the war, was a member of the lower house of the North Carolina legislature four times (once as speaker), a member of the state senate twice, and a member of Congress twice. During the convention he took no part in the debates and was absent for over a month during July and August. In July he wrote to his brother: "I must confess notwithstanding all I heard in favor of this system I am not in sentiment with my colleagues for as I have said before I still think we shall ultimately and [in] not many years just be separate and distinct governments, perfectly independent of each other." On September 17, the day of signing the Constitution, Hugh Williamson referred to Blount as being one of the members "who disliked the Constitution." Blount did sign, explaining, however, that this was not to indicate approval but merely to "attest the fact that the plan was the unanimous act of the states in convention." Blount also voted for ratification in the North Carolina convention. Later he had a political career in Tennessee, where he achieved the dubious distinction of being the only man ever expelled from the U.S. Senate—for conspiracy to bring about an attack by Britain on Spanish Florida and Louisiana.

X

Delegates from Delaware

John Dickinson

DICKINSON'S pre-Revolutionary activity and his authorship of the Dickinson draft of the Articles have already been discussed. Although he practiced law in Philadelphia, Dickinson had grown up in Delaware and had maintained his connections there, so that actually he was a citizen of both states. He represented Delaware in Congress and during the 1780's was governor, in successive terms, of both Delaware and Pennsylvania. In 1785 he left Philadelphia and returned to Delaware where he went into semi-retirement.

Dickinson never lost his preference for monarchy over republican government, but he was a realist. Early in the convention he referred to a limited monarchy as "one of the best governments in the world. It was not certain," he said, "that the same blessings were derivable from any other form. It was certain that equal blessings had never yet been derived from any of the republican form. A limited monarchy however was out of the question. The spirit of the times, the state of . . . affairs, forbade the experiment, if it were desirable."

Dickinson accepted the necessity, even the desirability, of continuing the state governments. On June 2 he said that he "had no idea of abolishing the state governments as some gentlemen seemed inclined to do. The happiness of this country in his opinion required that considerable power be left in the hands of the states." Dickinson believed that "one branch of the legislature should be drawn immediately from the people; and that the other should be chosen by the legislatures of the states. This combination of the state governments with the national government was as politic as it was unavoidable." Although Dickinson favored a strong national government, he felt that the states should retain a "considerable agency in the system." Without any powers, the states could not act as a check on the national government. Abolition of the states as entities, Dickinson felt, "would degrade the councils of our country, would be impracticable, would be ruinous." The proposed national system was like the solar system; as "planets," the states "ought to be left to move freely in their proper orbits."

The appearance of the New Jersey plan prompted Dickinson to tell Madison that this was "the consequence of pushing things too far." Some of the smaller states, he told Madison, wish for "a good national government," but will not "be deprived of an equality of suffrage, in both branches of the legislature." It is clear, however, that Dickinson saw the need for national supremacy over the states. On June 8 he spoke on behalf of the congressional negative, since he saw the greater potential danger coming from the states.

Dickinson also opposed compensation of congressmen by the states: the general government should avoid this kind of dependence. Nor should it have to be invited into states to control domestic violence. In still another area, Dickinson favored general jurisdiction: the Constitution should not authorize the states severally to import slaves. "The true question was whether the national happiness would be promoted or impeded by the importation, and this question ought to be left to the national government, not to the states particularly interested." After the convention Dickinson urged ratification of the Constitution in his letters signed "Fabius." But his political career was over.

George Read

READ, a lawyer, had been a member of both the First and Second Continental Congresses, and although he voted against independence he did sign the Declaration. He was active in the Delaware constitutional convention of 1776, a prominent leader in the legislature thereafter, and a delegate to the Annapolis convention.

Throughout the convention Read was outspoken against the sovereignty of the states. On June 6 he declared that the delegates seemed unduly attached to state governments. "A national government must soon of necessity swallow all of them up," he said. "They will soon be reduced to the mere office of electing the national Senate." He hoped the convention would abandon all thought of trying to patch up the old confederation. "It would be like putting new cloth on an old garment." We must establish a general government based on new principles, Read said. "The state magistrates may disagree but the people are with us."

Read's distrust of distinct states was also apparent in his opposition to a resolution that would have guaranteed "republican government and territory to each state." He hoped to do "away with states altogether and unite them all into one great society." He told small states "that it was their interest that we should become one people as much as possible, that state attachments should be extinguished as much as possible, that the Senate should be so constituted as to have the feelings of citizens of the whole."

Read desired a general government that was "truly national," without "too much of a federal mixture in it. . . . In order to obtain one the whole states must be incorporated. If the states remain, the representatives of the large ones will stick together, and carry every thing before them. The executive also will be chosen under the influence of this partiality, and will betray it in his administration. These jealousies are inseparable from the scheme of leaving the states in existence." On July 10, Read said that he "hoped the objects of the general government would be much more numerous than seemed to be expected by some gentlemen, and that they would become more and more so." And on August 8, speaking against a state residence requirement for Congressmen, Read reminded a supporter of the motion that "we were now forming a national government and [that] such a regulation would correspond little with the idea that we were one people."

Read naturally was in favor of the congressional negative and also advocated life membership for Senators. He was instrumental in bringing about approval of the Constitution in Delaware, which became the first state to ratify. As one of Delaware's first Senators, Read was a staunch Federalist. He resigned in 1793 to become chief justice of Delaware, a post he held until his death.

Gunning Bedford

A PRINCETON graduate, lawyer, and large landowner, Bedford had been a state legislator, a member of Congress, attorney-general of Delaware, and a delegate to the Annapolis convention. At Philadelphia, however, he was not particularly active in the debates.

Originally he was in favor of merely strengthening the Articles of Confederation. On June 30 he contended that there was no middle way between a perfect consolidation and a mere confederacy of the states. "The first is out of the question, and in the latter they must continue if not perfectly, yet equally sovereign. . . . We must like Solon make such a government as the people will approve." Like Read, Bedford felt that the people were agreeable to enlarging the powers of the general government. He was certain that "the large states dare not dissolve the confederation. If they do, the small ones will find some foreign ally of more honor and good faith, who will take them by the hand and do them justice." This would be a natural consequence, said Bedford, "which ought to be avoided by enlarging the federal powers, not annihilating the federal system. This is what the people expect. All agree in the necessity of a more efficient government and why not make such an one as they desire?" For his reference to the possibility of the small states seeking foreign alliances, Bedford was rebuked by Rufus King, and he later apologized to the convention.

In June he opposed the congressional negative, saying that, "after all, if a state does not obey the law of the new system, must not force be resorted to as the only ultimate remedy, in this as in any other system? It seems as if Pennsylvania and Virginia by the conduct of their deputies wished to provide a system in which they would have an enormous and monstrous influence. Besides, how can it be thought that the proposed negative can be exercised? Are the laws of the states to be suspended in the most urgent cases until they can be sent seven or eight hundred miles, and undergo the deliberations of a body who may be incapable of judging of them? Is the national legislature too to sit continually in order to revise the laws of the states?"

But in July, once the states were assured of equal representation in the Senate, he moved to expand the legislative power of Congress beyond that set forth in the original Virginia plan. He was subsequently appointed a United States district judge in 1789 and held the post until his death.

Richard Bassett

THE SON of a tavern-keeper, Bassett was later adopted by a lawyer, from whom he learned his profession and inherited a sizable estate. He had attended the Delaware constitutional convention, served in both houses of the state legislature, and participated as a delegate to the Annapolis convention. Bassett, an ardent Methodist, was the only religious enthusiast at the convention. He did not participate in the debates but is recorded as having voted against the congressional negative. A leading member of the ratification convention, he was a Federalist Senator from 1789 to 1793. He was chief justice of the Delaware court of common pleas from 1793 to 1799, and governor from 1799 to 1801. Bassett was one of the "midnight judges" appointed by President John Adams just before Adams left office. The commissions were withheld by Jefferson, and the famous case of *Marbury v. Madison* was the result.

Jacob Broom

BROOM, as the son of a blacksmith, had origins as humble as Bassett's. Broom became a prosperous businessman of many interests—real estate, insurance, and cotton mills—and served several terms in the Delaware legislature. At the convention he seldom spoke, but he is known to have favored a life term for the executive and the congressional negative. He is probably the least known of all the delegates to the convention.

XI

Delegates from Georgia

Abraham Baldwin

LIKE Jacob Broom, Baldwin was a blacksmith's son. Born in Connecticut, he managed to graduate from Yale and become a licensed minister. He taught religion at Yale and was an army chaplain during the Revolution. Turning to the law, he went to Georgia, entered politics immediately, and served both in Congress and in the legislature. Although he was probably the ablest of the Georgia delegates at Philadelphia, Baldwin participated little in the debates at the convention. He did speak out strongly in favor of the Senate's being the representative of property owners.

Envisioning Georgia as a populous state, Baldwin was originally in favor of proportional representation. His subsequent defection, probably influenced by the Connecticut delegation, helped make possible the adoption of the compromise. Baldwin said that he "would have wished that the powers of the general legislature had been defined, before the mode of constituting it had been agitated," and also that it "appears to be agreed that the government we should adopt ought to be energetic and formidable, yet I would guard against the danger of becoming too formidable." He was against a provision prohibiting slavery, saying that he "had conceived national objects alone to be before the convention, not such as like the present were of a local nature."

Baldwin served in the House from 1789 to 1799 and in the Senate from 1799 until his death in 1807. During this period he was a faithful Jeffersonian, opposing the Hamilton politics, voting against the Alien and Sedition Laws, voting to repeal the Judiciary Act of 1801, and voting to convict Justice Chase.

William Few

BROOM, Baldwin, and Bassett to the contrary, the convention was dominated by men drawn from the upper classes. Few was remarkable in that he was a product of the small farmer class. His family had been involved in the Regulator movement in North Carolina. Burned out by the British, the family went to Georgia where they became ardent revolutionists. William Few saw military duty, became a lawyer, served in the Georgia legislature, and was twice elected a delegate to Congress. At the convention he did not enter into the debates, but he signed the Constitution and supported it in the Georgia ratification convention. He was a U.S. Senator from 1789 to 1793 and federal judge from 1796 to 1799. Resigning, he went to New York where he eventually became a bank president.

William Pierce

LITTLE is known of Pierce's background and early life. After serving with distinction in the Revolution, he settled in Savannah, where he engaged in a general mercantile and banking business and was a delegate to Congress in 1787. He too took no active part in the debates and is remembered chiefly for his lively and interesting character sketches of the other delegates.

In two situations, however, he revealed that he was no believer in state sovereignty. On May 31 he said that it "appeared clear" to him "that unless we established a government that should carry at least some of its principles into the mass of the people, we might as well depend upon the present confederation. If the influence of the states is not lost in some part of the new government we never shall have anything like a national institution. But in my opinion it will be right to show the sovereignty of the state in one branch of the legislature, and that should be in the Senate." And at the end of June he stated: "The great difficulty in Congress arose from the mode of voting. Members spoke on the floor as state advocates, and were biased by local advantages. What is federal? No more than a compact between states; and the one heretofore formed is insufficient. We are now met to remedy its defects, and our difficulties are great, but not, I hope, insurmountable. State distinctions must be sacrificed so far as the general government shall render it necessary without, however, destroying them altogether. Although I am here as a representative from a small state, I consider myself as a citizen of the United States, whose general interest I will always support."

Pierce left the convention in August and was not present for the signing of the Constitution. He wrote to a friend that he most certainly would have signed—"with all my heart"—if pressing business had not taken him to New York.

William Houstoun

SON OF a royal officer in the government of Georgia, Houstoun was educated and studied law in England. The recorded details of his life are meager. Like all the other delegates from Georgia, Houstoun was a member of Congress in 1787 and served in a dual capacity to save the state travel expenses. His role in the convention was insignificant, and he left when it was about half over. Commenting on the proposal to guarantee the states a republic form of government, he said that he "was afraid of perpetuating the existing constitutions of the states. That of Georgia was a very bad one, and he hoped [it] would be revised and amended." The constitution he referred to was the one drawn up by anti-nationalists in 1777, providing for a unicameral legislature and broad suffrage rights. Houstoun also opposed the equal representation of the states in the Senate.

XII

Delegates from New York

Alexander Hamilton

BORN in the West Indies, this authentic genius entered Columbia College in 1773, and one year later, at the age of nineteen, he wrote brilliant and penetrating pamphlets on the relations between the colonies and England. In 1777 Hamilton became Washington's aide and secretary, rendering invaluable service until he resigned in 1781. The next year, after three months' study, he was admitted to the New York bar and was immediately elected to Congress.

Hamilton was one of the first Americans to think along truly national lines, and even before the Articles had been ratified he correctly diagnosed their fatal weakness and prescribed the necessary remedy. Writing to James Duane in 1780, Hamilton said: "The idea of an uncontrollable sovereignty in each state over its internal police will defeat the other powers given to Congress, and make our union feeble and precarious." In order to remedy this weakness, Hamilton suggested "calling immediately a convention of all states, with full authority to conclude finally upon a general confederation" which would give Congress the necessary powers. Hamilton's drafting, at the Annapolis convention, the call for the Philadelphia convention has already been mentioned, as has his role in placing the New York legislature on record in favor of the move.

In 1787 he was thirty-two years old. Actually, his greatest contribution to the establishment of the Constitution was made before and after the convention rather than at Philadelphia. There he was consistently outvoted by Yates and Lansing in determining the New York vote. Hamilton finally left, returning only after his fellows had in turn departed. He stayed on then to sign the Constitution on behalf of New York.

On June 18, after the Virginia and New Jersey plans had both been advanced, Hamilton made his principal speech of the convention. He was unfriendly to both plans, feeling that the latter was especially unsuitable because it would allow the states to retain their sovereignty. After referring to the sovereignty of the states and "the ambition of their demagogues," Hamilton continued:

> How then are all these evils to be avoided? Only by such a complete sovereignty in the general government as will turn all the strong principles and passions above mentioned on its side. . . . The general power, whatever be its form if it preserves itself, must swallow up the state powers, otherwise it will be swallowed up by them. It is against all the principles of a good government to vest the requisite powers in such a body as Congress. Two sovereignties can not co-exist within the same limits. Giving powers to Congress must eventuate in a bad government or in no government. The plan of New Jersey therefore will not do.

When Hamilton looked about for a remedy, he was discouraged by the vastness of the country to be governed. The cost of maintaining a general government was equally formidable, unless the expenses of state governments could be reduced. Indeed, although he did not mean to shock public opinion with such a proposal, he felt that necessary economy could be effected by eliminating state governments and relying upon a general government alone. State governments, after all, served none of the "great purposes of commerce, revenue, or agriculture." Hamilton realized that subordinate authorities would be necessary—district tribunals and "corporations for local purposes. But *cui bono*, the vast and expensive apparatus now appertaining to the states? The only difficulty of a serious nature which occurred to him, was that of drawing representatives from the extremes to the center of the community."

Hamilton then offered his own plan for a government with "supreme" legislative, executive, and judicial branches. The legislature, in which the Senators were to hold office for life, was to have "power to pass all laws whatsoever" subject to the absolute veto of the executive who was also to hold office for life. In order to assure national supremacy, the plan provided that all "laws of the particular states contrary to the constitution or laws of the United States to be utterly void; and the better to prevent such laws being passed, the governor or president of each state shall be appointed by the general government and shall have a negative upon the laws about to be passed in the state of which he is governor or president." Hamilton's notes for his speech that day, after setting forth the objections to the confederation, contain the following comments:

There seem to be but three lines of conduct.

    I. A league offensive and defensive, treaty of commerce, and apportionment of the public debt.

    II. An amendment of the present confederation by adding such powers as the public mind seems nearest being matured to grant.

    III. The forming a new government to pervade the whole with decisive powers, in short, with complete sovereignty.

To avoid any misunderstanding of his position, Hamilton rose the next day to state that he had not been understood a day earlier. "By an abolition of the states, he meant that no boundary could be drawn between the national and state legislatures; that the former must therefor have indefinite authority. If it were limited at all, the rivalship of the states would gradually subvert it. Even as corporations, the extent of some of them as Virginia, Massachusetts, and others would be formidable. As states, he thought they ought to be abolished."

On June 21 Hamilton opposed a motion that the manner of electing the lower house of Congress be left to the state legislatures. He considered the motion as intended manifestly to transfer the election from the people to the state legislatures, which would essentially vitiate the plan. "It would increase that state influence which could not be too watchfully guarded against. All too must admit the possibility, in case the general government should maintain itself, that the state governments might gradually dwindle into nothing. The system therefore should not be engrafted on what might possibly fail." And on June 29 he opposed equal representation in Congress, asserting that "as states are a collection of individual men which ought we to respect most, the rights of the people composing them, or of the artificial beings resulting from the composition? Nothing could be more preposterous or absurd than to sacrifice the former to the latter." As quoted by Yates, Hamilton said, "The question, after all, is, is it our interest in modifying this general government to sacrifice individual rights to the preservation of the rights of an artificial being, called states?"

During his absence from the convention, Hamilton wrote to Washington on July 3 that the "prevailing apprehension among thinking men is, that the convention, from a fear of shocking the popular opinion, will not go far enough." After he returned to the convention on September 6, he confided "that he had been restrained from entering into the discussions by his dislike of the scheme of government in general; but as he meant to support the plan to be recommended, as better than nothing, he wished in this place to offer a few remarks."

Hamilton's contribution to the ratification of the Constitution by writing most of the *Federalist Papers* is well known. Even more remarkable, however, was his role in the ratification fight in New York, where he succeeded—in one of the most amazing individual performances ever in any popular assembly—in wangling approval from a hostile convention. His subsequent career as Washington's Secretary of the Treasury, his financial measures, and his advocacy of a broad construction of the powers of the central government to achieve the purposes of the Constitution were all consistent with the philosophy of nationalism which he had espoused from the beginning.

John Lansing

DESCENDED from an old Dutch family, Lansing was an Albany lawyer who had been in the legislature for six terms and served as speaker for two years. He had been mayor of Albany and was a member of Congress in 1784-1785. In Philadelphia, Lansing was an outspoken opponent of the idea of forming a national government, not only because he considered it beyond the power of the convention but also because he believed that such national power would destroy the sovereignty of the states.

On June 16 Lansing called for "the reading of the first resolution of each plan, which he considered as involving principles directly in contrast; that of Mr. Paterson, [New Jersey plan], says he, sustains the sovereignty of the respective states, that of Mr. Randolph [Virginia plan] destroys it. The latter requires a negative on all the laws of the particular states; the former, only certain general powers for the general good. The plan of Mr. Randolph, in short, absorbs all power except what may be exercised in the little local matters of the states which are not objects worthy of the supreme cognizance." Yate's notes for that same day record Lansing as comparing the Paterson plan with the one offered by Virginia: "This system is fairly contrasted with the one ready to be reported, the one federal, and the other national. In the first, the powers are exercised as flowing from the respective state governments. The second, deriving its authority from the people of the respective states, which latter must ultimately destroy or annihilate the state governments."

On June 20, addressing himself to the proposal for a congressional negative, Lansing wondered whether the general legislature would have time to pass upon all state laws. And how competent, Lansing asked, would the judges be? "Will a gentleman from Georgia be a judge of the expediency of a law which is to operate in New Hampshire? Such a negative would be more injurious than that of Great Britain heretofore was."

To be effectual, Lansing said, the national government would have to possess the influence which attends the granting of offices and honors. Since the states would not agree to this, they would have to be abolished, Lansing concluded. "Will any one say this would ever be agreed to?" Lansing doubted that any general government "equally beneficial to all" could be achieved. That form then under consideration, he was sure, "must be utterly unattainable."

The system was, among other things, "too novel and complex. No man could foresee what its operation will be either with respect to the general government or the state governments. One or other it has been surmised must absorb the whole." Yates's notes on the same day record Lansing as follows:

> I am clearly of opinion that I am not authorized to accede to a system which will annihilate the state governments, and the Virginia plan is declarative of such extinction. And I hold it as an undoubted truth, as long as state distinctions remain, let the national government be modified as you please, both branches of your legislature will be impressed with local and state attachments. This national government will, from their power, have great influence in the state governments; and the existence of the latter are only saved in appearance. And has it not been asserted that they expect their extinction?

Concluding that the convention was acting beyond its powers to create a national government destructive of state sovereignty and that they were powerless to stop it, Lansing and his colleague Yates left the convention on July 10, never to return. Lansing opposed the Constitution in the New York convention. Subsequently he served as a judge from 1790 to 1814, when he returned to his law practice. On a visit to New York in 1829, he disappeared. No trace was ever found of him, and the circumstances remain unknown.

Robert Yates

ANOTHER Albany lawyer, Yates had been a member of the various New York provincial congresses and was appointed in 1777 a judge of the New York supreme court. As a dedicated supporter of Governor Clinton during the 1780's Yates was very much an anti-nationalist. In the convention he voted on May 30 against the motion to establish a national government. In his notes for June 9 he recorded his own ideas as follows: "Upon the whole, every sovereign state according to a confederation must have an equal vote, or there is an end to liberty. As long therefore as state distinctions are held up, this rule must invariably apply; and if a consolidated national government must take place, then state distinctions must cease, or the states must be equalized."

Upon leaving the convention, Yates and Lansing set forth their reasons in a report to Governor Clinton.

> It is with the sincerest concern we observe, that, in the prosecution of the important objects of our mission, we have reduced to the disagreeable alternative, of either exceeding the powers delegated to us, and giving our assent to measures which we conceive destructive to the political happiness of the citizens of the United States, or opposing our opinions to that of a body of respectable men, to whom those citizens have given the most unequivocal proofs of confidence. Thus circumstanced, under these impressions, to have hesitated, would have been culpable. We, therefore, gave the principles of the constitution, which has received the sanction of a majority of the convention, our decided and unreserved dissent. But we must candidly confess that we should have been opposed to any system, however modified, which had in object the consolidation of the United States into one government.

Then, referring to the instructions which they had received on going to the convention, they continued: "We were led to believe, that a system of consolidated government could not in the remotest degree, have been in the contemplation of the legislature of this state." The adoption of measures which tended to deprive the states of their sovereignty was a procedure of such moment, Yates and Lansing assumed, that it could not properly be undertaken without express instructions to the delegates. "Reasoning in this manner, we were of opinion, that the leading feature of every amendment, ought to be the preservation of the individual states, in their uncontrolled constitutional rights." Lansing and Yates then listed reasons for their objecting to a general government. "These reasons were," they believed, "conclusive against any system of consolidated government: to that recommended by the convention, we suppose most of them very forcibly apply. . . . We were not present at the completion of the new Constitution, but before we left the convention, its principles were so well established, as to convince us, that no alteration was to be expected, to conform it to our ideas of expediency and safety. A persuasion, that our further attendance would be fruitless and unavailing, rendered us less solicitous to return."

Yates opposed the ratification of the Constitution in the New York convention. Accepting the result, however, he ran for governor the next year as a Federalist candidate against Clinton but was defeated. He became chief justice of the New York supreme court in 1790, serving until 1798. In 1795 he reverted to his Anti-federalism and ran again for governor, this time against John Jay, and was again defeated.

XIII

Delegates from
South Carolina

John Rutledge

ANOTHER English-educated delegate, Rutledge, a highly successful Charleston lawyer, was a seasoned veteran whose career went back to the Stamp Act Congress and also included service in both the First and Second Continental Congresses, where he took nationalist positions. He was the principal drafter of South Carolina's 1776 constitution and became the state's first governor. During the Revolution Rutledge rendered heroic efforts, assuming almost dictatorial powers.

At the convention Rutledge took a cautious approach toward national supremacy. Thus on June 5 he opposed "establishing any national tribunal except a single supreme one. The state tribunals are most proper to decide in all cases in the first instance. . . . The right of appeal to the supreme national tribunal being sufficient to secure the national rights and uniformity of judgments."

On August 23, however, he moved the adoption of a supremacy clause almost identical with the one eventually adopted, requiring state judges to be bound by the Constitution, laws, and treaties of the United States in cases of conflict with state constitutions and laws. Furthermore, he contemplated clearly that the Supreme Court would decide controversies between the states and also between the nation and the states. Thus on August 24 Rutledge said that "this provision for deciding controversies between the states was necessary under the Confederation, but will be rendered unnecessary by the national judiciary now to be established." He moved to strike the provision. And on August 27, opposing a motion to make Supreme Court judges removable by the President on recommendation of Congress, Rutledge said, "If the Supreme Court is to judge between the U.S. and particular states, this alone is an insuperable objection to the motion."

Rutledge believed that Congress' powers should be enumerated. On the proposition to grant legislative power in all cases to which the state legislatures were individually incompetent, he "objected to the vagueness of the term *incompetent,* and said they could not well decide how to vote until they should see an exact enumeration of the powers comprehended by this definition."

Rutledge also opposed the congressional negative. "If nothing else," he said, "this alone would damn and ought to damn the Constitution. Will any state ever agree to be bound hand and foot in this manner? It is worse than making mere corporations of them whose by-laws would not be subject to this shackle."

Rutledge also believed that property should be part of the basis of representation, that Congress should be elected by the state legislatures, and that the President should be elected by Congress. He was against restrictions on the slave trade but thought the national government should assume state war debts.

As chairman of the highly important Committee of Detail, Rutledge assumed primary responsibility for preparing the draft which his committee reported back to the convention on August 6. Speaking of this draft, Rutledge's biographer states: "Nowhere in the document are the words nation or national used, and yet between every line and into almost every syllable is breathed something to create national power. This astounding indirection of expression is essentially Rutledgian. He had the faculty of making a simple assertion in plain language, seemingly quite innocent and irrefutable. Yet it contained a hidden power far transcending the direct postulate."

Rutledge, from 1789 to 1791, was an associate justice of the Supreme Court. He was appointed Chief Justice in 1795 but was denied confirmation by the Senate, probably because of an untimely speech condemning the Jay Treaty.

Charles Cotesworth Pinckney

ANOTHER prominent Charlestown lawyer, Pinckney had been educated in England and had studied law under Blackstone. Returning to America in 1769, he became active in colonial politics and government, serving in the colonial and state legislatures. During the revolution he rendered brilliant military service and rose to the rank of brigadier-general. He was (and is) referred to as "General Pinckney" to distinguish him from his younger cousin.

In the convention Pinckney set forth his general views on nation-state relations on June 6. He wished to have "a good national government" but also wanted to leave "a considerable share of power in the states." Because the people were so scattered, Pinckney said, election of either branch of the national government by the people was "totally impracticable." The legislatures, furthermore, would be more effective than the people in guarding against "bad measures." The South Carolina legislature, for instance, because it "had some sense of character," Pinckney said, refused to make paper money legal tender—this in opposition to the people's preferences. State legislatures, he continued, should be given some participation in the national government in order to prevent their attempts to thwart it.

Pinckney was acute enough to realize immediately that the New Jersey plan was put forth on behalf of equal representation for the small states and not in the interest of state sovereignty. Thus on June 16 he said that "the whole comes to this . . . Give New Jersey an equal vote, and she will dismiss her scruples, and concur in the national system. He thought the convention authorized to go any length in recommending, which they found necessary to remedy the evils which produced this convention."

Pinckney favored property qualifications for all members of all branches of the national government. He opposed paying salaries to Senators, because he wished to be assured that only the wealthy could serve. When this was voted down, however, Pinckney urged that the states take an active role in the general government. "If the Senate was to be appointed by the states, it ought in pursuance of the same idea to be paid by the states; and the states ought not to be barred from the opportunity of calling members of it into offices at home." Pinckney proposed a four-year term for Senators. "A longer term would fix them at the seat of government. They would acquire an interest there, perhaps transfer their property and lose sight of the states they represent. Under these circumstances the distant states would labor under great disadvantages," he said.

Pinckney's military experience persuaded him that the regulation and discipline of the militia should come within the province of the national government. "Uniformity was essential. The states would never keep up a proper discipline of their militia." Consequently, Pinckney opposed divided control. In renewing Mason's original motion, Pinckney said, "For a part to be under the general and a part under the state governments would be an incurable evil. He saw no room for such distrust of the general government." He defended slavery but opposed religious qualifications for office. Near the end of the convention, he said that he had overcome his prejudices against the eastern states, whose delegates, he found, were "as liberal and candid as any men whatever."

Pinckney was a member of the ratification convention in South Carolina, where he strongly supported the Constitution. Subsequently he was the Federalist candidate for Vice-President in 1800, and for President in 1804 and 1808.

Pierce Butler

ALWAYS vain about being a nobleman's son, Butler had been born in Ireland. In 1773 he emigrated to South Carolina, where he became a planter and politician. From 1778 to 1789 he was almost constantly in the state legislature, where, although he himself possessed wealth and property, he failed to align himself with the planter-merchant group (probably because of personal rivalry) and backed many of the reform measures of back-country democrats.

Butler was cautious in his approach to a strong central government. When the Virginia propositions were introduced on May 31, Butler feared that the proposed reduction of state powers would destroy "all that balance and security of interests among the States" which he felt should be preserved. He asked Randolph to explain his ideas further. Butler opposed the proposal to establish inferior tribunals. "The people, he said, "will not bear such innovations. The states will revolt at such encroachments. Supposing such an establishment to be useful, we must not venture on it. We must follow the example of Solon who gave the Athenians not the best government he could devise, but the best they would receive." State tribunals, Butler said, could handle the business for which the national sub-system of courts was being proposed. Butler was vehemently opposed to the congressional negative, "as cutting off all hope of equal justice to the distant states. The people there would not, he was sure, give it a hearing."

Butler was adamant on the principle that property as such should be represented in Congress. He advanced this idea on June 11, adding "that money was power; and that the states ought to have weight in the government in proportion to their wealth." Yates recorded Butler as having said on June 26 that the Senate should be considered as "the aristocratic part of our government." The Senate, in short, was "to represent the states according to their property." An extract from King's notes would indicate that Butler was more interested in protecting property rights than states rights. "I am against determining the mode of election," said Butler, "until the ratio of representation is fixed. If that proceeds on a principle favorable to wealth as well as numbers of free inhabitants, I am content to unite with Delaware in abolishing the state legislatures, and becoming one nation instead of a confederation of republics." Butler was in favor of "submitting the whole militia to the general authority, which had the care of the general defence." A slaveholder, he insisted on the inclusion of a rendition clause.

Butler defended the Constitution in South Carolina but was not a member of the ratification convention. He was elected a Federalist Senator in 1789 and again in 1802, each time resigning during his term and never bothering to follow party lines very closely.

Charles Pinckney

LIKE his father, Pinckney was a wealthy planter and lawyer in Charlestown. He had served in the state legislature and had been a member of Congress from 1784 to 1787. There he had sought to increase central powers, and had served on a committee which made extensive recommendations in that direction. These not being adopted, he supported the idea of a general convention.

In 1787 he was just thirty years old. On May 29, after the Virginia plan had been presented, Pinckney submitted to the convention his own draft of a plan for a new government. Just what happened to it is not known, and the exact contents of the missing "Pinckney draft" have been a historical puzzle since then. He had also prepared a speech in connection with his presentation of the plan. It was never delivered, but it was published shortly after the convention was over. This pamphlet therefore accurately reflects Pinckney's views at the time of the convention on the question of national supremacy and state sovereignty.

"I apprehend," said Pinckney, that "the true intention of the states in uniting, is to have a firm national government, capable of effectually executing its acts, and dispensing its benefits and protection. In it alone can be vested those powers and prerogatives which more particularly distinguish a sovereign state." The old notion of state sovereignty must be abandoned, Pinckney said, since "it is absurd to suppose there can be more than one sovereignty within a government."

Pinckney defined the areas of power further:

The states should retain nothing more than that mere local legislation, which, as districts of a general government, they can exercise more to the benefit of their particular inhabitants, than if it was vested in the supreme council; but in every foreign concern, as well as those internal regulations, which respecting the whole to be uniform and national, the states must not be suffered to interfere. No act of the federal government in pursuance of its constitutional powers ought by any means to be within control of the state legislatures; if it is, experience warrants me in asserting, they will assuredly interfere and defeat its operation. . . . It is agreed that a reform of our government is indispensable, and that a stronger federal system must be adopted; but it will ever be found, that let your system upon paper be as complete and guarded as you can make it, yet still if the state assemblies are suffered to legislate without restriction or revision, your government will remain weak, disjointed, and inefficient.

Despite what we may have thought in the past about state sovereignty, Pinckney continued, the states interests lie

. . . in concentrating as much as possible, the force and resources of the Union in one superintending government, where alone they can be exercised with effect. In granting to the federal government certain exclusive national powers, you invest all their incidental rights. The term exclusive involves every right or authority necessary to their execution. . . . Though our present disorders must be attributed in the first instance, to the weakness and inefficacy of our government, it must still be confessed, they have been precipitated by the refractory and inattentive conduct of the states; most of which have neglected altogether the performance of their federal duties, and whenever their state-policy, or interests prompted, used their retained sovereignty, to the injury and disgrace of the federal head. Nor can any other conduct be expected, while they are suffered to consider themselves as distinct sovereignties, or in any other light, than as parts of a common government.

In short, Pinckney felt that unless the state powers were retrenched with "as much force and vigor" as possible concentrated in the Union, we would "soon be a divided, and consequently an unhappy people."

He doubted that the convention would at first go as far as he wished, "but," he said, "this I think may be safely asserted, that upon a clear and comprehensive view of the relative situation of the Union, and its members, we shall be convinced of the policy of concentering in the federal head, a complete supremacy in the affairs of government; leaving only to the states, such powers as may be necessary for the management of their internal concerns."

Like Madison, Pinckney believed that the congressional negative was essential to the maintenance of national supremacy. On June 8 Pinckney moved "that the national legislature should have authority to negative all laws which they should judge to be improper." He also urged:

. . . that such a universality of the power was indispensably necessary to render it effectual; that the states must be kept in due subordination to the nation; that if the states were left to act of themselves in any case, it would be impossible to defend the national prerogatives, however extensive they might be on paper; that the acts of Congress had been defeated by this means; nor had foreign treaties escaped repeated violations; that this universal negative was in fact the cornerstone of an efficient national government; that under the British government the negative of the Crown had been found beneficial, and the states are more one nation now, than the colonies were then.

He urged the negative again July 17, and as late in the convention as August 23 Pinckney moved to add as an additional power of Congress the right to negative all laws passed by the states which in its opinion interfered with the general interests and harmony of the Union, "provided that two-thirds of the members of each House assent to the same."

On the other hand, Pinckney did not believe that the states should be obliterated but considered that they would be useful, even necessary, for local purposes. Thus on June 25 he stated that no position appeared more true to him than this: "that the general government cannot effectually exist without reserving to the states the possession of their local rights. They are the instruments upon which the Union must frequently depend for the support and execution of their powers, however immediately operating upon the people, and not upon the states."

After supporting ratification in the South Carolina convention, Pinckney served as governor from 1789 to 1792, and again from 1796 to 1798. Gradually he became Republican in his politics, was elected to the Senate in 1798, and served as Jefferson's manager in South Carolina, for which service he was rewarded with the appointment as minister to Spain from 1801 to 1805. Subsequently he was again elected governor and served in the state legislature and in Congress.

XIV

Delegates from Massachusetts

Nathaniel Gorham

A MERCHANT from Charlestown who also engaged in large-scale land speculation, Gorham had served in the colonial assembly, the provincial congress, the state constitutional convention, and the state legislature, of which he was speaker three times. He was a delegate to Congress in 1782-1783 and again in 1785-1787, serving as president during the latter term.

In Philadelphia, Gorham was a consistent advocate of national power. On June 29 he addressed himself to the fears of the small states by stressing the advantages of a strong union. "The states as now confederated have no doubt a right to refuse to be consolidated, or to be formed into any new system," Gorham felt. But, he continued, the smaller states, "which seemed most ready to object," had the most to lose in any rupture with the union. "The weak therefore were most interested in establishing some general system for maintaining order. If among individuals, composed partly of weak, and partly of strong, the former most need the protection of law and government, the case is exactly the same with weak and powerful states." Gorham proceeded to specifics:

> What would be the situation of Delaware in case of a separation of the states? Would she not lie at the mercy of Pennsylvania? Would not her true interest lie in being consolidated with her, and ought she not now to wish for such a union with Pennsylvania under one government as will put it out of the power of Pennsylvania to oppress her? Nothing can be more ideal than the danger apprehended by the states, from their being formed into one nation. . . . On the whole he considered a Union of the states as necessary to their happiness, and a firm general government as necessary to their Union. He should consider it as his duty if his colleagues viewed the matter in the same light he did to stay here as long as any other state would remain with them in order to agree on some plan that could with propriety be recommended to the people.

Since Gorham felt that extant state governments would tend to encroach constantly upon the general government, he advocated redivision of the Union as soon as possible, preferably into small units. If the general government were strong enough at the outset, it would not be so important to the states whether they were great or small. On July 23 he emphasized that the "strength of the general government will lie not in the largeness, but in the smallness of the states."

Gorham supported the plan for inferior tribunals and upheld the power of the national government to forcibly suppress rebellion within a state.

> Mr. Gorham thought it strange that a rebellion should be known to exist in the empire, and the general government should be restrained from interposing to subdue it. At this rate an enterprising citizen might erect the standard of monarchy in a particular state, might gather together partisans from all quarters, might extend his views from state to state, and threaten to establish a tyranny over the whole and the general government be compelled to remain an inactive witness of its own destruction. With regard to different parties in a state; as long as they confine their disputes to words they will be harmless to the general government and to each other. If they appeal to the sword it will then be necessary for the general government, however difficult it may be to decide on the merits of their contest, to interpose and put an end to it.

On August 9 Gorham supported the power of Congress to control the conduct of congressional elections. He felt it would be as improper to take this power from the national legislature as to restrain the British Parliament from regulating elections.

Gorham was a member of the state convention, where he actively urged ratification of the Constitution. Shortly thereafter, as a result of his speculations, he became insolvent and died.

Rufus King

A HANDSOME and eloquent Harvard graduate, King had been in both the state legislature and Congress, where as late as 1785 he was opposed to any radical change in the Articles. Shortly thereafter he married the daughter of a New York City nationalist and by the time of the convention, when he was thirty-two, King was committed to a strong central government. Writing to Elbridge Gerry in early 1787 he stated: "Events are hurrying to a crisis; prudent and sagacious men should be ready to seize the most favorable circumstances to establish a more permanent and vigorous government."

King was one of those who denied that the states had ever been sovereign in the fullest sense of the word, even before and during the Articles. On June 19, in supporting the Randolph proposal that a national government be established,

> King wished as everything depended on this proposition, that no objections might be improperly indulged against the phraseology of it. He conceived that the import of the terms "states," "sovereignty," "national," and "federal" had been often used and applied in the discussion inaccurately and delusively. The states were not "sovereigns" in the sense contended for by some. They did not possess the peculiar features of sovereignty. They could not make war, nor peace, nor alliances, nor treaties. Considering them as political beings, they were dumb, for they could not speak to any foreign sovereign whatever. They were deaf, for they could not hear any propositions from such sovereign. They had not even the organs or faculties of defense or offence, for they could not of themselves raise troops, or equip vessels, for war. On the other side, if the Union of the states comprises the idea of a confederation, it comprises that also of consolidation. A Union of the states is a union of the men composing them, from whence a national character results to the whole. Congress can act alone without the states. They can act and their acts will be binding against the instructions of the states. If they declare war, war is *de jure* declared, captures made in pursuance of it are lawful. No acts of the states can vary the situation or prevent the judicial consequences. If the states therefore retained some portion of their sovereignty, they had certainly divested themselves of essential portions of it. If they formed a confederacy in some respects, they formed a nation in others. The convention could clearly deliberate on and propose any alterations that Congress could have done under the federal articles, and could not Congress propose by virtue of the last article, a change in any article whatever; and as well that relating to the equality of suffrage, as any other. . . . He doubted much the practicability of annihilating the states; but thought that much of their power ought to be taken from them.

Aware of the rivalry between the states and the central government, King opposed the election of members of Congress by the state legislatures. He supposed that legislatures would constantly choose men subservient to their own views as contrasted to the general interest, and that they might even devise modes of election that would be subversive of the end in view.

King was opposed to equality of representation in the Senate because he thought it tended to perpetuate ideas of state sovereignty. On June 30 he stated that he was

. . . filled with astonishment that if we were convinced that every man in America was secured in all his rights, we should be ready to sacrifice this substantial good to the phantom of state sovereignty: that his feelings were more harrowed and his fears more agitated for his country than he could express, that he conceived this to be the last opportunity of providing for its liberty and happiness: that he could not therefore but repeat his amazement that when a just government, founded on a fair representation of the people of America was within our reach, we should renounce the blessing, from an attachment to the ideal freedom and importance of states: that should this wonderful illusion continue to prevail, his mind was prepared for every event, rather than sit down under a government founded in a vicious principle of representation and which must be as short-lived as it would be unjust.

Although King decried state sovereignty, he believed that the states should continue to perform important functions. Thus on June 30 King was for preserving the states in a subordinate degree. "As the fundamental rights of individuals are secured by express provisions in the state constitutions, why may not a like security be provided for the rights of states in the national constitution?"

Although King believed that the general government ought to be paramount, he did not think that Congress would have to meet every year. The essential concerns of the Congress were few. Once the chief of these —commerce and revenue—were settled, King felt, "alterations would be rarely necessary and easily made."

King was a member of the important Committee on Style which put the Constitution in its final form, and was a leading advocate of ratification in the Massachusetts convention. He then moved to New York, where he was elected to the Senate in 1789 and in 1795. There he was one of the most able of the Federalists and supported all the nationalist proposals of the administration. Appointed minister to England in 1796, he was so successful that he continued in this post under Jefferson, finally being relieved at his own request. He was the Federalist candidate for Vice-President in 1804 and again in 1808, was twice thereafter re-elected to the Senate, and was the Federalist candidate for President in 1816.

Elbridge Gerry

A MERCHANT's son and a Harvard graduate who married into a merchant family, Gerry signed both the Declaration of Independence and the Articles of Confederation and had twice been a delegate to Congress.

In the convention he was one of the most frequent speakers, but his positions were often inconsistent, and he lacked the ability to distinguish the important from the trivial. Consequently his influence, although significant, was not commensurate with the extent of his participation. One of the delegates described him as "a man of sense, but a Grumbletonian. He was of service by objecting to every thing he did not propose."

Gerry started out by supporting a strong central government. On June 29 he urged that "we never were independent states, were not such now, and never could be even on the principles of the Confederation." The states and the advocates for them were "intoxicated with the idea of their sovereignty." As a member of Congress when the Articles were framed, Gerry voted for allowing each state an equal vote, but against his judgment "and under the pressure of public danger, and the obstinacy of the lesser states." Gerry lamented the persistent disagreement in the convention. He felt that, instead of "coming here like a band of brothers, belonging to the same family, we seemed to have brought with us the spirit of political negotiators."

Both state governments and the federal government, he said on July 23, "have been too long acquiesced in, to be now shaken. He considered the Confederation to be paramount to any state constitution." His opposition to a motion to bypass the states in the election of the president was based on expediency rather than state attachment. "He thought the community not yet ripe for stripping the states of their powers, even such as might not be requisite for local purposes. He was for waiting till people should feel more the necessity of it."

On the other hand, on July 6 Gerry did not agree that the large states ought to be cut up. "This policy has been inculcated by the middling and smaller states, ungenerously and contrary to the spirit of the Confederation. Ambitious men will be apt to solicit needless divisions, till the states be reduced to the size of counties. If this policy should still actuate the small states, the large ones could not confederate safely with them, but would be obliged to consult their safety by confederating only with one another."

He was also opposed to the congressional negative:

He could not see the extent of such a power, and was against every power that was not necessary. He thought a remonstrance against unreasonable acts of the states would reclaim them. If it should not, force might be resorted to. He had no objection to authorize a negative to paper money and similar measures. When the Confederation was depending before Congress, Massachusetts was then for inserting the power of emitting paper money among the exclusive powers of Congress. He observed that the proposed negative would extend to the regulations of the militia, a matter on which the existence of a state might depend. The national legislature with such a power may enslave the states. Such an idea as this will never be acceded to. . . . The states too have different interests and are ignorant of each other's interests. The negative therefore will be abused.

On the matter of representation Gerry "thought that representation ought to be in the combined ratio of numbers of inhabitants and of wealth, and not of either singly." And on the compromise providing for equal representation in the Senate, Gerry said that this was "the critical question. He had rather agree to it than have no accommodation. A government short of a proper national plan if generally acceptable, would be preferable to a proper one which if it could be carried at all, would operate on discontented states." On July 14 he "favored the reconsideration with a view not of destroying the equality of votes, but of providing that the states should vote per capita, which he said would prevent the delays and inconveniences that had been experienced in Congress and would give a national aspect and spirit to the management of business."

Gerry was vehement in his resistance to national control of the militia. On August 18 he was convinced that this was "the last point remaining to be surrendered. If it be agreed to by the convention, the plan will have as black a mark as was set on Cain. [Gerry] had no such confidence in the general government as some gentlemen possessed, and believed it would be found that the states have not." In August he felt that federal dominance in this area was "making the states drill-sergeants. He had as leave let the citizens of Massachusetts be disarmed, as to take the command from the states, and subject them to the general legislature. It would be regarded as a system of despotism." And the same day, he said, "let us at once destroy the state governments, have an executive for life or hereditary, and a proper Senate, and then there would be some consistency in giving full powers to the general government. But as the states are not to be abolished, [Gerry] wondered at the attempts that were made to give powers inconsistent with their existence. He warned the convention against pushing the experiment too far. Some people will support a plan of vigorous government at every risk. Others of a more democratic case will oppose it with equal determination. And a civil war may be produced by the conflict."

In the end Gerry refused to sign the Constitution. The gist of his opposition was what he considered the excessive and unlimited scope of the powers vested in the new national government and the absence of sufficient limitations on those powers. He opposed the ratification of the Constitution in Massachusetts and in 1788 ran for Governor unsuccessfully as an Anti-federalist. His inconsistency cropped out again when he went to Congress in 1789 and supported Federalist policies and programs. He was later elected governor as a Republican, when he immortalized himself by his use of what became known as the gerrymander, and was thereafter elected Vice-President in 1812.

Caleb Strong

ANOTHER Harvard graduate and a lawyer of Northampton, Strong had been a county attorney, a member of the state constitutional convention of 1789, and a state senator from 1780 to 1789. Business took him away from the convention in August, and during his attendance he spoke only occasionally. Although he was not present for the signing, he was a leading supporter of the Constitution in the Massachusetts ratifying convention. He was elected Senator in 1789 and became a Federalist bulwark. Re-elected in 1793, Strong resigned three years later. In 1800, despite the Jeffersonian sweep, he was elected governor as a Federalist, defeating Gerry, and was subsequently re-elected six times. During the War of 1812 he refused to furnish state troops for national use.

XV

Delegates from Maryland

Daniel of St. Thomas Jenifer

THE HOLDER of various offices under the proprietary government and a man of considerable wealth, Jenifer had been president of the Maryland state senate and a delegate to Congress. He was a bachelor and a close friend of Washington. The senior man in his delegation, Jenifer played a minor role in the convention, but his few recorded positions were nationalist. Thus he was opposed to mere amendment of the Articles, to equality of state representation in the Senate, and to having state governors share in the power to appoint officers of the United States. He signed the Constitution and supported its ratification.

Daniel Carroll

EDUCATED in Flanders, the heir of a large estate, Carroll had served as a delegate to Congress and in the state legislature. In the convention he represented the movement in Maryland "in favor of centralized government powers." Although his participation was not extensive, Carroll's responses and reactions to the proceedings of the convention indicate that he was a strong nationalist.

Carroll "did not think the Confederation could be amended to answer its intentions." He was opposed to having state governors share in appointing officers of the United States, and he did not believe that members of Congress should be dependent on the states for their compensation. On this point, he said that he "had been much surprised at seeing this clause in the report. The dependence of both houses on the state legislatures is complete; especially as the members of the former are eligible to state offices. The state can now say: If you do not comply with our wishes, we will starve you: if you do we will reward you. The new government in this form was nothing more than a second edition of Congress in two volumes, instead of one. . . . The Senate was to represent and manage the affairs of the whole, and not to be the advocate of state interests. They ought then not to be dependent on nor paid by the states."

In 1789 Carroll was chosen as one of Maryland's first Senators, and in 1791 he became one of the first commissioners of the District of Columbia, which was located on land that he had owned.

Luther Martin

SON OF a farmer, Martin had graduated from Princeton and, after a stint as a schoolteacher, studied law and was admitted to the bar. He had been a delegate to Congress, where he proved to be extremely state-minded. In 1778 he was appointed attorney-general of Maryland, a position he held until 1805.

During the sessions in Philadelphia, Martin was an outspoken advocate of state sovereignty. His basic views were set forth in a speech delivered on June 20. "Mr. Luther Martin agreed with Colonel Mason as to the importance of the state governments. He would support them at the expense of the general government, which was instituted for the purpose of that support. At the separation from the British Empire, the people of America preferred the establishment of themselves into thirteen separate sovereignties instead of incorporating themselves into one. To these they look up for the security of their lives, liberties, and properties. To these they must look up. The federal government they formed, to defend the whole against foreign nations, in case of war, and to defend the lesser states against the ambition of the larger. They are afraid of granting powers unnecessarily, lest they should defeat the original end of the Union; lest the powers should prove dangerous to the sovereignties of the particular states which the Union was meant to support, and expose the lesser to being swallowed up by the larger." According to Yates's notes for that day Martin said he would support state government at the expense of the union, since he considered the present system "a system of slavery."And King's notes quoted Martin as saying, "I think the Confederation was formed for the protection and safety of the particular states and not for those of the U.S. I will not support the general government at the expense of the particular states, but I will contend for the safety and happiness of the particular states at the expense of the U.S."

On June 27 Martin "contended at great length and with great eagerness that the general government was meant merely to preserve the state governments, not to govern individuals; that its power ought to be kept within narrow limits; that if too little power was given to it, more might be added; but that if too much, it could never be resumed." Unfortunately for Martin's cause, he was a boring and prolix speaker. Yates, who was sympathetic to Martin's views, noted that Martin spoke on one occasion for almost three hours. "As his arguments were too diffuse," said Yates "and in many instances desultory, it was not possible to trace him through the whole, or to methodize his ideas into a systematic or argumentative arrangement." Another discourse of Martin's, Yates said, was characterized by "diffuseness and considerable vehemence."

Martin's positions on particular issues in the convention were consistent with his general philosophy. Unlike other delegates from small states, he was for state equality of representation because to him it was a corollary of state sovereignty. Thus on June 19 he took the position that the separation from Great Britain placed the thirteen states in a state of nature toward each other; that they would have remained in that state till this time but for the Confederation; that they entered into the Confederation on the footing of equality; that they met now to amend it on the same footing; and that he could never accede to a plan that would introduce an inequality and lay ten states at the mercy of Virginia, Massachusetts, and Pennsylvania.

On June 27 Martin stated that "an equal vote in each state was essenial to the federal idea, and was founded in justice and freedom, not merely in policy: that though the states may give up this right of sovereignty, yet they had not, and ought not: that the states like individuals were in a state of nature equally sovereign and free. . . . that the states, particularly the smaller, would never allow a negative to be exercised over their laws: that no state in ratifying the Confederation had objected to the equality of votes; that the complaints at present run not against this equality but the want of power."

Naturally, he was opposed to the congressional negative, considering such power "as improper and inadmissable. Shall all the laws of the states be sent up to the general legislature before they shall be permitted to operate?" he asked. He was also opposed to giving Congress the power to create inferior tribunals, which would create "jealousies and oppositions" within the state courts whose jurisdiction they might preempt. Martin would have left the states "to suppress rebellions themselves," or would have required that any "extraneous force" enter in only at the request and with the consent of the troubled state. He further opposed per capita voting in the Senate and payment of Senators by the national government.

Perceiving that his views in support of state sovereignty and in opposition to a strong central government were almost invariably overridden by the other delegates, Martin left the convention in disgust early in September. He expressed his opposition to the Constitution in a strong address to the Maryland legislature in November 1787, and the next year, as a member of the state convention, he fought against ratification. Due largely to a personal dispute with Jefferson, Martin later allied himself politically with the Federalists. He was one of the counsel who defended Justice Chase in his impeachment trial, and Aaron Burr in his trial for treason. He was reappointed attorney-general in 1818 and argued the case of *McCulloch v. Maryland* for the state. Resigning in 1822, he spent his remaining years in New York in the Burr home.

John Francis Mercer

BORN in Virginia to a wealthy plantation owner-lawyer, Mercer was a graduate of William and Mary and had an active military career during the Revolution. He became a lawyer, served twice in the Virginia legislature and also as a delegate to Congress, then moved to Maryland. Mercer did not arrive at the convention until August and left two weeks later. On a state residence requirement for election to Congress, he said that a regulation of this kind "would present a greater alienship among the states than existed under the old federal system. It would interweave local prejudices and state distinctions in the very Constitution which is meant to cure them." He referred to "those speculating legislatures which are now plundering [the people] throughout the United States." And on another occasion he asked, "What led to the appointment of this convention? The corruption and mutability of the legislative councils of the states. If the plan does not remedy these, it will not recommend itself; and we shall not be able in our private capacities to support and enforce it; nor will the best part of the citizens exert themselves for the purpose."

According to McHenry, Mercer stated his disbelief that the Articles could be saved by amendment. And yet he stated that it was "a great mistake to suppose that the paper we are to propose will govern the United States. It is the men whom it will bring into the government and interest in maintaining it that is to govern them. The paper will only mark out the mode and the form. Men are the substance and must do the business. All government must be by force or influence."

When the Constitution was submitted for ratification, Mercer cast his lot with Luther Martin in opposition. Quickly he became the trenchant leader of the Anti-federalist faction in Maryland and was forever thereafter an opponent of a strong central government. He served in the Maryland legislature during 1788-1791, in Congress during 1791-1794, and later as Republican Governor of Maryland.

James McHenry

BORN and educated in Ireland, McHenry came to Baltimore in 1771. There his father established an importing house which the son inherited. James McHenry studied medicine, served as a surgeon during the early years of the war, and was later on the staff of Washington and Lafayette. Abandoning medicine for politics, he served in the Maryland legislature and as a delegate to Congress. Not a man of marked ability, he was absent from the convention during June and July and made no significant contribution to the Constitution.

During his attendance he took notes which indicate that he was more mindful of state interests than nationalist in his participation. Thus he believed that the Confederation was "susceptible of a revision which would sufficiently invigorate it for the exigencies of the times." He also thought the states should participate in the selection of the ports of entry, and that state governors should share in the power of appointment of officers of the national government. He nevertheless signed the Constitution, even though he was opposed to many parts of the system. His reasons were his distrust of his own judgment, his confidence in the leadership of the convention, and his comparison of the "inconveniences and the evils which we labor under and may experience from the present Confederation, and the little good we can expect from it—with the possible evils and probable benefits and advantages promised us by the new system."

McHenry was a member of the state ratification convention and became a confirmed Federalist, serving in the state legislature from 1789 to 1796 and as Secretary of War from 1796 to 1800.

XVI

Delegates from Connecticut

William Samuel Johnson

A YALE graduate with a Master's degree from Harvard and a Doctor of Laws from Oxford, Johnson was probably the best educated man in the convention. He had been a delegate to the Stamp Act Congress but declined appointment to the First Continental Congress because he could not in conscience support the movement toward independence. He therefore undertook no military or political career during the Revolution but was able notwithstanding to retain his personal popularity. He served in Congress during 1785-1787, and in 1787, just before the convention, he was chosen president of Columbia College.

Johnson attended sessions of the convention diligently and came to be widely respected by the other delegates. He assumed the position of a strong nationalist who nevertheless recognized the importance of the states. On June 21 he analyzed the situation:

> On a comparison of the two plans which had been proposed from Virginia and New Jersey, it appeared that the peculiarity which characterized the latter was its being calculated to preserve the individuality of the states. The plan from Virginia did not profess to destroy this individuality altogether, but was charged with such a tendency. One gentleman alone (Colonel Hamilton), in his animadversions on the plan of New Jersey, boldly and decisively contended for an abolition of the state governments. Mr. Wilson and the gentleman from Virginia, who also were adversaries of the plan of New Jersey, held a different language. They wished to leave the states in possession of a considerable though a subordinate jurisdiction. They had not yet however shown how this could consist with, or be secured against the general sovereignty and jurisdiction, which they proposed to give to the national government. If this could be shown in such a manner as to satisfy the patrons of the New Jersey propositions, that the individuality of the states would not be endangered, many of their objections would no doubt be removed. If this could not be shown their objections would have their full force. He wished it therefore to be well considered whether in case the states, as was proposed, should

retain some portion of sovereignty at least, this portion could be preserved, without allowing them to participate effectually in the general government, without giving them each a distinct and equal vote for the purpose of defending themselves in the general councils.

King's notes for the day record Johnson as saying that Hamilton was "praised by every gentleman, but supported by no gentleman. He goes directly to the abolition of the state governments and the erection of a general government. All other gentlemen agree that the national or general government should be more powerful, and the state governments less so. Provision is made in the Virginia project to secure the general government but no provision is made for the security of the state government. The plan from New Jersey provides for the security of the state and general governments. If the advocates for the general government agreeable to the Virginia Plan can show that the state governments will be secure from the general government we may all agree."

At the end of June, Johnson set forth the basis of the compromise which was eventually reached:

> The fact is that the states do exist as political societies, and a government is to be formed for them in their political capacity, as well as for the individuals composing them. Does it not seem to follow, that if the states as such are to exist they must be armed with some power of self-defense? This is the idea of Colonel Mason who appears to have looked to the bottom of this matter. Besides the aristocratic and other interests, which ought to have the means of defending themselves, the states have their interests as such, and are equally entitled to like means. . . . As in some respects the states are to be considered in their political capacity, and in others as districts of individual citizens, the two ideas embraced on different sides, instead of being opposed to each other, ought to be combined; that in one branch the people ought to be represented; in the other, the states.

But although Johnson believed that the states were entitled to representation as states in the Congress, he did not consider that, as between national and state governments, the states retained their sovereignty. This is clear from his remarks on August 20 concerning the provision relating to treason. "He contended that treason could not be both against the United States and individual states; being an offense against the sovereignty which can be but one in the same community. Doctor Johnson was still of opinion there could be no treason against a particular state. It could not even at present, as the Confederation now stands;

the sovereignty being in the Union; much less can it be under the proposed system." He referred to "the sovereign, the supreme sovereign, the United States."

Johnson was a member both of the Compromise Committee and the Committee on Style. He signed the Constitution and worked for its ratification. Elected to the Senate in 1789, he resigned two years later so that he could devote full time to Columbia College, where he served until 1800.

Roger Sherman

A FARMER'S son who became a shoemaker with no formal education, Sherman was an outstanding example of a self-made and a self-educated man. By sheer hard work and common sense he became a lawyer, a landowner, treasurer of and recipient of an honorary degree from Yale, and a state judge from 1776 to 1789. He was one of the most influential members of Congress during his tenure in 1774-1781 and again in 1783-1784, during which time he tried unsuccessfully to bring about an increase in Congress' powers. He had the unique distinction of being the only man to sign all three documents—the Declaration of Independence, the Articles of Confederation, and the Constitution.

In Philadelphia, Sherman favored increasing the powers of the central government but was not an advocate of sweeping changes in the direction of nationalism. He was more solicitous than most delegates of the powers of the states. Thus on May 30, taking his seat, Sherman admitted "that the Confederation had not given sufficient power to Congress and that additional powers were necessary; particularly that of raising money which he said would involve many other powers. He admitted also that the general and particular jurisdictions ought in no case to be concurrent. He seemed however not to be disposed to make too great inroads on the existing system, intimating as one reason, that it would be wrong to lose every amendment, by inserting such as would not be agreed to by the states."

On June 6 he elaborated:

If it were in view to abolish the state governments, the elections ought to be by the people. If the state governments are to be continued, it is necessary in order to preserve harmony between the national and state governments that the elections to the former should be made by the latter. The right of participating in the national government would be sufficiently secured to the people by their election of the state legislatures. The objects of the Union, he thought were few. 1. Defense against foreign danger. 2. Defense against internal disputes and a resort to force. 3. Establishment of treaties with foreign nations. 4. Regulating foreign commerce, and drawing revenue from it. These and perhaps a few lesser objects alone rendered a Confederation of the states necessary. All other matters civil and criminal would be much better in the hands of the states. The people are more happy in small than large states. States may indeed be too small, as Rhode Island, and thereby be too subject to faction. Some others were perhaps too large, the powers of government not being able to pervade them. He was for giving the general government power to legislate and execute within a defined province.

On June 20 Sherman stated that each state "like each individual had its peculiar habits, usages, and manners, which constituted its happiness. It would not therefore give to others a power over this happiness, any more than an individual would do, when he could avoid it." And on the same day, King records that Sherman said, "I am for an increase of the powers of Congress, and wish to preserve the state governments, and am against a consolidation or Union."

Sherman agreed that the national government should be supreme within its own sphere. On June 30 he said: "I acknowledge there have been failures in complying with the federal requisition. Many states have been defective, and the object of our convention is to amend these defects." And on July 14 Sherman signified that his expectation was that the general legislature would in some cases act on the federal principle of requiring quotas. But he thought it ought to be empowered to carry their own plans into execution, if the states should fail to supply their respective quotas."

Sherman thought that the congressional negative ought to be exercised only in specifically defined situations. Later, because he thought national supremacy would be recognized, he saw no need for the negative. On July 17 he therefore "thought it unnecessary, as the courts of the states would not consider as valid any law contravening the authority of the Union, and which the legislature would wish to be negatived. . . . Such a power involves a wrong principle, to wit, that a law of a state contrary to the articles of the Union, would if not negatived, be valid and operative."

On the other hand, Sherman sought to protect the states against national encroachments. For this reason he supported state equality in the Senate. He proposed, for example, "that the proportion of suffrage in the first branch should be according to the respective numbers of free inhabitants; and that in the second branch or Senate, each state should have one vote and no more." Since the states would still possess "certain individual rights," each one should "be able to protect itself; otherwise a few large States will rule the rest." Later Sherman urged the equality of votes not so much as a security for the small states as for the state governments which could not be preserved unless they were represented and had a negative in the general government." He believed that election of Senators by state legislatures was desirable for the same reason.

In addition to seeking political protection for the states, Sherman tried twice without success to insert in the Constitution a specific assurance of the states' power over their internal police. In July he noted that "it would be difficult to draw the line between the powers of the general legislatures, and those to be left with the states; that he did not like the definition contained in the resolution, and proposed instead 'to make laws binding on the people of the United States in all cases which may concern the common interests of the Union; but not to interfere with the government of the individual states in any matters of internal police which respect the government of such states only, and wherein the general welfare of the United States is not concerned.'" One month later Sherman "expressed his fears that three-fourths of the states might be brought to do things fatal to particular states, as abolishing them altogether or depriving them of their equality in the Senate." He moved accordingly that no state without its consent could be affected in its internal police, or deprived of its equal suffrage in the Senate. Only the latter clause was adopted.

On the basis of his general views, Sherman took stands against certain specific provisions. Thus he opposed "the requirement of an oath of state officers to observe the national Constitution and laws . . . as unnecessarily intruding into the state jurisdictions." And on the compensation of members of Congress, Sherman "contended for referring both the quantum and the payment of it to the state legislatures."

Despite his fears, however, Sherman took an active role in supporting ratification. He later served in the House during 1789-1791 and in the Senate from 1791 until his death two years later.

Oliver Ellsworth

THE SON of a wealthy farmer, Ellsworth first attended Yale, then transferred and was graduated from Princeton, eventually becoming a lawyer. He almost starved during three years of rural practice, but on moving to Hartford he was immediately successful and quickly rose to wealth and power at the bar. He had served as a state's attorney, as a judge, and as a member of Congress from 1779 to 1783.

Ellsworth emerged as a moderate nationalist at the convention. He voted in favor of a general legislative power in Congress in all cases where the states individually were incompetent, but he contemplated that the business of Congress "would relate to a few great national objects only." And yet, within this area, he had no doubt that "the laws of the United States are to be paramount." Ellsworth feared and repeatedly cautioned against a Constitution that was too nationalist in its design and would therefore arouse such opposition as to defeat its adoption. Thus on June 22 Ellsworth said, "If we are jealous of the state governments they will be so of us. If on going home I tell them we gave the general government such powers because we could not trust you, will they adopt it? Without their approbation it is a nullity." And on June 25 Ellsworth observed that, the people of the states being "strongly attached to their own constitutions," they would oppose any system of general government that destroyed their constitutional rights.

Ellsworth did not agree that if state governments were retained they and the central government should be employed as balances. "On the contrary," Ellsworth thought, "the only chance we have to support a general government is to graft it on the state governments. I want to proceed on this ground, as the safest, and I believe no other plan is practicable. In this way, and in this way only, can we rely on the confidence and support of the people." Ellsworth was not in general a halfway man, yet he preferred doing "half the good we could, rather than do nothing at all. The other half may be added, when the necessity shall be more fully experienced."

Furthermore, Ellsworth considered that area and distance largely precluded central government and rendered a continuation of state governments essential. On June 25 he therefore urged the necessity of maintaining the existence and agency of the states. Without their cooperation he thought it would be impossible to support a republican government over so great an extent of country. An army could scarcely render it practicable. "The largest states are the worst governed," Ellsworth observed. "Virginia is obliged to acknowledge her incapacity to extend her government to Kentucky. Massachusetts cannot keep the peace one hundred miles from her capitol and is now forming an army for its support. How long Pennsylvania may be free from a like situation can not be foreseen. If the principles and materials of our government are not adequate to the extent of these single states, how can it be imagined that they can support a single government throughout the United States? The only chance of supporting a general government lies in engrafting it on that of the individual states."

He felt, therefore, that Senators should be chosen by the state legislatures. Since wisdom, Ellsworth said on June 25, was to be one of the express ends for which the Senate was designed, would not more of it issue from the legislatures than from direct election by the people? He advocated equal representation in the Senate on the ground that the Union was "partly national; partly federal. The proportional representation in the first branch was conformable to the national principle and would secure the large states against the small. An equality of voices was conformable to the federal principle and was necessary to secure the small states against the large. He trusted that on this middle ground a compromise would take place."

Originally, Ellsworth favored payment of Senators by the states, but eventually he changed his mind because "in reflecting on this subject he had been satisfied that too much dependence on the states would be produced by this mode of payment." That Ellsworth seems to have contemplated a division of sovereignty is indicated by his remark made during debate on the treason provision: "The U.S. are sovereign on one side of the line dividing the jurisdictions, the states on the other. Each ought to have power to defend their respective sovereignties."

Having left the convention almost a month before it ended, Ellsworth was not present for the signing of the Constitution. He supported ratification, however, in his well-known *Letters of a Landholder*. He was elected to the Senate in 1789 where he became, in the words of John Adams, "the firmest pillar in [Washington's] whole administration." He personally wrote most of the Judiciary Act of 1789, including the famous Section 25, which declared the appellate jurisdiction of the Supreme Court over state courts. It was this section which the advocates of state sovereignty later repeatedly and vainly sought to repeal. Ellsworth was Chief Justice of the United States from 1796 to 1800.

XVII

Architects of a Nation

CERTAIN general and collective summary conclusions may be drawn from the foregoing examination of the views of the individual delegates. Throughout the Revolutionary and Confederation periods there was a basic division of thought as to the nature of the American system of government: whether there should be a strong national government possessing authority and powers (including power of enforcement) paramount to the states, or a weak federal government in which the central authority was limited and subordinate to the political sovereignty of the states. For purposes of brevity, these views have been summarized in the phrases "national supremacy" and "state sovereignty." On this question there is no room for doubt that almost all of the delegates to the Constitutional Convention were personally committed to the nationalist philosophy. Some of the delegates went farther in their nationalism than others did, and these differences in degree manifested themselves in disagreement over certain specific matters such as the extent of the powers of Congress and the limitations on those powers, the amount of independence and autonomy which should be left to the states, and the best method of assuring and enforcing the supremacy of national law.

Twelve of the delegates comprised what might be called the "advanced nationalists." This group included George Washington, who thought that the states should be to the nation as counties to a state, and who advocated a "radical cure" for the evils of "thirteen sovereignties pulling against each other"; James Madison, who believed the national government should have "a negative in all cases whatsoever on the legislative acts of the states" to protect national supremacy and confine the states to areas where they could be "subordinately useful"; James Wilson, who said that in forming a general government "we ought to proceed by abstracting as much as possible from the idea of state governments" and who denied that a sovereign state could retain its sovereignty within the new system; Gouverneur Morris, who declared that "state attachments and state importance have been the bane of this country" and that the happiness of America would not be affected "if all the charters and constitutions of the states were thrown into the fire, and all their demagogues into the ocean"; Alexander Hamilton, who desired "a complete sovereignty in the general government," even to the extent of national appointment of state governors with an absolute veto over all state laws; Charles Pinckney, who thought that the "idea which has been so long and falsely entertained of each being a sovereign state, must be given up"; John Langdon, who believed the "extent of the national constitution" should be judged by the national and not by the state governments; George Read, who said that state attachments "should be extinguished as much as possible" and who hoped "the objects of the general government would be much more numerous" than some expected and that "they would become more and more so"; and Nathaniel Gorham, who thought that "it was of importance therefore that the extent of the states should be reduced as much and as fast as possible." In this group should be included also Benjamin Franklin, and, on the basis of collateral evidence, Robert Morris and Jared Ingersoll. Four of this group—Washington, Madison, Wilson, and Gouverneur Morris—were among the most influential members of the convention.

Twenty-one delegates were what might be called "moderate nationalists." These men agreed that a strong national government should be created which would be supreme over the states and equipped with some means of enforcing its supremacy. They disagreed with the "advanced nationalists" on the extent of the powers which the national government should have, on how its supremacy should be enforced against the states, and on how much power should be left to the states. In this group were John Dickinson, who "was for a strong national government but for leaving the states a considerable agency in the system," and who warned Madison against "the consequences of pushing things too far," a lesson he had no doubt learned from the fate of the Dickinson draft of the Articles of Confederation; John Rutledge, who supported national supremacy and visualized the Supreme Court as the arbiter of disputes between the national government and the states, but who wanted an enumeration of congressional powers and warned against creating "unnecessary obstacles" to the adoption of the new system; General Pinckney, who agreed that "the federal government cannot be made efficient" and who "wished to have a good national government and at the same time to leave a considerable share of power in the states"; Rufus King, who was astonished that some "should be ready to sacrifice . . . substantial good to the phantom of state sovereignty, but who "was for preserving the states in a subordinate degree," and who contemplated that "the most numerous objects of legislation belong to the states . . . those of the national legislature were but few"; William Samuel Johnson, who denied that the states would retain their sovereignty under the new system, but who thought that since they would continue to "exist as political societies" they should be armed with "some power of self-defense"; Oliver Ellsworth, who recognized that "the laws of the United States are to be paramount" but thought the national government "could only embrace objects of a general nature" and who warned that "not too much should be attempted, by which all may be lost"; Roger Sherman, who "admitted the Confederation had not given sufficient power to Congress" and who denied that "a law of a state contrary to the Articles of the Union" would be "valid and operative," but who tried twice, each time in vain, to write into the Constitution a specific protection of the power of the states over their internal police; William Paterson, who insisted on equality of state representation and forced a compromise providing for it in the Senate, but whose motives were correctly assessed by Pinckney when he said that if New Jersey were given an equal vote, "she will dismiss her scruples, and concur in the national system," which Paterson thereafter did; and Hugh Williamson, who was willing to support the congressional negative as to "such laws only as will encroach on the national government," but who believed that the "state legislatures ought to possess independent powers in cases purely local." Also included in the group of "moderate nationalists," but exercising much less influence, were James McClurg, David Brearly, Jonathan Dayton, Richard Dobbs Spaight, William Richardson Davie, Gunning Bedford, Abraham Baldwin, William Pierce, Pierce Butler, James McHenry, Daniel of St. Thomas Jenifer, and Daniel Carroll.

The three delegates who refused to sign the Constitution may also properly be included in the group of "moderate nationalists." It was not a fundamental disagreement with the basic postulates of the nationalist philosophy that prompted the decision of Randolph, Mason, and Gerry, although Mason had at one time been an adherent of state sovereignty. The common denominator of their unwillingness to sign was a belief that excessive power had been granted to the new national government without sufficient limitation. Their disagreement was based on degree rather than basic principle. Thus, while Randolph was "convinced that radical changes in the system of the Union were necessary," he gave as his reason for not signing "the indefinite and dangerous power" which the Constitution gave to Congress. Similarly, Mason agreed that "a more efficient government is necessary" but felt that "whatever power may be necessary for the national government, a certain portion must necessarily be left in the states." It was "the dangerous power and structure of the government" that Mason saw in the powers of Congress and the jurisdiction of the United States courts which persuaded him that the nationalists had overreached themselves. And Gerry, who had started out in the convention by complaining that the "states and the advocates for them were intoxicated with the idea of their sovereignty," ended up by warning the convention "against pushing the experiment too far," and refusing to sign when he concluded that his warning had gone unheeded.

A third group, which might be called the "uncommitted," was comprised of fourteen delegates who during sessions of the convention did not reveal their views on the issue of "national supremacy" or "state sovereignty". These men were John Blair, George Wythe, William Livingston, William C. Houston, Nicholas Gilman, Thomas Mifflin, George Clymer, Thomas Fitzsimmons, Alexander Martin, Richard Bassett, Jacob Broom, William Few, William Houstoun, and Caleb Strong. These are the delegates whose participation and influence in the proceedings of the convention, so far as the records show, were insignificant. What little evidence is available would indicate that half a dozen of them—Blair, Livingston, Clymer, Fitzsimmons, Broom, and Strong—were probably "moderate nationalists," but since they did not express themselves on the matter, it is safer to list them as "uncommitted."

Only the five remaining delegates composed a group dedicated to the preservation of a system of "state sovereignty" wherein the central government was the subservient creature of states which were *de facto* and *de jure* supreme. This group included John Lansing, who doubted "whether any general government equally beneficial to all can be attained," and who said he was "not authorized to accede to a system which will annihilate the state governments"; Robert Yates, who wrote to his governor that the convention was creating "a system of consolidated government" that would "deprive the state government of its most essential rights of sovereignty, and . . . place it in a dependent situation"; Luther Martin, who contended that "the general government ought to be formed for the states, not for individuals," who would "rather see partial confederacies take place, than the plan on the table," and who said that he "would support the state government at the expense of the Union"; and John Francis Mercer, who did not defend state sovereignty during the convention, and who is included in this group only because of his subsequent alignment with Martin in opposing ratification of the Constitution. William Blount, who was "not in sentiment" with his fellows and who "disliked the Constitution," is included on the assumption that the wish was father to the thought when he predicted that "we shall ultimately and in not many years just be separate and distinct governments, perfectly independent of each other."

Not only were the adherents of "state sovereignty" in the convention pitifully few, they were almost completely without influence on the proceedings. Lansing and Yates left the convention early in July—for the stated reason that they believed state sovereignty was being destroyed —and did not return; Mercer attended for only about two weeks and participated but little in the debates, while Blount was absent for almost two months and did not participate in the debates at all. Only Martin made any sustained defense of state sovereignty, and even he eventually concluded it was hopeless and left the convention early in September.

The overall conclusion is irrefutably clear. Only a handful of delegates to the Constitutional Convention of 1787 believed in the perpetuation of a system which has been described as a compact of sovereign states, and this handful was almost completely without influence in the convention. The Constitution was drafted by men who clearly revealed themselves as committed to the nationalist philosophy of a strong central government, supreme over the states and equipped with ample means to execute its increased powers and to enforce and maintain its supremacy. The vision of the Founding Fathers did not contemplate a system based on "state sovereignty."

Part Three:
The Drafting
of the
Constitution

XVIII

A Short View of the

Constitutional Convention

THE CONVENTION was formally organized on Friday, May 25, 1787. George Washington was unanimously elected president, and a committee headed by George Wythe was appointed to draw up standing rules to govern the proceedings. Monday was devoted to discussion and adoption of the committee's report, and it was not until Tuesday, May 29, that the convention began its deliberations. Edmund Randolph opened the main business by suggesting that the convention's goal should be a government "to secure 1. against foreign invasion; 2. against dissensions between members of the Union, or seditions in particular states; 3. to procure to the several states various blessings, of which an isolated situation was incapable; 4. to be able to defend itself against encroachments; and 5. to be paramount to the state constitutions." Speaking of the defects of the Articles of Confederation, Randolph "professed a high respect for its authors, and considered them as having done all that patriots could do, in the then infancy of the science of constitutions." He recognized that "perhaps nothing better could be obtained from the jealousy of the states with regard to their sovereignty." The defects in the Articles which he enumerated included the following: "that the federal government could not check the quarrels between states, nor a rebellion in any, not having constitutional power nor means to interpose according to the exigency; . . . that the federal government could not defend itself against the encroachments from the states; . . . that it was not even paramount to the state constitutions, ratified as it was in many of the states."

As a remedy for the existing state of affairs, Randolph then offered the Virginia plan—a series of fifteen resolutions which had been drawn up by that state's delegates before the opening of the convention, with

James Madison as the principal architect. Of particular relevance to the issue of national supremacy and state sovereignty were the following proposals: a national legislature of two houses in which state representation would be based either on the number of free inhabitants or the amount of property; power in this legislature "to enjoy the legislative rights vested in Congress by the Confederation and moreover to legislate in all cases to which the separate states are incompetent, or in which the harmony of the United States may be interrupted by the exercise of individual legislation"; power "to negative all laws passed by the several states, contravening in the opinion of the national legislature the articles of Union"; and power "to call forth the force of the Union against any member of the Union failing to fulfill its duty under the articles thereof"; a national executive armed with "a general authority to execute the national laws" and also "to enjoy the executive rights vested in Congress by the Confederation"; a national judiciary holding office during good behavior, whose jurisdiction was to extend to "questions which may involve the national peace and harmony"; and a requirement that "the legislative, executive, and judiciary powers within the several states ought to be bound by oath to support the articles of Union."

Resolving itself next day into a committee of the whole, the convention considered the Virginia plan for two weeks and on June 13 reported favorably on nineteen resolutions. These resolutions included all of the proposals set forth in the preceding paragraph, with one exception: the power to call forth the armed force of the Union against a state was omitted. In all other respects the nationalist features of the Virginia plan were approved. On June 14, Paterson of New Jersey took the floor and "observed to the convention that it was the wish of several deputations, particularly that of New Jersey, that further time might be allowed them to contemplate the plan reported from the committee of the whole, and to digest one purely federal, and contradistinguished from the reported plan." The next day Paterson laid before the convention the New Jersey plan consisting of nine resolutions.

A comparison of the essential features of the two plans reveals the following significant differences. The New Jersey plan proposed that "the Articles of Confederation ought to be so revised, corrected, and enlarged, as to render the federal Constitution adequate to the exigencies of government," thereby contemplating the retention of a confederation rather than the creation of a national government. No provision was made for any change in the structure of Congress or the basis of its representation; the New Jersey plan thus would have continued the unicameral Congress provided under the Articles, a Congress which was merely the agent of the states and in which each state had one vote.

The New Jersey plan would have provided only modest and express increases in the power of Congress: a limited revenue power in the form of duties on imports, stamp taxes, and postage fees, supplemented by a continuation of the state requisition system with additional powers of collection; and a power to pass acts for the regulation of trade and commerce with foreign nations and between the states themselves. A "federal executive" was provided for with "general authority to execute the federal acts," but this was to be a plural executive appointed by Congress and removable by Congress on the application of a majority of the state governors. A "federal judiciary" of judges holding office during good behavior was provided, but its jurisdiction was limited commensurately with the power of Congress. The sixth New Jersey resolution provided for the supremacy of all acts of Congress and all treaties of the United States over state laws, and authorized the executive to "call forth the power of the confederated states" to compel obedience by recalcitrant states or individuals.

So that the New Jersey plan might be given "fair deliberation," it was referred to the committee of the whole, and "in order to place the two plans in due comparison," the Virginia plan was recommitted. The convention thus had before it a clear-cut choice between two systems—on the one hand, a national government of virtually unlimited powers, armed with a complete and absolute supremacy over the states, and on the other, a confederation in which the central authority had enforceable supremacy only in sharply limited areas, with the states retaining their sovereignty in all others.

For three days the convention considered the New Jersey plan. Paterson and Lansing defended it, the latter declaring that the two plans involved "principles directly in contrast; that of Mr. Paterson . . . sustains the sovereignty of the respective states, that of Mr. Randolph destroys it." Hamilton, Wilson, and Madison—the advanced nationalists —spoke strongly against the New Jersey plan. Then, on June 19, King moved that "Mr. Randolph's propositions be re-reported without alteration, which was in fact a question whether Mr. Randolph's should be adhered to as preferable to those of Mr. Paterson." The convention voted and made its choice: seven states "Aye" (Massachusetts, Connecticut, Pennsylvania, Virginia, North Carolina, South Carolina, and Georgia); three states "Nay" (New York, New Jersey, and Delaware); one state,

Maryland, divided. Thus, only three weeks after it began its deliberations, the convention rejected the continuation of a system based on
state sovereignty and decided in favor of a system based on national
supremacy. It was a decision which was never changed.

With this fundamental determination made, the convention next proceeded to consider the nineteen resolutions reported by the committee
of the whole, which included all but one of the nationalist features of the
original Virginia plan. It quickly became apparent that there was a
sharp conflict of opinion on the question of representation in Congress.
The larger states insisted on representation based on population, which
would have given them dominance of the new government. The small
states, not wishing to be overwhelmed by numbers, insisted on equality
of representation, which had been the rule in Congress under the Articles. By July 2 the convention had reached an impasse on this question.
As Sherman tersely put it, "We are now at a full stop."

To resolve the matter a committee was appointed—consisting of
Gerry, Franklin, Mason, Davie, Rutledge, Ellsworth, Yates, Paterson,
Bedford, Martin, and Baldwin—and the convention adjourned over the
holiday until July 5. On this day the committee reported recommendations that offered a compromise in which representation was to be based
on population in the first house, but each state was to have an equality
of vote in the second house. Debate then continued, but finally, on July
16, the compromise was adopted by the close vote of five states to four
—Connecticut, New Jersey, Delaware, Virginia, and North Carolina
voting "Aye," and Pennsylvania, Maryland, South Carolina, and Georgia voting "Nay," with Massachusetts divided this time.

Debate on the resolutions of the committee of the whole continued until July 26. By this time the convention had adopted twenty-three resolutions which were referred to a Committee of Detail which was "to report a constitution conformable to the resolutions. . . ." It is important to
note that these resolutions included all of the nationalist features which
had been found in the resolutions of the committee of the whole. The
convention then adjourned until August 6 so that the Committee of Detail might have time to prepare a draft of a constitution.

The committee which had thus been assigned the task of drawing up
the first form of the Constitution of the United States was composed of
Rutledge, Randolph, Ellsworth, Gorham, and Wilson—three "moderate" and two "advanced" nationalists. The report which this committee submitted on August 6 was a document consisting of a preamble
and twenty-three articles, many of which were broken down into separate sections totaling forty-one.

In general and in most particulars, this first draft of the Constitution conformed to the resolutions referred to the committee by the convention; in certain areas, however, the committee had made substantive changes on its own. The most striking developments which had been wrought during this stage were: the transformation of the broad, indefinite, general legislative power of Congress into an enumeration of expressly delineated powers; the inclusion of certain specific prohibitions on congressional power; the transformation of the broad, almost unlimited jurisdiction of the national judiciary into specific subjects of jurisdiction; and the inclusion of additional restrictions on the powers of the states.

On August 6 the convention resumed its deliberations, now focused upon the draft constitution reported by the Committee of Detail. The convention meticulously considered the draft article by article and section by section. For over a month the detailed process of revision, modification, elaboration, and correlation continued. Finally, on September 10, the convention turned its work over to a Committee of Style and Arrangement to cast the convention's decisions into orderly form and precise phraseology. This committee was composed of Johnson, Hamilton, Gouverneur Morris, Madison, and King—three "advanced" and two "moderate" nationalists. This final draft was virtually the sole handiwork of Gouverneur Morris, who completed the task—incredibly—in two days. When one considers that these were the words over which subsequent generations of Americans were to debate all over again the issue of "national supremacy" and "state sovereignty," the fact that they were written by one of the most advanced nationalists in the convention is obviously of enormous historical and legal significance.

Receiving the report of the Committee of Style on Wednesday, September 12, the convention spent four days considering its provisions, time consumed principally in rejecting proposed alterations. On Saturday, September 15, "on the question to agree to the Constitution, as amended, all the states, Aye. The Constitution was then ordered to be engrossed." On Monday, September 17, thirty-nine delegates signed the Constitution on behalf of the twelve states represented, and the convention adjourned.

XIX

The Fabric of a National Government— The Legislature

ON MAY 30, the day after the Virginia plan was presented, the convention, acting as a committee of the whole, had approved its very first resolution: "that a national government ought to be established consisting of a supreme legislative, executive, and judiciary." On May 31 resolutions were approved in favor of a "national" legislature chosen by popular election and invested with both an indefinite legislative power and a negative on state laws. On June 1 the convention adopted resolutions that a "national" executive be instituted with general authority to carry into effect the "national" laws. On June 4 a resolution was adopted that a "national" judiciary be established. Thus, less than a week after it began its deliberations, the convention had approved the necessary structure for the type of government desired by the group of nationalists who had brought about the convention and who composed its membership almost entirely. Throughout the rest of the convention, whenever reference was made to the government being set forth in the new Constitution, it was viewed constantly as a "national" government. Today we refer to our system as a "federal" system and to the United States government as the "federal" government. To the Founding Fathers, however, the word "federal" meant something entirely different. They used the term "federal" to describe the type of government that existed under the Articles—a compact or league of states which were *de jure* and *de facto* sovereign, in which the central "government" was no more than the subordinate common agent of sovereign states. It was precisely this kind of government that the nationalists were determined to eradicate and replace; in distinction to it and as descriptive of the kind of government they favored, they used the term "national."

Just what was the difference in the minds of the Founders when they referred to a "national" government as opposed to a "federal" government? Madison, the "father of the Constitution," discussed the matter most fully in the convention. On May 30, on the question of the basis of representation in Congress, Madison "observed that whatever reason might have existed for the equality of suffrage when the Union was a federal one among sovereign states, it must cease when a national government should be put into the place. In the former case, the acts of Congress depended so much for their efficacy on the cooperation of the states, that these had a weight both within and without Congress, nearly in proportion to their extent and importance. In the latter case, as the acts of the general government would take effect without the intervention of the state legislatures, a vote from a small state would have the same efficacy and importance as a vote from a large one, and there was the same reason for different numbers of representatives from different states as from counties of different extents within particular states."

On June 19 Madison left no doubt as to what sort of plan of government was being consciously abandoned. Describing a "federal" plan, Madison said: "One characteristic was that in a federal government, the power was exercised not on the people individually, but on the people collectively, on the states. . . . The other characteristic was, that a federal government derived its appointments not immediately from the people, but from the states which they respectively composed." On July 23 he said that he considered "the difference between a system founded on the legislatures only, and one founded on the people, to be the true difference between a league or treaty, and a Constitution." In opposing equality of representation, Madison emphasized the truly national character of the new government:

> But it had been said that the government would in its operation be partly federal, partly national; that although in the latter respect the representatives of the people ought to be in proportion to the people, yet in the former it ought to be according to the number of states. If there was any solidity in this distinction he was ready to abide by it, if there was none it ought to be abandoned. In all cases where the general government is to act on the people, let the people be represented and the votes be proportional. In all cases where the government is to act on the states as such, in like manner as Congress now acts on them, let the states be represented and the votes be equal. This was the true

ground of compromise if there was any ground at all. But he denied that there was any ground. He called for a single instance in which the general government was not to operate on the people individually. The practicability of making laws, with coercive sanctions, for the states as political bodies, had been exploded on all hands.

In later years Madison reiterated this point of view. In a letter written in 1826 he said that the term "national" was used "not in contradistinction to a limited, but to a federal government. As the latter operated within the extent of its authority through requisitions on the confederated states, and rested on the sanction of the state legislatures, the government to take its place, was to operate within the extent of its powers directly and coercively on individuals, and to receive the higher sanction of the people of the states." A letter written by Madison in 1831 stated that "the term national as contradistinguished from federal was not meant to express more than that the powers to be vested in the new government were to operate as in a national government directly on the people, and not as in the old Confederacy on the states only. And in still another letter in 1833, discussing the term "national," Madison wrote: "In the first place. It contradistinguished the proposed government from the Confederacy which it was to supersede. Second. As the system was to be a new and compound one, a nondescript without a technical appellation for it, the term national was very naturally suggested by its national features. 1. In being established not by the authority of state legislatures but by the original authority of the people. 2. In its organization into legislative, executive, and judiciary departments. and 3. In its action on the people of the states immediately, and not on the government of the states, as in a confederacy."

Madison's conception of a "national" government, then, was one whose powers were to be exercised directly upon individuals without any "intervention of the state legislatures," and enforced by its own agencies rather than through the states. Such a government could never be formed upon any league of sovereign states; it could be brought into existence and operation only through a constitution "founded on the people."

That Madison's view expressed the general understanding of the convention is clear. Not a single delegate took issue with it during the convention; on the contrary, each delegate who addressed himself specifically to the subject revealed a coincidence of opinion with Madison. Thus on June 16 Randolph said that the "true question is whether we shall adhere to the federal plan, or introduce the national plan. The insufficiency of the former has been fully displayed by the trial already made. . . . We must resort therefore to a national legislation over individuals." And Mason on May 30 observed that "the present confederation was not only deficient in not providing for coercion and punishment against delinquent states, but . . . punishment could not, in the nature of things, be executed on the states collectively, and therefore . . . such a government was necessary as could directly operate on individuals, and would punish those only whose guilt required it." On June 6 Mason said: "Under the existing Confederacy, Congress represents the states, not the people of the states. Their acts operate on the states, not on the individuals. The case will be changed in the new plan of government. The people will be represented; they therefore ought to choose the representatives."

On May 30 Gouverneur Morris also explained "the distinction between a federal and a national, supreme government, the former being a mere compact resting on the good faith of the parties, the latter having a complete and compulsive operation. He contended that in all communities there must be one supreme power, and only one." On June 25, opposing election of Congress by state legislatures, Wilson said that in "explaining his reasons it was necessary to observe the twofold relation in which the people would stand. 1. As citizens of the general government. 2. As citizens of their particular state. The general government was meant for them in the first capacity, the state governments in the second. . . . The general government is not an assemblage of states, but of individuals for certain political purposes—it is not meant for the states, but for the individuals composing them. The individuals, therefore, not the states, ought to be represented in it."

Hamilton, on June 18, referring to the Virginia plan, stated that the "plan last proposed departs from the federal idea, as understood by some, since it is to operate eventually on individuals." And Lansing, speaking of the New Jersey plan, said that "this system is fairly contrasted with the one ready to be reported—the one federal, and the other national. In the first, the powers are exercised as flowing from the respective state governments—the second, deriving its authority from the people of the respective states, which latter must ultimately destroy or annihilate the state governments." King on June 11 "observed that it would be better first to establish a principle, that is to say, whether we will depart from federal grounds in forming a national government." On June 19 he declared that "a union of the states is a union of the men composing them, from whence a national character results to the whole,

Congress can act alone without the states—they can act and their acts will be binding against the instructions of the states." On July 14 King added that he "considered the proposed government as substantially and formally, a general and national government over the people of America. There never will be a case in which it will act as a federal government on the states and not on the individual citizens."

The action of the convention on June 20 was significant: when the first proposition of the committee of the whole came up for debate, Ellsworth "moved to alter it so as to run 'that the government of the United States ought to consist of a supreme legislative, executive, and judiciary.' This alteration, he said, would drop the word national, and retain the proper title 'the United States.'" The motion was agreed to without debate.

The question may be asked: Did this action mean that the convention had abandoned its commitment to a "national" government? It is clear from the subsequent proceedings that the change was in nomenclature only, and not in substance.

Years later Madison gave the explanation. In a letter of 1826 he wrote: "With respect to the term 'national' as contradistinguished from the term 'federal,' it was not meant to express the extent of power, but the mode of its operation, which was to be not like the power of the old Confederation operating on states; but like that of ordinary governments, operating on individuals; and the substitution of 'United States' for 'national' noted in the journal, was not designed to change the meaning of the latter, but to guard against a mistake or misrepresentation of what was intended." Again, writing in 1831, Madison stated: "Some exulting inferences have been drawn from the change noted in the journal of the convention, of the word national into 'United States.' The change may be accounted for by a desire to avoid a misconception of the former, the latter being preferred as a familiar caption. That the change could have no effect on the real character of the government was and is obvious; this being necessarily deduced from the actual structure of the government and the quantum of its powers."

It is clear that the Founding Fathers intended that the Constitution should establish a "national" government to replace the "federal" system of the Articles; that whereas the "federal" system had operated on and through the states, the new "national" government was to operate directly on individuals; and finally, that these results were to be accomplished without the participation and intervention of the individual states.

Structure of the National Legislature

A BICAMERAL BODY

Article I, Section I of the Constitution provides that "All legislative powers herein granted shall be vested in a Congress of the United States, which shall consist of a Senate and a House of Representatives." There was thus established a bicameral legislature, in contrast to the unicameral Congress which had existed under the Articles of Confederation. Following the example of Parliament, all the colonial assemblies and all the succeeding state legislatures, excepting only Pennsylvania and Georgia, were composed of two houses. The Continental Congress, on the other hand, both before and after the adoption of the Articles, was always one house only.

The reason for the difference lay in the governmental systems of which each was a part. The state legislatures represented the people of the state and enacted laws which were operative directly upon individuals within the state. Having two houses in the legislature, each of which could act as a check on the other and with the concurrence of both necessary to the enactment of legislation, was some assurance against undue accumulation of power and the passage of unwise or oppressive laws. A bicameral legislature was considered necessary as a means of protection of individuals against legislative power which operated directly upon them. The Congress created by the Articles of Confederation, however, did not operate (except in a few minor instances) directly upon individuals. The system of government under the Articles was, as we have seen, merely a compact or league of sovereign states, the enactments of Congress being operative only on states and enforceable only by states. A unicameral Congress, in which each state was equally represented, was therefore a body sufficient to the purposes of the Articles and also one in which each state was amply protected.

With the abolition of a system based on state sovereignty and the creation of a national government whose powers were to operate directly on individuals, the provision for a bicameral legislature was intended to assure those individuals of protection against abuse of those national powers. This purpose was expressed by several of the delegates at various times throughout the convention. Madison, for example, on June 7 stated that the "use of the Senate is to consist in its proceeding with more coolness, with more system, and with more wisdom, than the popular branch. Enlarge their number and you communicate to them the vices which they are meant to correct." Later on June 26, when the

Senate was under consideration, Madison said that in order "to judge of the form to be given to this institution, it will be proper to take a view of the ends to be served by it. These were, first, to protect the people against their rulers; secondly, to protect the people against the transient impressions into which they themselves might be led." On the same day he declared: "One great end of the institution was that, being a firm, wise and impartial body, it might . . . give stability to the general government in its operations on individuals."

Randolph on May 31 said he observed "that the general object was to provide a cure for the evils under which the U.S. labored; that in tracing these evils to their origin every man had found it in the turbulence and follies of democracy; that some check therefore was to be sought for against this tendency of our governments; and that a good Senate seemed most likely to answer the purpose." Again, on June 12 Randolph declared: "The democratic licentiousness of the state legislatures proved the necessity of a firm Senate. The object of this second branch is to control the democratic branch of the national legislature. If it be not a firm body, the other branch being more numerous, and coming immediately from the people, will overwhelm it."

Similarly, Gouverneur Morris on July 2 stated that the object of the Senate was "to check the precipitation, changeableness, and excesses of the first branch. Every man of observation had seen in the democratic branches of the state legislatures, precipitation, in Congress changeableness, in every department excesses against personal liberty, private property, and personal safety." And King on July 14 stated that "The second [branch] was admitted to be necessary, and was actually meant, to check the first branch, to give more wisdom, system, and stability to the government, and ought clearly as it was to operate on the people to be proportioned to them."

It is not surprising, therefore, that the third resolution of the Virginia plan was "that the national legislature ought to consist of two branches." This was agreed to on May 31 without debate or dissent. The New Jersey plan on the other hand, contemplated the continuation of a unicameral Congress. Consequently, when the resolution was taken up on June 20 there was a brief but revealing debate. Lansing, the state sovereignty advocate, observed "that the true question here was, whether the convention would adhere to or depart from the foundation of the present confederacy; and moved instead of the second resolution 'that the powers of legislation be vested in the United States in Congress.'" Sherman "seconded and supported Mr. Lansing's motion. He admitted two branches to be necessary in the state legislatures, but saw no necessity for them in a confederacy of states." And Martin "saw no necessity for two branches," inasmuch as "Congress represented the legislatures."

In reply, Mason said that "he believed the mind of the people of America, as elsewhere, was unsettled as to some points, but settled as to others." There was no doubt that the people preferred a republican government with more than one legislative branch. That the state constitutions already inclined toward these forms, Mason said, "must either have been a miracle, or have resulted from the genius of the people. The only exceptions to the establishment of two branches in the legislatures are the state of Pennsylvania and Congress, and the latter the only single one not chosen by the people themselves. What has been the consequence? The people have been constantly averse to giving that body further powers." Mason was supported by Madison and Wilson who, being advanced nationalists, saw the necessity for a bicameral body. Lansing's motion was defeated, and the second of the resolutions of the convention submitted to the Committee of Detail on July 26 was that "The Legislature of the United States ought to consist of two branches."

It is clear, therefore, that the adoption of a bicameral Congress was consistent with, and indeed demanded by, the establishment of a "national" government.

NATIONAL METHODS OF SELECTION

The Articles of Confederation had provided, in Article V, that the legislature of each state make annual appointments of delegates to meet in Congress every November. This was a completely natural method of choosing delegates in a confederation of sovereign states. The Founding Fathers did not deem it consistent, however, with the establishment of a "national" government, to leave such a matter to the choice of individual states. Instead they chose to prescribe a uniform method by which members of the bicameral Congress should be chosen in each state. The Constitution provided, therefore, in Article I, Section 2, Clause 1, that: "The House of Representatives shall be composed of members chosen every second year by the people of the several states." And Article I, Section 3, Clause 1, stated: "The Senate of the United States shall be composed of two Senators from each state, chosen by the legislature thereof, for six years."

The election of representatives by the people was considered by the advanced nationalists as an essential ingredient of their system. Since the laws of the "national" government were to operate directly upon individuals, i.e., the people, it was a corollary principle that the people should elect the members of the national legislature which enacted the laws. Consequently, the fourth of Randolph's original resolutions included a provision that "the members of the first branch of the national legislature ought to be elected by the people of the several states."

When this resolution was taken up on May 31, a short debate ensued. Sherman "opposed the election by the people, insisting that it ought to be by the state legislatures." Gerry affirmed that the "evils we experience flow from the excess of democracy," and said that he "did not like the election by the people." And Butler also "thought an election by the people an impracticable mode."

On the other hand, Mason "argued strongly for an election of the larger branch by the people. It was to be the grand depository of the democratic principle of the government. It was, so to speak, to be our House of Commons. It ought to know and sympathize with every part of the community, and ought therefore to be taken not only from different parts of the whole republic, but also from different districts of the larger members of it." Madison too "considered the popular election of one branch of the national legislature as essential to every plan of free government. . . . He thought too that the great fabric to be raised would be more stable if it should rest on the solid formation of the people themselves, than if it should stand merely on the pillars of the legislatures." And Wilson "contended strenuously for drawing the most numerous branch of the legislature immediately from the people. He was for raising the federal pyramid to a considerable altitude, and for that reason wished to give it as broad a basis as possible. . . . He also thought it wrong to increase the weight of the state legislatures by making them electors of the national legislature. All interference between the general and local governments should be obviated as much as possible. On examination, it would be found that the opposition of states to federal measures had proceeded more from the officers of the states than from the people at large." The resolution providing for election by the people then carried.

On June 6 the matter was brought up again. On this day General Pinckney moved "that the first branch of the national legislature be elected by the state legislatures, and not by the people." In support of his motion, the General said that he "wished to have a good national government and at the same time to leave a considerable share of power in the states. . . . The state legislatures also, he said, would be more jealous and more ready to thwart the national government if excluded from a participation in it." Supporting Pinckney, Sherman asserted that if "it were in view to abolish the state governments, the elections ought to be by the people. If the state governments are to be continued, it is necessary in order to preserve harmony between the national and state governments, that the elections to the former should be made by the latter." Gerry said his "idea was that the people should nominate certain persons in certain districts, out of whom the state legislatures should make the appointment."

The opposition was led by Mason and Madison, supported by Read, Dickinson, and Pierce. Mason's point was that since the new government was to operate on individuals, they "ought therefore to choose the representatives." Madison "considered an election of one branch at least of the legislature by the people immediately as a clear principle of free government, and . . . this mode under proper regulations has the additional advantage of securing better representatives, as well as avoiding too great an agency of the state governments in the general one." Read said bluntly: "Too much attachment is betrayed to the state governments. We must look beyond their continuance. A national government must soon of necessity swallow all of them up." Dickinson "considered it as essential that one branch of the legislature should be drawn immediately from the people, and as expedient that the other should be chosen by the legislatures of the states. . . . He was for a strong national government but for leaving the states a considerable agency in the system." Pierce favored "an election by the people as to the first branch and by the states as to the second branch, by which means the citizens of the states would be represented both individually and collectively." After this debate, Pinckney's motion was defeated and election by the people retained.

On June 21 Pinckney tried again, moving this time "that the first branch, instead of being elected by the people, should be elected in such manner as the legislature of each state should direct." This, of course, was the system provided by the Articles. The motion was seconded by Martin and supported by Rutledge, who stated that the "delegates to Congress he thought had also been fitter men than would have been appointed by the people at large." Sherman said that he "would like an election by the legislatures best, but is content with the plan as it stands."

In opposition, Hamilton said that the whole plan would be weakened by the motion, which obviously intended to "transfer the election from the people to the state legislatures." "It would increase that state influence," said Hamilton, "which could not be too watchfully guarded against. All too must admit the possibility, in case the general government should maintain itself, that the state governments might gradually dwindle into nothing. The system therefore should not be engrafted on what might possibly fail." King, also against the motion, "supposed the legislatures would constantly choose men subservient to their own views as contrasted to the general interest. . . . He remarked several instances in which the views of a state might be at variance with those of the general government." With Mason and Wilson also expressing opposition, the Pinckney proposal was defeated, and the matter was settled permanently in favor of popular election of representatives.

On the method of choosing Senators, the Virginia plan had provided that "the members of the second branch of the national legislature ought to be elected by those of the first." When this resolution first came up for discussion on May 31, it was received with general dissatisfaction. Wilson "thought both branches of the national legislature ought to be chosen by the people," whereas Spaight "contended that the second branch ought to be chosen by the state legislatures."

The upshot was that the resolution was defeated without anything else being substituted in its place. On June 7 Dickinson moved "that the members of the second branch ought to be chosen by the individual legislatures." Sherman seconded, "observing that the particular states would thus become interested in supporting the national government, and that a due harmony between the two governments would be maintained." In support of his motion, Dickinson argued that the "preservation of the states in a certain degree of agency is indispensable. It will produce that collision between the different authorities which should be wished for in order to check each other. . . . If the state governments were excluded from all agency in the national one, and all power drawn from the people at large, the consequence would be that the national government would move in the same direction as the state governments now do, and would run into all the same mischiefs. The reform would only unite the thirteen small streams into one great current pursuing the same course without any opposition whatever."

Gerry and the younger Pinckney also supported the proposal, but Mason's argument was the decisive one:

Whatever power may be necessary for the national government, a certain portion must necessarily be left in the states. It is impossible for one power to pervade the extreme parts of the United States so as to carry equal justice to them. The state legislatures also ought to have some means of defending themselves against encroachments of the national government. In every other department we have studiously endeavored to provide for its self-defense. Shall we leave the states alone unprovided with the means for this purpose? And what better means can we provide than the giving them some share in, or rather to make them a constituent part of, the national establishment? There is danger on both sides, no doubt; but we have only seen the evils arising on the side of the state governments. Those on the other side remain to be displayed. The example of Congress does not apply. Congress had no power to carry their acts into execution as the national government will have.

The matter of affording the states, as states, some method of self-protection within the framework and operation of a national system was, of course, behind the divergence over the question of representation in the Congress. Mason's comment here reveals that the two questions—method of selection and basis of representation—were inseparably linked by this common element. And this was recognized, for Butler would take no stand at this time on the method of selection, stating that he "was anxious to know the ratio of representation before he gave any opinion."

Opposing the motion, Wilson asserted that any national government ought to flow from the people at large. If one branch were chosen by the legislatures and the other by the people, the two branches would rest on different foundations and dissensions would naturally arise. Wilson was supported by Morris and Madison. Read advocated the highly centralized method of appointment by the executive from persons nominated by the state legislatures. When the vote was taken, Dickinson's motion carried, and the decision that Senators should be elected by the state legislatures was never again seriously challenged.

In this manner the system of the Articles of Confederation, in which each sovereign state was free to choose its own manner of selecting delegates to Congress, was consciously abandoned in favor of a system more consistent with a national government: a uniform method prescribed by national law which each state would be required to follow. Where members of the House were concerned, the system was even more nationalistic, with election by the people on whom the national laws were to operate. Not until 1913, when the Seventeenth Amendment substituted popular election of Senators for election by the state legislatures, was the United States Congress to rest completely upon the broadest grounds of democratic nationalism. At the same time, the provision for election of Senators by state legislatures actually underscored the fact that state sovereignty was to be extinguished by the Constitution. For it was the fact that the states were no longer to be sovereign that made it necessary to give them political representation in the Congress as a means of protecting themselves against the sovereign power of the new national government.

QUALIFICATIONS FOR DELEGATES TO THE NATIONAL LEGISLATURE

The Articles of Confederation had imposed no qualifications on the delegates that a state might send to Congress. It was consistent with a system based on state sovereignty that each state should determine for itself what qualifications, if any, should be required of its delegates in Congress. But the Founding Fathers did not consider that such a matter should be left for individual choice in a "national" government; rather, the Constitution itself should prescribe uniform qualifications for all members of Congress. Consequently, Article I, Section 2, Clause 2, provides: "No person shall be a representative who shall not have attained to the age of twenty-five years, and been seven years a citizen of the United States, and who shall not, when elected, be an inhabitant of that state in which he shall be chosen." And Article I, Section 3, Clause 3, states: "No person shall be a Senator who shall not have attained to the age of thirty years, and been nine years a citizen of the United States, and who shall not, when elected, be an inhabitant of that state for which he shall be chosen." These qualifications are remarkably few as compared with those which existed in the states as requisite for election to the legislatures. They are also markedly more liberal and republican than those pertaining to state legislatures in that they make no requirements as to residence, religion, or property ownership, all of which were standard in the states.

Since the new "national" government was to operate directly on individuals rather than on the states, it is clear that a new relationship was being created: between the new "national" government and the individuals on whom it was to operate. Wilson in the convention had referred to the twofold future relation of the people: as citizens of the Union and as citizens of their own states. This concept of dual citizenship was incorporated into the Constitution. State citizenship was expressly recognized in Article III, Section 2, which extended the judicial power of the United States to controversies "between a state and citizens of another state; between citizens of different states; between citizens of the same state claiming lands under grants of different states, and between a state, or the citizen thereof, and foreign states, citizens or subjects." And it was also specified in Article IV, Section 2, which provided that the "citizens of each state shall be entitled to all privileges and immunities of citizens in the several states."

In three other provisions the Constitution recognized a United States citizenship. Article I, Section 2, setting the qualifications for members of the House of Representatives, prohibited any person who had not "been seven years a citizen of the United States." Similarly, Section 3 of the same article provided that Senators must have been nine years "a citizen of the United States." Both sections prohibited the offices to persons "who shall not, when elected, be an inhabitant of the state in which he shall be chosen." This language seems further to demonstrate that a distinction was intended between the two kinds of citizenship, for although a person could be elected to Congress without being a citizen of the state in which elected, it was mandatory that he be a citizen of the United States. The third provision is in Section 1 of Article II: "No person except a natural born citizen of the United States, at the time of the adoption of this Constitution, shall be eligible to the office of President." The phrase "citizen of the United States" is not to be found in the Articles of Confederation, although the Articles did refer to the "free inhabitants of each of these states" and also to "free citizens in the several states."

The Constitution, therefore, expressly recognized something which had not been expressly recognized prior to that time: a citizenship of the United States, which, it seems clear, was from the time of ratification on to be something distinct and different from citizenship of a state. That this was the conscious design of the Founders is demonstrated from the proceedings in the convention. On July 26 the convention enacted a resolution "that the Committee of Detail be instructed to receive a clause requiring certain qualifications of landed property and citizenship of the United States in members of the Legislature." As the Committee of Detail referred the draft Constitution to the Convention on August 6, the requirement for members of the House of Representatives and Senators was that each candidate "shall have been a citizen in the United States" for the specified number of years. The journal of the convention records that on August 8 the convention changed the qualification for the House from "a citizen in the United States" to "a citizen of the United States," and on August 9 made the same alteration as to the qualification for Senators. The records contain no discussion of these amendments, but the importance of the change is apparent. The phrase "citizen in the United States" arguably might mean no more than citizenship in one of the states in the United States. The "of" in the altered phrase, however, changes the meaning in an important way. The revised phrase is in marked contrast to the explicit designations of state citizenship in other sections.

Now, whereas the Constitution uses the term "citizen" and recognizes a distinction between state citizenship and United States citizenship, it does not contain any definition of "citizen" or any rules defining who were to be "citizens." Historical research has revealed that Americans of that day used the term "citizen" as synonymous with "subject," the one term being more appropriate for a republic, the other for a monarchy. Under the common law at that time, "subjects" of the King were all persons of British nationality. It seems clear that to the Founding Fathers a "citizen," like a "subject," was one who belonged to a particular state. "Citizenship" and "nationality" being thus equated, the phrase "citizen of the United States" necessarily projected a national political entity. And this, of course, is completely consistent with the repeated reference throughout the convention to a "national" government.

The debate on the requirement of habitance in the state was short but illuminating. As reported to the convention by the Committee of Detail, the section required that the representative be at the time of election a "resident" of the state from which he was chosen. It was moved that "resident" be struck out and "inhabitant" inserted, since great disputes had arisen in the states over the term "residence," whereas "inhabitant" apparently had a more settled meaning. Madison said that "both [terms] were vague, but the latter least so in common acceptation, and would not exclude persons absent occasionally for a considerable time on public or private business." Rutledge opposed the motion and held out for "residence" as a qualification for representatives. Read thereupon "reminded him that we were now forming a national government and such a regulation would correspond little with the idea that we were one people." And Mercer declared that "a regulation of this kind would present a greater alienship among the states than existed under the old federal system. It would interweave local prejudices and state distinctions in the very Constitution which is meant to cure them." On the vote, "inhabitant" was inserted in place of "resident." The same action was taken with regard to parallel language in the qualifications for Senator.

Thus the fact that qualifications were prescribed in the Constitution itself, plus the considerations prompting the usage of the terms "citizen of the United States" and "inhabitant," again reveal the conscious movement from a federal system of sovereign states toward a national government.

NATIONAL COMPENSATION

The Articles of Confederation had provided, in Article V, that each state "shall maintain its own delegates in a meeting of the states, and while they act as members of the committee of the states." In a confederation of sovereign states, with a Congress in which each delegate was merely an agent of his state, it was fitting and proper that the compensation of each delegate should be paid by the state which he represented. But the Founding Fathers did not consider such a method of compensation suitable for the members of a "national" legislature. The Constitution, therefore, provides in Article I, Section 6, Clause 1, that "Senators and Representatives shall receive a compensation for their services, to be ascertained by law, and paid out of the Treasury of the United States." Thus it provided that members of Congress were to be paid by the "national" government of which they were officers. This provision was not won without a struggle, and the debates in the convention reveal clearly how the drive for a truly national government had to overcome considerations based on deep-seated state attachments.

Randolph's original resolutions of May 29 had provided that members of the national legislature should "receive liberal stipends by which they may be compensated for the devotion of their time to public service," but they had contained no reference to the source of such payments. When this provision first came up for debate on June 12, Madison moved that the compensation be "fixed" and observed "that it would be improper to leave the members of the national legislature to be provided for by the state legislatures because it would create an improper dependence." Mason seconded the motion, adding that "it would be improper, for other reasons, to leave the wages to be regulated by the states—first, the different states would make different provisions for their representatives, and an inequality would be left among them, whereas he thought they ought to be in all respects equal." Pierce's motion that "the wages should be paid out of the national treasury" then passed without debate. Butler and Rutledge subsequently proposed that "the members of the second branch should be entitled to no salary or compensation for their services." Madison included a footnote at this point, that the voting probably "turned chiefly on the idea that if the salaries were not here provided for, the members would be paid by their respective states." This proposal was defeated, and it was then agreed that the clause should be the same for both houses. Accordingly, the committee of the whole reported to the convention on June 19 resolutions that members of the two branches should "receive fixed stipends by which they may be compensated for the devotion of their time to the public service to be paid out of the national treasury."

When the resolution relating to the first branch came up for consideration on June 22, Ellsworth promptly "moved to substitute payment by the state, out of their own treasuries." Williamson and Sherman both supported the move, with Sherman recommending that "both the quantum and the payment of it" be referred to the state legislatures. The reaction of the nationalists was vigorous. Randolph was afraid that "popular prejudices" were exerting too much pressure; national legislators paid by the states would almost certainly be dependent on those states. The whole system would therefore be vitiated unless funds came from the national treasury. King and Wilson also warned against creating financial dependence on the states. Madison "concurred in the necessity of preserving the compensations for the national government independent of the state governments." And Hamilton said he "was strenuous against making the national council dependent on the legislative rewards of the states. Those who pay are the masters of those who are paid. . . . He expatiated emphatically on the difference between the feelings and views of the *people* and the *governments* of the states, arising from the personal interest and official inducements which must render the latter unfriendly to the general government. . . . He pressed the distinction between the state governments and the people. The former would be the rivals of the general government. The state legislatures ought not, therefore, to be the paymasters of the latter." Against this barrage, Ellsworth protested that "If we are jealous of the state governments, they will be so of us."

The vote was close—four states supported the Ellsworth motion, five were opposed, and two were divided. At this point Madison added another footnote: "It appeared that Massachusetts concurred, not because they thought the state treasury ought to be substitued but because they thought nothing should be said on the subject, in which case it would silently devolve on the national treasury to support the national legislature." The convention then agreed without debate that "adequate compensation" should be substituted in place of "fixed stipends." But when Butler moved "that a question be taken on both points jointly, to wit, 'adequate compensation to be paid out of the national treasury,' " the vote was five states for, five against, and one divided. "So the question was lost, and the sentence was not inserted."

When the matter came up again on June 26 in connection with the compensation of Senators, Ellsworth made another try, this time moving to strike out "to be paid out of the national treasury" and to insert "to be paid by their respective states." He argued that if "the Senate was meant to strengthen the government, it ought to have the confidence of the states."

In reply, Madison said that he "considered this as a departure from a fundamental principle. . . . Senators would, if this motion should be agreed to, hold their places during the pleasure of the state legislatures. . . . The motion would make the Senate, like Congress, the mere agents and advocates of state interests and views, instead of being the impartial umpires and guardians of justice and the general good." And Dayton said that he "considered the payment of the Senate by the states as fatal to their independence. He was decided for paying them out of the national treasury."

Again the vote was close—five states in support of Ellsworth's motion, and six against. Immediately thereafter, however, a question was taken whether the words "to be paid out of the public treasury" should stand, and this was also defeated by a five to six division, North Carolina inexplicably voting against both modes of payment.

The sources differ as to the resolution referred to the Committee of Detail. Prescott's version is that the convention resolved that "members of the first branch ought . . . to be paid out of the public treasury." In Farrand, no reference was made to compensation for representatives. The resolution as to Senators was that they should "receive a compensation" without reference to its source. It is clear, however, that the convention had twice specifically rejected, as proposed by Ellsworth, the method of payment by the states. Notwithstanding this fact, when the Committee of Detail reported back a draft Constitution to the convention, it provided that the "members of each house shall receive a compensation for their services, to be ascertained and paid by the state in which they shall be chosen." This was the system of the Articles all over again and of course was inconsistent with the whole idea of a national legislature as part of a national government. It must have come as quite a surprise to many members of the convention that this method of payment should have been included by the Committee of Detail after having twice been expressly rejected by the convention.

But an even greater surprise was yet to come. For when this provision came up for consideration on August 6, Ellsworth, who had twice sought its inclusion by the convention and who was a member of the Committee of Detail, now spoke out against the proposal. He said that "in reflecting on this subject, he had been satisfied that too much dependence on the states would be produced by this mode of payment." He therefore moved to strike it out and insert "that they should be paid out of the treasury of the United States." He was supported by Morris, Langdon, and Madison. But Butler pressed "for payment by the states, particularly in the case of the Senate, who will be so long out of their respective states that they will lose sight of their constituents unless dependent on them for their support." In reply, Gerry said that "The observation of Mr. Butler has weight in it. On the other side, the state legislatures may turn out the Senators by reducing their salaries." Mason added: "It has not yet been noticed that the clause as it now stands makes the House of Representatives also dependent on the state legislatures; so that both houses will be made the instruments of the politics of the states, whatever they may be."

Broom, in one of his rare utterances, said that he "could see no danger in trusting the general legislature with the payment of themselves." Carroll and Dickinson both spoke out strongly. Carroll said he "had been much surprised at seeing this clause in the report. The dependence of both houses on the state legislatures is complete, especially as the members of the former are eligible to state offices." And Dickinson said that he "took it for granted that all were convinced of the necessity of making the general government independent of the prejudices, passions, and improper views of the state legislatures. The contrary of this was effected by the section as it stands. . . . If the general government should be left dependent on the state legislatures, it would be happy for us if we had never met in this room."

Luther Martin, the state sovereignty diehard, said that as "the Senate is to represent the states, the members of it ought to be paid by the states." To this Carroll replied that the "Senate was to represent and manage the affairs of the whole and not to be the advocates of state interests. They ought then not to be dependent on nor paid by the states." The convention then voted, nine states to two, to pay members of the national legislature out of the national treasury. And so on this question, so vital to the creation of a national government, which in the most practical way required a clear choice between national supremacy and state sovereignty, the convention's original decision of May 29 in favor of national payment was in the end supported by an overwhelming vote, in the face of persistent and determined efforts to change it.

NATIONAL PREROGATIVES

Census and Allotment of Representatives. The Articles of Confederation had provided that no state "shall be represented in Congress by less than two, nor by more than seven members." In replacing a unicameral with a bicameral Congress, the Constitution dealt with the number of members in a different manner. In the Senate, there were to be two Senators from each state. In the House, Article I, Section 2, Clause 3, provided that "Representatives and direct taxes shall be apportioned among the several states which may be included within this Union, according to their respective numbers, which shall be determined by adding to the whole number of free persons, including those bound to service for a term of years, and excluding Indians not taxed, three-fifths of all other persons. The actual enumeration shall be made within three years after the first meeting of the Congress of the United States, and within every subsequent term of ten years, in such manner as they shall by law direct." There followed a listing of the number of representatives each state should have until the enumeration was made.

This section was the result of a motion made by Randolph on July 10 that "in order to ascertain the alterations in the population and wealth of the several states the Legislature should be required to cause a census, and estimate to be taken within one year after its first meeting; and every — years thereafter, and that the Legislature arrange the representation accordingly." There was some debate as to whether the matter should be dealt with in the Constitution or left to the discretion of Congress. Morris "opposed it as fettering the Legislature too much." Read also "thought the Legislature ought not to be too much shackled." Wilson "had himself no objection to leaving the Legislature entirely at liberty."

On the other hand, Mason said that the "greater the difficulty we find in fixing a proper rule of representation, the more unwilling ought we to be, to throw the task from ourselves, on the general legislature." Sherman said "he was at first for leaving the matter wholly to the discretion of the Legislature; but he had been convinced by the observations of Mr. Randolph and Mr. Mason that the periods and the rule of revising the representation ought to be fixed by the Constitution." Gorham's view was that if the convention, "who are comparatively so little biased by local views are so much perplexed, how can it be expected that the Legislature hereafter under the full bias of those views, will be able to settle a standard. He was convinced by the arguments of others and his own reflections, that the convention ought to fix some standard or other." No one, however, disagreed with Randolph when, on July 11, speaking in behalf of a substitute offered by Williamson, he stated that "the census must be taken under the direction of the general legislature. The states will be too much interested to take an impartial one for themselves."

So it was that the Constitution provided that there should be a national allotment of representatives based on the national population as determined by a census taken in accordance with national law. All of which, of course, was consistent with the idea of a national legislature.

Tenure. The Articles of Confederation provided in Article V that "delegates should be annually appointed in such manner as the legislature of each state shall direct . . . with a power reserved to each state, to recall its delegates, or any of them, at any time within the year, and to send others in their stead, for the remainder of the year." The same article also stated that "no person shall be capable of being a delegate for more than three years in any term of six years." The power of the state to recall and the limitation on consecutive service both served to minimize the likelihood that any state delegate should become too attached to national or general interests. Together with the provision already noted that delegates were to be financially maintained by the states, these clauses assured a complete dominion of the state over the delegate and effectively precluded his becoming anything more than an agent of state interests. These provisions, completely natural and normal in a confederation of sovereign states, were completely inconsistent with a national legislature. Accordingly, it is not surprising that both provisions were eliminated in the Constitution. Curiously enough, both were found in the original Randolph resolutions, but both were struck out, on motion of Pinckney on June 12, without any debate and without a dissenting vote. Consequently, as befits members of a national legislature, representatives and Senators enjoy fixed terms immune from state recall, with no limitation on re-eligibility for office.

Contested Elections. Under the Articles of Confederation the Congress had no control whatever over the selection of the delegates from the states. On June 21 Pinckney sought to replace the popular election of representatives, as provided for in the Virginia plan, with the system which had prevailed under the Articles; namely, election "in such manner as the legislature of each state shall direct." One of the arguments offered by Pinckney in support of his motion was "that otherwise disputed elections must be referred to the general legislature which would be attended with intolerable expense and trouble to the distant parts of the republic." Wilson and Madison, on the other hand, opposed the motion for the very reason, among others, that "the returns may be made to the legislatures of the several states—they may judge of contested elections."

Pinckney's motion was defeated, but the Convention took no further action at the time on the judging of contested elections. The Committee of Detail, however, included a provision in its draft that each house should be the judge of the elections, returns, and qualifications of its own members. On August 10 this provision was agreed to without debate and without dissent. On September 14 a motion to reconsider was defeated without debate. Consequently the Constitution provides, in Article I, Section 5, Clause 1: "Each house shall be the judge of the elections, returns, and qualifications of its own members." The states were thus completely precluded from any participation in disputes over the election or qualifications of members of Congress. These were matters to be determined by the national legislature itself.

Quorum and Attendance. The Articles of Confederation, as noted, had provided that no state should be represented by less than two members. Furthermore, Article IX prohibited Congress from exercising its most important powers "unless nine states assent to the same," and from taking any action at all (except adjourning from day to day) "unless by the votes of a majority of the united states in congress assembled." The paralysis which resulted from the requirement of a quorum of states and the declining attendance in Congress after the war has already been discussed in Chapter Two. This was in keeping, of course, with a confederation of sovereign states. But a national legislature could not exercise national powers effectively under any such legislative arrangement. Consequently the Constitution radically transformed this system by providing, in Article I, Section 5, Clause 1, that "a majority of each house shall constitute a quorum to do business; but a smaller number may adjourn from day to day, and may be authorized to compel the attendance of absent members, in such manner, and under such penalties as each house may provide."

This section originated with the Committee of Detail, which had included in its draft a provision that a majority in each house should constitute a quorum to do business. When this came up for consideration on August 10, Gorham contended that "less than a majority in each house should be made of quorum, otherwise great delay might happen in business, and great inconvenience from the future increase of numbers." Mercer "was also for less than a majority. So great a number will put it in the power of a few by seceding at a critical moment to introduce convulsions, and endanger the government. . . . He was for leaving it to the Legislature to fix the quorum."

Mason, however, argued "This is a valuable and necessary part of the plan. In this extended country, embracing so great a diversity of interests, it would be dangerous to the distant parts to allow a small number of members of the two houses to make laws. . . . He thought the Constitution as now molded was founded on sound principles, and was disposed to put into it extensive power. At the same time he wished to guard against abuses as much as possible." Morris observed that "the secession of a small number ought not to be suffered to break a quorum. Such events in the states may have been of little consequence. In the national councils, they may be fatal." Ellsworth said that it would give the people confidence to know "that no law or burden could be imposed on them by a few men." He suggested, therefore, that the "inconveniency of secessions may be guarded against by giving to each house an authority to require the attendance of absent members." Randolph and Madison moved to add to the provision as it stood: "and may be authorized to compel the attendance of absent members in such manner and under such penalties as each house may provide." This was agreed to, and the section as amended was then adopted without further debate. It is significant that at no time did any one suggest that a quorum should be in any way related to the number of states represented, not even in the Senate, where each state had an equality of representation. Both of the actions of the convention—setting a numerical majority as a quorum and empowering Congress to make attendance compulsory—was a clear repudiation of the state sovereignty which had prevailed on these matters under the Articles.

Discipline of Membership. The Articles of Confederation granted Congress no authority over individual delegates. The Thomas Burke incident recounted in Chapter One demonstrated that Congress was powerless to discipline a member, even one who had deliberately destroyed a quorum by refusing to attend. For their conduct in Congress, delegates were amenable only to the states which they represented. This was consistent with a compact of sovereign states, but not with a national legislature. Consequently, the Constitution provided, in Article I, Section 5, Clause 2: "Each house may determine the rules of its proceedings, pun-

ish its members for disorderly behavior, and, with the concurrence of
two-thirds, expel a member." This section was inserted originally by
the Committee of Detail. When Section 2 came up for consideration on
August 10, Madison "observed that the right of expulsion was too important to be exercised by a bare majority of a quorum, and in emergencies of faction might be dangerously abused. He moved that 'with
the concurrence of two-thirds' might be inserted between 'may' and
'expel.' " Although Morris thought that the majority might be entrusted
with such power, the amendment carried and as amended the section
passed without debate and without dissent. In the future, no member
would humiliate the new national legislature as Thomas Burke had humiliated the old Congress. Again state sovereignty had been abandoned
in favor of national supremacy.

Impeachment. The foregoing provisions indicate the extent to which
the states were stripped of all formal control over members of Congress.
States were also denied participation in the process whereby members
of the executive and judicial branches of the national government could
be impeached. An attempt was made, however, to include state participation in the removal of the President. On June 2 Dickinson moved
"that the executive be made removable by the national legislature on
the request of a majority of the legislatures of individual states." In support of his motion, he said that it was "necessary . . . to place the power of
removing somewhere. He did not like the plan of impeaching the great
officers of state. He did not know how provision could be made for removal of them in a better mode than that which he had proposed. He had
no idea of abolishing the state governments as some gentlemen seemed
inclined to do. The happiness of this country in his opinion required
considerable powers to be left in the hands of the states."

Madison and Wilson promptly objected on the ground that such a plan
"would open a door for intrigues against [the President] in states
where his administration though just might be unpopular, and might
tempt him to pay court to particular states whose leading partisans he
might fear, or wish to engage as his partisans. They both thought it bad
policy to introduce such a mixture of the state authorities, when their
agency could be otherwise supplied." The motion was defeated, all
states except Delaware, Dickinson's own state, being opposed. Where
the removal of judges was concerned, an interesting incident occurred
later in the convention. Dickinson sought on August 27 to provide for
their removal by the President on application of Congress. Rutledge
opposed the motion on the ground that if the Supreme Court "is to judge

between the United States and particular states, this alone is an insuperable objection to the motion."

In the end, the method of removal decided on by the convention was the one most consistent with a national government. Article II, Section 4, provided: "The President, Vice-President, and all civil officers of the United States, shall be removed from office on impeachment for, and conviction of, treason, bribery, or other high crimes and misdemeanors." And Article I, Section 2, Clause 5, provided that the House of Representatives "shall have the sole power of impeachment." Thus, high officers of the national government were subject to impeachment by the branch of the national legislature representing the people on whom that government was to be directly operative.

The sum total of what has been said regarding the national legislature in various respects—its bicameral structure, its nationally prescribed methods of selection, its nationally prescribed qualifications, its national compensation, and its national prerogatives of allotment, tenure, judging contested elections and qualifications, quorum and compulsory attendance, discipline, and impeachment—reveals clearly the complete antithesis between the nature of the Congress of the Articles of Confederation and the Congress created by the Constitution.

Under the Articles every provision and practice was what it was because the Congress was merely a convention of agents representing sovereign states. With the abolition of state sovereignty and its replacement by a national government operating directly upon the people, the national legislature simply had to be freed from dependence on and control by the states. The foregoing discussion amply demonstrates the completeness with which this was accomplished.

In only three respects were the states accorded any recognition or participation in the selection or composition of the national legislature.

(1) State Equality of Representation in the Senate. This topic will be examined later in connection with the powers of the national legislature. At that time further consideration will be given to the significance of the selection of Senators by the state legislatures.

(2) State Determination of Suffrage Requirements. The Constitution, in Article I, Section 2, Clause 3, after providing for popular election of representatives, then states that "the electors in each state shall have the qualifications requisite for electors of the most numerous branch of the state legislature." This provision originated with the Committee of Detail, and the records indicate that the committee originally contemplated nationally prescribed standards. One committee draft was that

the qualifications of electors should be the same as in the states "unless the Legislature (i.e., Congress) shall hereafter direct some uniform qualification to prevail through the states." Another committee draft would have limited the suffrage to freeholders of fifty acres, at least twenty-one years old, with one year's residence in the United States. The temptation to prescribe qualifications nationally undoubtedly arose from the diversity of suffrage requirements in the states, where there was a wide variance in such factors as residence, property ownership, payment of taxes, and so on. In no two states, as a matter of fact, were the requirements exactly the same. On the other hand, this very diversity rendered it almost impossible to devise a national scheme which would meet with general satisfaction.

When the matter came before the convention on August 7, Morris moved to strike out the committee recommendation "in order that some other provision might be substituted which would restrain the right of suffrage to freeholders." According to King, however, the motion was "to leave it to the Legislature (i.e., Congress) to establish the qualifications of electors and elected, or to add a clause that the Legislature may hereafter alter the qualifications." Morris was not only opposed to voting by non-freeholders; he also thought that another "objection against the clause as it stands is that it makes the qualifications of the national legislature depend on the will of the states, which he thought not proper." Madison favored a limitation to freeholders but thought that "the right of suffrage is certainly one of the fundamental articles of republican government, and ought not to be left to be regulated by the Legislature." Wilson took the view that the committee had considered this part of the report well enough so that it could not be improved upon. "It was difficult," he said, "to form any uniform rule of qualifications for all the states." Mason believed that a power "to alter the qualifications would be a dangerous power in the hands of the Legislature." And Ellsworth "thought the qualifications of the electors stood on the most proper footing. The right of suffrage was a tender point, and strongly guarded by most of the state constitutions. The people will not readily subscribe to the national constitution if it should subject them to be disfranchised. The states are the best judges of the circumstances and temper of their own people." Morris' motion was then defeated, and the matter was never thereafter raised again. Inasmuch as the suffrage requirements in the states were constitutionally prescribed, the method provided by the Constitution represents a compromise between congressional or state legislative control. It is clear, therefore, that this constitutional provision is based on a concept of popular sovereignty rather than on state sovereignty.

(3) State Determination of Electoral Processes. The draft submitted to the convention by the Committee of Detail contained a provision that the "times and places and the manner of holding the elections of the members of each House shall be prescribed by the legislatures of each state; but their provisions concerning them may, at any time, be altered by the Legislature of the United States." When the matter came up for discussion on August 9, the first part was agreed to without debate and without dissent. The second part, recognizing a controlling authority in Congress, occasioned some debate. The younger Pinckney and Rutledge moved to strike this second part. "The states, they contended, could and must be relied on in such cases."

The nationalist opposition to this motion was vigorous. Gorham said that "It would be as improper to take this power from the national legislature, as to restrain the British Parliament from regulating the circumstances of elections, leaving this business to the counties themselves." Madison argued that in this manner:

> The necessity of a general government presupposes that the state legislatures will sometimes fail or refuse to consult the common interest at the expense of their local conveniency or prejudices . . . the legislatures of the states ought not to have the uncontrolled right of regulating the times, places, and manner of holding elections. These were words of great latitude. It was impossible to foresee all the abuses that might be made of the discretionary power. . . . Whenever the state legislatures had a favorite measure to carry, they would take care so as to mould their regulations as to favor the candidates they wished to succeed. . . . It seemed as improper in principle, though it might be less inconvenient in practice, to give to the state legislatures this great authority over the election of the representatives of the people in the general legislature as it would be to give to the latter like power over the election of their representatives in the state legislatures.

King asserted, "If this power be not given to the national legislature, their right of judging of the returns of their members may be frustrated. No probability has been suggested of its being abused by them. Although this scheme of erecting the general government on the authority of the state legislatures has been fatal to the federal establishment, it would seem as if many gentlemen still foster the dangerous idea." And Morris "observed that the states might make false returns and then make no provisions for new elections." Even Sherman "did not know but it might be best to retain the clause, though he had himself sufficient confidence in the state legislatures." The motion of Pinckney and Rutledge was then defeated.

Immediately thereafter, on a motion by Read, the word "their" was struck out and "regulations in such cases" inserted in place of "provisions concerning them," the clause then reading "but regulations, in each of the foregoing cases, may at any time be made or altered by the legislature of the United States." The explanation given for this motion was that this "was meant to give the national legislature a power not only to alter the provisions of the states, but to make regulations in case the states should fail or refuse altogether." The result of the debate, therefore, was that the ultimate and controlling power of Congress was confirmed and even expanded. On September 14 one further change was made. The words "except as to the places of choosing Senators" were added at the end of the clause. This amendment resulted from the feeling that the state legislatures, who were to choose the senators, should be free to control their own place of meeting.

The final form, in Article I, Section 4, Clause 1, reads as follows: "The times, places and manner of holding elections for Senators and Representatives, shall be prescribed in each state by the legislature thereof; but the Congress may at any time by law make or alter such regulations, except as to the places of choosing Senators." It is clear that this clause, even though it recognized initial state power over the electoral process, was not included because of any solicitude for state sovereignty. On the contrary, the insistence that ultimate power rests with Congress is an express assertion of national supremacy.

Powers of the National Legislature

BY 1787 the insufficiency of the powers of Congress under the Articles of Confederation was recognized and admitted even by most of the antinationalists. Increased central powers had been a nationalist article of faith since before the adoption of the Articles. Consequently, it is not surprising that the Virginia plan dealt with this matter in the sweeping fashion it did. The sixth resolution introduced by Randolph provided that "the national legislature ought to be empowered to enjoy the legislative rights vested in Congress by the Confederation and moreover to legislate in all cases to which the separate states are incompetent, or in which the harmony of the United States may be interrupted by the exercise of individual legislation."

When the convention, acting as a committee of the whole, considered this resolution on May 31, a short discussion ensued. Pinckney and Rutledge felt that the term "incompetent" was vague and said "they could not well decide how to vote until they should see an exact enumeration of the powers comprehended by this definition." Butler was still afraid that the convention was being "extreme in taking away the powers of the states, and called on Mr. Randolph for the extent of his meaning." At this, Randolph "disclaimed any intention to give indefinite powers to the national legislature, declaring that he was entirely opposed to such an inroad on the state jurisdictions." Madison's comment was most discreet. He said

> that he had brought with him into the convention a strong bias in favor of an enumeration and definition of the powers necessary to be exercised by the national legislature; but had also brought doubts concerning its practicability. His wishes remained unaltered; but his doubts had become stronger. What his opinion might ultimately be he could not yet tell. But he should shrink from nothing which should be found essential to such a form of government as would provide for the safety, liberty, and happiness of the community. This being the end of all our deliberations, all the necessary means for attaining it must, however reluctantly, be submitted to.

Then, on the question for giving powers in cases to which the states were not competent, the committee expressed its approval, nine states to none, with one state divided. The other two clauses of the resolution were approved without debate or dissent. The committee of the whole thus approved the resolution as first proposed by Randolph.

When the resolution in that form came before the convention on July 16, the first clause was approved without debate or dissent. The second and third clauses, however, granting power to legislate in cases to which the states were incompetent or in which individual legislation would interrupt the harmony of the United States, occasioned some discussion. Butler called for "some explanation of the extent of this power; particularly of the word 'incompetent.' The vagueness of the terms," Butler said, "rendered it impossible for any precise judgment to be formed." To this Gorham replied that the very "vagueness of the terms constitutes the propriety of them. We are now establishing general principles, to be extended hereafter into details which will be precise and explicit." Rutledge then "urged the objection started by Mr. Butler and moved that the clause should be committed to the end that a specification of the powers comprised in the general terms might be reported." On this question the states were equally divided, five to five, and the motion was lost.

The next day, July 17, Sherman "observed that it would be difficult to draw the line between the powers of the general legislatures, and those to be left with the states; that he did not like the definition contained in the resolution." Accordingly, he proposed to substitute, in place of the two clauses under discussion, the following: "to make laws binding on the people of the United States in all cases which may concern the common interests of the Union; but not to interfere with the government of the individual states in any matters of internal policy which respect the government of such states only, and wherein the general welfare of the United States is not concerned." Gouverneur Morris opposed the motion: "The internal police, as it would be called and understood by the states, ought to be infringed in many cases, as in the case of paper money and other tricks by which citizens of other states may be affected." On the question, Sherman's vote was decisively defeated, eight to two.

Bedford then moved that the resolution be altered so as to include the clause "and moreover to legislate in all cases for the general interests of the Union." The addition of this power expanded the legislative power of Congress even beyond the broad coverage of the Virginia resolution—so much so that even Randolph was taken aback. He was moved to say, "This is a formidable idea indeed. It involves the power of violating all the laws and constitutions of the states, and of intermeddling with their police." In other words, it accomplished the very thing he had earlier disclaimed would be accomplished by his own resolution. Bedford responded that "it is not more extensive or formidable than the clause as it stands; no state being separately competent to legislate for the general interest of the union." On the vote, Bedford's motion carried, six to four, and the entire clause as amended was then approved, eight to two.

Up to this point, then, the convention had approved a general broad legislative power in Congress; had rejected a proposal to enumerate specifically the powers of Congress; had rejected a proposal to protect the internal police power of the states against the power of Congress; and, finally, had amended the legislative power to make it even more sweeping and comprehensive than it had originally been. The resolution submitted by the convention to the Committee of Detail was that "the Legislature of the United States ought to possess the legislative rights vested in Congress by the Confederation; and moreover to legislate in all cases for the general interests of the Union, and also in those cases to which the states are separately incompetent, or in which the harmony of the United States may be interrupted by the exercise of individual legislation." The draft constitution reported to the convention by the Committee of Detail revealed a substantial change in form and language. An enumeration of particular powers was substituted for the broad general grant. This policy of enumeration was adopted by the convention, with the result that Article I, Section 8, of the Constitution lists eighteen separate powers of Congress, and other powers are set forth in other sections. The significance of enumeration of legislative powers rather than general grant will be commented on subsequently. First, however, the powers themselves will be considered in light of their relationship to the question of state sovereignty.

FISCAL POWERS

Two fiscal powers were granted to Congress by the Articles of Confederation. Congress was vested with the power of "regulating the alloy and value of coin struck by their own authority, or by that of the respective states." This power was carried forward, modified, and amplified under the Constitution, which authorized Congress to "coin money, regulate the value thereof, and of foreign coin." The reference to the coin of the states was deleted inasmuch as the states were specifically prohibited, in Article I, Section 10, from coining money. The power to regulate value of foreign as well as domestic coin was one which had not existed in Congress under the Articles. Being a power incident to sovereignty, it affords one illustration of the conscious shift of sovereignty from states to nation. The Articles had also granted to Congress the power "to borrow money, or emit bills on the credit of the United States, transmitting every half year to the respective states an account of the sums of money so borrowed or emitted." This power was also carried over into the Constitution, naturally omitting any necessity of accounting to the states and also deleting the express power of emitting bills of credit.

It has been noted that the absence of any power of taxation in Congress was one of the most glaring inadequacies of the Articles of Confederation. The Articles had merely provided that "All charges of war, and all other expenses that shall be incurred for the common defense or general welfare, and allowed by the United States in Congress assembled, shall be defrayed out of a common treasury, which shall be supplied by the several states, in proportion to the value of all land within each state. . . . The taxes for paying that proportion shall be laid and levied by the authority and direction of the legislatures of the several states. . . ." Under this system, obviously, Congress had no power to obtain any revenue by laying taxes directly upon individual citizens. Congress could only make requisitions upon the states, but Congress lacked any power to compel the states to comply with such requisitions. Such a system was consistent, of course, with the constitutional assertion made before and during the Revolution that there should be no taxation without representation. Under the Articles the people were not represented in the Congress and therefore it could not tax them. Since they could be taxed only by their representatives, the taxing power was confined to the state legislatures where the people were represented. The revenue system of the Articles, therefore, was exactly what it should have been in a compact of sovereign states.

The almost fatal consequences of state sovereignty in this area before and after the Revolution, and the repeated refusal of the states to grant any additional power to Congress, have been chronicled in Chapter Two. By 1787 the necessity of a national power of taxation was accepted by almost everyone. Even the New Jersey plan, clinging as it did to a federal system, would have authorized Congress "to pass acts for raising a revenue" and "to make rules and regulations for the collection thereof." And it is probably not a coincidence that, when the Committee of Detail decided to enumerate the powers of Congress, the very first one vested a "power to lay and collect taxes, duties, imposts, and excises." When this language came up for consideration on August 16, there was not a dissenting voice raised against the grant of power. The only discussion which occurred related to the question of whether the power should extend to exports. On the vote, only Gerry voted against the grant of power.

It may be safely said that no other section in the Constitution more conclusively demonstrates the transition from a confederation of sovereign states to a national government operating directly upon individuals than the first clause of Article I, Section 8: "The Congress shall have the power to lay and collect taxes, duties, imposts, and excises, to pay the debts and provide for the common defense and general welfare of the United States." This broad and sweeping power was qualified in only three ways, none of very great importance from the standpoint of ability to raise revenue. The granting clause itself contains one limitation—that "all duties, imposts, and excises shall be uniform throughout the United States." A second limitation is found in both Article I, Section 3, and Article I, Section 9, which contain a requirement that direct taxes be apportioned among the states in accordance with their population as determined by the national census. The third limitation, also found in Article I, Section 9, prohibits a tax on articles exported from any state. It seems clear that these limitations were placed upon the national power for the protection of individuals upon whom the power was to operate, and not because of any consideration of state sovereignty. This is readily apparent as to the uniformity and apportionment requirements; that it is also true of the export limitation is plain, since the Constitution in Article I, Section 10, placed the same restriction upon the states.

COMMERCIAL POWERS

Under the Articles of Confederation, the powers of Congress relating to trade and commerce were very limited. Virtually this entire domain was subject to the sovereign will of the several states. The Articles did grant to Congress the power of "fixing the standard of weights and measures throughout the United States," and this power was carried forward into the Constitution. Congress also had, under the Articles, the power of "establishing and regulating post offices from one state to another, throughout all the United States, and exacting such postage on the papers passing through the same as may be requisite to defray the expenses of the said office." This power was also carried forward into the Constitution in simplified form, Article I, Section 8 granting the power in Clause 7 "To establish post offices and post roads." The third and final power of Congress in this area was of "regulating the trade and managing all affairs with the Indians, not members of any of the states, provided that the legislative right of any state within its own limits be not infringed or violated." Not only was this power over trade confined to Indians, but the proviso effectively nullified the grant and left the authority of the states supreme.

It was in the realm of commercial intercourse among the states themselves and with foreign nations that the Articles of Confederation were inadequate, for in these vital areas Congress had no power whatever. (The disastrous consequences have been summarized in Chapter One.) Commercial reform was, of course, the stated reason for the convening of the Annapolis convention, which led to the calling of the Philadelphia convention. In the light of this background, it is not surprising that the draft reported to the convention by the Committee of Detail contained the broad and unqualified grant of power to Congress "to regulate commerce with foreign nations and among the several states." Nor is it surprising that when this clause came up for consideration on August 16, it was approved by the convention without discussion and without dissent. So easily and readily was a huge and vitally important area of legislative power transferred from the states to the nation. On motion of Brearly, the convention added the words "and with the Indian tribes," thereby removing this once important area from the jurisdiction of the states.

The draft submitted by the Committee of Detail had contained a provision requiring a two-thirds majority in each house for the passage of navigation acts. On referral to a committee it was recommended that this provision be stricken. When the committee report came up on August 29, the younger Pinckney moved to postpone it in order to take up the following proposition: "That no act of the Legislature for the purpose of regulating the commerce of the United States with foreign powers, or among the several states, shall be passed without the assent of two-thirds of the members of each House."

This proposal went further even than the committee draft, since it would have required an extraordinary majority for any regulation of commerce and not merely for navigation acts. Because the states were to be equally represented in the Senate, the adoption of the Pinckney proposition would have represented an approval and continuation of the system that had existed under the Articles (the approval of nine states in Congress was required for any acts of importance). Pinckney was supported by Mason, who stated that the "majority will be governed by their interests. The southern states are the minority in both houses. It is to be expected that they will deliver themselves bound hand and foot to the eastern states?" Williamson and Randolph also spoke in favor of the proposition.

Wilson responded in opposition. "The majority, he said, would be no more governed by interest than the minority. It was surely better to let the latter be bound hand and foot than the former. Great inconveniences had, he contended, been experienced in Congress from the Article of Confederation requiring nine votes in certain cases." And Sherman also reminded the convention that "to require more than a majority to decide a question was always embarrassing as had been experienced in cases requiring the votes of nine states in Congress." Some southern delegates refused to take a provincial view of the matter. General Pinckney said that "it was the true interest of the southern states to have no regulation of commerce, but considering the loss brought on the commerce of the eastern states by the revolution, their liberal conduct toward the views of South Carolina (i.e., on the slavery question) and the interest the weak southern states had in being united with the strong eastern states, he thought it proper that no fetters should be imposed on the power of making commercial regulations; and that his constituents, though prejudiced against the eastern states, would be reconciled to this liberality. He had himself, he said, prejudices against the eastern states before he came here, but would acknowledge that he had found them as liberal and candid as any men whatever." And Rutledge was also "against the motion of his colleague. It did not follow from a grant of power to regulate trade, that it would be abused. At the worst a navigation act could bear hard a little while only on the southern states. As we are laying the foundation for a great empire, we ought to take a permanent view of the subject and not look at the present moment only."

It was Madison, however, who best expressed the wisdom of the national point of view. He observed:

> The disadvantage to the southern states from a navigation act lay chiefly in a temporary rise of freight, attended however with an increase of southern as well as northern shipping, with the emigration of northern seamen and merchants to the southern states, and with a removal of the existing and injurious retaliations among the states on each other. The power of foreign nations to obstruct our retaliating measures on them by a corrupt influence would also be less if a majority should be made competent than if two-thirds of each house should be required to legislate acts in this case. An abuse of the power would be qualified with all these good effects. . . . He added that the southern states would derive an essential advantage in the general security afforded by the increase of our maritime strength. He stated the vulnerable situation of them all, and of Virginia in particular. The increase of the coasting trade, and of seamen, would also be favorable to the southern states, by increasing the consumption of their produce. If the wealth of the eastern should in a still greater proportion be augmented, the wealth would contribute the more to the public wants, and be otherwise a national benefit.

Confronted with the choice between a full national power or one fettered by the requirement of a two-thirds majority, the convention rejected the Pinckney proposition. On September 15 Mason tried again to qualify the power with a two-thirds majority, this time only until 1808, but again the convention rejected the proposal.

One particular subject of commerce—the slave trade—received special consideration. The resolutions approved by the committee of the whole contained no reference to this subject. The draft submitted by the Committee of Detail, however, explicitly reserved the matter for state power by providing that "No tax or duty shall be laid by the legislature . . . on the migration or importation of such persons as the several states shall think proper to admit; nor shall such migration or importation be prohibited." When this came before the convention on August 21, Luther Martin's detestation of slavery overcame his devotion to state sovereignty, and he proposed to vary this article "so as to allow a prohibition or tax on the importation of slaves," arguing that "such a clause would leave an encouragement to this traffic" and that "it was inconsistent with the principles of the Revolution and dishonorable to the American character to have such a feature in the Constitution."

This motion was supported by Mason, who asserted that the "present question concerns not the importing states alone but the whole Union." After discoursing on the evils of slavery, Mason said, "As to the states being in possession of the right to import, this was the case with many other rights, now to be properly given up. He held it essential to every point of view that the general government should have power to prevent the increase of slavery." Dickinson said he "Considered it inadmissible, on every principle of honor and safety, that the importation of slaves should be authorized to the states by the Constitution. The true question was whether the national happiness would be promoted or impeded by the importation, and this question ought to be left to the national government, not to the states particularly interested." And Langdon was "strenuous for giving the power to the general government. He could not, with a good conscience, leave it with the states, who could then go on with the traffic, without being restrained by the opinions here given, that they will themselves cease to import slaves."

Southern opposition to the Martin proposal was vigorous, even threatening. "Religion and humanity had nothing to do with this question," Rutledge asserted. "Interest alone is the governing principle with nations. The true question at present is whether the southern states shall or shall not be parties to the Union." Rutledge continued by declaring that "If the convention thinks that North Carolina, South Carolina, and Georgia will ever agree to the plan, unless their right to import slaves be untouched, the expectation is vain. The people of those states will never be such fools as to give up so important an interest." The younger Pinckney stated that "South Carolina can never receive the plan if it prohibits the slave trade," and affirmed that "If slavery be wrong, it is justified by the example of all the world. . . . In all ages one half of mankind have been slaves. If the southern states were let alone, they will probably of themselves stop importations. He would himself, as a citizen of South Carolina, vote for it. An attempt to take away the right, as proposed, will produce serious objections to the Constitution, which he wished to see adopted." General Pinckney also argued that "the importation of slaves would be for the interest of the whole Union" and declared that he "should consider a rejection of the clause as an exclusion of South Carolina from the Union." Baldwin said he had "conceived national objects alone to be before the convention, not such as, like the present, were of a local nature." And Williamson said he "thought the southern states could not be members of the Union, if the clause should be rejected, and that it was wrong to force any thing down not absolutely necessary, and which any state must disagree to."

Some support was forthcoming from northern delegates. Ellsworth said that he was "for leaving the clause as it stands. Let every state import what it pleases. The morality or wisdom of slavery are considerations belonging to the states themselves. What enriches a part enriches the whole, and the states are the best judge of their particular interest." He urged that the convention refrain from meddling. "Slavery in time," Ellsworth said, "will not be a speck in our country." And Sherman "was for leaving the clause as it stands. He disapproved of the slave trade, yet as the states were now possessed of the right to import slaves, as the public good did not require it to be taken from them, and as it was expedient to have as few objections as possible to the proposed scheme of government, he thought it best to leave the matter as we find it." He said "it was better to let the southern states import slaves than to part with them, if they made that a *sine qua non*."

The matter was referred to a committee which, on August 24, recommended the substitution of a provision which prohibited Congress from outlawing the slave trade prior to 1800, but authorized a tax at a rate "not exceeding the average of the duties laid on imports." This clause represented a substantial departure from the former one which prohibited all exercise of congressional power over the subject. The power of Congress to prohibit the slave trade was now being expressly recognized, even though its exercise was to be postponed. Surprisingly enough, this compromise arrangement was agreeable to the southern delegates, who were content with amendments advancing the year to 1808 and limiting the tax to $10 per person. In its final form the clause is found in Article I, Section 9, of the Constitution: "The migration or importation of such persons as any of the states now existing shall think proper to admit, shall not be prohibited by the Congress prior to the year one thousand eight hundred and eight, but a tax or duty may be imposed on such importation, not exceeding ten dollars for each person." Although the product of sectional compromise, the evolution of the clause clearly and expressly demonstrated the conscious shift from state to national power over the subject matter.

MILITARY POWERS

The powers of the Confederation in the field of the military were more impressive, in terms of the scope of their grant and the efficacy of their exercise, than in any other field. Nonetheless, the powers of Congress enumerated in the draft of the Committee of Detail not only carried forward all powers extant under the Articles but, in two important respects, granted centralized power where it had not previously existed. Under the Articles, Congress had the "sole and exclusive right and power of determining on peace and war." These powers were separated in the Constitution. Congress was given the power "to declare war," the verb "declare" being used rather than "make" in order to leave "to the executive power to repel sudden attacks." The power to make peace was comprehended under the treaty power. The Articles had empowered Congress to establish "rules for deciding in all cases what captures on land and water shall be legal, and in what manner prizes taken by land and naval forces in the service of the United States shall be divided or appropriated." The Constitution gave Congress the power "to make rules concerning captures on land and water." The Articles also empowered Congress "to build and equip a navy." In the Constitution this became the power "to provide and maintain a navy." Under the Articles, Congress had the power of "making rules for the government and regulation of the said land and naval forces, and directing their operations." The Constitution also granted Congress the power to "make rules for the government and regulation of the land and naval forces."

It was in connection with the land forces that the Constitution provided two important extensions of power. As to the raising of armies, the system of the Articles was a reflection of state sovereignty. Congress was given the power "to agree upon the number of land forces, and to make requisitions from each state for its quota, in proportion to the number of white inhabitants in such state." Then there followed an elaboration of the assembling, clothing, and equipping of the men. The tragic inadequacy of this quota and requisition system for raising the Continental Army has already been discussed. With state sovereignty no longer a necessary consideration, the Constitution provided simply that Congress should have power "to raise and support armies."

The convention agreed to all of the foregoing provisions without dissent. The subject of the state militia, however, raised a sharp debate over national and state power. During the Revolution each state had maintained its own militia which was immune from congressional power and control. The draft of the Committee of Detail went beyond the Articles so far as to grant Congress the power "to call forth the aid of the militia, in order to execute the laws of the Union, enforce treaties, suppress insurrections, and repel invasions." No one opposed this clause, which was subsequently approved on August 23 after the deletion of the words "enforce treaties," on the ground that they were superfluous because treaties were comprehended under "the laws of the Union." The provision would have left with the states the organization and regulation of the militia.

When this provision came up on August 18, Mason urged the amplification of national power and brought up the problem of "regulating the militia." He said he "thought such a power necessary to be given to the general government. . . . Thirteen states will never concur in any one system if the disciplining of the militia be left in their hands. If they will not give up the power over the whole, they probably will over a part as a select militia." He therefore moved, as an additional power, "to make laws for the regulation and discipline of the militia of the several states, reserving to the states the appointment of the officers." Mason considered uniformity necessary in the regulation of the militia throughout the Union. General Pinckney agreed that uniformity "was essential. The states would never keep up a proper discipline of the militia."

Ellsworth was more state-minded. He said he was "for going as far, in submitting the militia to the general government, as might be necessary, but thought the motion of Mr. Mason went too far. . . . The whole authority over the militia ought by no means to be taken away from the states, whose consequence would pine away to nothing after such a sacrifice of power. He thought the general authority could not sufficiently pervade the Union for such a purpose, nor could it accommodate itself to the local genius of the people. It must be vain to ask the states to give the militia out of their hands." In this view he had the support of Dickinson: "the states never would nor ought to give up all authority over the militia."

Confronted by this disagreement, Mason retreated to "the idea of a select militia. He was led to think that would be, in fact, as much as the general government could advantageously be charged with. He was afraid of creating insuperable objections to the plan." He therefore withdrew his original motion and instead moved for "a power to make laws for regulating and disciplining the militia, not exceeding one-tenth part in any one year, and reserving the appointment of officers to the states."

But Mason's retreat did not satisfy the proponents of stronger national power in this area. Butler urged "the necessity of submitting the whole militia to the general authority, which had the care of the general defense." General Pinckney urged a return to Mason's original motion. "For a part to be under the general and a part under the state governments," the elder Pinckney said, "would be an incurable evil. He saw no room for such distrust of the general government." Langdon seconded Pinckney's renewal, saying that he "saw no more reason to be afraid of the general government than of the state governments." Madison also supported this view. He "thought the regulation of the militia naturally appertaining to the authority charged with the public defense. It did not seem, in its nature, to be divisible between two distinct authorities. If the states would trust the general government with a power over the public treasury, they would, from the same consideration of necessity, grant it the direction of the public force. Those who had a full view of the public situation would, from a sense of the danger, guard against it. The states would not be separately impressed with the general situation, nor have the due confidence in the concurrent exertions of each other." The younger Pinckney thought "the power such a one as could not be abused, and that the states would see the necessity of surrendering it." Gerry, on the other hand, "thought this the last point remaining to be surrendered. If it be agreed to by the convention," Gerry said, "the plan will have as black a mark as was set on Cain. He had no such confidence in the general government as some gentlemen possessed, and believed it would be found that the states have not."

The upshot was that the matter was referred to a committee. The report submitted by the committee on August 21 was a distinct victory for the nationalists. It recommended that Congress have the power "to make laws for organizing, arming, and disciplining the militia, and for governing such part of them as may be employed in the service of the United States, reserving to the states, respectively, the appointment of the officers, and the authority of training the militia, according to the discipline prescribed by the United States." This broad grant gave Congress complete power over the subject except for the appointment of officers. On August 23, when the matter was taken up again, Ellsworth observed that the term "discipline" was of vast extent "and might be so expounded as to include all power on the subject." Gerry at this point depicted the states as being reduced to little more than drill sergeants. Ellsworth and Sherman thereupon sought to modify the power by substituting the following: "To establish an uniformity of arms, exercise, and organization for the militia, and to provide for the government of them when called into the service of the United States," explaining that the "object of this proposition was to refer the plan for the militia to the general government, but to leave the execution of it to the state governments."

But even this dilution of national power was opposed. Langdon said "he could not understand the jealousy expressed by some gentlemen. The general and state governments were not enemies to each other but different institutions for the good of the people of America. As one of the people, he could say the national government is mine, the state government is mine. In transferring power from one to the other, I only take out of my left hand what it cannot so well use and put it into my right hand where it can be better used." Madison was vigorous in support of national power:

> The primary object is to secure an effectual discipline of the militia. This will no more be done if left to the states separately than the requisitions have been hitherto paid by them. The states neglect their militia now, and the more they are consolidated into one nation, the less each will rely on its own interior provisions for its safety, and the less prepare its militia for that purpose, in like manner as the militia of a state would have been still more neglected if each county had been independently charged with the care of its militia. The discipline of the militia is evidently a *national* concern, and ought to be provided for in the *national* Constitution.

And Randolph said that he "was for trammeling the general government whenever there was danger, but here there could be none. He urged this as an essential point, observing that the militia were everywhere neglected by the state legislatures, the members of which courted popularity too much to enforce a proper discipline. Leaving the appointment of officers to the states protects the people against every apprehension that could produce murmur." On the vote, all states were opposed to Ellsworth's motion except his own, Connecticut.

Madison then sought to increase national power even further by a motion to amend the clause so that the reservation to the states of the appointment of officers should be confined to those "under the rank of general officers." Sherman said he "considered this as absolutely inadmissible." And Gerry was bitter. "Let us at once destroy the state governments, have an executive for life or hereditary, and a proper Senate; and then there would be some consistency in giving full powers to the general government; but as the states are not to be abolished, he wondered at the attempts that were made to give powers inconsistent with their exercise. He warned the convention against pushing the experiment too far." Madison replied that since the greatest danger was that of disunion of the states, it was necessary to guard against it by sufficient powers to the common government; "and as the greatest danger to liberty is from large standing armies, it is best to prevent them by an effectual provision for a good militia." The majority, however, evidently feeling that the states should have the sop of appointing the officers, defeated Madison's motion, eight to three.

The committee recommendation was then approved and appears verbatim in the Constitution. The action of the convention on this subject affords good reason for the subsequent disuse of the phrase "state militia" and the adoption of the more accurate title of "national guard."

NATURALIZATION

The Articles of Confederation made no mention of any national citizenship, only state citizenship being recognized. This was natural since the Articles created no nation but merely a compact of sovereign states. Consequently each state legislated for itself on the admission of foreigners to citizenship, and Congress had no power whatever on the subject. As would be expected, the state laws varied considerably from each other. In the convention Mason noted that the "states have formed different qualifications themselves for enjoying different rights of citizenship." And the younger Pinckney remarked "that the laws of the states had varied much the terms of naturalization in different parts of America and contended that the United States could not be bound to respect them on such an occasion as the present. It was a sort of recurrence to first principles."

It has been noted that the Constitution, unlike the Articles, explicitly recognized a citizenship of the United States. The Constitution did not, however, define this citizenship. It seems to have been tacitly assumed that anyone who was a citizen of his state before the adoption of the Constitution would be a citizen of the United States after ratification. This concept was even made retroactive in order to permit the election of a Congress at the outset of the new government, for one of the requirements for membership in the House and Senate was citizenship in the

United States for seven and nine years, respectively. Aside from this, there remained the questions of who was to decide what constituted United States citizenship and how it was to be acquired. The Constitution was silent on the acquisition of citizenship by birth and on the relationship between state and national citizenship, which were later the subjects of intense disagreement in the controversy over slavery, and which were finally settled by the Fourteenth Amendment.

The convention was more concerned with the expectation that after the Constitution was ratified there would be a tide of immigration from the Old World. The acquisition of citizenship by naturalization therefore assumed an immediate importance, and there was unanimous agreement that it was a matter to be vested within the exclusive power of Congress. The Committee of Detail made the recommendation which was approved on August 16, without debate or dissent, and which appears in Clause 4 of Article I, Section 8, as the power "to establish a uniform rule of naturalization . . . throughout the United States." Inasmuch as there would be no uniform rule if the states retained concurrent power, the grant was of necessity exclusive, and inasmuch as the power to confer citizenship is a power incident to sovereignty, the grant is one more example of the conscious creation of a national sovereignty.

SPECIFIED CRIMES

Under the Articles, Congress had the "sole and exclusive power" of "appointing courts for the trial of piracies and felonies committed on the high seas." But the power to define the crimes was not granted, and common law as to felonies varied among the states. The Committee of Detail recommended that Congress have the power "to declare the law and punishment of piracies and felonies committed on the high seas . . . and offenses against the law of nations." When this clause came up for discussion on August 17, Mason observed that he "doubted also the propriety of taking the power in all these cases wholly from the states." But Morris and Madison moved to amend the power to one "to define and punish." Madison asserted that "If the laws of the states were to prevail on this subject, the citizens of different states would be subject to different punishments for the same offense at sea. There would be neither uniformity nor stability in the law. The proper remedy for all these difficulties was to vest the power proposed by the term 'define' in the national legislature." This view prevailed, and the grant appears in Article I, Section 8, Clause 10, as the power "to define and punish piracies and felonies committed on the high seas, and offenses against the law of nations." The last clause is further proof that the framers of the Constitution were consciously creating a nation.

PATENTS AND COPYRIGHTS

Under the Articles, Congress had no power over patents and copyrights. Most of the states had enacted copyright legislation which varied among the states, and patents were usually granted by special acts. Only if the national government possessed power over these matters could authors and inventors enjoy protection in their rights uniformly throughout the United States. Consequently, Madison on August 18 suggested the inclusion of such a power. A clause recommended by the committee on unfinished business was approved on September 5 without discussion and debate. It appears in Article I, Section 8, Clause 8, as the power to "promote the progress of science and useful arts, by securing for limited times to authors and inventors the exclusive right to their respective writings and discoveries."

SEAT OF GOVERNMENT

There was no seat of government under the Articles nor any power to provide for one. Until 1783 Congress assembled in Philadelphia, from which they fled when the local authorities failed to protect them against mutinous troops. They reassembled at Princeton, then sat alternately at Trenton and Annapolis until 1785, when they removed to New York and sat until the adoption of the Constitution.

There seems to have been unanimous agreement in the convention that the new national government should have a capital of its own. On July 26 Mason "observed that it would be proper, as he thought, that some provision should be made in the Constitution against choosing for the seat of the general government the city or place at which the seat of any state government might be fixed. There were two objections against having them at the same place, which, without mentioning others, required some precaution on the subject. The first was that it tended to produce disputes concerning jurisdiction. The second and principal one was that the intermixture of the two legislatures tended to give a provincial tincture to the national deliberations." Gerry also said that he thought "it to be the general sense of America that neither the seat of a state government nor any large commercial city should be the seat of the general government." The younger Pinckney also thought "the seat of a state government ought to be avoided." And Butler was "for fixing, by the Constitution, the place, and a central one, for the seat of the national government."

On August 18 Madison submitted a proposal to accomplish this objective, and a clause reported by the committee on unfinished business on September 5 was approved without discussion or dissent. It appears in Article I, Section 8, Clause 17, as the power to "exercise exclusive legislation in all cases whatsoever, over such district (not exceeding ten miles square) as may, by cession of particular states, and the acceptance of Congress, become the seat of the government of the United States."

The proposal of the committee on unfinished business also contained the power "to exercise like authority over all places purchased for the erection of forts, magazines, arsenals, dockyards, and other needful buildings." Gerry objected that "this might be made use of to enslave any particular state by buying up its territory, and that the strongholds proposed would be a means of awing the state into an undue obedience to the general government." King replied, saying that he "thought, himself, the provision unnecessary, the power being already involved, but would move to insert after the word 'purchased' the words 'by the consent of the legislature of the state.' This would certainly make the power safe." The motion was adopted, and the clause was agreed to as amended.

FULL FAITH AND CREDIT

"Full faith and credit," said the Articles of Confederation, "shall be given in each of these states to the records, acts and judicial proceedings of the courts and magistrates of every other state." It will be noted that this provision related only to "courts and magistrates." Further, it contained no mention of the method of proving the "records, acts and judicial proceedings," nor did it deal with the effect which should be given to them, once proved. As to these matters—proof and effect—the laws of the states were controlling. The general guarantee of the Articles was therefore subject to the will of sovereign states for meaningful application. The draft of the Committee of Detail read, "Full faith shall be given in each state to the acts of the legislatures, and to the records and judicial proceedings of the courts and magistrates, of every other state." This proposal went further than the Articles in that it also applied to the acts of the legislatures.

When this provision came up for discussion on August 29, Williamson moved "to substitute, in place of it, the words of the Articles of Confederation on the same subject." Wilson, Johnson, and Gorham supported the original proposal, however, and Madison wanted to go even further. He said he "wished the legislature might be authorized to provide for the *execution* of judgments in other states, under such regulations as might be expedient. He thought that this might be safely done, and was justified by the nature of the Union." To this Randolph replied that "there was no instance of one nation executing judgments of the courts of another nation." Gouverneur Morris then offered a proposition which, for the first time, granted to Congress new and broad power over the subject. "Full faith," his version read, "ought to be given in each state to the public acts, records, and judicial proceedings, of every other state; and the legislature shall, by general laws, determine the proof and effect of such acts, records, and proceedings." The draft proposal, Randolph's proposal, and Morris' proposition were all then referred to a committee.

The committee report on September 1 adopted Morris' proposal that Congress be vested with power over the subject. "Full faith and credit ought to be given in each state to the public acts, records, and judicial proceedings of every other state; and the legislature shall, by general laws, prescribe the manner in which such acts, records, and proceedings shall be proved, and the effect which judgments obtained in one state shall have in another." This provision went further than the draft proposal in that it authorized a broad national power, but it did not go as far as Morris' proposition, since the power of Congress to determine effect was confined to state judgments. Morris therefore moved to accomplish his original purpose by substituting the word "thereof" for all after "effect." Johnson recognized that "the amendment, as worded, would authorize the general legislature to declare the effect of legislative acts of one state in another state." Randolph, who by September was increasingly disenchanted with the trend of the convention, objected. He said that the general objection to the plan was strengthened because the plan's "definition of the powers of the government was so loose as to give it opportunities of usurping all the state powers. He was for not going further than the report, which enables the legislature to provide for the effect of *judgments.*" But Morris' motion was approved, six states to three. Then, on motion of Madison, "ought" was changed to "shall" in the first part of the provision, thereby making full faith and credit mandatory on the states; and "shall" was changed to "may" in the second part of the provision, making the power of Congress discretionary. As finally approved, the provision appears in Section 1 of Article IV of the Constitution: "Full faith and credit shall be given in each state to the public acts, records, and judicial proceedings of every other state. And the Congress may by general laws prescribe the manner in which such acts, records, and proceedings shall be proved, and the effect thereof." The progress of this provision through the convention reveals clearly a steady and conscious enhancement of national power.

ADMISSION OF NEW STATES

The Articles of Confederation had contained the following provision: "Canada acceding to this Confederation, and joining in the measures of the United States, shall be admitted into, and entitled to all the advantages of this union: but no other colony shall be admitted into the same, unless such admission be agreed to by nine states." The ambiguity of language in the second clause had created considerable doubt as to the Confederation's power to admit as a new state any portion of one of the original thirteen states. This doubt created opposition to the admission of Vermont, Kentucky, and Franklin. Furthermore, there was no provision in the Articles which contemplated the formation and admission of states out of the great territory to the west. Notwithstanding the absence of any authorization in the Articles, Congress had encouraged and accepted the cession of the western land from the states, asserting title under a resolution which promised that such land should be formed into distinct republican states, which should be admitted on an equal footing with present members of the Confederation. The Northwest Ordinance of 1787, enacted by Congress on July 13 while the convention was in session, provided for five new states to be formed from lands north of the Ohio River, to be admitted on an equal footing with the original states.

The absence of power over this subject was remedied by the convention. The Virginia plan had provided for "admission of states lawfully arising within the limits of the United States, whether from a voluntary junction of government and territory, or otherwise, with the consent of a number of voices in the national legislature less than the whole." This was a radical departure from state sovereignty in that it would permit admission of new states by voice vote in the legislature rather than by vote of the states as such. The proposal was approved by the committee of the whole without change.

The draft of the Committee of Detail was more specific. It provided that new states "lawfully constituted or established within the limits of the United States may be admitted by the Legislature into this government; but to such admission the consent of two-thirds of the members present in each house shall be necessary. If a new state shall arise within the limits of any of the present states, the consent of the legislatures of such states shall be also necessary to its admission. If the admission be consented to, the new states shall be admitted on the same terms with the original states."

This proposition was debated on August 29 and 30, with the result that the requirement of a two-thirds vote and the provision for equality of new states were both deleted. The language respecting the territorial integrity of the states was modified, and it is interesting to note that it was strongly opposed by Luther Martin. Although Martin was one of the few defenders of state sovereignty in the convention, he was also from a small state and was therefore not averse to carving up the large ones. "Nothing," he said "would so alarm the limited states as to make the consent of the large states claiming the western lands necessary to the establishment of new states within their limits." But Wilson, the nationalist, replied that he "knew nothing that would give greater or juster alarm than the doctrine that a political society is to be torn asunder without its own consent." The final version is found in Section 3 of Article IV: "New states may be admitted by the Congress into this Union; but no new state shall be formed or erected within the jurisdiction of any other state; nor any state be formed by the junction of two or more states, or parts of states, without the consent of the legislatures of the states concerned as well as of the Congress." The provision affords one more example of the conscious departure from a compact of sovereign states.

TERRITORIES AND OTHER PROPERTIES

The Articles of Confederation contained no provision for the ownership of territory by the United States. Congress, of course, had nevertheless accepted title in the name of the United States to an enormous expanse of territory in the West. The power of Congress to admit new states from this territory was no longer in doubt, as a result of the action just described. But what of the government of the territory prior to the admission of new states or of territory which would possibly not be included in new states? This deficiency in the power of Congress was provided for on August 30 when Morris moved the provision which was accepted without discussion or dissent, appearing in Article IV, Section 3, Clause 2, of the Constitution: "The Congress shall have power to dispose of and make all needful rules and regulations respecting the territory or other property belonging to the United States."

NECESSARY AND PROPER LAWS

Article II of the Articles of Confederation read: "Each state retains its sovereignty, freedom, and independence, and every power, jurisdiction, and right, which is not by this Confederation expressly delegated to the United States, in Congress assembled." Upon this provision foundered the many efforts to enlarge by implication the powers of Congress during the Confederation. As noted earlier, the Virginia plan originally contemplated a broad general legislative power which was amplified even more by the committee of the whole and approved in the following form: "Resolved, that the national legislature ought to possess the legislative rights vested in Congress by the Confederation; and moreover, to legislate in all cases for the general interests of the Union, and also in those to which the states are separately incompetent, or in which the harmony of the United States may be interrupted by the exercise of individual legislation."

The draft submitted by the Committee of Detail substituted for this broad general grant an enumeration of specific powers of Congress. Most of these are found in Section 8 of Article I, which deals with the legislative branch. Others, however, are found in other sections of Article I, and many powers of Congress are scattered throughout the Constitution in various other articles. The powers which have been discussed deal with specific subjects—taxation, commerce, military forces, naturalization, elections, and so forth. One power of Congress which the Committee of Detail recommended, however, was not a specific but a general one. The last clause of Section 8 grants to Congress the power to "make all laws which shall be necessary and proper for carrying into execution the foregoing powers, and all other powers vested by this Constitution in the government of the United States, or in any department or officer thereof." When this provision came before the convention on August 20, Madison and the younger Pinckney moved to insert the words "and establish all offices" after the word "laws," on the ground that it was "liable to cavil that the latter was not included in the former." But Gouverneur Morris, Wilson, Rutledge, and Ellsworth all insisted "that the amendment could not be necessary," and it was defeated, nine to two. There was no further discussion, and the convention approved the clause without dissent.

Opponents of the Constitution later referred to this provision as the "sweeping clause," and its scope was a matter of intense debate in the ratification campaign. There seems to be no room for doubt that the function of the clause, at the very least, was to permit the exercise of implied powers and thus to repudiate Article II of the Articles of Confederation. It is arguable that much more was accomplished by the clause. On its face it amplifies not only the previously listed specific powers of Congress but all other powers of the government of the United States—the legislative powers set forth elsewhere in the Constitution, the executive powers, and the judicial powers. It might also be noted that there is nothing in the records of the convention to indicate that the convention intended that Congress should have less power after enumeration than was contemplated under the former general grant; the sum of one hundred is no less when ten is listed ten times than when the full sum is set forth in one figure. For the purpose of this book, however, it is sufficient to state that the scope of this power was indeterminate, for whatever its scope it represented to that extent a still further assimilation in Congress of what had formerly been within the legislative power of sovereign states.

SELF-PROTECTION BY THE STATES

Although the powers of Congress were enumerated, they were not defined. No precise or particularized meaning automatically or inevitably attached to such words and phrases as, for example, "the common defense and general welfare," or "regulate commerce . . . among the several states," or, above all, "laws which may be necessary and proper." The fact that the enumerated powers of Congress were latitudinal in nature afforded one of the principal grounds of opposition to the ratification of the Constitution. The fact was of enormous practical significance to the question of state sovereignty and state power, for the powers of Congress were to be exercised, without the intervention of the states, directly upon individuals in areas formerly within the exclusive province of the states. The express limitations in the Constitution on these national powers were few and of limited scope. The extent to which state sovereignty and state power would be reduced and displaced by the legislative powers of the national government would depend upon two factors. One was the scope and breadth of the meaning and application which would be given to the national powers, and the other was the extent to which those powers actually would be used in the operation of the national government. Even under a minimal view, the displacement of state by national power was considerable. Potentially, the inroad on the powers and jurisdiction of the states was enormous. Unless the purpose was virtually to annihilate the powers of the states, as opponents of the Constitution charged, some limiting factor was required. As will be seen later, the power to determine the scope of national power was confined to the instrumentalities of the national government, with some degree of remedial power in the states through the amending process. In determining the extent to which the legislative powers would be actually used, however, the states as such were given an important control for their own self-protection. This control lay in the provision adopted by the convention and found in Article I, Section 3, Clause 1, of the Constitution: "The Senate of the United States shall be composed of two Senators from each state, chosen by the legislature thereof."

The requirement of equal representation of states in the Senate has usually been depicted as a device whereby the small states would be protected against the large states. Without gainsaying the validity of this or the other purpose of the Senate—its role as the upper house in a bicameral legislature—the debates in the convention clearly reveal a third purpose. This was to enable the states as such, whether large or small, to participate in the political process whereby the national legislative powers were to be exercised, and thus to be afforded an opportunity to protect themselves against the exercise of what were recognized as potentially destructive powers. For this purpose, appointment of Senators by the state legislatures was fully as important as equality of representation. Sherman on July 14 "urged the equality of votes not so much as a security for the small states, as for the state governments, which could not be preserved unless they were represented and had a negative in the general government." There was agreement among all shades of opinion in the convention as to whom the Senate was to represent. Madison, the advanced nationalist, "observed that the Senate represented the states alone." Mason, the moderate nationalist, stated that "the Senate did not represent the *people,* but the *states* in their political character." And Luther Martin, the state sovereignty advocate, agreed that "the Senate is to represent the states."

Statements made by other delegates indicate a general understanding as to the function of the Senate as a forum for the protection of state interests against national power. Thus Dickinson on June 6 said he "considered it essential that one branch of the legislature should be drawn immediately from the people, and as expedient that the other should be chosen by the legislatures of the states. . . . This combination of the state governments with the national government was as politic as it was unavoidable. . . . He was for a strong national government, but for leaving the states a considerable agency in the system." Again on June 7 Dickinson argued for equal representation in this fashion: "The preservation of the states in a certain degree of agency is indispensable. It will produce that collision between the different authorities which should be wished for in order to check each other. . . . If the state governments were excluded from all agency in the national one, and all power drawn from the people at large, the consequence would be that the national government would move in the same direction as the state governments now do, and would run into all the same mischiefs. The reform would only unite the thirteen small streams into one great current pursuing the same course without any opposition whatever."

Wilson also recognized the position, although he disagreed with it. On June 21 he stated: "As the plan now stood, though indeed contrary to his opinion, one branch of the general government, the Senate or second branch, was to be appointed by the state legislatures. The state legislatures, therefore, by this participation in the general government, would have an opportunity of defending their rights." On June 28 Wilson noted that the "leading argument of those who contend for equality of votes among the states is that the states as such being equal, and being represented not as districts of individuals, but in their political and corporate capacities, are entitled to an equality of suffrage." And on July 14 he stated that the "justice of the general principle of proportional representation has not in argument at least been yet contradicted. But it is said that a departure from it so far as to give the states an equal vote in one branch of the Legislature is essential to their preservation." In addition to Wilson, Pierce on May 31 said that "If the influence of the states is not lost in some part of the new government, we shall never have anything like a national institution. But in my opinion it will be right to show the sovereignty of the state in one branch of the legislature, and that should be in the Senate."

The position was elaborated to the fullest, however, by Mason and Johnson. On June 7 Mason declared that "whatever power may be necessary for the national government, a certain portion must necessarily be left in the states. It is impossible for one power to pervade the extreme parts of the United States so as to carry equal justice to them. The state legislatures also ought to have some means of defending themselves against encroachments of the national government. In every other department we have studiously endeavored to provide for its self-defense. Shall we leave the states alone unprovided with the means for this purpose? And what better means can we provide than the giving them some share in, or rather make them a constituent part of, the national establishment?" And on June 25 Mason crystallized the position: "It has been agreed on all hands that an efficient government is necessary, that to render it such it ought to have the faculty of self-defense, that to render its different branches effectual each of them ought to have the same power of self-defense. He did not wonder that such an agreement should have prevailed in these points. He only wondered that there should be any disagreement about the necessity of allowing the state governments the same self-defense. If they are to be preserved, as he conceived to be essential, they certainly ought to have this power, and the only mode left of giving it to them, was by allowing them to appoint the second branch of the national legislature."

Johnson, who discussed this point on June 21, took the same position. "On a comparison of the two plans which had been proposed from Virginia and New Jersey," he said, "it appeared that the peculiarity which characterized the latter was its being calculated to preserve the individuality of the states. The plan from Virginia did not profess to destroy this individuality altogether, but was charged with such a tendency. . . . He wished it therefore to be well considered whether in case the states, as was proposed, should retain some portion of sovereignty at least, this portion could be preserved without allowing them to participate effectually in the general government, without giving them each a distinct and equal vote for the purpose of defending themselves in the general councils."

On June 29, discussing the matter of representation, Johnson returned to the same point.

> The controversy must be endless whilst gentlemen differ in the grounds of their arguments, those on one side considering the states as districts of people composing one political society, those on the other considering them as so many political societies. The fact is that the states do exist as political societies, and a government is to be formed for them in their political capacity, as well as for the individuals composing them. Does it not seem to follow, that if the states as such are to exist, they must be armed with some power of self-defense? . . . Besides the aristocratic and other interests, the states have their interests as such, and are equally entitled to like means. On the whole . . . as in some respects the states are to be considered in the political capacity, and in others as districts of individual citizens, the two ideas embraced on different sides, instead of being opposed to each other, ought to be combined, that in one branch the people ought to be represented, in the other, the states.

On June 16 the younger Pinckney made an acute observation: "Give New Jersey an equal vote, and she will dismiss her scruples, and concur in the national system." The record bears out this estimate. The convention on July 16 approved the compromise under which the states were accorded equal representation in the Senate. The very next day the states which had fought for this equal representation joined in approving a general legislative power in Congress to "enjoy the legislative rights vested in Congress by the Confederation, and moreover to legislate in all cases for the general interests of the Union, and also in those to which the states are separately incompetent, or in which the harmony of the United States may be interrupted by the exercise of individual legislation."

It is clear, therefore, that equality of representation in the Senate, with appointment of Senators by the state legislatures, was considered by the convention as providing a political means whereby the states could protect themselves against what they considered excessive exercise of national powers. The fact that such a self-protective device was considered necessary demonstrates the understanding that there were few definite legal limits to the possible exercise of national power, and a recognition that the existence of state power was not one of these limitations. This meant that without some means of self-protection, the states would be virtually helpless, and this of course is merely another way of saying that, in relation to the national government, the states under the Constitution were no longer to be sovereign either in law or in fact.

But even this provision for the participation by the states in the exercise of national legislative power was diluted by the provision for individual voting in the Senate. Although representation was equal, per capita voting rather than voting by states raised the possibility of the Senators from a state voting differently, and thus dissipating the influence of their state as such in the making of decisions. Curiously, it was Gerry who first suggested that the vote in the Senate should be individual, rather than by states. On July 14 he said he favored "providing that the states should vote per capita, which he said would prevent the delays and inconveniences that had been experienced in Congress and would give a national aspect and spirit to the management of business." Sherman said he "had no objection to the members in the second branch voting per capita." No action was taken, however, until July 23, when Gouverneur Morris and King moved that Senators should vote per capita. It is interesting and significant that the only objection to this proposal was made by Luther Martin, defender of state sovereignty, who "was opposed to voting per capita, as departing from the idea of the *states* being represented in the second branch." The motion carried, nine states to one. The Committee of Detail included in its draft such a provision, and it was approved on August 9 in spite of a move to postpone it. In final form the provision is part of Article I, Section 3, Clause 1: "each Senator shall have one vote."

XX

Prohibitions on the States

As THE preceding chapter demonstrates, the Constitution significantly diminished state sovereignty by arranging for transfer to the national government of powers which had belonged previously to the States. In addition, the Constitution placed substantial restrictions upon the political powers of the states which reduced still further what had previously been unlimited sovereignty. Article VI of the Articles of Confederation had, of course, listed certain restrictions on the states, but the states ignored them consistently because the Articles did not provide any power to enforce these restrictions. All of the restrictions set forth in the Articles were carried forward into the Constitution. To these, however, the Founding Fathers made many additions which further impaired the states as entities.

The original Virginia plan as introduced by Randolph had contained no specific limitations on the powers of the states. This did not represent a concession to state sovereignty, however, since under the Virginia plan Congress was to have not only an unlimited general legislative power but also the power to negative all state laws which, in the opinion of Congress, contravened the Constitution. With this power in Congress, there seemed to be no need for any specific limitations on the states. The correctness of this analysis is substantiated by subsequent events.

The convention finally, on July 17, over the strenuous protest of Madison and other advanced nationalists, rejected the congressional negative. The resolutions referred to the Committee of Detail on July 26, however, still included the unlimited general legislative power. The Committee of Detail had substituted for the general legislative power an extensive enumeration of express powers. It was in the committee's draft Constitution that the listing of express limitations on the states first appeared. The reason would seem clear. With the congressional negative and the general legislative power both eliminated, it was considered necessary as a means of protecting the national government against intrusions by the states to expressly prohibit or limit the exercise of state power in certain areas.

Accordingly, two articles to accomplish this purpose were included in the committee draft, one listing certain powers denied absolutely to the states, the other listing certain qualified prohibitions—powers, that is, which were not to be exercisable by the states without the consent of Congress. This requirement of consent is readily seen as a method of protecting national interests.

The convention acted on these proposals in two ways, both of which reveal the general tenor of the proceedings and the attitude of the delegates toward state sovereignty. First, some of the qualified restrictions were elevated to absolute prohibitions, and second, new absolute prohibitions, not proposed by the committee, were added by the convention. As finally agreed to, the following prohibitions on the states, absolute and qualified, appear in Article I, Section 10, of the Constitution.

"No state shall enter into any treaty, alliance, or confederation." Under both the Articles of Confederation and the draft of the Committee of Detail, this was a qualified restriction only. It was placed in the category of absolute prohibitions by Gouverneur Morris and the Committee on Style on September 12, and was approved by the convention. It never occasioned either discussion or opposition. The threat to the national government would be obvious if a treaty-making power remained in the states. But the absolute prohibition serves also to show that the states were to be completely excluded from the area of foreign affairs, and that the only sovereignty which could deal with other sovereign powers of the world was to be the national government.

"No state shall . . . grant letters of marque and reprisal." The Articles of Confederation had contained only a qualified prohibition in this area; states were free to issue such letters under the Articles after a declaration of war by Congress. The proposal of the Committee on Style made this an absolute prohibition, applicable in peace as well as war. This prohibition must be considered along with the grant to Congress of the power to declare war. Letters of marque and reprisal were usually preludes to, or the accompaniments of, hostilities between nations. No one state, therefore, could be permitted to exercise a power which might embroil the entire nation in a war. This denial of power to the states also serves to underscore the creation of a national sovereignty with exclusive powers over external affairs. It was accepted by the convention without discussion and without opposition.

"No state shall coin money." Under the Articles of Confederation

the power to coin money was concurrent with Congress and the states, the sole qualification on state power being that Congress could regulate the alloy and value of the state coin. But this supervisory authority could not eliminate variations in sizes and weights, and under the Articles, therefore, it was not possible to achieve a uniform national currency, the pressing need for which has been discussed in Chapter One. The Committee of Detail's recommendation that there be an absolute prohibition on state power in this respect was adopted by the convention without discussion or opposition. Congress was granted the power "to coin money" and "regulate the value thereof." The addition of a prohibition on the states served to render this vitally important power of sovereignty exclusive with the national government.

"No state shall . . . emit bills of credit; make anything but gold and silver coin a tender in payment of debts." The Articles of Confederation had not limited the states in this way. Indeed, as has been noted in a previous chapter, the issuance of paper money and the passage of tender laws by the states had become especially abhorrent to the creditor class, which wanted national protection against such activities by the states. The draft of the Committee of Detail laid qualified prohibitions on these two powers. But the convention went all the way. On August 28, when the article dealing with absolute prohibitions was taken up, Wilson and Sherman moved to insert after the words "coin money," the words "nor emit bills of credit, nor make anything but gold and silver coin a tender in payment of debts," and to make these prohibitions absolute instead of making the measures allowable, as in the thirteenth article, with the consent of the Legislature of the United States." On this proposal Gorham was doubtful, thinking that "the purpose would be as well secured by the provision of Article XIII, which makes the consent of the general legislature necessary; and that in that mode no opposition would be excited, whereas an absolute prohibition of paper money would rouse the most desperate opposition from its partisans." Sherman, however, "thought this a favorable crisis for crushing paper money. If the consent of the legislature could authorize emission of it, the friends of paper money would make every exercise to get into the legislature in order to license it." Rather than transfer the political struggle over paper money from the state legislature to Congress, the convention voted eight states to one, with one state divided, in favor of an absolute prohibition against state emission of bills of credit. The remaining part of the motion, relating to legal tender, was then passed without opposition. Thus at last nationalists incorporated long-held de-

sires into two very important restrictions on the sovereignty of the states.

"No state shall . . . pass any bill of attainder, ex post facto law, or law impairing the obligation of contracts." The Articles of Confederation had contained no such limitations. Nor were they included in the draft submitted by the Committee of Detail. On August 22, however, the convention had agreed to prohibit Congress from passing bills of attainder and *ex post facto* laws.

On August 28, just after the convention had voted to prohibit the states from emitting bills of credit, King "moved to add, in the words used in the ordinance of Congress establishing new states, a prohibition on the states to interfere in private contracts." The reference was to the Northwest Ordinance, into which the Confederation Congress had written a prohibition against laws which interfered with or affected private contracts. Morris was opposed, asserting that this "would be going too far. There are a thousand laws relating to bringing actions, limitations of actions, etc., which affect contracts. The judicial power of the United States will be a protection in cases within their jurisdiction." Madison was in favor of the motion but thought a negative on state laws would be better. Mason, like Morris, objected that "This is carrying the restraint too far. Cases will happen that cannot be foreseen, where some kind of interference will be proper and essential. He mentioned the case of limiting the period for bringing actions on open account—that of bonds after a certain lapse of time—asking whether it was proper to tie the hands of the states from making provision in such cases." Wilson answered that "retrospective interferences only are to be prohibited." To this Madison put the question, "Is not that already done by the prohibition of *ex post facto* laws, which will oblige the judges to declare interferences null and void?" Madison thus indicated his view that the *ex post facto* prohibition was applicable to civil laws. At this point Rutledge moved, in lieu of King's motion, to insert "nor pass bills of attainder, nor retrospective laws," and this motion was carried, seven states to three.

On August 29 Dickinson "mentioned to the house that on examining Blackstone's Commentaries, he found that the term '*ex post facto*' related to criminal cases only; that they would not consequently restrain the states from retrospective laws in civil cases; and that some further provision for this purpose would be requisite." Madison's notes reveal no discussion on this point. On September 14 Mason moved to strike from the limitations on the powers of Congress in Article I, Section 9, the prohibition against *ex post facto* laws. "He thought it not sufficiently clear that the prohibition meant by this phrase was limited to cases of a criminal nature; and no legislature ever did or can altogether avoid them in civil cases." Gerry seconded the motion, "but with a view to extend the prohibition to 'civil cases,' which he thought ought to be done." All the states voted no. On the same day the first clause of Article I, Section 10, was approved in its final form. Thus it is arguable as an original proposition whether the convention intended the *ex post facto* and impairment prohibitions to apply to retroactive criminal and civil laws respectively, or whether *ex post facto* applied to both retroactive criminal and civil laws, thereby giving the contract impairment clause a broader meaning. Whatever they intended, in either event the prohibitions made substantial inroads into what had previously been the sovereign powers of the states.

"No state shall . . . grant any title of nobility." The Articles had laid this prohibition on both Congress and the states. The Committee of Detail included a like provision in its draft. On August 23 the convention adopted such a prohibition on Congress, and on August 28 the same as to the states. Such titles would, of course, have been completely inconsistent with republican principles.

"No state shall, without the consent of Congress, lay any imposts or duties on imports or exports, except what may be absolutely necessary for executing its inspection laws; and the net produce of all duties and imposts laid by any state on imports or exports, shall be for the use of the treasury of the United States; and all such laws shall be subject to the revision and control of the Congress." The Articles of Confederation, in Article VI, had provided that no state should lay any imposts or duties which interfered with treaties entered into by Congress. This denial of power was effectually nullified in Article IX, however, by a proviso that Congress' power to enter into treaties should not restrain the power of the states to impose reciprocal imposts or to prohibit completely the export or import of any goods or commodities whatsoever.

The Constitution, of course, granted Congress the power "to lay and collect taxes, duties, imposts, and excises," and also "to regulate commerce with foreign nations, and among the several states." In addition to endowing the national government with these great powers not possessed by Congress under the Articles, the Committee of Detail proposed a qualified limitation that no state, without the consent of Congress, should lay imposts or duties on imports. When this provision

came up for discussion on August 28, Madison moved to make the prohibition on the states an absolute one but was voted down, seven to four.
On motion of King, the convention did, however, extend the prohibition
to exports as well as imports. Then, on Sherman's motion, the convention voted nine to two that proceeds of all state duties on imports and
exports should be carried into the national treasury. The purpose was
to prevent the eastern states, through whose ports goods must pass,
from unfairly taxing, to their own advantage, the producing states.

On September 12 Mason brought the clause up for reconsideration
and urged a proviso that the states should be permitted to lay duties for
the purpose of defraying the costs of state inspections. Madison agreed,
pointing out that the "best guard against an abuse of the power of the
states on this subject was the right in the general government to regulate trade between state and state." Gorham and Langdon both thought
that "there would be no security, if the proviso should be agreed to,
for the states exporting through other states, against these oppressions
of the latter." They then inquired, "How was redress to be obtained, in
case duties should be laid beyond the purpose expressed?" Madison's
reply was significant: "There will be the same security as in other
cases. The jurisdiction of the Supreme Court must be the source of
redress." So far provision had been made only against injurious acts
of the states. Madison thought this insufficient. A negative on the state
laws alone could meet all the shapes these might assume—but this had
been overruled. On September 15 Mason won his point, but the concession was restricted by the provision that "all such laws shall be subject
to the revision and control of Congress."

The power of the states to lay duties was, in short, circumscribed in
several ways. Such duties could be laid without the consent of Congress only for purposes of defraying inspection costs and even then only
to the extent "absolutely necessary." In all other situations the consent of Congress was required. In all cases, whether with or without
the consent of Congress, the net produce of the duties was to go into
the treasury of the United States, and all state laws were to be subject
to the revision and control of Congress. In this important area, therefore, the sovereign power which the states had enjoyed under the Articles was completely shackled under the Constitution.

*"No state shall, without the consent of the Congress, lay any duties of
tonnage."* No such limitation existed under the Articles of Confederation, of course, and the Committee of Detail had made no recommendations on such levies. The provision was the result of a motion made on

September 14 by McHenry and Carroll of Maryland that "no state shall be restrained from laying duties of tonnage for the purpose of clearing harbors and erecting lighthouses." In support, Mason explained that the reason was "the situation in the Chesapeake, which peculiarly required expenses of this sort."

An interesting colloquy then ensued. Morris maintained that "the states are not restrained from laying tonnage, as the Constitution now stands. The exception proposed will imply the contrary, and will put the states in a worse condition than the gentleman wishes." But Madison replied that "Whether the states are now restrained from laying tonnage duties depends on the extent of the power 'to regulate commerce.' These terms are vague, but seem to exclude the power of the states. They may certainly be restrained by treaty." Madison observed "that there were other objects for tonnage duties, as the support of seamen, etc. He was more and more convinced that the regulation of commerce was in its nature indivisible, and ought to be wholly under one authority." Sherman asserted that the United States' power to regulate trade was supreme and therefore could control interferences of the state regulations when such interferences happen, "so that there is no danger to be apprehended from a concurrent jurisdiction." And Langdon then insisted that "the regulation of tonnage was an essential part of the regulation of trade, and that the states ought to have nothing to do with it." The motion was then changed to provide that "no state shall lay duty on tonnage without the consent of Congress," and in this form passed, six to four, with one state divided. It is clear, therefore, that Madison's view of the scope of Congress' commerce power was accepted by the majority.

"No state shall, without the consent of the Congress, . . . keep troops, or ships of war in time of peace, enter into any agreement or compact with another state, or with a foreign power, or engage in war, unless actually invaded, or in such imminent danger as will not admit of delay." Comparable qualified prohibitions had existed under the Articles of Confederation and had been carried forward in much simplified form into the draft of the Committee of Detail. These were approved by the convention on August 28 without discussion or opposition, and again in final form on September 14. Generally, these limitations on the states had the same purpose and policy as the absolute prohibitions against the states entering into treaties, alliances, or confederations and granting letters of marque and reprisal: to lodge the powers over foreign relations and war and peace in the national government.

Special notice should be taken of the provision relating to agreements or compacts. It will be recalled that the prohibition against the states' entering into any treaty, alliance, or confederation was absolute. The qualified prohibition refers to "any agreement or compact with another state, or with a foreign power." Neither the debates nor literature of the times reveal exactly what difference the Founders had in mind between a "treaty, alliance, or confederation" and an "agreement or compact." It may safely be assumed, however, that the separate phrases were not used without any purpose. Whatever the Framers had in mind, it is clear that the effect of the qualified prohibition, so far as it concerned the power of the states to maintain relations with foreign nations, was to destroy completely what had previously been the area of state sovereignty. Furthermore, the extension of the prohibition from the external to the internal arena by the inclusion of the phrase "with another state" even further constricted the range within which the states were formerly free to move.

XXI

The Supremacy of National Law

THE PRINCIPLE defect of the Articles of Confederation, the cumulative consequence of all of its provisions, was the weakness and inadequacy of the central government. This resulted partly from the way in which power was distributed between Congress and the states. Powers delegated to Congress were too few and too narrow, and the express reservation of power by the states in Article II precluded the existence of any implied national powers. As the two preceding chapters have demonstrated, the Constitution remedied this aspect of weakness by vastly increasing the powers granted to Congress, by supplementing them with the "necessary and proper" power, and by greatly increasing the express prohibitions on the power of the states.

But insufficiency of powers in Congress was only part of the problem under the Articles. There was also the lack of any means to enforce the Articles in the face of the failure and refusal of the states to abide by them. The Articles, after all, had granted some powers to Congress and denied some powers to the states. But if the states were unwilling to abide by even the modest provisions of the Articles, were they any more likely to abide by the much stronger provisions of the Constitution? Sovereign powers could be granted to the national government and denied to the states on paper, but unless there was some way to effectuate such provisions in practice, the Constitution would be as futile an instrument of government as its predecessor had been. Of equal, if not greater, importance, therefore, was the necessity of finding some means of enforcing whatever constitution might be adopted.

Article XIII of the Articles had provided: "Every state shall abide by the determinations of the United States in congress assembled, on all questions which by this Confederation are submitted to them. And the Articles of this Confederation shall be inviolably observed by every state." The language here clearly contemplated that central power and central law, within their area of narrow and express authorization, would be complied with, as evidenced by the casting upon the states of a duty of obedience. The duty, however, was unenforceable. There was no method whereby such compliance could be achieved when it was not voluntarily forthcoming.

This was entirely consistent with the true nature of the Articles, described in Article III as a "league of friendship," or, to use another term, a "compact of sovereign states." As has been noted, the determination of the Founders was revealed at the very beginning of the convention to abandon the confederation principle, in which the central authority operated on the states, and to adopt a national government whose powers would be exercised directly upon individuals. But the convention did not at first realize the implication of this transformation on the problem of enforcing the supremacy of the central authority. The sixth resolution of the Virginia plan, after granting a general indefinite legislative power to Congress, then granted the powers "to negative all laws passed by the several states, contravening in the opinion of the national legislature the Articles of Union or any treaty subsisting under the authority of the Union; and to call forth the force of the Union against any member of the Union failing to fulfill its duty under the Articles thereof." The fourteenth resolution stated that "the legislative, executive and judiciary powers within the several states ought to be bound by oath to support the Articles of Union."

Armed Force

THE USE of force against a recalcitrant state is obviously much more consistent with the idea of a confederation government acting on states in all instances than it is with the idea of a national government acting directly upon individuals. Furthermore, the use of physical coercion against states would be apt to keep the nation in a state of constant unrest and turmoil. It is probably no coincidence that Madison, the advanced nationalist, was the one to first recognize these inconsistencies. On May 31 he "observed that the more he reflected on the use of force, the more he doubted the practicability, the justice, and the efficacy of it, when applied to people collectively and not individually. A union of the states containing such an ingredient seemed to provide for its own destruction. The use of force against a state would look more like a declaration of war than an infliction of punishment; and would prob-

ably be considered by the party attacked as a dissolution of all previous compacts by which it might be bound." Madison hoped "that such
a system would be framed as might render this recourse unnecessary,
and moved that the clause be postponed." On his motion the clause was
abandoned without further discussion and without dissent. The sixth
resolution of the New Jersey plan, submitted to the convention on June
15, contained a provision authorizing the executive to forcibly compel
obedience to laws of Congress and treaties, but was never discussed
or acted on. Another part of this sixth resolution, however, was to become exceedingly important.

The Congressional Negative

COINCIDENT with the convention's eliminating the power of coercion
was its approval on May 31 of the other clause of the Virginia plan which
authorized a congressional negative over state laws that contravened
"the Articles of Union, or any treaty subsisting under the authority of
the Union." On June 8 the younger Pinckney launched an effort to
vastly expand this power by moving that "the national legislature
should have authority to negative all laws which they should judge to
be improper." This motion touched off a lively debate, with Pinckney
urging

> that such a universality of the power was indispensably necessary to render
> it effectual; that the states must be kept in due subordination to the nation;
> that if the states were left to act of themselves in any case, it would be impos-
> sible to defend the national prerogatives, however extensive they might be on
> paper; that the acts of Congress had been defeated by this means; nor had
> foreign treaties escaped repeated violations; that this universal negative
> was in fact the cornerstone of an efficient national government; that under
> the British government, the negative of the Crown had been found beneficial,
> and the *states* are more one nation now than the *colonies* were then.

Adoption of the congressional negative was one of Madison's most
cherished goals, and he continued to urge its acceptance until the very
end of the convention. Now Madison, convinced that the negative was
essential to a perfect system, seconded Pinckney's motion. The states
had attempted constantly "to encroach on the federal authority; to
violate national treaties; to infringe the rights and interests of each
other; to oppress the weaker party within their respective jurisdictions.
A negative," Madison felt, "was the mildest expedient that could be

devised for preventing these mischiefs." Without such a check, the central government could resort only to coercion. "The negative," said Madison, "would render the use of force unnecessary. The states could of themselves pass no operative act, any more than one branch of the Legislature, where there are two branches, can proceed without the other. But in order to give the negative this efficacy, it must extend to all cases. A discrimination would only be a fresh source of contention between the two authorities. In a word, to recur to the illustrations borrowed from the planetary system, this prerogative of the general government is the great pervading principle that must control the centrifugal tendency of the states which, without it, will continually fly out of their proper orbits, and destroy the order and the harmony of the political system."

In opposition to the motion, Williamson said he opposed "giving a power that might restrain the states from regulating their internal police." And Gerry said that he "could not see the extent of such a power, and was against every power that was not necessary. He thought a remonstrance against unreasonable acts of the states would restrain them. If it should not, force might be resorted to. He had no objection to authorize a negative to paper money and similar measures. . . . He observed that the proposed negative would extend to the regulations of the militia, a matter on which the existence of the state might depend. The national legislature, with such a power, may enslave the states. Such an idea as this will never be acceded to. It has never been suggested or conceived among the people. No spectacular projector —and there are enough of that character among us, in politics as well as in other things—has, in any pamphlet or newspaper, thrown out the idea." Sherman was for considering the matter further. "The cases in which the negative ought to be exercised," he said, "might be defined. He wished the point might not be decided till a trial at least should be made for that purpose."

Wilson then joined in support of Pinckney and Madison. He would not speculate as to what "modifications of the proposed power might be practicable or expedient. But however novel it might appear, the principle of it, when viewed with a close and steady eye, is right.

There is no instance in which the laws say that the individual should be bound in one case and at liberty to judge whether he will obey or disobey in another. The cases are parallel. Abuses of the power over the individual persons may happen as well as over the individual states. Federal liberty is to the states what civil liberty is to private individuals; and states are not more unwilling to purchase it, by the necessary concession of their political sovereignty, than the savage is to purchase civil liberty by the surrender of the personal sovereignty, which he enjoys in a state of nature. A definition of the cases in which the negative should be exercised is impracticable. A discretion must be left on one side or the other—will it not be most safely lodged on the side of the national government?"

Wilson noted that it was the convention's business to correct the "vices" of the Articles. One of these vices was want of an effectual control "in the whole over its parts. What danger is there that the whole will un-necessarily sacrifice a part? But reverse the case, and leave the whole at the mercy of each part, and will not the general interest be continually sacrificed to local interests?"

Dickinson also voiced his support of Madison and Pinckney. He said he thought it "impossible to draw a line between the cases proper and improper for the exercise of the negative. We must take our choice of two things. We must either subject the states to the danger of being injured by the power of the national government, or the latter to the danger of being injured by that of the states. . . . To leave the power doubtful would be opening another spring of discord, and he was for shutting as many of them as possible."

Bedford, in opposition, emphasized the helpless position of the small states if the congressional negative should be combined with representation based on population.

In answer to his colleague's question, where would be the danger to the states from this power, [Bedford] would refer him to the smallness of his own state, which may be injured at pleasure without redress. It was meant, he found, to strip the small states of their equal right of suffrage. In this case, Delaware would have about one-ninetieth for its share in the general councils, while Pennsylvania and Virginia would possess one-third of the whole. Is there no difference of interests, no rivalship of commerce, of manufactures? Will not these large states crush the small ones, whenever they stand in the way of their ambitions or interested views? . . . Besides, how can it be thought that the proposed negative can be exercised? Are the laws of the states to be suspended in the most urgent cases until they can be sent seven or eight hundred miles and undergo the deliberation of a body who may be incapable of judging of them? Is the national legislature, too, to sit continually in order to revise the laws of the states?

Madison spoke again, observing "that the difficulties which had been stated were worthy of attention, and ought to be answered before the question was put." Urgent legislation could be provided for "by some emanation of the power from the national government into each state, so far as to give a temporary assent at least." Madison "supposed that the negative might be very properly lodged in the Senate alone, and that the more numerous and expensive branch therefore might not be obliged to sit constantly." The last word came from Butler, who was "vehement against the negative in the proposed extent, as cutting off all hope of equal justice to the distant states. The people there would not, he was sure, give it a hearing."

On the vote, the motion was defeated, seven states to three, with one state divided. With this broader version of the negative defeated, the scope of the congressional negative which was included in the resolutions approved by the committee of the whole on June 19 remained in the form introduced in the Virginia plan and as formerly approved on May 31: applying to state laws which, in the opinion of Congress, contravened the Articles of Union or treaties subsisting thereunder. To even this relatively milder version, however, the few defenders of state sovereignty were naturally opposed. On June 16 Lansing had stated that the "states will never feel a sufficient confidence in a general government to give it a negative on their laws. The scheme is itself totally novel. There is no parallel to it to be found." On June 20 Lansing took a stand against the negative for reasons already mentioned: the sheer bulk of state laws would overburden Congress, and its members might not be competent to pass on laws involving regional problems with which they were not familiar. And Luther Martin on June 27 asserted that "the states, particularly the smaller, would never allow a negative to be exercised over their laws."

By July 2 the convention had reached an impasse, along large and small state lines, over the question of representation. As a result of this, a committee was appointed which made its compromise report on July 5. The report was debated for ten days and finally adopted on July 16. It seems probable that the question of the negative was adding to the disgruntlement of the small states, for during this period of debate Randolph offered five resolutions designed to conciliate the small states. The fourth of these provided that "although every negative given to the law of a particular state shall prevent its operation, any state may appeal to the national judiciary against a negative; and that such negative if adjudged to be contrary to the power granted by the articles of the Union, shall be void." Events indicated the reason for the proposal's never being considered. Not only had the small states succeeded in exacting equal representation in the Senate, as approved on July 16; they had also maneuvered the congressional negative into position for the kill. It came the very next day, July 17.

When the question came up on that day, Gouverneur Morris launched the attack upon "this power as likely to be terrible to the states, and not necessary if sufficient legislative authority should be given to the general government." Morris was clearly no state sovereignty man; he was, in fact, one of the most advanced of the nationalists. Earlier on this very day he had opposed Sherman's amendment designed to protect state power from congressional power, saying that the "internal police, as it would be called and understood by the states, ought to be infringed in many cases." Morris' opposition is explained by the latter part of his statement emphasizing a sufficient national legislative power. It has already been noted that, once they were assured of equal representation in the Senate, the small state men abandoned their opposition to strong national powers. The conclusion is clear that part of the deal also was the abandonment of the negative. Now, supporting Morris, Sherman said he thought it "unnecessary, as the courts of the states would not consider as valid any law contravening the authority of the Union, and which the national legislature would wish to be negatived." And Martin thought the power was both "improper and inadmissible. Shall all the laws of the states be sent up to the general legislature before they shall be permitted to operate?"

Madison arose in defense of his brainchild, looking upon

the negative on the laws of the states as essential to the efficacy and security of the general government. The necessity of a general government proceeds from the propensity of the states to pursue their particular interests in opposition to the general interest. This propensity will continue to disturb the system unless effectually controlled. Nothing short of a negative on their laws will control it. They will pass laws which will accomplish their injurious objects before they can be repealed by the general legislature, or set aside by the national tribunals. Confidence cannot be put in the state tribunals as guardians of the national authority and interests. In all the states, these are more or less dependent on the legislatures. . . . A power of negativing the improper laws of the states is at once the most mild and certain means of preserving the harmony of the system. . . . As to the sending all laws up to the national legislature, that might be rendered unnecessary by some emanation of the power into the states, so far at least as to give a temporary effect to laws of immediate necessity.

Morris, however, "was more and more opposed to the negative. The

proposal of it would disgust all the states. A law that ought to be negatived will be set aside in the judiciary department; and if that security
should fail, may be repealed by a national law." This remark reveals
starkly that state sovereignty did not lie behind Morris' opposition to the
negative. Although the power to negative was to be dropped, the power
of Congress to repeal a state law was to remain, as well as the power of
the national courts to invalidate it. It is obvious that congressional
power to repeal an operative state law and power in the national courts
to invalidate it were as inconsistent with state sovereignty as the power
to approve or disapprove before it could become operative. With the
negative abandoned, the states would be more autonomous, but they
would not be any more sovereign. Sherman then added the thought
that such power would involve "a wrong principle, to wit, that a law of
a state contrary to the Articles of the Union would, if not negatived, be
valid and operative." The principle of national supremacy, then, according to Sherman, would be enough to invalidate state laws contrary to the Constitution. The younger Pinckney "urged the necessity
of the negative," but it was defeated, seven states to three. It is clear
from the discussion which preceded the vote, however, that the result
was not based on considerations of state sovereignty.

The Supremacy Clause

THE RECORD reveals that immediately after the above vote Martin
moved the following: "That the legislative acts of the United States
made by virtue and in pursuance of the Articles of Union, and all treaties
made and ratified under the authority of the United States, shall be the
supreme law of the respective states, as far as those acts or treaties
shall relate to the said states, or their citizens and inhabitants; and
that the judiciaries of the several states shall be bound thereby in their
decisions, anything in the respective laws of the individual states to
the contrary notwithstanding." This resolution, agreed to without discussion and without debate, was taken almost verbatim from the sixth
resolution of the New Jersey plan. Martin, of course, was one of the
few state sovereignty men in the convention, and his introduction of
the resolution at this time was a shrewd maneuver. The convention,
clearly in favor of the principle of national supremacy, was grappling
with the problem of how the principle could best be effectuated. Coercion and the congressional negative now had both been rejected. The
supremacy clause as introduced by Martin was skillfully designed to

express the principle while at the same time leaving its effectuation where he wanted it left—to the states.

Closer scrutiny reveals that, although the clause submitted by Martin was a considerable advance over the Articles, it did not provide for a complete national supremacy. For one thing, state laws were to be measured against acts of Congress and treaties of the United States only, and not against the Constitution itself. Put another way, in the absence of an affirmative exercise of national power, the Constitution alone would not be a source or standard by which invalidity of a state law could be determined. For another thing, only state "laws" were to yield to national supremacy; state "constitutions" were to be superior. That this was Martin's intent is revealed in his later correspondence. Finally, even this limited degree of national supremacy was to be enforced by "the judiciaries of the several states . . . in their decisions," thereby leaving with state instrumentalities the ultimate power of interpretation and determination of conflict.

But these subtleties in the art of drafting were not lost upon the nationalists, who were themselves adept manipulators of language. The resolution as it came back from the Committee of Detail had undergone two significant alterations. The phrase "judiciaries of the several states" had been replaced by the phrase "judges in the several states." The importance of this change lies in the fact that the convention had on June 4 approved the power in Congress to create national tribunals inferior to the Supreme Court. On July 18, the day after Martin's version of the supremacy clause was approved, he had sought unsuccessfully to eliminate this power of Congress. Under the committee version, the federal judges sitting in the states would also be empowered to enforce national supremacy instead of leaving it to the state judges. The second change of the Committee of Detail was equally important. The word "constitutions" was added to "laws" so that, as amended, national laws, and treaties were to be given supremacy, "anything in the constitutions or laws of the several states to the contrary notwithstanding." The third deficiency in the Martin version was cured on August 23, when, on Rutledge's motion, the phrase "this Constitution" was added anterior to "laws of the United States." On August 25 the treaty clause was amended to read "all treaties made, or which shall be made," to make certain that pre-existing as well as future treaties were contemplated.

In its final form, the supremacy clause, found in Article VI, Clause 2, of the Constitution, reads: "This Constitution, and the laws of the

United States which shall be made in pursuance thereof, and all treaties made, or which shall be made, under the authority of the United
States, shall be the supreme law of the land; and the judges in every
state shall be bound thereby, anything in the Constitution or laws of
any state to the contrary notwithstanding." Here was the answer which
the convention had been seeking to the basic problem of how to effect
national supremacy. The substitution of the supremacy clause for the
congressional negative represented a shift from the idea of a prior
legislative restraint on state law to the concept of a subsequent judicial
review. Instead of considering national supremacy as a political matter
to be dealt with by Congress, the convention made it a legal principle
enforceable in the courts, and this, of course, is more consistent with a
national government operating upon individuals. While serving as a
sufficient protection of national law against state interference, the supremacy clause provided for a minimum of direct control and review
of state law. While it repudiated state sovereignty, it recognized a full
degree of state autonomy.

It is one of the ironies of the convention that out of Luther Martin's
effort to protect state sovereignty there evolved what subsequent constitutional history proved to be the principal bulwark of national supremacy.

Oath of Support of Constitution

IN ADDITION to the provisions already noted, the Virginia plan also
sought to assure national supremacy by proposing, in its fourteenth
resolution, "that the legislative, executive, and judiciary powers within
the several states ought to be bound by oath to support the Articles of
Union." When this resolution came up for discussion on June 11, Sherman "opposed it as unnecessarily intruding into the state jurisdictions."
Randolph replied that the oath would preclude "competition between
the national Constitution and laws, and those of the particular states,
which had already been felt. The officers of the states are already
under oath to the states. To preserve a due impartiality, they ought
to be equally bound to the national government. The national authority
needs every support we can give it. The executive and judiciary of
the states, notwithstanding their nominal independence on the state
legislatures, are in fact so dependent on them that unless they be
brought under some tie to the national system, they will always lean
too much to the state systems, whenever a contest arises between the

two." Gerry "did not like the clause. He thought there was as much reason for requiring an oath of fidelity to the states from national officers as vice versa." Luther Martin, whose primary loyalty was always with his state, "moved to strike out the words requiring such an oath from the state officers, viz., 'within the several states,' observing that if the new oath should be contrary to that already taken by them, it would be improper; if coincident, the oaths already taken will be sufficient." This motion was defeated, seven to four, and the Virginia resolution was then adopted, six to five.

Unchanged by the Committee of Detail, the resolution came up on July 23, when Williamson suggested "that a reciprocal oath should be required from the national officers, to support the governments of the states." This was the very thing which Gerry had suggested on June 11. Now Gerry inconsistently "moved to insert, as an amendment, that the oath of the officers of the national government also should extend to the support of the national government."

This was agreed to without dissent. Wilson said "he was never fond of oaths, considering them as a left-handed security only. A good government did not need them, and a bad one could not or ought not to be supported." He also thought the oath might "prove an obstacle" to the amending clause which had just been approved. Gorham "did not know that oaths would be of much use," but he saw no inconsistency between the oath and the provision for amendment. Agreeing with Gorham on this point, Gerry added that on "the other side, he thought one good effect would be produced by it. Hitherto the officers of the two governments had considered them as distinct from, and not a part of, the general system, and had, in all cases on interference given a preference to the state governments. The proposed oath will cure that error." The resolution was then agreed to without dissent. On August 30 the words "or affirmation" were added after "oath," so that in its final form in Article VI, Clause 3, of the Constitution, it reads: "The senators and representatives before mentioned, and the members of the several state legislatures, and all executive and judicial officers, both of the United States and of the several states, shall be bound by oath or affirmation to support this Constitution."

XXII

The Fabric of a National
Government — The Executive

THE LACK of a unified executive was one of the conspicuous inadequacies of the governmental system before the Constitution. Not until 1781 did the Continental Congress agree to put the three departments of War, Marine, and Treasury (which had previously operated as adjuncts to congressional committees) under individual heads responsible to Congress. As Burnett states: "Thus, almost when the war was coming to a close, Congress at last put its principal administrative and executive business upon such a basis as, if it had been done in the beginning of the contest, would have saved that devoted body from many blunders and would have proved of incalculable advantage in the conduct of its affairs." The intentional exclusion from the Articles of Confederation of any provisions looking toward a permanent and potentially strong executive has already been noted.

In the light of this situation, it is not surprising that the seventh proposition of the Virginia plan was "that a national executive be instituted . . . and that besides a general authority to execute the national laws, it ought to enjoy the executive rights vested in Congress by the Confederation." On June 1 the convention unanimously approved the first part of this clause. On the same day Madison moved to strike the part relating to the powers of the executive and to insert instead the following: "with power to carry into effect the national laws; to appoint to offices in cases not otherwise provided for; and to execute such other powers, not legislative nor judiciary in their nature, as may from time to time be delegated by the national legislature." On motion of the younger Pinckney, the last words of Madison's clause were struck because "they were unnecessary, the object of them being included in the 'power to carry into effect the national laws.'" On June 4, acting on Wilson's motion, the convention noted in favor of a single executive. At the end of the first week, therefore, the convention had resolved in favor of "a national executive, to consist of a single person, with power to carry into effect the national laws, to appoint to offices not otherwise provided for." In this fashion the convention, dominated entirely by nationalists of varying degree, at the very outset provided a cure for one of the principal defects, as demonstrated by experience, of a system based on state sovereignty.

Method of Selection

THE METHOD of selecting the executive involved one of the most trouble-some decisions which confronted the convention. It is sufficient here to note that the convention emphatically rejected any method which would have placed the power of selection in the states. On May 29 Wilson re-sumed "his declarations in favor of an appointment by the people. He wished to derive not only both branches of the Legislature from the people without the intervention of the state legislatures, but the execu-tive also, in order to make them as independent as possible of each other, as well as of the states." And on June 2 Wilson restated "his argu-ments in favor of an election without the intervention of the states."

Gerry's motion on June 9, however, was that "the national executive should be elected by the executives of the states." In his own support, Gerry argued that the method of appointment by the state executives was "most analogous to the principle observed in electing the other branches of the national government; the first branch being chosen by the people of the states and the second by the legislatures of the states, he did not see any objection against letting the executive be appointed by the executives of the states." Answer to this argument came from Randolph, who strongly urged

the inexpediency of Mr. Gerry's mode of appointing the national executive. The confidence of the people would not be secured by it to the national magis-trate. . . . Bad appointments would be made, the executives of the states being little conversant with characters not within their own small spheres. The state executives too, notwithstanding their constitutional independence, being in fact dependent on the state legislatures, will generally be guided by the views of the latter, and prefer either favorites within the states, or such as it may be expected will be most partial to the interests of the state. A national executive thus chosen will not be likely to defend with becoming vigilance and firmness the national rights against state encroachments. . . . He could not suppose, either, that the executives would feel the interest in supporting the national executive which had been imagined. They will not cherish the great oak which is to reduce them to paltry shrubs.

On the question for referring the appointment of the national executive to the state executives, as proposed by Gerry, nine states were opposed, one was divided, and none was in favor.

Gerry brought his proposal up again later in the convention. On July 19 he urged "the expediency of an appointment of the executive by electors to be chosen by the state executives. The people of the states will then choose the first branch; the legislatures of the states, the second branch of the national legislature; and the executives of the states, the national executives." This he thought would form "a strong attachment in the states to the national system." But the suggestion found no listeners. On July 24 Gerry moved "that the legislatures of the states should vote by ballot for the executive," but on a question to postpone a previous motion to take Gerry's motion under consideration, "the noes were so predominant that the states were not counted." The next day he proposed once more that "the executive be appointed by the governors and presidents of the states." This time it was Madison who made the reply. In the course of a survey of the various methods of choosing the executive, Madison considered the possibility of choice by the states.

The existing authorities in the states are the legislative, executive, and judiciary. The appointment of the national executive by the first was objectionable in many points of view, some of which had already been mentioned. He would mention one which of itself would decide his opinion. The legislatures of the states had betrayed a strong propensity to a variety of pernicious measures. One object of the national legislature was to control this propensity. One object of the national executive, so far as it would have a negative on the laws, was to control the national legislature, so far as it might be infected with a similar propensity. Refer the appointment of the national executive to the state legislatures, and this controlling purpose may be defeated. The legislatures can and will act with some kind of regular plan, and will promote the appointment of a man who will not oppose himself to a favorite object. Should a majority of the legislatures, at the time of election, have the same object, or different objects of the same kind, the national executive would be rendered subservient to them. An appointment by the state executives was liable, among other objections, to this insuperable one, that being standing bodies, they could and would be courted, and intrigued with by the candidates, by their partisans, and by the ministers of foreign powers. The state judiciaries had not been, and he presumed would not be, proposed as a proper source of appointment.

On the same day that Madison made the above statements, Dickinson also declared that election by either state executives or state legislatures invited "insuperable objections."

REPRESENTATION OF NATIONAL INTERESTS

Throughout the convention it was clear that the national executive was to be the representative of national rather than sectional interests, of the people rather than the states. More often than not this thought was implicit in the many discussions of the executive power, as a reading of the debates will demonstrate. Frequently, however, individual delegates made the thought explicit in their remarks. Butler, for example, on June 2 felt that a "single magistrate" would be "most likely to answer the purpose of the remote parts. If one man should be appointed, he would be responsible to the whole, and he would be impartial to its interests. If three or more be taken from as many districts, there would be a constant struggle for local advantages." Gouverneur Morris, holding forth at great length July 19, remarked on the vastness of the Union. "We must either then renounce the blessings of the Union or provide an executive with sufficient vigor to pervade every part of it. . . . It is necessary, then, that the executive magistrate should be the guardian of the people. . . . The executive, therefore, ought to be so constituted as to be the great protector of the mass of the people. . . . If he is to be the guardian of the people, let him be appointed by the people." Madison on August 24 declared that the President was to serve not the states but the people. And on September 6 Wilson, complaining of the excessive powers of the Senate as then provided, said that under extant provisions, "the President will not be the man of the people, as he ought to be."

In furtherance of this concept of the executive, the convention also rejected proposals which would have made state and sectional interests part of the executive structure. Many delegates realized that a single executive would be less susceptible to influence by such interests, as Butler's remark above indicates. The New Jersey plan would have created a plural executive, consistent with a confederation form of government. The sentiment behind a plural executive was expressed on July 24 by Williamson, who said he "did not like the unity in the executive. He had wished the executive power to be lodged in three men, taken from three districts, into which the states would be divided. As the executive is to have a kind of veto on the laws, and there is an essential difference of interest between the northern and southern states, particularly in the carrying trade, the power will be dangerous if the executive is to be taken from part of the Union to the part from which he is not taken." Williamson, however, received no support. On September 7 Mason moved to establish "an executive council as a Council of State for the President of the United States, to consist of six members, two of which from the eastern, two from the middle, and two from the southern states." This proposal, which would also have injected state and sectional interests into the executive structure, was defeated, eight states to three. All of this confirms the statement made earlier that the states as such were to be represented in the national government only in the Senate.

REMOVAL

It is also worth noting that in the provision for removing the executive the convention consciously avoided any mention of state participation in the process. The Virginia plan contained no provision on this subject. The New Jersey plan, however, would have made the executive "removable by Congress on application by a majority of the executives of the several states." The convention on June 2 voted in committee of the whole in favor of removability and approved this recommendation on July 20, but without specifying what body should impeach. The Committee of Detail gave this power to the House of Representatives. This choice was approved by the convention, and so it is provided in the Constitution, Article II, Section 6, and Article I, Section 2. Remembering that the House of Representatives was to be chosen by and be representative of the people, the vesting in this body of the power to impeach the executive is further evidence that the executive was intended by the convention to be a national figure representing national interests.

POWER OF APPOINTMENT

In accordance with the decision of the convention made on June 1, the Committee of Detail provided in its report that the executive should "appoint officers in all cases not otherwise provided for by this Constitution." On August 24 Randolph observed that "the power of appointments was a formidable one both in the executive and legislative hands; and suggested whether the legislature should not be left at liberty to refer appointments, in some cases, to some state authority." Dickinson then moved to annex to the appointing power the clause "except where by law the appointment shall be vested in the legislatures or executives of the several states." Upon Sherman's objection, the movers excised the term, "legislatures." As for the remainder of the motion, Gouverneur Morris offered the observation that "This would be putting it in the power of the states to say, 'you shall be viceroys, but we will be viceroys over you.' " On the vote, the defeat of Dickinson's motion showed conclusively the convention's disapproval of any distribution between national and state authority of the power to appoint national officers.

The power of appointment of ambassadors and judges of the Supreme Court, as well as the power to make treaties, were cases especially provided for, and in the report of the Committee of Detail these powers were vested in the Senate. Considerable opposition was expressed. Madison, for example, stated that "the Senate represented the states alone; and that for this as well as other obvious reasons, it was proper that the President should be an agent in treaties." The clause was never approved, and on August 31 it and other matters were referred to a committee on unfinished business. This committee on September 4 recommended the scheme finally approved, under which the powers were vested in the President, subject to the consent of the Senate. This action of the convention thus represented a shift of power from the representative of the states to the representative of the people. It also affords further evidence of the contemplated role of the Senate as the voice of the states in a national government exercising supreme powers over states no longer sovereign.

XXIII

The Fabric of a National Government — The Judiciary

ONE OF the characterizing aspects of the system created by the Articles of Confederation was the almost complete absence of any judicial power. Article IX provided that Congress itself should "be the last resort on appeal in all disputes and differences now subsisting or that hereafter may arise between two or more states concerning boundary, jurisdiction, or any other cause whatever." On petition by a state of Congress and notice to the other state, the contending states were directed jointly to appoint judges to decide the question. A complicated procedure for the selection of judges was provided to handle situations in which the appointment process bogged down. The court so chosen should then proceed to hear the case and announce a judgment, which was solemnly declared to be "final and conclusive." No method of enforcement was provided, however. In essence, therefore, an arbitral rather than judicial process was established. The same system was made available for the settlement of private rights claimed under the land grants of different states. Article IX also granted to Congress the power of "appointing courts for the trial of piracies and felonies committed on the high seas and establishing courts for receiving and determining finally appeals in all cases of captures," and also of "establishing rules for deciding in all cases what captures on land or water shall be legal, and in what manner prizes taken by land or naval forces in the service of the United States shall be divided or appropriated." These are among the few examples in which congressional power was exercisable directly over individuals, and the only instance of a United States court's exercising appellate jurisdiction over the state courts. In all other instances, the enforcement of congressional measures and treaties depended upon the instrumentalities of the states and the state's willingness to use them in support of Congress. The power to act coercively upon individuals was, with the rare exceptions noted above, a jealously guarded prerogative of state sovereignty.

The abandonment of state sovereignty in favor of a national government acting directly on individuals logically and practically demanded the creation of a national judiciary. Reflecting this need, the ninth resolution of the Virginia plan was "that a national judiciary be established." This was agreed to without debate or dissent on June 4 and was never thereafter questioned. The limited amount of discussion during the convention on the judicial power and the various decisions concerning it all serve to underscore the basic approach.

INFERIOR TRIBUNALS

The Virginia plan provided that the national judiciary should "consist of one or more supreme tribunals, and of inferior tribunals." This clause was also approved on June 4 without debate or dissent. On June 5, however, Rutledge, having "obtained a rule for reconsideration of the clause for establishing inferior tribunals under the national authority, now moved that that part of the clause in the ninth resolution should be expunged; arguing that the state tribunals might and ought to be left in all cases to decide in the first instance, the right of appeal to the supreme national tribunal being sufficient to secure the national rights and uniformity of judgments; that it was making an unnecessary encroachment on the jurisdiction of the states, and creating unnecessary obstacles to the adoption of the new system."

Madison spoke in opposition, observing

> that unless inferior tribunals were dispersed throughout the republic with final jurisdiction in many cases, appeals would be multiplied to a most oppressive degree; that, besides, an appeal would not in many cases be a remedy. What was to be done after improper verdicts, in state tribunals, obtained under the biased directions of a dependent judge, or the local prejudices of an undirected jury? To remand the cause for a new trial would answer no purpose. To order a new trial at the supreme bar would oblige the parties to bring up their witnesses, though ever so distant from the seat of the court. An effective judiciary establishment commensurate to the legislative authority was essential. A government, without a proper executive and judiciary, would be the mere trunk of a body, without arms or legs to act or move.

Wilson also opposed the motion "on like grounds." And Dickinson argued "strongly that if there was to be a national legislature, there ought to be a national judiciary, and that the former ought to have authority to institute the latter." Despite these objecions, Rutledge's motion was approved, six states to four, with one state divided.

Immediately following this vote, Wilson and Madison moved, "in pursuance of the idea expressed above by Mr. Dickinson, to add to the ninth resolution the words following: 'that the national legislature be empowered to institute inferior tribunals.' They observed that there was a distinction between establishing such tribunals absolutely and giving a discretion to the Legislature to establish them or not to establish them. They repeated the necessity of some such provision."

Butler was against the motion, saying that the people would not bear such innovations. King made the practical observation, "as to the comparative expense, that the establishment of inferior tribunals would cost infinitely less than the appeals that would be prevented by them." On the vote, the Madison-Wilson motion was approved, eight states to two, with one state divided. On June 15 the New Jersey plan was submitted, proposing that "a federal judiciary be established to consist of a supreme tribunal" with no provision for inferior tribunals, thus contemplating that the state courts should exercise all original jurisdiction. But on June 19 the committee of the whole approved resolutions that "a national judiciary be established, to consist of one supreme tribunal," and that "the national legislature be empowered to appoint inferior tribunals."

When these resolutions came before the convention on July 18, the former was agreed to without debate or dissent. The latter touched off a brief debate which covered old ground. Butler said he thought the state tribunals alone would be sufficient for the nation's needs. Luther Martin concurred: a national judiciary, interfering with established jurisdiction, would certainly "create jealousies and oppositions in the state tribunals."

Gorham replied that federal courts, "with jurisdiction for trial of piracies [and similar depredations] committed on the seas," already exist in the states. "No complaints have been made by the states or the courts of the states. Inferior tribunals are essential to render the authority of the national legislature effectual." Randolph did not feel that state courts could "be trusted with the administration of the national laws. The objects of jurisdiction," he said, "are such as will often place the general and local policy at variance." Gouverneur Morris and Mason concurred on the need for a national judiciary power. And even Sherman, who had seconded Rutledge's motion of June 5, now agreed to give the power to the Legislature, but wished them to "make use of the state tribunals, whenever it could be done with safety to the general interest." The resolution was then approved without dissent. No substantive change was made by the Committee of Detail. In final form the Constitution provides in Article III that "The judicial power of the United States shall be vested in one Supreme Court, and in such inferior courts as the Congress may from time to time ordain and establish." Article I, Section 3, confers upon Congress the power "to constitute tribunals inferior to the Supreme Court."

APPOINTMENT OF JUDGES

The method of appointment of judges was also the occasion for discussion. The Virginia plan provided that the national judiciary should be "chosen by the national legislature." On June 5, after some discussion, this was stricken without providing any substitute method. On June 13 the committee of the whole resolved that appointments should be made by the Senate, in which at that time, representation, as in the House, was proportional to population. When this resolution came before the convention on July 18, Wilson offered a substitution, "that the judges be appointed by the executive," which was seconded by Morris. By this time it had been decided that representation in the Senate should be equal for all states. Luther Martin strenuously asked "for an appointment by the second branch. Being taken from all the states, it would be best informed of characters, and most capable of making a fit choice." Sherman agreed with Martin, "adding that the judges ought to be diffused, which would be more likely to be attended to by the second branch than by the executive." After some debate, in which Madison, Morris, and Gorham supported the Wilson motion and Mason, Sherman, Randolph, and Bedford opposed it, the motion was defeated two states to six, with one state absent. Gorham then moved "that the judges be nominated and appointed by the executive, by and with the advice and consent of the second branch." But this also failed to carry, and Madison then moved "that the judges should be nominated by the executive, and such nomination should become an appointment if not disagreed to within—days by two-thirds of the second branch." The motion was seconded by Morris, but by "common consent, the consideration of it was postponed." As of that time, therefore, appointment still remained in the Senate.

On July 21 the convention resumed consideration of Madison's motion of June 18, and in support thereof Madison offered the following argument:

> . . . that as the second branch was very differently constituted, when the appointment of the judges was formerly referred to it, and was now to be com-

posed of equal votes from all the states, the principle of compromise which had prevailed in other instances required that in this there should be a concurrence of two authorities, in one of which the people, in the other the state, should be represented. The executive magistrate would be considered as a national officer, acting for and equally sympathizing with every part of the United States. If the second branch alone should have this power, the judges might be appointed by a minority of the people, though by a majority of the states, which could not be justified on any principle, as their proceedings were to relate to the people rather than to the states, and as it would, moreover, throw the appointments entirely into the hands of the northern states, a perpetual ground of jealousy and discontent would be furnished to the southern states.

Gouverneur Morris supported the motion, arguing differently from Madison that "the states, in their corporate capacity, will frequently have an interest staked on the determination of the judges. As in the Senate the states are to vote, the judges ought not to be appointed by the Senate. Next to the impropriety of being judge in one's own cause, is the appointment of the judge." Randolph was also in favor of the motion, with Ellsworth, Gerry, and Mason opposed. On the vote, Madison's motion failed, three states to six. Then by a six to three vote the convention again approved appointment of judges by the Senate. And so it was provided in the draft of the Committee of Detail.

A committee on unfinished business was appointed August 31 to deal with various matters on which decision had been postponed or agreement not reached, which included the power to make treaties and appoint ambassadors. This committee's report not only vested these powers in the President but also reversed the decision of the convention of July 21 as to the appointment of judges by the Senate. The proposal of the committee was that "The President, by and with the advice and consent of the Senate, shall have power to . . . appoint . . . judges of the Supreme Court." This was the same proposal advanced by Gorham on July 18 and rejected. The proposal was agreed to on September 7 without discussion or debate, so far as the records indicate—a rather remarkable about-face considering the earlier action. The political maneuvering in committee which brought about this substantial change can only be a matter of speculation. It should suffice here to note that the views of the advanced nationalists, Madison and Gorham, ultimately prevailed and that the final decision on this very important matter represented a definite shift of power from the legislative body which represented the states to the executive officer who represented the people.

Jurisdiction

CONSIDERING the subsequent importance of the jurisdiction of the national judiciary, it is notable that there was very little discussion of the subject during the convention. The Virginia plan had provided for original jurisdiction in the inferior and appellate jurisdiction in the supreme tribunal of cases involving piracies, felonies on the high seas, enemy captures, foreigners, collection of the national revenue, impeachments, and also—in sweeping and inclusive language—of "questions which may involve the national peace and harmony." The committee of the whole had approved the latter three of the above jurisdictional grants. On July 18 the convention, on Madison's motion, amended the clause to the form in which it went to the Committee of Detail: "that the jurisdiction of the national judiciary shall extend to cases arising under laws passed by the general legislature; and to such other questions as involve the national peace and harmony." It is interesting to compare the generality of this clause respecting judicial authority with that of the grant of legislative power which was submitted to the Committee of Detail. As it had done with the legislative power, so now the committee also reduced the general statement of judicial authority to numerous particulars. The committee's revision was substantially as ultimately approved, but several relevant items should be mentioned here.

COEXTENSIVE WITH SUPREMACY CLAUSE

We have already seen how the convention met the problem of effecting national supremacy. After rejecting coercion of arms and the congressional negative, it had provided that the Constitution, laws, and treaties of the United States should be "the supreme law of the land," anything in the state constitutions or laws to the contrary notwithstanding. In order that this legal principle of national supremacy should be judicially enforceable, it was necessary that the national judiciary should have jurisdiction commensurate with the language of the supremacy clause. The record leaves no doubt that this was the conscious intent and plan of the convention. The draft of the Committee of Detail made acts of Congress and treaties of the United States the supreme laws of the land, but provided only that "the jurisdiction of the Supreme Court shall extend to all laws passed by the Legislature of the United States." The convention on August 23, it will be recalled, added the words "this Constitution" to the supremacy clause. On August 27 Johnson moved to amend the judicial jurisdiction clause by inserting the words "this Constitution and the" before "laws." This emendation was agreed to without dissent. Then, on Rutledge's motion, the words "and treaties made or which shall be made under their authority" were inserted after "United States," as the record states, "conformably to a preceding amendment in another place," i.e., in the supremacy clause. The supremacy clause of the Committee of Detail draft had made that supremacy enforceable by "the judges in the several states" instead of, in Luther Martin's language, "the judiciaries of the several states." National supremacy could therefore be protected by the inferior tribunals which Congress was authorized to create. This purpose was made doubly clear on August 27 when, on motion of Madison and Morris, "the judicial power" was substituted for "the jurisdiction of the Supreme Court." The "judicial power," was of course vested in one Supreme Court and such inferior courts as Congress might establish. In its final form the clause appears in Article III as follows: "The judicial power of the United States shall extend to all cases, in law and equity, arising under this Constitution, the laws of the United States, and treaties made, or which shall be made, under their authority." The symmetry between the supremacy clause and the judicial power was thus perfected, and the convention had provided a national judiciary clothed with sufficient authority to enforce the national supremacy in all respects.

APPELLATE JURISDICTION OVER STATE COURTS

In later years, after the Constitution had been adopted, advocates of state sovereignty urged that the Supreme Court had no appellate jurisdiction over state courts. It is interesting to note that the proceedings of the convention give no support whatever to this contention. Available evidence, as a matter of fact, is directly to the contrary. The entire argument against any provision for inferior national tribunals was predicated upon the assumption that such appellate jurisdiction would exist. Thus Rutledge could argue "that the state tribunals might and ought to be left in all cases to decide in the first instance, the right of appeal to the supreme national tribunal being sufficient to secure the national rights and uniformity of judgments."

And although Congress was authorized to create inferior national tribunals whose judicial power should extend to cases arising under the Constitution, laws, and treaties of the United States, there was no suggestion that this would deprive the state courts of all such jurisdiction.

Indeed, the convention clearly contemplated, as the language of the supremacy clause itself demonstrated, that the state courts would continue to exercise jurisdiction over such cases. Even though the supremacy clause adjured the state courts to effectuate national supremacy, it was stated openly in the convention by Randolph that "the courts of the states cannot be trusted" since "the general and local policy" would often be "at variance." This distrust was one of the principal sources of support for a power in Congress to create inferior national tribunals. But the existence of inferior tribunals would be insufficient assurance that national supremacy would be protected, so long as the state courts had concurrent jurisdiction. Madison's statement of June 5 clearly revealed that the authorization of inferior tribunals was intended to be in addition to, and not in substitution for, appeals from state courts to the supreme national tribunal. It is impossible to impute to the convention any intention to depart from the original contemplation that the supreme national tribunal should have appellate jurisdiction over state courts.

CONTROVERSIES BETWEEN STATES

One further point having to do with jurisdiction should be mentioned: the matter of controversies between states. The method of settlement provided by the Articles was arbitral and unenforceable. This method's assumption that such controversies were political matters was consistent with the fact that the states were then indeed sovereign. The first mention of this problem in the convention appeared in the draft prepared by the Committee of Detail, wherein it was provided that the jurisdiction of the Supreme Court should extend "to controversies between two or more states (except such as shall regard territory or jurisdiction)."

This in itself was a substantial inroad upon state sovereignty, since the arbitral method of the Articles applied to controversies concerning boundaries and jurisdiction, and to disputes arising from "any other cause whatever." The latter category of disputes (i.e., all other than boundaries or jurisdiction) was now brought under the jurisdiction of the Supreme Court. The committee draft provided, however, that "In all disputes and controversies now subsisting, or that may hereafter subsist between two or more states, respecting jurisdiction or territory, the Senate shall possess the following powers." The arbitral method of the Articles was then set forth, with the Senate, in its role and function as the representatives of the states, substituted for Congress. This vestige of state sovereignty as well was eliminated by the convention. On August 24 "Rutledge said this provision (for deciding controversies between the states) was necessary under the Confederation, but will be rendered unnecessary by the national judiciary now to be established, and moved to strike it out." Williamson "was for postponing instead of striking out, in order to consider whether this might not be a good provision, in cases where the judiciary were interested or too closely connected with the parties." Gorham also "had doubts as to striking out. The judges might be connected with the states being parties. He was inclined to think the mode proposed in the clause would be more satisfactory than to refer such cases to the judiciary." The convention, however, voted seven to three against postponing, and then eight to two in favor of striking out the provision.

As finally approved, the Constitution provides in Article III, Section 2, Clause 1, that the "judicial power shall extend . . . to controversies between two or more states," and in Clause 2 that in "all cases . . . in which a state shall be party, the Supreme Court shall have original jurisdiction." Comparison of the Articles with the Constitution on this matter affords one of the most striking illustrations of the transition from state sovereignty to national supremacy.

TREASON

Finally, attention should be given to the provision relating to treason, which is found in the same article that deals with the judicial power. It is not surprising that there was no mention of treason in the Articles of Confederation. Since treason is a crime against sovereignty, and since under the Articles sovereignty remained in the states, treasonous matters were governed by state law. The creation of a national government supreme over the states demanded some treatment of the subject. The first mention in the convention was in the draft of the Committee of Detail, which stated in part that treason against the Union "shall consist only in levying war against the United States, or any of them; and in adhering to the enemies of the United States, or any of them. The Legislature of the United States shall have power to declare the punishment of treason."

When this provision came up for debate on August 20, a lively discussion ensued. Gouverneur Morris said he was "for giving the Union an exclusive right to declare what should be treason. In case of a contest between the United States and a particular state, the people of the latter must, under the disjunctive terms of the clause, be traitors to one or other authority." Johnson "contended that treason could not be both against the United States and individual states; being an offense against the sovereignty, which can be but one in the same community." Wilson and Johnson then moved that the words "or any of them" after the words "United States" be struck out, and this was done without discussion or debate. This action left the provision dealing only with "treason against the United States." By thus unanimously rejecting treason against a state as proper for inclusion in the Constitution, the convention clearly revealed that it was consciously creating a national sovereignty.

The question still remained, however, whether treason against a state was still possible. Madison was of the opinion that "as the definition here was against the United States, it would seem that the individual states would be left in possession of a concurrent power, so far as to define and punish treason particularly against themselves, which might involve double punishment." Madison thought the amendment striking out the words "or any of them" had not "removed the embarrassment. The same act might be treason against the United States, as here defined, and against a particular state, according to its laws." Johnson, however, "was still of opinion there could be no treason against a particular state. It could not, even at present, as the Confederation now stands, the sovereignty being in the Union, much less can it under the proposed system." Mason countered with the view that "The United States will have a qualified sovereignty only. The individual states will retain a part of the sovereignty. An act may be treason against a particular state, which is not so against the United States. He cited the rebellion of Bacon in Virginia as an illustration of the doctrine." To this Johnson replied that "that case would amount to treason against the sovereign, the supreme sovereign, the United States."

In order to clarify the situation, someone moved "to strike out 'against the United States' after 'treason,' so as to define treason generally." The motion carried, eight states to two. King then "moved to insert, before the word 'power' the word 'sole' giving the United States the exclusive right to declare the punishment of treason." He explained that his amendment resulted from the vote defining treason generally, by striking out 'against the United States,' which excludes any treason against particular states." Inexplicably, the convention voted against King's motion, six states to five. Wilson immediately pointed out that the clause as it stood was ambiguous. " 'Sole' ought either to have been inserted, or 'against the United States' to be reinstated." King now said, "No line can be drawn between levying war and adhering to the enemy against the United States and against an individual state. Treason against the latter must be so against the former." And Dickinson also took the view that war or insurrection "against a member of the Union must be so against the whole body, but the Constitution should be made clear on this point."

Sherman, however, thought that resistance "against the laws of the United States, as distinguished from resistance against the laws of a particular state, forms the line." And Ellsworth asserted that the "United States are sovereign on one side of the line, dividing the jurisdictions—the states on the other. Each ought to have the power to defend their respective sovereignties." The clause was then reconsidered, with Wilson and Ellsworth moving to reinstate "against the United States" after the word "treason." This motion carried, six states to five. There is no doubt that a concession had been made to state sovereignty, but it was a formal rather than a substantive one, as evidenced by Ellsworth's own observation that there could "be no danger to the general authority from this, as the laws of the United States are to be paramount." In its final form in Article III, Section 3, the definition reads: "Treason against the United States shall consist only in levying war against them, or in adhering to their enemies, giving them aid and comfort."

XXIV

Miscellaneous Provisions
of the Constitution

Interstate Privileges and Immunities

THE ARTICLES of Confederation provided that "the free inhabitants of each of these states . . . shall be entitled to all privileges and immunities of free citizens in the several states; and the people of each state shall have free ingress and regress to and from any other state, and shall enjoy therein all the privileges of trade and commerce, subject to the same duties, impositions, and restrictions as the inhabitants thereof respectively." This was cumbersome language, confusing as it did the terms "free inhabitants," "free citizens," and "people," and superimposing "all the privileges of trade and commerce" upon "all privileges and imunities of free citizens." The Committee of Detail recommended the abbreviated and simplified version which was adopted without debate and without change and is found in Article IV, Section 2, Clause 1, of the Constitution: "The citizens of each state shall be entitled to all privileges and immunities of citizens in the several states."

This provision deals primarily with the relation between the states themselves, and, like the "full faith and credit clause" already discussed, it recognizes that, in the absence of some overriding provision of national law, the states would be under no obligation to respect the laws or policies of sister states, that they would be, in law and in fact, independent and sovereign as between each other. If such a provision was desirable under a confederation of sovereign states, it was *a fortiori* even more a necessity under a Constitution one of whose stated purposes was "to form a more perfect union." The inclusion of such a provision would be a futility, however, in the absence of some superior authority to enforce the obligation upon the states, as was the situation under the Articles. Under the Constitution the interstate privileges and immunities clause stands not only as a limitation on the power of the states as between each other, but also as a repudiation of state sovereignty as between the states and the national government. For the clause, being included in the Constitution, not only became a part of "the supreme law of the land," but also became an enforceable limitation upon state authority under the judicial power which extends to "all cases arising under the Constitution," by the executive power "to take care that the laws be faithfully executed," and by the legislative power to make "all laws which shall be necessary and proper" to carry the judicial and executive powers into effect.

Interstate Extradition

THE ARTICLES of Confederation provided that "If any person guilty of, or charged with treason, felony, or other high misdemeanor in any state, shall flee from justice, and be found in any of the United States, he shall upon demand of the governor or executive power of the state from which he fled, be delivered up and removed to the state having jurisdiction of his offense." The Committee of Detail made a comparable recommendation which finally emerged, without significant debate, as Clause 2 of Article IV, Section 2, of the Constitution: "A person charged in any state with treason, felony, or other crime, who shall flee from justice, and be found in another state, shall on demand of the executive authority of the state from which he fled, be delivered up to be removed to the state having jurisdiction of the crime."

Everything which was said in the preceding paragraphs on interstate privileges and immunities applies equally to this interstate extradition clause.

National Guarantee to States

As NOTED in Part I, Shays' Rebellion in Massachusetts during the winter of 1786-1787 had frightened many people throughout the states. For a time there was real doubt whether Massachusetts would be able to suppress the uprising with its own forces alone. The Articles, however, recognized no power in Congress to use Continental troops to suppress an insurrection against a state. In order to cope with such an eventuality in the future, the Virginia plan provided that "a republican government . . . ought to be guaranteed by the United States to each state." On June 11, "alterations having been made in the resolution" so as to make it read "that a republican constitution, and its existing laws, ought to be guaranteed to each state by the United States," it was agreed to without debate or dissent.

When this resolution came up for discussion on July 18, Wilson explained that the object was "merely to secure the states against dangerous commotions, insurrections, and rebellions." Randolph said that the resolution "has two objects—first, to secure a republican government; secondly, to suppress domestic commotions." Mason thought that if "the general government should have no right to suppress rebellions against particular states, it will be in a bad situation indeed. As rebellions against itself originate in and against individual states, it must remain a passive spectator to its own subversion." But Luther Martin, being a state sovereignty man, was "for leaving the states to suppress rebellions themselves." Gorham replied that he thought it "strange that a rebellion should be known to exist in the empire and the general government should be restrained from interposing to subdue it. At this rate an enterprising citizen might erect the standard of monarchy in a particular state, might gather together partisans from all quarters, might extend his views from state to state, and threaten to establish a tyranny over the whole, and the general government be compelled to remain an inactive witness of its own destruction." Carroll said he believed that "some such provision is essential. Every state ought to wish for it." Rutledge thought "it unnecessary to insert any guarantee. No doubt could be entertained but that Congress had the authority, if they had the means, to cooperate with any state in subduing a rebellion. It was and would be involved in the nature of the thing." The matter was resolved for a time by the adoption of a motion by Wilson "that a republican form of government shall be guaranteed to each state, and that each state shall be protected against foreign and domestic violence."

The draft of the Committee of Detail dealt with the subject in two provisions. One was an express grant to Congress "to subdue a rebellion in any state, on the application of its Legislature." The other was a modification of the Wilson motion: "The United States shall guarantee to each state a republican form of government; and shall protect each state against foreign invasion, and, on the application of its Legislature, against domestic violence."

When the first of these provisions came before the convention on August 17, the younger Pinckney moved to strike out "on the application of its Legislature." Luther Martin opposed this deletion "as giving a dangerous and unnecessary power. The consent of the state ought to precede the introduction of any extraneous force whatever." And Gerry said he was "against letting loose the myrmidons of the United States on a state, without its own consent." Langdon, on the other hand, supported Pinckney's motion, stating that the "apprehension of the national force will have a salutary effect in preventing insurrections." And Morris noted that the convention was playing "a very strange part. We first form a strong man to protect us, and at the same time wish to tie his hands behind him. The Legislature [i.e., the Congress] may surely be trusted with such a power to preserve the public tranquillity." Ellsworth said that "In many cases the general government ought not to be able to interpose unless called upon." He suggested varying the motion to add "or without it, when the Legislature cannot meet." This was agreed to, five to three, with two states divided. Madison and Dickinson then moved to insert "as explanatory" after the word "state" the words "against the government thereof," for the reason that there "might be a rebellion against the United States." Agreement to this motion without dissent made it clear that in these provisions the convention was dealing with rebellions and insurrections against a state and not against the national government. Inexplicably, after the convention had approved both the Ellsworth and the Madison-Dickinson amendments, the clause then failed to carry by a divided vote, four to four.

There remained the second provision recommended by the Committee of Detail. When this came up on August 30, Dickinson moved to strike out the words "on the application of its Legislature, against." He said he "thought it of essential importance to the tranquillity of the United States that they should in all cases suppress domestic violence, which may proceed from the state legislature itself." But this motion was defeated by a vote of eight to three. Then, on motion of Dickinson, "executive" was added to the clause. As finally approved, the provision appears as Article IV, Section 4, of the Constitution: "The United States shall guarantee to every state in this Union a republican form of government, and shall protect each of them against invasion; and on application of the legislature, or of the executive (when the legislature cannot be convened) against domestic violence."

Bearing in mind that both clauses recommended by the Committee of Detail were designed as guarantees to the states, and also the convention's approval of the Madison-Dickinson motion, it seems clear that the "domestic violence" referred to is that directed against the state and not against the national government. Any other view would render the national government powerless to protect itself against domestic violence from a state without the request of such state, an obvious absurdity which the debates make clear was not contemplated. That the clause was not intended as a limitation against the power of the national government to deal with domestic violence against itself is also conclusively demonstrated by other parts of the Constitution. For Congress was empowered in Article I, Section 8, to "provide for calling forth the militia to execute the laws of the Union, suppress insurrections and repel invasions." And Article I, Section 9, which sets forth limitations on the power of the national government, prohibited suspension of the privilege of the writ of habeas corpus "unless when in cases of rebellion or invasion the public safety may require it."

Method of Amendment

THE ARTICLES of Confederation had said, of themselves, "nor shall any alteration at any time hereafter be made in any of them, unless such alteration be agreed to in a congress of the United States, and be afterwards confirmed by the legislatures of every state." This provision, requiring the consent of the legislatures of every state, had throughout the Confederation blocked all efforts to strengthen the powers of Congress by formal amendment, for there was always at least one state which was opposed. At the same time, however, it was inherent in the nature of a Confederation of sovereign states that no one state should have amendments of the compact thrust upon it without its consent. The Virginia plan was vague on the question, proposing "that provision ought to be made for the amendment of the Articles of Union, whensoever it shall seem necessary, and that the assent of the national legislature ought not to be required thereto." On June 11, this provision being considered, "several members did not see the necessity of the resolution at all, nor the propriety of making the consent of the national legislature unnecessary." Mason, however, urged "the necessity of such a provision. . . . It would be improper to require the consent of the national legislature, because they may abuse their power, and refuse their assent on that very account." In this he was backed by Randolph, but the convention, notwithstanding, approved the provision without the clause "without requiring the consent of the national legislature."

The draft of the Committee of Detail provided that "on the application of the legislatures of two-thirds of the states in the Union, for an amendment of this Constitution, the legislature of the United States shall call a convention for that purpose." This proposal was approved on August 30 without discussion or dissent. On September 10, however, Gerry moved to reconsider the provision. "This Constitution, he said, is to be paramount to the state constitutions. It follows, hence, from this article, that two-thirds of the states may obtain a convention, a majority of which can bind the Union to innovations that may subvert the state constitutions altogether. He asked whether this was a situation proper to be run into." Hamilton seconded the motion but, he said, with a different view. He did not object to the consequences stated by Gerry. There was "no greater evil in subjecting the people of the United States to the major voice than the people of a particular state." He urged that an easier method of amendment than that of the Articles was desirable, but argued that the state legislatures "will not apply for alterations, but with a view to increase their own powers. The national legislature will be the first to perceive, and will be most sensible to, the necessity of amendments, and ought to be empowered, whenever two-thirds of each branch should concur, to call a convention. There could be no danger in giving this power, as the people would finally decide in the case." Gerry's motion to reconsider the provision then carried.

Sherman then moved to add to the provision an alternate method, "or the legislature may propose amendments to the several states for their approbation, but no amendments shall be binding until consented to by the several states." To avoid the requirement of unanimous consent, Wilson moved to make ratification by two-thirds of the states sufficient, and, this being defeated, he then moved for three-fourths consent, which was approved. Thus the convention refused to follow the unanimity rule of the Articles. At this stage, Madison proposed a substitute which was approved, under which Congress, either on two-thirds vote of both houses or on the application of two-thirds of the state legislatures, could propose amendments, to be ratified either by three-fourths of the state legislatures or by conventions in three-fourths of the states, whichever Congress should provide. On September 15 the convention approved a motion by Morris providing for a convention, on application of two-thirds of the states, to propose amendments. Motions by Sherman and Gerry, which would have required ratification to be unanimous, were then rejected by the convention.

On September 12 the convention had agreed to a limitation on the amending power, proposed by Rutledge, which prohibited amendments directed against slavery prior to 1808. Three days later Sherman sought a further limitation in favor of state sovereignty. He expressed "his fears that three-fourths of the states might be brought to do things fatal to particular states, as abolishing them altogether, or depriving them of their equality in the Senate. He thought it reasonable that the proviso in favor of the states importing slaves should be extended so as to provide that no state should be affected in its internal police, or deprived of its equality in the Senate." He therefore moved, "according to his idea above expressed, to annex at the end of the article a further proviso that no state shall, without its consent, be affected in its internal police, or deprived of its equal suffrage in the Senate." Madison objected: "Begin with these special provisos, and every state will insist on them, for their boundaries, exports, etc." Sherman's motion was then defeated, eight to three. Next, his motion to strike the entire amendment was also defeated. Gouverneur Morris then made a conciliatory motion "that no state, without its consent, shall be deprived of its equal suffrage in the Senate," and the motion, "being dictated by the circulating murmurs of the small states, was agreed to without debate, no one opposing it or, on the question, saying no."

In final form the amending provision appears as Article V of the Constitution:

> The Congress, whenever two-thirds of both houses shall deem it necessary, shall propose amendments to this Constitution, or, on the application of the legislatures of two-thirds of the several States, shall call a convention for proposing amendments, which, in either case, shall be valid to all intents and purposes, as part of this Constitution, when ratified by the legislatures of three-fourths of the several states, or by conventions in three-fourths thereof, as the one or the other mode of ratification may be proposed by the Congress; provided that no amendment which may be made prior to the year one thousand eight hundred and eight shall in any manner affect the first and fourth clauses in the ninth section of the first article; and that no state, without its consent, shall be deprived of its equal suffrage in the Senate.

Thus the convention repudiated state sovereignty by adopting an amending process under which a state could be bound without its consent, either in the proposal or in the ratification of an amendment. The convention expressly required the participation of Congress in the amending process, thereby giving protection to the national government, and expressly refused to limit the amending power to protect the police power of the states. Congress was also given the discretionary power to bypass the state legislatures and go to the people, acting through conventions, for ratification. Even the proviso protecting state equality in the Senate from amendment emphasizes, rather than refutes, the repudiation of state sovereignty, for it offers further proof of the contemplation that the states, since they were no longer to be sovereign, should be represented as states in the national government which was to exercise the powers of sovereignty on behalf of the people.

XXV

Ratification by the People

THE MOST dramatic and conclusive proof of the conscious transition from a confederation of sovereign states to a national government was the choice made by the convention for a method of ratifying the Constitution. The Articles of Confederation, operative only on the states as such, appropriately had been ratified by the states as such. Article XIII, after declaring that the Union created therein should be perpetual, continued: "nor shall any alteration at any time hereafter be made in any of them; unless such alteration be agreed to in a Congress of the United States, and be afterwards confirmed by the legislature of every state." This was the unanimity rule on which all the efforts to strengthen the Articles had foundered. The resolution of Congress in February 1787, calling for a convention, stated:

> Whereas there is provision in the Articles of Confederation and perpetual union for making alterations therein by the assent of a Congress of the United States and of the legislatures of the several states, and whereas experience has evinced that there are defects in the present Confederation, as a means to remedy which several of the states and particularly the state of New York by express instructions to their delegates in Congress have suggested a convention for the purposes expressed in the following resolution, and such convention appearing to be the most probable means of establishing in these states a firm national government; Resolved, that in the opinion of Congress it is expedient that on the second Monday in May next a convention of delegates who shall have been appointed by the several states be held at Philadelphia for the sole and express purpose of revising the Articles of Confederation and reporting to Congress and the several legislatures such alterations and provisions therein as shall when agreed to in Congress and confirmed by the states render the federal government adequate to the exigencies of government and the preservation of the Union.

This resolution not only limited the purpose of the convention solely and expressly to revising the Articles, but also contemplated that the method set forth in the Articles for approving amendments should be followed as to any recommendations of the convention.

The Virginia plan included a resolution "that the amendments which shall be offered to the Confederation by the convention, ought at a proper time, or times, after the approbation of Congress, to be submitted to an assembly or assemblies of representatives, recommended by the several legislatures, to be expressly chosen by the people to consider and decide thereon." The provision for "assemblies expressly chosen by the people" was of course utterly foreign to the Articles, and there was some support in the convention for ratification by the state legislatures. This position was essentially legalistic—that this was the only method which was provided for by the Articles. Thus, when the proposition in the Virginia plan came up on June 5, Sherman said he "thought such a popular ratification unnecessary, the Articles of Confederation providing for changes and alterations with the assent of Congress and ratification of state legislatures." Gerry also expressed opposition to popular ratification, which was nevertheless strongly defended by Madison, King, Wilson, and the younger Pinckney, and subsequently approved on June 12 by the committee of the whole, six states to three, with two states divided.

When this proposal came before the convention on July 23, Ellsworth and Paterson "moved that the Constitution framed by this convention be referred to the legislatures of the states for ratification." Arguing in support of the motion, Ellsworth "observed that a new set of ideas seemed to have crept in since the Articles of Confederation were established. Conventions of the people, or with power derived expressly from the people, were not then thought of. The legislatures were considered as competent. Their ratification has been acquiesced in without complaint. To whom have Congress applied on subsequent occasions for further powers? To the legislatures, not to the people. The fact is that we exist at present, and we need not inquire how, as a federal society, united by a charter one article of which is that alterations therein may be made by the legislative authority of the states." Gerry said that he "considered the Confederation to be paramount to any state constitution. The last article of it authorizing alterations must consequently be so as well as the others, and everything done in pursuance of the article must have the same high authority with the article. Great confusion, he was confident, would result from a recurrence to the people." Mason, Randolph, Gorham, Morris, King, and Madison all spoke strongly against the Ellsworth motion, which was defeated, seven states to three. The convention then approved, nine states to one, the proposal for ratification by assemblies chosen by the people expressly for that purpose.

Examination of the arguments against ratification by the state legislatures and of the reasons supporting ratification by conventions of the people conclusively demonstrates that the Constitution, unlike the Articles, was not predicated upon state sovereignty.

First, there was the question whether the convention had any power to go beyond amending the Articles and draft a totally new Constitution. Although the Virginia plan described itself as "amendments . . . to the Confederation," it proposed, as we have seen, a fundamentally different governmental system. It will be remembered that on May 30, the day after the Virginia plan was introduced, Randolph submitted the three basic postulates upon which it was based: "1. that a union of the states merely federal will not accomplish the objects of . . . common defense, security of liberty, and general welfare. 2. that no treaty or treaties among the whole or part of the states, as individual sovereignties, would be sufficient. 3. that a national government ought to be established consisting of a supreme legislative, executive, and judiciary." There was never any doubt that what was being proposed was a new organic instrument of government radically different from the old. It is interesting to note that as early as June 5 Madison's notes refer to the convention's taking up the fifteenth proposition "for recommending conventions under appointment of the people to ratify the new Constitution."

On May 30 General Pinckney "expressed a doubt whether the act of Congress recommending the convention, or the commissions of the deputies to it, could authorize a discussion of a system founded on different principles from the federal Constitution." And Gerry "seemed to entertain the same doubt." On June 9 Paterson made "some remarks on the nature, structure, and powers" of the convention:

> The convention, he said, was formed in pursuance of an act of Congress, that this act was recited in several of the commissions, particularly that of Massachusetts, which he required to be read; that the amendment of the Confederacy was the object of all the laws and commissions on the subject; that the Articles of the Confederation were therefore the proper basis of all the proceedings of the convention. We ought to keep within its limits, or we should be charged by our constituents with usurpation; that the people of America were sharpsighted and not to be deceived. But the commissions under which we acted were not only the measure of our power, they denoted also the sentiments of the states on the subject of our deliberation. The idea of a na-

tional government as contradistinguished from a federal one, never entered into the mind of any of them, and to the public mind we must accommodate ourselves. We have no power to go beyond the federal scheme, and if we had the people are not ripe for any other. We must follow the people; the people will not follow us.

And again on June 16 Paterson, arguing in support of his own New Jersey plan, said that he "preferred it because it accorded 1. with the powers of the convention, and 2. with the sentiments of the people. If the confederacy was radically wrong, let us return to our states, and obtain larger powers, not assume them of ourselves." Lansing on the same day said he was persuaded

> that the power of the convention was restrained to amendments of a federal nature, and having for their basis the Confederacy in being. The act of Congress, the tenor of the acts of the states, the commissions produced by the several deputations all proved this, and this limitation of the power to an amendment of the Confederacy marked the opinion of the states, that it was unnecessary and improper to go farther. He was sure that this was the case with his state. New York would never have concurred in sending deputies to the convention, if she had supposed the deliberations were to turn on a consolidation of the states, and a national government.

In reply to this charge that the convention was proceeding *ultra vires*, a less legalistic approach was taken by some delegates on grounds of necessity and on a distinction drawn between the power to propose and the power to adopt a new system. Thus, Randolph said that he "was not scrupulous on the point of power. When the salvation of the Republic was at stake, it would be treason to our trust, not to propose what we found necessary." The younger Pinckney "thought the convention authorized to go any length in recommending which they found necessary to remedy the evils which produced this convention." Wilson said, concerning the convention's power, that "he conceived himself authorized to conclude nothing, but to be at liberty to propose anything." And Hamilton stated that he "agreed moreover with the honorable gentleman from Virginia, Mr. Randolph, that we owed it to our country to do on this emergency whatever we should deem essential to its happiness. The states sent us here to provide for the exigencies of the Union. To rely on and propose any plan not adequate to these exigencies, merely because it was not clearly within our powers, would be to sacrifice the means to the end."

Mason, Morris, King, and Madison, going further, sought to justify the course of conduct of the convention on broader grounds. Mason and

Morris frankly conceived the function of the convention to be extra-legal but thought that approval by the people would validate it. On June 4, for example, Mason said that he considered "the federal government as in some measure dissolved by the meeting of this convention." On June 20, noting that "the principal objections against the plan of Mr. Randolph were the want of power and the want of practicability," Mason affirmed that there "can be no weight in the first as the fiat is not to be here, but in the people." A month later, Morris put it as follows: "If the Confederation is to be pursued, no alteration can be made without the unanimous consent of the legislatures: legislative alterations not conformable to the federal compact would clearly not be valid. The judges would consider them as null and void. Whereas in case of an appeal to the people of the United States, the supreme authority, the federal compact may be altered by a majority of them, in like manner as the constitution of a particular state may be altered by a majority of the people of the state. The amendment moved by Mr. Ellsworth erroneously supposes that we are proceeding on the basis of the Confederation. This convention is unknown to the Confederation." King then stated that "he preferred a reference to the authority of the people expressly delegated to conventions as the most certain means of obviating all disputes and doubts concerning the legitimacy of the new Constitution." Madison, on June 19, noted that considerable "stress had been laid by some gentlemen on the want of power in the convention to propose any other than a federal plan." On August 31 he answered this objection succinctly. "The people were in fact the fountain of all power, and by resorting to them, all difficulties were got over. They could alter constitutions as they pleased. It was a principle in the bills of rights that first principles might be resorted to." The position was thus made clear. Since all power was derived from the people, a ratification of the Constitution by an exercise of popular sovereignty would cure any want of original power in the convention.

For another thing, the nature of the new government to be created by the Constitution cast doubt upon the power of state governments to ratify it. True, the state governments had ratified the Articles on behalf of the people of each state. But since the duties and obligations of the Articles rested upon the states as such, and since under the Articles the states remained sovereign, there could be no question of the power of the state governments, representing the sovereignty of their respective peoples, to ratify the Articles. Nor could there be any question of the power of state legislatures to make alterations in the

Articles, so long as the unanimous consent requirement protected state sovereignty. But the government to be created by the Constitution was to be a national government, exercising its great powers directly upon individuals without the intervention of the states. Its laws were to apply to the individual inhabitants of a state, even though that state's representatives might have opposed such laws. And the new Constitution itself was subject to amendment by Congress and three-fourths of the states, any new amendments being binding both on dissident states and their inhabitants. Was it within the competence of the state governments to create such power over their constituentts, or was it necessary that such power be granted by the people themselves?

Hamilton raised the question on June 18 and suggested the answer at the same time. "It may be said that the states can not ratify a plan not within the purview of the Articles of Confederation providing for alterations and amendments. But may not the states themselves in which no constitutional authority equal to this purpose exists in the legislatures, have had in view a reference to the people at large?" When the convention debated the question of ratification on July 23, other delegates took a similar view. Mason said he "considered a reference of the plan to the authority of the people as one of the most important and essential of the resolutions. The legislatures have no power to ratify it. They are the mere creatures of the state constitutions," Mason said, "and can not be greater than their creators. And he knew of no power in any of the constitutions, he knew there was no power in some of them, that could be competent to this object. Whither then must we resort? To the people with whom all power remains that has not been given up in the constitutions derived from them. It was of great moment, he observed, that this doctrine should be cherished as the basis of free government."

King remarked that "among other objections made in the state of New York to granting powers to Congress, one had been that such powers as would operate within the states could not be reconciled to the state constitution, and therefore were not grantable by the legislative authority. He considered it as of some consequence also to get rid of the scruples which some members of the state legislatures might derive from their oaths to support and maintain the existing constitutions."

Madison then stated that he "thought it clear that the legislatures were incompetent to the proposed changes. These changes would make essential inroads on the state constitutions, and it would be a novel and dangerous doctrine that a legislature could change the constitution under which it held its existence. There might indeed be some constitutions within the Union which had given a power to the legislature to concur in alterations of the federal compact. But there were certainly some which had not, and in the case of these, a ratification must of necessity be obtained from the people." Thus the consensus was that, although the state governments might not be competent to create a national government acting directly upon the people, there was no doubt of the power of the people themselves to create such a government. Its base was to be the sovereignty of the people and not of the states.

Furthermore, the convention recognized that any system founded on the consent of the state governments could never be anything more than a compact or treaty among sovereign states, and that a national government with supremacy over the states could be founded on consent of the people only. Madison made this point on June 5 when the Virginia plan proposal first came up. He said he believed this was an essential provision.

> The Articles of Confederation themselves were defective in this respect, resting in many of the states on the legislative sanction only. Hence in conflicts between acts of the states and of Congress, especially where the former are of posterior date and the decision is to be made by state tribunals, an uncertainty must necessarily prevail, or rather perhaps a certain decision in favor of the state authority. He suggested also that as far as the Articles of Union were to be considered as a treaty only of a particular sort, among the governments of independent states, the doctrine might be set up that a breach of any one article, by any of the parties, absolved the other parties from the whole obligation. For these reasons as well as others, he thought it indispensable that the new Constitution should be ratified in the most unexceptionable form, and by the supreme authority of the people themselves.

On July 23, in debate on the proposal, Mason observed that even if the legislatures had a "competent authority, it would be wrong to refer the plan to them, because succeeding legislatures having equal authority could undo the acts of their predecessors, and the national government would stand in each state on the weak and rotten foundation of an act of assembly." And Randolph noted that, among other objections against a ratification by legislative authority only, was the fact that there have been instances in which the authority of the common law has been set up in particular states against that of the Confederation which has had no higher sanction than legislative ratification."

On the same day Madison made the most succinct statement on this issue:

> He considered the difference between a system founded on the legislatures only, and one founded on the people, to be the true difference between a league or treaty, and a constitution. The former in point of *moral obligation* might be as inviolable as the latter. In point of *political operation* there were two important distinctions in favor of the latter. First, a law violating a treaty ratified by a pre-existing law might be respected by the judges as a law, though an unwise or perfidious one. A law violating a constitution established by the people themselves would be considered by the judges as null and void. Secondly, the doctrine laid down by the law of nations in the case of treaties is that a breach of any one article by any of the parties, frees the other parties from their engagements. In the case of a union of people under one constitution, the nature of the pact has always been understood to exclude such an interpretation. Comparing the two modes in point of expediency, he thought all the considerations which recommended the convention in preference to the legislatures for examining and adopting it.

Only through ratification by the people could there be an express repudiation of a compact or confederation of sovereign states.

Another powerful consideration supporting popular ratification was of supreme practical importance: the expectation that the state governments would furnish the most formidable opposition to the Constitution, and that prospects for ratification would be enhanced if the decision were made by the people themselves. Thus, King thought on June 5 that a "convention being a single house, the adoption may more easily be carried through it than through the legislatures where there are several branches. The legislatures also being reluctant to lose power, will be most likely to raise objections. The people having already parted with the necessary powers, it is immaterial to them by which government they are possessed, provided they be well employed." And Randolph on July 23 stated that one idea "has pervaded all our proceedings, to wit, that opposition as well from the states as from individuals will be made to the system to be proposed. Will it not then be highly imprudent to furnish any unnecessary pretext by the mode of ratifying it?" The local demagogues whose importance was threatened, Randolph said, were the most likely source of opposition to the system. These men would try to prevent the people's being enlightened as to the virtues of the plan. "It is of great importance, therefore, that the consideration of this subject should be transferred from the legislatures where this class of men have their full influence to a field in which their efforts can be less mischievous," Randolph concluded.

On the same day Gorham set himself up against referring the plan to the legislatures.

> 1. Men chosen by the people for the particular purpose will discuss the subject more candidly than members of the legislature who are to lose the power which is to be given up to the general government.   2. Some of the legislatures are composed of several branches. It will consequently be more difficult in these cases to get the plan through the legislatures than through a convention.   3. In the states, many of the ablest men are excluded from the legislatures but may be elected into a convention. Among these may be ranked many of the clergy who are generally friends to good government. Their services were found to be valuable to the formation and establishment of the constitution of Massachusetts.   4. The legislatures will be interrupted with a variety of little business, by artfully pressing which, designing men will find means to delay from year to year, if not to frustrate altogether, the national system.

And Williamson agreed that "conventions were to be preferred as more likely to be composed of the ablest men in the states."

On August 31 Madison recommended that conventions be required: "among other reasons, for this, that the powers given to the general government, being taken from the state governments, the legislatures would be more disinclined than conventions composed in part at least of other men; and if disinclined, they could devise modes apparently promoting, but really thwarting, the ratification." On the same day Gouverneur Morris said "his object was to impress in stronger terms the necessity of calling conventions in order to prevent enemies to the plan from giving it the go-by. When it first appears, with the sanction of this convention, the people will be favorable to it. By degrees the state officers and those interested in the state governments will intrigue and turn the popular current against it."

Along with the fear of opposition by the state governments was the realization that if legislative ratification were tied to the unanimous consent requirement of the Articles, ratification would be impossible. As early as June 5 Wilson wished "to lead the committee by a train of observations to the idea of not suffering a disposition in the plurality of states to confederate anew on better principles, to be defeated by the inconsiderate or selfish opposition of a few states. He hoped the provision for ratifying would be put on such a footing as to admit of such a partial union, with a door open for the accession of the rest." Gorham on July 23 observed that, according to the last of the Articles, "the unanimous concurrence of the states will be necessary. But will any one say that all the states are to suffer themselves to be ruined, if Rhode Island should persist in her opposition to general measures? Some other states might also tread in her steps. The present advantage which New York seems to be so much attached to, of taxing her neighbors by the regulation of her trade, makes it very probable that she will be of the number. It would therefore deserve serious consideration whether provision ought not to be made for giving effect to the system without waiting for the unanimous concurrence of the states."

To obviate this difficulty, the draft of the Committee of Detail provided that "The ratification of the conventions of—states shall be sufficient for organizing this Constitution." On August 30, when this provision came before the convention, various proposals were made to fill the blank with the figures seven, eight, nine, and ten. Carroll moved to fill the blank with thirteen, "unanimity being necessary to dissolve the existing Confederacy which had been unanimously established."

It is interesting to note the views expressed by Madison and King as indicating their attitude toward state sovereignty. Madison remarked "that if the blank should be filled with 'seven,' 'eight,' or 'nine'—the Constitution as it stands might be put in force over the whole body of the people, though less than a majority of them should ratify it." And King, in response to Carroll's motion, "thought this amendment necessary; otherwise as the Constitution now stands, it will operate on the whole though ratified by a part only." Wilson, on the other hand, stated that as the Constitution stood, only the states which ratify could be bound. "We must," he said, "in this case go to the original powers of society. The house on fire must be extinguished, without a scrupulous regard to ordinary rights." To clarify this point, King the next day "moved to add to the end of Article XXI the words 'between the said states' so as to confine the operation of the government to the states ratifying it." This motion, which recognized the state sovereignty that existed under the Articles, carried, nine states to one.

Sherman then said he was not sure of "the propriety of authorizing less than all the states to execute the Constitution, considering the nature of the existing Confederation." Then Morris, somewhat inconsistently, considering his earlier position, moved "to strike out 'conventions of the' after 'ratifications,' leaving the states to pursue their own modes of ratification." He explained that he "meant to facilitate the adoption of the plan by leaving the modes approved by the several state constitutions to be followed." King objected, stating that "striking out 'conventions' as the requisite mode was equivalent to giving up the business altogether. Conventions alone, which will avoid all the obstacles from the complicated formation of the legislatures, will succeed and if not positively required by the plan," conventions will be opposed by the plan's enemies. Madison spoke out against this idea, and Gorham and the younger Pinckney "urged the expediency of 'conventions' for reasons formerly urged on a discussion of this question." Luther Martin held out for "a reference to the state legislatures. He urged the danger of commotions from a resort to the people and to first principles in which the governments might be on one side and the people on the other." The Morris motion was defeated, six states to four. Then Carroll's motion to fill the blank with "thirteen" was rejected, all the states against except Maryland. The convention also rejected "ten" and then voted, eight states to three, to fill the blank with "nine."

The convention made one further repudiation of state sovereignty before it completed its deliberations on ratification. The draft of the Committee of Detail, following a similar requirement in the original Virginia proposal, contained a provision that "This Constitution shall be laid before the United States in Congress assembled for their approbation." The difficulty with this proposal was that such approbation by Congress would have to be unanimous, since Congress operated under the Articles, and it was probable that Rhode Island (which was represented in Congress although not in the convention), Maryland, and New York, or any one of them, would vote against the Constitution. To preclude such an unfortunate occurrence, **Gouverneur Morris and the** younger Pinckney on August 31 moved "to strike out the words 'for their approbation.'" This motion carried, eight states to three. On September 10 Gerry moved to reconsider this action, stating that he "objected to proceeding to change the government without the approbation of Congress, as being improper and giving just umbrage to that body. He repeated his objections also to an annulment of the Confederation with so little scruple and formality," and also "urged the indecency and pernicious tendency of dissolving in so slight a manner, the solemn obligations of the Articles of Confederation."

But Wilson was vigorous in his opposition:

> He expressed in strong terms his disapprobation of the expedient proposed, particularly the suspending the plan on the approbation of Congress. He declared it to be worse than folly to rely on the concurrence of the Rhode Island members of Congress in the plan. Maryland has voted on this floor for

requiring the unanimous consent of the thirteen states to the proposed change in the federal system. New York has not been represented for a long time past in the convention. Many individual deputies from other states have spoken much against the plan. Under these circumstances, can it be safe to make the assent of Congress necessary? After spending four or five months in the laborious and arduous task of forming a government for our country, we are ourselves at the close throwing insuperable obstacles in the way of its success.

Gerry's motion to reinstate the words "for the approbation of Congress" was then defeated unanimously, thereby preventing an abortion of the Constitution by an exercise of state sovereignty.

XXVI

Blueprint for a Nation

IN THE end, thirty-nine of the forty-two delegates who were present at the close of the convention affixed their signatures to the completed Constitution. Luther Martin had returned to Maryland before the convention ended, and only Randolph, Mason, and Gerry refused to sign. Some of the reasons they gave are relevant. Randolph, for example, objected to what he called "the indefinite and dangerous power given by the Constitution to Congress," and particularly to "the general clause concerning necessary and proper laws." He protested against "the want of a more definite boundary between the general and state legislatures" and said he "considered it as strengthening the general objection against the plan that its definition of the powers of the government was so loose as to give it opportunities of usurping all the state powers." Although Randolph said he "had from the beginning . . . been convinced that radical changes in the system of the Union were necessary," the final product of the convention's labors was so nationalistic that he was unwilling "to promote the establishment of a plan which he verily believed would end in tyranny."

Mason declared on August 31 that "he would sooner chop off his right hand than put it to the Constitution as it now stands." He protested "the dangerous power and structure of the government, concluding that it would end either in monarchy, or a tyrannical aristocracy." He listed many specific objections, one of which was that, through "the general clause at the end of the enumerated powers, the Congress may . . . extend their powers as far as they shall think proper, so that the state legislatures have no security for the powers now presumed to remain to them, or the people for their rights." Another was that the "judiciary of the United States is so constructed and extended as to absorb and destroy the judiciaries of the several states." Mason concluded that "This government will set out a moderate aristocracy. It is at present impossible to foresee whether it will, in its operation, produce a monarchy, or a corrupt, tyrannical aristocracy. It will most probably vibrate some years between the two, and then terminate in the one or the other."

Gerry objected specifically to "the general power of the Legislature to make what laws they may please to call necessary and proper," and to the fact that "the times, places, and manner of choosing representatives [were] subjected to the general government." More generally, he alleged that the "sovereignty or liberty of the states will be destroyed, and the judicial will be oppressive."

In truth, the differences between the Articles and the Constitution were enormous. The Articles provided for a compact of sovereign states; the Constitution created a national government operating directly upon individuals. The Articles provided for a Congress which was an assemblage of ambassadors; the Constitution created a national legislature, with nationally prescribed methods of selection and qualifications, nationally compensated and endowed with national prerogatives with respect to such matters as tenure, contested elections, quorum, attendance, discipline, and so forth. The Congress provided by the Articles possessed relatively few powers; the Congress created by the Constitution was vested with vast and far-reaching powers whose scope and application were indeterminate. Under the Articles the prohibitions on the states were relatively few; under the Constitution they were greatly increased. Under the Articles there was no executive, no judiciary, no means of enforcing the few powers which Congress had or the few prohibitions on the states; under the Constitution there was a clear-cut and comprehensive declaration of the supremacy of national law over state law, with a national executive and a national judiciary as instrumentalities for the enforcement of that supremacy. Under the Articles, amendment required the consent of every state legislature; the Constitution could bind the states by amendments without their consent. The Articles were adopted by sovereign states; the Constitution was ratified by an act of popular sovereignty.

As one compares the two documents and studies the debates in the convention itself, it is impossible not to be impressed by the extent to which the nationalist philosophy was reflected in the Constitution and by the negligible effect of considerations based on state sovereignty. On fundamental principles, there was almost unanimous agreement: the state sovereignty diehards were few. On matters of detail and implementation, the nationalists repeatedly disagreed among themselves. As Part Two suggests, there was a nucleus of "advanced nationalists" headed by Madison, Wilson, and Gouverneur Morris. A larger group of delegates have been described as "moderate nationalists" to indicate that although sometimes they agreed with the "advanced" group, they frequently took positions more favorable to state power. The superior intellectual and forensic leadership of the "advanced" group served as a center to which were drawn a group of "moderates" whose composition varied on different questions. Almost invariably, the coalition was numerous enough to carry the vote for the "advanced" position. The outstanding exception to this pattern, of course, was produced by the question of representation.

What may be said of the position of the states in the new scheme of government set forth in the Constitution? The Constitution is crowded with provisions dealing specifically with the states. The states, for example, were to serve as electoral districts for members of both houses of Congress. Qualifications to vote for members of the House were to be the same as for the most numerous branch of the state legislature. Senators were to be elected by the state legislatures. The states were also to have the initial power to prescribe the times, places, and manner of holding national elections. Congress was given the power to regulate commerce among the several states. The states were to appoint presidential electors. In the event of no electoral majority, voting in the House was to be by states. The amending process was predicated upon the existence of the states. States were guaranteed their territorial integrity and a republican form of government. And prohibitions on the states demonstrate an *a fortiori* recognition of state power.

In sum, the Constitution expressly recognized the existence of the states as geographic and governmental entities with autonomous power, and contemplated their continued existence as essential constituent parts of the system. The convention recognized that, notwithstanding the increase in national power, there would remain an extensive range of functions and activities which were not of national importance. The framers contemplated that, in the performance of these local duties, the states would play a useful and essential role in the new system. In their relationship to each other, the states were recognized as separate and independent political units. This had been the pattern under the Articles and was to continue under the Constitution, as attested by the fact that, where the nature of the Union demanded, the Constitution provided otherwise. Thus, full faith and credit was to be given in every state to the public acts, records, and judicial proceedings of every other state, and the citizens of each state were to be entitled to all privileges and immunities of citizens in the several states. Throughout American constitutional history, judicial and political literature has referred to "state sovereignty" and "sovereign states" in instances where it is clear from the context that these terms were intended to mean: 1) the states as geographic and political entities; 2) the autonomy of the state's governmental power; or 3) the relationship of the states to each other.

The term "state sovereignty" has been used here, however, in the context of the relationship of the states to the central government. The states were sovereign under the Articles because there was no superior authority, either in law or in fact, to which they were required to yield; the states were therefore *de jure* and *de facto* supreme. In this sense, the record leaves little room for doubt that the Founding Fathers consciously and intentionally abandoned and repudiated a system based on state sovereignty. This conclusion is supported by a comparative analysis of the Articles and the Constitution and the study of the actual drafting of the Constitution. Furthermore, this was the understanding of the delegates themselves. Yates and Lansing left the convention in July for the very reason that the plan being developed was destructive of state sovereignty. Randolph, Mason, and Gerry refused to sign for the reason, among others, that the Constitution was too destructive of state power. And on October 24, 1787, Madison, setting forth his observations of the work of the convention in a letter to Jefferson in Paris, wrote: "It appeared to be the sincere and unanimous wish of the convention to cherish and preserve the Union of the states. No proposition was made, no suggestion was thrown out, in favor of a partition of the empire into two or more Confederacies. It was generally agreed that the objects of the Union could not be secured by any system founded on the principle of a confederation of sovereign states."

Part Four:
The Ratification
of the
Constitution

XXVII

The Formation
of Public Opinion

IMMEDIATELY after the signing of the Constitution on September 17, 1787, the convention resolved that "the preceding Constitution be laid before the United States in Congress assembled, and that it is the opinion of the convention, that it should afterwards be submitted to a convention of delegates, chosen in each state by the people thereof, under the recommendation of its legislature, for their assent and ratification, and that each convention assenting to, and ratifying the same, should give notice thereof to the United States in Congress assembled." Then there followed a recommended procedure for establishing and inaugurating the operation of the new government.

As president of the convention, Washington sent along with the constitution a transmittal letter which significantly emphasized the transcendence of national over local interests:

The friends of our country have long seen and desired, that the power of making war, peace, and treaties, that of levying money and regulating commerce, and the corresponding executive and judicial authorities should be fully and effectually vested in the general government of the Union. . . . It is obviously impracticable in the federal government of these states, to secure all rights of independent sovereignty to each, and yet provide for the interest and safety of all. . . . It is at all times difficult to draw with precision the line between those rights which must be surrendered, and those which may be reserved; and on the present occasion this difficulty was increased by a difference among the several states as to their situation, extent, habits, and particular interests. . . . In all our deliberations on this subject we kept steadily in our view, that which appears to us the greatest interest of every true American, the consolidation of our Union, in which is involved our prosperity, felicity, safety, perhaps our national existence.

Congress, which was sitting in New York at the time, received the

Constitution, the convention resolution, and Washington's transmittal letter on September 20. Although, as Bancroft put it, the impression was that Congress was being invited by these documents "to light its own funeral pyre," a clear majority in Congress was in favor of submitting the Constitution to the states for popular decision. Ten of the thirty-three members of Congress had been delegates to the convention. This majority would have liked the submission to be unanimous and to carry with it the recommendation and approval of Congress.

There was, however, a strong opposition organized under the leadership of Richard Henry Lee, Nathan Dane of Massachusetts, and Melancton Smith of New York. This group first argued that Congress had no power under the Articles to accede to the convention's recommendation. Failing in this, they sought then to attach amendments to the Constitution before it went forth to the people. It soon became obvious that the opposition could not prevent the submission but could prevent its being unanimous. Their price for unanimous submission was that Congress should use no words which would constitute a stamp of approval of the Constitution. Under this compromise, therefore, Congress on September 28 unanimously resolved "that the said report with the resolutions and letter accompanying the same be transmitted to the several legislatures in order to be submitted to a convention of delegates chosen in each state by the people thereof in conformity to the resolves of the convention made and provided in that case."

In the meantime, the Constitution had been reprinted in all the leading journals and newspapers of the states, with the result that supporters and opponents were already forming into recognizable and cohesive groups, which quickly became known as Federalists and Antifederalists. Actually, the term "federal" had been used previously as a word of art to designate the confederation-type government of the Articles, whereas the government created by the Constitution was denominated in the convention a "national" one. According to this previously accepted meaning, the opponents of the Constitution were the true federalists and its supporters were nationalists. The politically sagacious supporters of the Constitution realized that to campaign for its ratification as "Nationalists" might arouse the fears of many people. They therefore shrewdly pre-empted for themselves the label Federalists, simultaneously placating popular opinion and leaving to the opponents of the Constitution the negative style of Anti-federalists.

For the next year debate and discussion over the Constitution was the principal topic of interest throughout the states. In public meetings and private conversation, in letters to the newspapers, in essays and pamphlets, by every means of communication available, the merits and demerits of the Constitution were analyzed and explicated. In several of the state conventions the struggle over ratification was bitter and hard fought and the victory of the Constitution a narrow one. During the course of the ratification campaigns, dozens of objections were levied against the Constitution, but it seems fair to say that most of these were comprehended under two general headings—that the Constitution would destroy the sovereignty of the states, and that the Constitution had no bill of rights as a protection of personal freedom. The purpose of this part is to examine a representative sampling of the contemporary literature and the debates in the state conventions, to determine the understanding of the people of America as to the effect the Constitution would have upon the sovereignty of the states.

Literature Opposing the Constitution

LETTERS OF A FEDERAL FARMER

Richard Henry Lee had represented Virginia in the Continental Congress and had moved the resolutions which had led to the Declaration of Independence and the Articles of Confederation. He served also in the Confederation Congress and had been appointed a member of the Philadelphia convention, although he had declined to serve. As an aristocrat, Lee was notable for his sympathy with democratic causes; he was a long-time political ally of Patrick Henry. He opposed the Constitution in Congress on its referral by the convention, and continued his opposition throughout the ratification campaign. His *Letters of a Federal Farmer* were perhaps the ablest of the Anti-federalist writings. The first series of these letters, upon which the ensuing discussion is based, were published first in October 1787; they were widely reprinted and circulated throughout the states.

Lee stated at the outset that on careful examination of the plan of government proposed by the convention, he considered it "to be a plan retaining some federal features; but to be the first important step, and to aim strongly at one consolidated government of the United States." Admitting the inadequacy of the Articles, Lee said: "Our object has been all along to reform our federal system, and to strengthen our governments—to establish peace, order, and justice in the community —but a new object now presents. The plan of government now proposed is evidently calculated totally to change, in time, our condition as a people. Instead of being thirteen republics, under a federal head, it is clearly designed to make us one consolidated government."

To Lee it was clear that the Constitution was the culmination of a carefully planned program on the part of nationalists. "This consolidation of the states has been the object of several men in this country for some time past. . . . To have a just idea of the government before us, and to show that a consolidated one is the object in view, it is necessary not only to examine the plan, but also its history, and the politics of its particular friends." Referring to the Confederation, Lee found, therefore, "members of Congress urging alterations in the federal system almost as soon as it was adopted." Adverting to the enactment by state legislatures of tender, suspension, and paper money laws, Lee said that through these and other precedents, "several orders of men in the community have been prepared, by degrees, for a change of government; and this very abuse of power in the legislatures, which in some cases has been charged upon the democratic part of the community, has furnished aristocratical men with those very weapons, and those very means, with which, in great measure, they are rapidly effecting their favorite object."

Lee then elaborated upon the unfolding of the plot. After men's minds had grown sufficiently uneasy, partly because of acknowledged evils, and partly because of "secret instigations of artful men," Lee said, "a bold step was taken. . . . A general convention for mere commercial purpose was moved for—the authors of this measure saw that the people's attention was turned solely to the amendment of the federal system; and that, had the idea of a total change been started, probably no state would have appointed members to the convention. The idea of destroying ultimately, the state governments, and forming one consolidated system, could not have been admitted—a convention, therefore, merely for vesting in Congress power to regulate trade was proposed. . . . September, 1786, a few men from the middle states met at Annapolis, and hastily proposed a convention to be held in May, 1787, for the purpose, generally, of amending the Confederation." There was still no mention, Lee said, of destroying the old Constitution or framing a new one.

The states still unsuspecting, and "not aware that they were passing the Rubicon," appointed members to the new convention for the sole and express purpose of revising and amending the Confederation —and "probably not one man in ten thousand in the United States, till within these ten or twelve days, had an idea that the old ship was to be destroyed, and he put to the alternative of embarking in the new ship presented, or of being left in danger of sinking—the states, I believe, universally supposed the convention would report alterations in the Confederation, which would pass an examination in Congress, and after being agreed to there, would be confirmed by all the legislatures, or be rejected. . . . Here the favorite moment for changing the government was evidently discerned by a few men, who seized it with address."

With some self-reproach, Lee lamented the failure of "many good republican characters" to attend the convention. "The non-attendance of eight or nine men, who were appointed members of the convention, I shall ever consider as a very unfortunate event to the United States. Had they attended, I am pretty clear that the result of the convention would not have had that strong tendency to aristocracy now discernible in every part of the plan. There would not have been so great an accumulation of power, especially as to the internal police of this country in a few hands as the Constitution reported proposes to vest in them—the young visionary men, and the consolidating aristocracy, would have been more restrained than they have been." As a matter of fact, he continued, "these aristocrats support and hasten the adoption of the proposed Constitution, merely because they think it a stepping stone to their favorite object. I think I am well founded in this idea; I think the general politics of these men support it, as well as the common observation among them, that the proffered plan is the best that can be got at present, it will do for a few years, and lead to something better."

As Lee read the Constitution, it was clear to him that the potential was there for eventually accomplishing such a degree of centralized power and law as to virtually reduce the states to political ciphers. "The powers lodged in the general government, if exercised by it, must intimately affect the internal police of the states, as well as external concerns." All essential powers, Lee said, will be in possession of the central government, "at least on paper, and those of the states a mere shadow of power. And therefore, unless the people shall make some great exertions to restore to the state governments their powers in matters of internal police; as the powers to lay and collect, exclusively, internal taxes, to govern the militia, and to hold the decisions of their own judicial courts upon their own laws final, the balance cannot possibly continue long; but the state governments must be annihilated, or continue to exist for no purpose."

Lee said that it was necessary to scrutinize the extent of the proposed powers and how they might operate.

> These powers, legislative, executive, and judicial, respect internal as well as external objects. Those respecting external objects, as all foreign concerns, commerce, imposts, all causes arising on the seas, peace and war, and Indian affairs, can be lodged nowhere else, with any propriety, but in this government. Many powers that respect internal objects ought clearly to be lodged in it; as those to regulate trade between the states, weights and measures, the coin or current monies, post offices, naturalization, etc. These powers may be exercised without essentially affecting the internal police of the respective states. But powers to lay and collect internal taxes, to form the militia, to make bankrupt laws, and to decide on appeal, questions arising on the internal laws of the respective states, are of a very serious nature, and carry with them almost all other powers. These taken in connection with the others, and powers to raise armies and build navies, proposed to be lodged in this government, appear to me to comprehend all the essential powers in this community, and those which will be left to the states will be of no great importance.

Lee also called attention to the latitudinal nature of the "necessary and proper" clause. "It is proper the national laws should be supreme, and superior to state or district laws; but then the national laws ought to yield to unalienable or fundamental rights—and national laws, made by a few men, should extend only to a few national objects. This will not be the case with the laws of Congress. To have any proper idea of their extent, we must carefully examine the legislative, executive, and judicial powers proposed to be lodged in the general government, and consider them in connection with a general clause in Article I, Section 8, in these words . . ." At this point, Lee quoted the "necessary and proper" clause. "The powers of this government, as has been observed, extend to internal as well as external objects, and to those objects to which all others are subordinate; it is almost impossible to have a just conception of their powers, or of the extent and number of the laws which may be deemed necessary and proper to carry them into effect, till we shall come to exercise those powers and make the laws." And when that time came, Lee said, there was a presumption "that men who govern will in doubtful cases construe laws and constitutions most favorably for increasing their own powers."

Referring to the supremacy clause, Lee gave a solemn warning: adoption of the Constitution would be the "last and supreme act" of the people. The Constitution and all laws proceeding from it would, whenever the occasion arose, abolish completely "the ancient customs, rights, . . . laws, or the [state] constitutions heretofore established in the United States." Treaties made under the aegis of the United States would also be "the supreme law. It is not said that these treaties shall be made in pursuance of the Constitution—nor are there any constitutional bounds set to those who shall make them. The President and two-thirds of the Senate will be empowered to make treaties indefinitely, and when these treaties shall be made, they will also abolish all laws and state constitutions incompatible with them."

THE LETTERS OF AGRIPPA

Eighteen of these letters appeared in the *Massachusetts Gazette* between November 1787 and February 1788. They were the most effective Anti-federalist writings published in Massachusetts, authorship being attributed to James Winthrop. One of the letters asserts that speculation concerning the identity of the writer is "conjectural," but Winthrop himself did not deny their authorship. The letters are, in any event, consistent with Winthrop's own views, for his opposition to the Constitution defeated his election from Cambridge as a delegate to the Massachusetts convention.

The best kind of government for America, thought Agrippa, was "a *Federal Republic*. By this kind of government each state reserves to itself the right of making and altering its laws for internal regulation, and the right of executing those laws without any external restraint, while the general concerns of the empire are committed to an assembly of delegates, each accountable to his own constituents. This is the happy form under which we live." Proceeding, Agrippa observed that the country is "now, in the strictest sense of the term, a federal republic. Each part has within its own limits the sovereignty over its citizens, while some of the general concerns are committed to Congress." The only deficiencies Agrippa could discover in the old plan could have been cured by two new articles. "By one a limited revenue would be given to Congress with a right to collect it, and by the other a limited right to regulate our intercourse with foreign nations."

The Constitution, on the other hand, was something different. Agrippa felt that the Constitution contained built-in problems quite like those in state constitutions. "It is a compact among the *people* for the purposes of government, and not [like the Articles] a compact between states. It begins in the name of the people, and not of the states." Furthermore, Agrippa said, "It is evident . . . that the new Constitution proposes to delegate greater powers than are granted to our own government." It would, he said, give "more numerous and extensive powers" to Congress "than to any state legislature upon the continent." So limitless, in fact, were the powers of Congress that "the direct tendency of the proposed system is to consolidate the whole empire into one mass and, like the tyrant's bed, to reduce all to one standard."

Throughout his letters Agrippa continually sought to demonstrate "that the proposed Constitution is an actual consolidation of the separate states into one extensive commonwealth." In the fourth letter, he wrote:

> Yet there is, I believe, not one point of legislation that is not surrendered in the proposed plan. Questions of every kind respecting property are determinable in a continental court, and so are all kinds of criminal causes. The continental legislature has, therefore, a right to make rules in all cases by which their judicial courts shall proceed and decide causes. No rights are reserved to the citizens. The laws of Congress are in all cases to be the supreme law of the land, and paramount to the constitutions of the individual states. The Congress may institute what modes of trial they please, and no plea drawn from the Constitution of any state can avail. The new system is, therefore, a consolidation of all the states into one large mass, however diverse the parts may be of which it is to be composed.

Agrippa said in his fifth letter, that the "idea of consolidation is further kept up in the right given to regulate trade. Though this power under certain limitations would be a proper one for the department of Congress, it is in this system carried much too far, and much farther than is necessary." Agrippa returned to this point in the thirteenth letter: "By Section 8 of Article I, Congress are to have the unlimited right to regulate commerce, external and *internal*. . . . They have also the unlimited right to imposts and all kinds of taxes, as well to levy as to collect them. They have indeed very nearly the same powers claimed formerly by the British Parliament."

The scope of Congress' powers also concerned Agrippa in the tenth letter. "By Article 3, Section 2, Congress are empowered to appoint courts with authority to try civil causes of every kind, and even offenses against particular states. By the last clause of Article I, Section 8, which defines their legislative powers, they are authorized to make laws for carrying into execution all the 'powers vested by this Constitution in the government of the United States, or in *any department* or officer thereof;' and by Article VI, the judges in every state are to be bound by the laws of Congress. It is therefore a complete consolidation of all the states into one, however diverse the parts of it may be." The thirteenth letter amplified this point:

> In Article III, Section 2, it is declared, that 'the judicial power shall extend to all cases in law and equity arising under this Constitution, the laws of the United States, and treaties made or which shall be made under their authority.' Among the cases arising under this new Constitution are reckoned, 'all controversies between citizens of different states,' which include all kinds of civil causes between those parties. The giving Congress a power to appoint courts for such a purpose is as much, there being no stipulation to the contrary, giving them power to legislate for such causes, as giving them a right to raise an army is giving them a right to direct the operations of the army when raised. But it is not left to implication. The last clause of Article I, Section 8, expressly gives them power.

Here, Agrippa, like Lee, quoted the "necessary and proper" clause. Agrippa concluded that Congress therefore has, under the Constitution, the power to pass almost every kind of law

> respecting property between citizens of different states. That this power extends to all cases between citizens of the same state, is evident from the sixth article, which declares all continental laws and treaties to be the *supreme law* of the land, and that all state judges are bound thereby, *anything in the constitution or laws of any state to the contrary notwithstanding.'* If this is not binding the judges of the separate states in their own office, by continental rules, it is perfect nonsense. There is then a complete consolidation of the legislative powers in all cases respecting property. . . . These are necessary parts of the new system, and it will never be complete till they are reduced to practice. They effectually prove a consolidation of all the states.

Agrippa realized that these changes would not all come about in a single year. But six years would probably be enough. Once the system was adopted, "in every doubtful case it is an established rule to decide in favor of authority."

Agrippa closed his letters with this final warning: "It is to be remembered too, that if you are so far charmed with eloquence, and misled by fair representation and charitable constructions, as to adopt an undefined system, there will be no saying afterwards that you were mistaken, and wish to correct it. *It will then be the Constitution of our country, and entitled to defense.*"

THE LETTERS OF CATO

Another Roman worthy's name was chosen for the pseudonym of George Clinton, whose seven "Cato" letters appeared in the *New York Journal* between September 1787 and January 1788. Clinton, elected governor of New York seven times, served consecutively from 1777 to 1795. Due to the commercial advantages accruing to New York because of its strategic geographic situation, Clinton had opposed the grant of national revenue and commercial powers to Congress during the Confederation and likewise opposed the Constitution. In addition, as governor, he had built a powerful political machine. His defense of state sovereignty was therefore based in part at least upon his fear of playing a reduced role in a new national system. The *Letters of Cato* ended abruptly, but additional epistles probably had been contemplated. These may have been left unwritten because of the convening of the New York assembly and Clinton's preoccupation with other political matters.

Cato first gave a historical glimpse of the convention and Congress:

> The states in Congress suggested that the Articles of Confederation had provided for making alterations in the Confederation—that there were defects therein, and as a means to remedy which, a convention of delegates, appointed by the different states, was resolved expedient to be held for the sole and express purpose of revising it, and reporting to Congress and the different legislatures such alterations and provisions therein as should (when agreed to in Congress and confirmed by the several states) render the federal Constitution adequate to the exigencies of government. . . . For the sole and express purpose aforesaid a Convention of delegates is formed at Philadelphia. What have they done? Have they revised the Confederation, and has Congress agreed to their report? Neither is the fact. This Convention have exceeded their authority given to them, and have transmitted to Congress a new political fabric, essentially and fundamentally distinct and different from it, in which the different states do not retain separately their sovereignty and independence, united by a Confederate league—but one entire sovereignty, a consolidation of them into one government—in which new provisions and powers are not made and vested in Congress, but in an assembly, Senate and President, who are not known in the Articles of Confederation. . . . This new government, therefore, was founded in usurpation.

According to Cato, the new form of government would consolidate all thirteen parts into "one great whole." This consolidation, Cato felt was unattainable. "But whoever seriously considers the immense extent of territory comprehended within the limits of the United States, together with the variety of its climates, productions, and commerce, the difference of extent, and number of inhabitants in all; the dissimilitude of interest, morals, and politics, in almost every one, will receive it as an intuitive truth, that a consolidated republican form of government therein, can never *form a perfect union, establish justice, insure domestic tranquility, promote the general welfare, and secure the blessings of liberty to you and your posterity."* He then asked: "From this picture, what can you promise yourselves, on the score of consolidation of the United States into one government?" Answering his own inquiry, Cato warned that "you must risk much, by indispensably placing trusts of the greatest magnitude, into the hands of individuals whose ambition for power, and aggrandizement, will oppress and grind you —where from the vast extent of your territory, and the complication of interests, the science of government will become intricate and perplexed, and too mysterious for you to understand and observe."

Cato emphasized the indefinite nature of the powers granted to the new national government. After noting that "the language of the article relative to the establishment of the executive of this new government was vague and inexplicit," he added that he could not "help remarking that inexplicitness seems to pervade this whole political fabric," and asked his readers "whence is it therefore that you are about to precipitate yourselves into a sea of uncertainty, and adopt a system so vague, and which has discarded so many of your valuable rights?" "Hitherto," he said, "we have tied up our rulers in the exercise of their duties by positive restrictions; if the cord has been drawn too tight, loosen it to the necessary extent, but do not entirely unbind them. I am no enemy to placing a reasonable confidence in them, but such an unbounded one as the advocates and framers of this new system advise you to, would be dangerous to your liberties; it has been the ruin of other governments, and will be yours, if you adopt with all its latitudinal power."

ADDRESS TO THE PEOPLE OF THE STATE OF NEW YORK, BY A PLEBEIAN
This address was written sometime in early 1788 by Melancton Smith, a prominent and influential merchant and lawyer. Smith was a member of the Continental Congress from New York from 1785 to 1788 and was a political ally of Governor Clinton. Smith opposed the Constitution as a member of the New York convention, but when news arrived of Virginia's ratification he broke the anti-federal ranks and announced his support.

Previous to the meeting of the convention, the subject of a new form of government had been little thought of, and scarcely written upon at all. It is true, it was the general opinion, that some alterations were requisite in the federal system. This subject had been contemplated by almost every thinking man in the Union. It has been the subject of many well-written essays, and it was the anxious wish of every true friend to America. But it was never in the contemplation of one in a thousand of those who had reflected on the matter to have an entire change in the nature of our federal government—to alter it from a confederation of states, to that of one entire government, which will swallow up that of the individual states. I will venture to say that the idea of a government similar to the one proposed, never entered the minds of the legislatures who appointed the convention, and of but very few of the members who composed it, until they had assembled and heard it proposed in that body; much less had the people any conception of such a plan until after it was promulgated. When it was agitated, the debates of the convention were kept an impenetrable secret, and no opportunities were given for well-informed men to offer their sentiments upon the subject.

Smith then undertook to "show that in the leading and most important objections that have been made to the plan, there has been and is an entire concurrence of opinion among writers and in public bodies throughout the United States." The very first one of these objections which the writer set forth was this: "It has been objected to that the new system, that it is calculated to, and will effect such a consolidation of the states, as to supplant and overturn the state governments. In this the minority of Pennsylvania, the opposition in Massachusetts, and all the writers of any ability or note in Philadelphia, New York, and Boston concur. It may be added that this appears to have been the opinion of the Massachusetts convention, and gave rise to that article in the amendments proposed, which confines the general government to the exercise only of powers expressly given."

Smith then listed some of the other objections which had been made to the Constitution. "The Constitution has been opposed because it gives to the legislature an unlimited power of taxation both with respect to direct and indirect taxes. . . . The opposers of the Constitution have said that it is dangerous because the judicial power may extend to many cases which ought to be reserved to the decision of the state courts. . . . The power of the general legislature to alter and regulate the time, place, and manner of holding elections, has been stated as an argument against the adoption of the system . . . the little degree of responsibility under which the great officers of government will be held, and the liberty granted by the system to establish and maintain a standing army without any limitation or restriction, are also objected to the Constitution."

WRITINGS OF LUTHER MARTIN

On November 29, 1787, Martin delivered to the Maryland legislature a report of the proceedings of the Constitutional Convention. Thereafter the speech was revised, considerably amplified and reprinted as a pamphlet entitled *Genuine Information,* which was circulated throughout the states by Anti-federalists.

There were in the convention, Martin said, three recognizable "parties":

> There was one party, whose object and wish it was to abolish and annihilate all state governments, and to bring forward one general government over this extensive continent. Those who openly avowed this sentiment were, it is true, but few; yet it is equally true that there was a considerable number, who did not openly avow it, who were . . . in reality favorers of that sentiment; and acting upon those principles, covertly endeavoring to carry into effect what they well knew openly and avowedly could not be accomplished. The second party was not for the abolition of the state governments . . . but they wished to establish such a system as could give their own states undue power and influence in the government over the other states. A third party was what I considered truly federal and republican. . . . This party were for proceeding upon terms of federal equality; they were for taking our present federal system as the basis of their proceedings.

What happened in the convention which made a document like the Constitution possible was that "those who wished the total abolition of state governments, well knowing that a government founded on truly federal principles, the basis of which were the thirteen state governments preserved in full force and energy, would be destructive of their views; and knowing they were too weak in numbers openly to bring forward their system; conscious also that the people of America would reject it if proposed to them—joined their interest with that party who wished a system giving particular states the power and influence over the others, procuring in return mutual sacrifices from them, in giving the government great and undefined powers as to its legislative and executive; well knowing that, by departing from a federal system, they paved the way for their favorite object, the destruction of the state governments."

Martin said he and other members of the third party had urged in the Convention that:

the government we were forming was not in reality a federal, but a national government, not founded on the principles of the preservation, but the abolition or consolidation of all state governments; . . . that we had not been sent to form a government over the inhabitants of America, considered as individuals; that as individuals, they were all subject to their respective state governments . . . that the system of government we were entrusted to prepare was a government over these thirteen states; but that, in our proceedings, we adopted principles which would be right and proper only on the supposition that there were no state governments at all, but that all the inhabitants of this extensive continent were, in their individual capacity, without government, and in a state of nature.

Martin noted that the Constitution "is, in its very introduction, declared to be a compact between the people of the United States, as individuals; and it is to be ratified by the people at large, in their capacity as individuals; all of which, it was said, would be quite right and proper if there were no state governments, if all the people of this continent were in a state of nature, and we were forming one national government for them as individuals."

He and his party, Martin said, had urged "that the principles on which a federal government over states ought to be constructed and ratified, are the reverse; that instead of the legislature consisting of two branches, one branch was sufficient . . . the representation, instead of being drawn from the people at large, as individuals, ought to be drawn from the states as states, in their sovereign capacity; that, in a federal government, the parties to the compact are not the people, as individuals, but the states, as states; and that it is by the states as states, in their sovereign capacity, that the system of government ought to be ratified, and not by the people, as individuals." Martin and his faction had therefore opposed the Constitution because they viewed it "as a national, not a federal government, as calculated and designed not to protect and preserve, but to abolish and annihilate the state governments."

As a matter of fact, Martin wrote, "so far were the friends of the system from pretending that they meant it, or considered it as a federal system, that on the question being proposed 'that a union of the states, merely federal, ought to be the sole object of the exercise of the powers vested in the convention,' it was negatived by a majority of the members, and it was resolved 'that a national government ought to be formed.'" Advocates of the system later excised the term "national," as potentially alarming, and now they call themselves "federalists."

But, said Martin, "in convention the distinction was quite the reverse; those who opposed the system were there considered and styled the federal party, those who advocated it, the anti-federal."

The only federal feature of the system, Martin wrote, was the equal representation in the Senate and appointment of Senators by state legislatures. But, he continued, this arrangement only *appeared* to be federal. To prove this, "and that the Senate as constituted could not be a security for the protection and preservation of the state governments, and that the Senators could not be justly considered the representatives of the states, as states," Martin called attention to the Senators' fixed term of office, their being paid out of the national treasury, and the states' lacking any power of recall, all of which made Senators unanswerable to the state as they would be in a truly federal system. The conclusion was that "for six years the Senators are rendered totally and absolutely independent of their states, of whom they ought to be the representatives, without any bond or tie between them. During that time, they may join in measures ruinous and destructive to their states, even such as should totally annihilate their state governments, and their states cannot recall them, nor exercise any control over them."

Martin then singled out certain powers of Congress for specific analysis and criticism. Congress' power to control the time, place, and manner of elections, he said, was "a provision expressly looking forward to, and, I have no doubt designed for, the utter extinction and abolition of all state governments; nor will this, I believe, be doubted by any person, when I inform you that some of the warm advocates and patrons of the system, in convention, strenuously opposed the choice of the Senators by the state legislatures, insisting that the state governments ought not to be introduced in any manner, so as to be component parts of, or instruments for carrying into execution, the general government."

Of Congress' power to lay and collect taxes, he remarked that "under the pretense of securing the collection of these duties, and to prevent the laws which imposed them from being evaded, the Congress may bring the decision of all questions relating to the conveyance, disposition, and rights of property, and every question relating to contracts between man and man, into the courts of the general government." He himself had proposed in the convention that this power of direct taxation of individuals should not be operative unless a state were delinquent in remitting its quota of revenue to the national treasury, but "the proposition was rejected by a majority, consistently with their aim and desire of increasing the power of the general government, as far as possible, and destroying the powers and influence of the states."

He opposed Congress' power to create tribunals inferior to the Supreme Court: "to have inferior courts appointed under the authority of Congress in the different states, would eventually absorb and swallow up the state judiciaries, by drawing all business from them to the courts of the general government, which the extensive and undefined powers, legislative and judicial, of which it is possessed, would easily enable it to do."

The militia, Martin observed, "the only defense and protection which the state can have for the security of their rights against arbitrary encroachments of the general government, is taken entirely out of the power of their respective states, and placed under the power of Congress." Indeed, members of the convention had admitted that congressional control of the militia could be used as a check upon the states. "They said that, as the states would be opposed to the general government, and at enmity with it, which, as I have already observed, they assumed as a principle, if the militia was under the control and the authority of the respective states, it would enable them to thwart and oppose the general government. They said, the states ought to be at the mercy of the general government, and therefore the militia ought to be put under its power, and not suffered to remain under the power of the respective states."

Martin also discussed the provision relating to treason. "The time may come when it shall be the duty of a state, in order to preserve itself from the oppression of the general government, to have recourse to the sword." Then both the state and its citizens would be guilty of treason. The provision therefore gives states no choice but "that they must tamely and passively yield to despotism, or their citizens must oppose it at the hazard of the halter if unsuccessful." Citizens "of the state which shall take arms" will be reduced "to a situation in which they must be exposed to punishment, let them act as they will; since, if they obey the authority of their state governments, they will be guilty of treason against the United States; if they join the general government, they will be guilty of treason against their own state." Martin said that in order to "save the citizens of the respective states from this disagreeable dilemma, and to secure them from being punishable as traitors to the United States, when acting expressly in obedience to the authority of their own state," he had introduced an amendment to the section which would have provided "that no act or acts done by one or more of the states against the United States, or by any citizen of any one of the United States, under the authority of one or more of the said states, shall be deemed treason, or punished as such; but, in case of war being levied by one or more of the states against the United States, the conduct of each party toward the other, and their adherents respectively, shall be regulated by the laws of war and of nations." Martin's provision, however, "was not adopted, being too much opposed to the great object of many of the leading members of the convention, which was, by all means to leave the states at the mercy of the general government, since they could not suceed in their immediate and entire abolition."

Martin wrote, in addition to the *Genuine Information,* a series of letters to the *Maryland Journal* which were published in January, February, and March, 1788. These letters started out as a reply to Oliver Ellsworth's *Letters of a Landholder* but expanded into a more general attack on the Constitution.

In one of these letters Martin explained his purpose in introducing what later became the supremacy clause of the Constitution and explained how it was transformed by the convention. "To place the matter in a proper point of view, it will be necessary to state, that as the propositions were reported by the committee of the whole house, a power was given to the general government to negative the laws passed by the state legislatures, a power which I considered as totally inadmissible; in substitution of this I proposed the following clause, which you will find very materially different from the clause adopted by the Constitution. . . ." (Here Martin set forth the clause as he introduced it.) When Martin's substitute clause was introduced, it still had not been established "that inferior continental courts should be appointed for trial of all questions arising on treaties and on the laws of the general government." Martin wished and hoped

that every question of that kind would have been determined in the first instance in the courts of the respective states; had this been the case . . . if such treaties or laws were inconsistent with our constitution and bill of rights, the judiciaries of this state would be bound to reject the first and abide by the last, since in the form I introduced the clause, notwithstanding treaties and the laws of the general government were intended to be superior to the laws of our state government, where they should be opposed to each other, yet that they were not proposed nor meant to be superior to our constitution and bill of rights. It was afterwards altered and amended (if it can be called an amendment) to the form in which it stands in the system now published, and as inferior continental, and not state courts, are originally to decide on those questions. It is now worse than useless, for being so altered as to render the treaties and laws made under the general government superior to our constitution, if the system is adopted it will amount to a total and unconditional surrender to that government, by the citizens of this state, of every right and privilege secured to them by our constitution, and an express compact and stipulation with the general government that it may, at its discretion, make laws in direct violation of those rights.

Martin said he was persuaded that "some of the principal framers of the Constitution" had as their object "the total abolition and destruction of all state governments, and the erection on their ruins of one great and extensive empire." As for the Constitution itself, Martin saw it as a "hotch-potch":

a system which is an innovation in government of the most extraordinary kind; a system neither wholly federal, nor wholly national—but a strange hotch-potch of both—just so much federal in appearance as to give its advocates in some measure, an opportunity of passing it as such upon the unsuspecting multitude, before they had time and opportunity to examine it, and yet so predominantly national as to put it in the power of its movers, whenever the machine shall be set agoing, to strike out every part that has the appearance of being federal, and to render it wholly and entirely a national government."

Martin used a striking analogy to illustrate his point. "The conduct of the advocates and framers of this system toward the thirteen states, in pretending that it was designed for their advantage, and gradually obtaining power after power to the general government, which could not but end in their slavery," Martin said, was like "the conduct of a number of jockeys who had thirteen young colts to break." At first, the jockeys make a show of kindness, giving to the colts "a lock of hay, or a handful of oats, and stroking them while they eat, until being rendered sufficiently gentle they suffer a halter to be put round their necks." Having won the colts' confidence, "the jockeys slip a curb bridle on their heads and the bit into their mouths, after which the saddle follows of course, and well booted and spurred, with good whips in their hands, they mount and ride them at their pleasure, and although [the colts] may kick and flounce a little at first, not being able to get rid of their riders, they soon become as tame and as passive as their masters could wish them."

Literature Supporting the Constitution

LETTERS OF A LANDHOLDER

Written by Oliver Ellsworth, these thirteen letters were published simultaneously in the *Connecticut Courant* at Hartford and the *American Mercury* at Litchfield. They appeared between November 1787 and March 1788, and were reprinted and circulated widely throughout the northern and middle states. Much of the material in the letters constituted attacks on Gerry and Martin, both of whom, of course, made replies.

The "Landholder" addressed his appeal for approval of the Constitution to other landholders, declaring, "Every foreign prohibition on American trade is aimed in the most deadly manner against the holders and tillers of the land, and they are the men made poor. Your only remedy is such a national government as will make the country respectable; such a supreme government as can boldly meet the supremacy of proud and self-interested nations. The regulation of trade ever was and ever will be a national matter. A single state in the American union cannot direct much less control it. This must be a work of the whole, and requires all the wisdom and force of the continent."

At the present time, "Landholder" said, the states "devour and take every advantage of each other" like "thirteen contentious neighbors." Whereas we were once "dependent only on Great Britain, now we are dependent on every petty state in the world and on every custom house officer of foreign ports. If the injured apply for redress to the assemblies of the several states, it is in vain, for they are not, and cannot be known abroad. If they apply to Congress, it is also vain, for however wise and good that body may be, they have not power to vindicate either themselves or their subjects." "Landholder" warned that the American people were probably having their last chance "to adopt a government which gives all protection to personal liberty, and at the same time promises fair to afford you all the advantages of a sovereign empire." He asserted that "A government capable of controlling the whole, and bringing its force to a point, is one of the prerequisites for national liberty."

Replying to Gerry's charge that some of the powers of Congress were ambiguous, and others indefinite and dangerous, "Landholder" observed that because of "the imperfection of language" any "human composition" could be called "ambiguous and indefinite." No two men, he continued, "will express the same sentiment in the same manner, and by the same words; neither do they connect precisely the same ideas with the same words. From hence arises an ambiguity in all language, with which the most perspicuous and precise writers are in a degree chargeable."

Actually, "Landholder" said, "this Constitution . . . is expressed with brevity, and in the plain, common language of mankind. Had it swelled into the magnitude of a volume . . . had it been expressed in the scientific language of the law . . . had the powers given to the legislature been loaded with provisos, and such qualifications as a lawyer who is so cunning as even to suspect himself would probably have intermingled," in such event, "Landholder" said, "the people who are to be its judges would have neither patience nor opportunity to understand it."; "to the great body of the people" it would have been "altogether obscure," and "there would have been much more of a deception in the case."

Replying to the charge that the powers granted to the national government were excessive, "Landholder" asserted that it was not difficult to demonstrate that every congressional power was "necessary for national defense and justice."

> Their courts are not to intermeddle with your internal policy, and will have cognizance only of those subjects which are placed under the control of a national legislature. It is as necessary there should be courts of law and executive officers, to carry into effect the laws of the nation, as that there be courts and officers to execute the laws made by your state assemblies. There are many reasons why their decisions ought not to be left to courts instituted by particular states. A perfect uniformity must be observed throughout the whole Union, or jealousy and unrighteousness will take place; and for a uniformity one judiciary must pervade the whole. . . . A legislative power, without a judicial and executive under their own control, is in the nature of things a nullity. . . . In all these matters and powers given to Congress, their ordinances must be the supreme law of the land, or they are nothing. They must have authority to enact any laws for executing their own powers, or those powers will be evaded by the artful and unjust.

"Landholder" was not alarmed by allegations that state governments would be so changed as to be, in effect, dissolved. "No alteration in the state governments is even now proposed, but they are to remain identically the same that they are now. Some powers are to be given into the hands of your federal representatives, but these powers are all in their nature general, such as must be exercised by the whole or not at all, and such as are absolutely necessary; or your commerce, the price of your commodities, your riches and your safety, will be the sport of every foreign adventurer." The Constitution, in other words, will link the states "indissolubly," "Landholder" said. Summarizing the states' role in electing Senators, "Landholder" concluded: "State representation and government is the very basis of the congressional power proposed."

THE LETTERS OF FABIUS

These nine letters were written by John Dickinson and published in a Delaware newspaper early in 1788.

Fabius answered the charge of consolidation in terms of delegated and reserved powers. The allegation that the states would end up being dissolved, Fabius said, "is begging a concession of the question, by inferring, that a manifest and great usefulness must necessarily end in abuse; and not only so, but it requires an extinction of the principle of all society; for the subordinate sovereignties, or, in other words, the undelegated rights of the several states, in a confederation, stand upon the very same foundation with the undelegated rights of individuals in a society, the federal sovereign will being composed of the subordinate sovereign wills of the several confederated states." Each state government, in short, would remain sovereign "in all matters that relate to each state only. It is to be subordinate barely in those matters that relate to the whole; and it will be their *own faults* if the several states suffer the federal sovereignty to interfere in things of their respective jurisdictions." The "trustees or servants" of the states will certainly guard state sovereignty, "*that justly darling object* of American affections, to which they are responsible, besides being endeared by all the charities of life."

Fabius emphasized the importance of the Senate as the forum for the representation of state interests. "Though small, let it be remembered, that it is to be created by the sovereignties of the several states; that is, by the persons, whom the people of each state shall judge to be most worthy, and who, surely, will be religiously attentive to making a selection, in which the interest and honor of their state will be so deeply concerned. It should be remembered too, that this is the same manner in which the members of Congress are now appointed; and that herein, the sovereignties of the states are so intimately involved, that however a renunciation of part of these powers may be desired by some of the states, it never will be obtained from the rest of them."

NOAH WEBSTER'S PAMPHLETS

This Yale graduate who became a famous lexicographer had such unsatisfactory experiences in seeking enactment of copyright laws by state legislatures that he became an early advocate of a strong central government. He published his views on the subject in 1785 in a pamphlet entitled "Sketches of American Policy," which attracted favorable attention from Washington and Madison. In 1787 he published another pamphlet, dedicated to Benjamin Franklin, which advocated adoption of the Constitution.

In this second pamphlet Webster complained that the present condition of the Union was hardly more than "a state of nature." "Our boasted state sovereignties are so far from securing our liberty and property, that they, every moment, expose us to the loss of both. The state which commands the heaviest purse and longest sword, may at any moment, lay its weaker neighbor under tribute; and there is no superior power now existing, that can regularly oppose the invasion or redress the injury. From such liberty, O Lord, deliver us!"

Discussing the charge that the powers granted to Congress by the Constitution were excessive, Webster sought to draw a line between national and state power. "The powers lodged in Congress are extensive; but it is presumed that they are not too extensive. The first object of the Constitution is to *unite* the states into one *compact society,* for the purposes of government." In answer to the question of what powers should belong to the legislature, Webster began by asserting that the Congress "must have exclusive jurisdiction in all matters in which the states have a mutual interest." Just as no state "has a right to supreme control, in any affair in which the other states have an interest," Webster continued, "Congress should not meddle in an affair which concerned a single state."

> This is the general line of division, which the convention have endeavored to draw, between the powers of Congress and the rights of the individual states. The only question therefore is, whether the new Constitution delegates to Congress any powers which do not respect the general interest and welfare of the United States. If these powers intrench upon the present sovereignty of any *state,* without having for an object the *collective interest* of the whole, the powers are too extensive. But if they do not extend to all concerns, in which the states have a mutual interest, they are too limited. If in any instance, the powers necessary for protecting the *general* interest interfere with the constitutional rights of an *individual* state, such state has assumed powers that are inconsistent with the safety of the United States, and which ought instantly to be resigned.

With the states "entering into a social compact" on equal terms and as individuals, "no state has a right to any power which may prejudice its neighbors. If therefore the federal Constitution has collected into the federal legislature no more power than is necessary for the *common defense and interest,* it should be recognized by the states, however, particular clauses may supersede the exercise of certain powers by the individual states."

No federal sovereignty can be established while states insist upon any degree of their own long-cherished sovereignty. "However flattered each state may be by its independent sovereignty," Webster said, "we can have no union, no respectability, no national character, and what is more, no national justice, till the states resign to one *supreme head* the exclusive power of *legislating, judging and executing,* in all matters of a general nature. Everything of a private or provincial nature must still rest on the ground of the respective state constitutions."

Rejecting the idea that the powers proposed for Congress were too extensive, Webster concluded that "the peace and independence of each state, will be more fully secured under such a constitution of federal government, than they will under a constitution with more limited powers; and infinitely safer than under our boasted distinct sovereignties. It appears to me that Congress will have no more power than will be necessary for our union and general welfare; and such power they must have or we are in a wretched state."

ADDRESS TO THE FREEMEN OF SOUTH CAROLINA

David Ramsay was a physician and historian of Charleston. He had been a delegate from South Carolina to the Confederation Congress, where he had supported various efforts to strengthen the central government. He was also a member of the South Carolina convention which ratified the Constitution.

Ramsay, like Webster, did not feel the proposed national powers were excessive. "If the thirteen states are to be united in reality, as well as in name, the obvious principle of the union will be, that the Congress, or general government, should have power to regulate all general concerns. . . . When several parishes, counties, or districts, form a state, the separate interests of each must yield to the collective interest of the whole. When several states combine in one government, the same principles must be observed. These relinquishments of natural rights are not real sacrifices; each person, county, or state gains more than it loses, for it only gives up a right of injuring others, and obtains in return aid and strength to secure itself in the peaceable enjoyment of all remaining rights." We should examine the new Constitution on the assumption "that all continental concerns should be managed by Congress. . . . Look over the eighth section, which enumerates the powers of Congress, and point out one that is not essential on the before recited principles of union. . . . The opposers of the Constitution cannot show a single power delegated to Congress, that could be spared consistently with the welfare of the whole, not a single one taken from the states, but such as can be more advantageously lodged in the general government, than in that of the separate states." Two questions, Ramsay said, should be asked of anyone "who objects to the powers of Congress: Is it not necessary that the supposed dangerous power should be lodged somewhere? And secondly, where can it be lodged, consistently with the general good, so well as in the general government?"

The Federalist Papers

THE MOST extensive and intensive scholarly analysis of the Constitution published during the ratification campaign was the series of essays which appeared in the New York press under the pseudonym of "Publius." These eighty-five papers were written by Hamilton, Madison, and John Jay. Although authorship of some of the papers is in doubt, most of them—fifty or more—were the work of Hamilton, with Madison producing about thirty and Jay writing only five.

ESSAYS BY HAMILTON

Hamilton characterized the Articles as an "imbecility" which had brought the Union to "almost the last stage of national humiliation." Under the Articles, "every important measure" required by the Union had required "the concurrence of thirteen distinct sovereign wills," which of course could not agree. "The measures of the Union have not been executed; the delinquencies of the states have, step by step, matured themselves to an extreme which has, at length, arrested all the wheels of the national government, and brought them to an awful stand."

Of those who merely advocated a stronger scheme of government under the system of the Articles, Hamilton said, "They seem still to aim at things repugnant and irreconcilable; at an augmentation of federal authority, without a diminution of state authority; at sovereignty in the Union, and complete independence in the members. They still, in fine, seem to cherish with blind devotion the political monster of an *imperium in imperio.*" The evils experienced under the Articles, he asserted, did "not proceed from minute or partial imperfections, but from fundamental errors in the structure of the building, which cannot be amended otherwise than by an alteration in the first principles and main pillars of the fabric." Thus Hamilton rejected any continuance of the conception of a confederation of sovereign states as found in the Articles.

The first step in the remedy was to change the basic characteristic of the Confederation. "The great and radical vice in the construction of the existing Confederation," Hamilton wrote:

is in the principle of legislation for states or governments, in their corporate or collective capacities, and as contradistinguished from the individuals of which they consist. Though this principle does not run through all the powers delegated to the Union, yet it pervades and governs those on which the efficacy of the rest depends. Except as to the rule of apportionment, the United States has an indefinite discretion to make requisitions for men and money; but they have no authority to raise either, by regulations extending to the individual citizens of America. The consequence of this is, that though in theory their resolutions concerning those objects are laws, constitutionally binding on the members of the Union, yet in practice they are mere recommendations which the states observe or disregard at their option.

He urged that "we must resolve to incorporate into our plan those ingredients which may be considered as forming the characteristic difference between a league and a government; we must extend the authority of the Union to the persons of the citizens—the only proper objects of government."

Later, Hamilton repeated the point: If we are truly "in earnest about giving the Union energy and duration, we must abandon the vain project of legislating upon the states in their collective capacities; we must extend the laws of the federal government to the individual citizens of America . . . a sovereignty over sovereigns, a government over governments, a legislation for communities, as contradistinguished from individuals, as it is a solecism in theory, so in practice it is subversive of the order and ends of civil polity."

Under such a system, operating on and through states, said Hamilton, laws enacted by Congress would always be unenforceable. "If, therefore, the measures of the Confederacy cannot be executed without the intervention of the particular administrations, there will be little prospect of their being executed at all. The rulers of the respective members, whether they have a constitutional right to do it or not, will undertake to judge of the propriety of the measures themselves."

Therefore, Hamilton wrote, the "next most palpable defect of the subsisting Confederation, is the total want of a sanction to its laws. The United States, as now composed, have no powers to exact obedience, or punish disobedience to their resolutions." No express power was granted, and any power resting on inference and construction was precluded by Article 2, which declared "that each State shall retain every power, jurisdiction, and right, not expressly delegated to the United States in Congress assembled." This provision, he noted, "has been of late a repeated theme of the eulogies of those who oppose the new Constitution, and the want of which, in that plan, has been the subject of much plausible animadversion, and severe criticism." Because of it, however, the United States afforded "the extraordinary spectacle of a government destitute even of the shadow of constitutional power to enforce the execution of its own laws."

Hamilton also observed that another circumstance which crowned the defects of the Confederation was the want of a judiciary power. "Laws are a dead letter without courts to expound and define their true meaning and operation." The same was true of treaties of the United States; to "produce uniformity in these determinations, they ought to be submitted, in the last resort, to one supreme tribunal. As long as each state has "a court of final jurisdiction, there may be as many different final determinations on the same point as there are courts . . . all nations have found it necessary to establish one court paramount to the rest, possessing a general superintendence, and authorized to settle and declare in the last resort a uniform rule of civil justice." This was particularly true in the United States. "This is the more necessary where the frame of the government is so compounded that the laws of the whole are in danger of being contravened by the laws of the parts. In this case, if the particular tribunals are invested with a right of ultimate jurisdiction, besides the contradictions to be expected from differences of opinion there will be much to fear from the bias of local views and prejudices, and from the interference of local regulations."

All of the foregoing defects indicated the kind of government Hamilton felt was necessary:

> The result of these observations to an intelligent mind must be clearly this, that if it be possible at any rate to construct a federal government capable of regulating the common concerns and preserving the general tranquillity, it must be founded, as to the objects committed to its care, upon the reverse

of the principle contended for by the opponents of the proposed Constitution. It must carry its agency to the persons of the citizens. It must stand in need of no intermediate legislations; but must itself be empowered to employ the arm of the ordinary magistrate to execute its own resolutions. The majesty of the national authority must be manifested through the medium of the courts of justice. The government of the Union, like that of each state, must be able to address itself immediately to the hopes and fears of individuals; and to attract to its support those passions which have the strongest influence upon the human heart. It must, in short, possess all the means, and have a right to resort to all the methods, of executing the powers with which it is intrusted, that are possessed and exercised by the governments of the particular states.

Hamilton devoted many of his essays to demonstrating the inadequacy of the powers of Congress under the Articles and defending the need for the powers conferred on Congress in the Constitution. His approach toward the latter was extremely latitudinarian. "A government ought to contain in itself every power requisite to the full accomplishment of the objects committed to its care, and to the complete execution of the trusts for which it is responsible, free from every other control but a regard to the public good and to the sense of the people." Referring to the military powers of Congress, he wrote, "These powers ought to exist without limitation, because it is impossible to foresee or define the extent and variety of national exigencies, or the corresponding extent and variety of the means which may be necessary to satisfy them." The same was true of Congress' power of taxation. "As revenue is the essential engine by which the means of answering the national exigencies must be procured, the power of procuring that article in its full extent must necessarily be comprehended in that of providing for those exigencies." And, he said, "as theory and practice conspire to prove that the power of procuring revenue is unavailing when exercised over the states in their collective capacities, the federal government must of necessity be invested with an unqualified power of taxation in the ordinary modes."

A proper evaluation of congressional powers rested on "certain primary truths, or first principles," which Hamilton likened to the maxims of geometry. "Of the same nature are those other maxims in ethics and politics, that there cannot be an effect without a cause; that the means ought to be proportioned to the end; that every power ought to be commensurate to its object; that there ought to be no limitation of a power destined to effect a purpose which is itself incapable of limitation." It was therefore "both unwise and dangerous to deny the federal government an unconfined authority, as to all those objects which are intrusted to its management." Furthermore, those objects were not susceptible of static ascertainment. Discussing the concurrent power of taxation, Hamilton predicted that "in a short course of time, the wants of the states will naturally reduce themselves within a very narrow compass." Comparing "the objects that will require a federal provision in respect to revenue, and those which will require a state provision," he said that the people shall "discover that the former are altogether unlimited, and that the latter are circumscribed within very moderate bounds."

The probability of expanded national activity due to future exigencies dictated the proper view to be taken of the extent of national powers:

> In pursuing this inquiry, we must bear in mind that we are not to confine our view to the present period, but to look forward to remote futurity. Constitutions of civil government are not to be framed upon a calculation of existing exigencies, but upon a combination of these with the probable exigencies of ages, according to the natural and tried course of human affairs. Nothing, therefore, can be more fallacious than to infer the extent of any power, proper to be lodged in the national government, from an estimate of its immediate necessities. There ought to be a capacity to provide for future contingencies as they may happen; and as these are illimitable in their nature, it is impossible safely to limit that capacity.

Hamilton's reply to the attacks on the "necessary and proper" and "supremacy" clauses was an ingenious evasion. "These two clauses . . . have been held up to the people in all the exaggerated colors of misrepresentation as the pernicious engines by which their local governments were to be destroyed . . . and yet, strange as it may appear . . . it may be affirmed with perfect confidence that the constitutional operation of the intended government would be precisely the same, if these clauses were entirely obliterated, as if they were repeated in every article. They are only declaratory of a truth which would have resulted by necessary and unavoidable implication from the very act of constituting a federal government, and vesting it with certain specified powers." To demonstrate the validity of this assertion, he asked: "What is a power, but the ability or faculty of doing a thing? What is the ability to do a thing, but the power of employing the *means* necessary to its execution? What is a legislative power, but a power of making laws? What are the *means* to execute a legislative power, but laws? What is the power of laying and collecting taxes, but a *legislative power,* or a power of *making laws,* to lay and collect taxes? What are the proper means of executing such a power, but *necessary* and *proper* laws?"

This approach, Hamilton felt, was applicable to all powers declared in the Constitution. It "is *expressly* to execute these powers," he said, "that the sweeping clause, as it has been affectedly called, authorizes the national legislature to pass all *necessary* and *proper* laws. If there is anything exceptionable, it must be sought for in the specific powers upon which this general declaration is predicated. The declaration itself, though it may be chargeable with tautology or redundancy, is at least perfectly harmless." Hamilton next asked, "Why then was it introduced?" His answer gave small comfort to the state sovereignty devotees. "The answer is, that it could only have been done for greater caution, and to guard against all cavilling refinements in those who might hereafter feel a disposition to curtail and evade the legitimate authorities of the Union. The convention probably foresaw, what it has been a principal aim of these papers to inculcate, that the danger which most threatens our political welfare is that the state governments will finally sap the foundations of the Union; and might therefore think it necessary, in so cardinal a point, to leave nothing to construction."

As for the supremacy clause, Hamilton asked what the laws of the Union would be if they were *not* supreme. "It is evident that they would amount to nothing. A law, by the very meaning of the term, includes supremacy. It is a rule which those to whom it is prescribed are bound to observe. This results from every political association. If individuals enter into a state of society, the laws of that society must be the supreme regulator of their conduct. If a number of political societies enter into a larger political society, the laws which the latter may enact, pursuant to the powers entrusted to it by its constitution, must necessarily be supreme over those societies, and the individuals of whom they are composed. It would otherwise be a mere treaty, dependent on the good faith of the parties, and not a government, which is only another word for political power and supremacy."

Extensive as the national powers were, however, Hamilton apparently recognized a constitutional division of power between nation and states. In the course of denying that Congress' power of taxation would deprive the states of a concurrent power, he wrote:

An entire consolidation of the states into one complete national sovereignty would imply an entire subordination of the parts; and whatever powers might remain in them, would be altogether independent of the general will. But as the plan of the convention aims only at a partial union or consolidation, the state governments would clearly retain all the rights of sovereignty which they before had, and which were not, by that act, exclusively delegated to the United States. This exclusive delegation, or rather this alienation, of state sovereignty, would only exist in three cases: where the Constitution in express terms granted an exclusive authority to the Union; where it granted in one instance an authority to the Union, and in another prohibited the states from exercising the like authority; and where it granted an authority to the Union, to which a similar authority in the states would be absolutely and totally *contradictory* and *repugnant*.

But was it not possible that the powers of Congress, extensive as they would be under the Constitution, would be used to invade the residual area of state authority? Hamilton was aware of the objection that national legislation for individual citizens "would tend to render the government of the Union too powerful, and to enable it to absorb those residual authorities, which it might be judged proper to leave with the States for local purposes." His answer was that he simply did not think it would happen. "The regulation of the mere domestic police of a state appears to me to hold out slender allurements to ambition. . . . The administration of private justice between the citizens of the same state, the supervision of agriculture and of other concerns of a similar nature, all those things, in short, which are proper to be provided for by local legislation, can never be desirable cares of a general jurisdiction."

The danger of encroachment, he thought, was from the other direction. "It should not be forgotten that a disposition in the state governments to encroach upon the rights of the Union is quite as probable as a disposition in the Union to encroach upon the rights of the state governments." Actually, said Hamilton, it "will always be far more easy for the state governments to encroach upon the national authorities, than for the national authorities to encroach upon the state authorities. The proof of this proposition turns upon the greater degree of influence which the state governments . . . will generally possess over the people."

While discounting the probability, Hamilton still admitted the possibility. Having asserted that under the Constitution the states would retain a concurrent power of taxation, he wrote: "And making this concession, I affirm that (with the sole exception of duties on imports and exports) they would, under the plan of the convention, retain that authority in the most absolute and unqualified sense; and that an attempt on the part of the national government to abridge them in the exercise of it, would be a violent assumption of power, unwarranted by any article or clause of the Constitution." And, after discussing the supremacy clause, he wrote: "But it will not follow from this doctrine that acts of the larger society which are *not pursuant* to its constitutional powers, but which are invasions of the residuary authorities of the smaller societies, will become the supreme law of the land. These will be merely acts of usurpation, and will deserve to be treated as such."

But who was to determine the extent of the powers of Congress and thus determine whether a usurpation had occurred? Hamilton's answer was: "first, that this question arises as well and as fully upon the simple grant of those powers as upon the declaratory clause; and . . . in the second place, that the national government, like every other, must judge, in the first instance, of the proper exercise of its powers, and its constituents in the last."

One medium through which the constituents could protest was the state legislatures, "who will always be not only vigilant but suspicious and jealous guardians of the rights of the citizens against encroachments from the federal government, will constantly have their attention awake to the conduct of the national rulers, and will be ready enough, if any thing improper appears, to sound the alarm to the people, and not only to be the voice, but, if necessary, the arm of their discontent." Hamilton wrote that it "may safely be received as an axiom in our political system, that the state governments will, in all possible contingencies, afford complete security against invasions of the public liberty by the national authority . . . they can at once adopt a regular plan of opposition, in which they can combine all the resources of the community. They can readily communicate with each other in the different states, and unite their common forces for the protection of their common liberty."

Whatever Hamilton had in mind when he wrote this, it seems clear he did not contemplate that the states should have the legal right to determine the question or to interpose their authority beween that of the national government and the citizens. As to the possibility that a state might throw off national authority and obstruct national laws, Hamilton's answer was to deny any such right in a system where the national government acted directly upon individuals. There was an

essential difference between a mere non-compliance and a direct and active resistance. If any interposition of the state legislatures be necessary to give effect to a measure of the Union, they have only not to act, or to act evasively, and the measure is defeated. . . . But if the execution of the laws of the national government should not require the intervention of the state legislatures, if they were to pass into immediate operation upon the citizens themselves, the particular governments could not interrupt their progress without an open and violent exertion of an unconstitutional power. No omissions nor evasions would answer the end. They would be obliged to act, and in such a manner as would leave no doubt that they had encroached on the national rights.

What protection, then, did the states have against unconstitutional exercises of national power? And who was to determine the question of constitutionality? "If the federal government should overpass the just bounds of its authority and make a tyrannical use of its powers," Hamilton replied, "the people, whose creature it is, must appeal to the standard they have formed, and take such measures to redress the injury done to the Constitution as the exigency may suggest and prudence justify."

Such an appeal to the standard was to be made through the judiciary. "The complete independence of the courts of justice is peculiarly essential in a limited constitution. By a limited constitution, I understand one which contains certain specified exceptions to the legislative authority. . . . Limitations of this kind can be preserved in practice no other way than through the medium of courts of justice, whose duty it must be to declare all acts contrary to the manifest tenor of the Constitution void." Hamilton denied "that the legislative body are themselves the constitutional judges of their own powers, and that the construction they put upon them is conclusive upon the other departments." Far more rational was the supposition "that the courts were designed to be an intermediate body between the people and the legislature, in order, among other things, to keep the latter within the limits assigned to their authority. The interpretation of the laws is the proper and peculiar province of the courts. A constitution is, in fact, and must be regarded by the judges, as a fundamental law. It therefore belongs to them to ascertain its meaning, as well as the meaning of any particular act proceeding from the legislative body."

Hamilton made it equally clear that the federal courts would enforce the supremacy of the Constitution and national law against the states. Of what use would restrictions on state legislatures be if the Constitution provided no mode of enforcing them? "The states, by the plan of the convention, are prohibited from doing a variety of things, some of which are incompatible with the interests of the Union, and others with the principle of good government. . . . No man of sense will believe, that such prohibitions would be scrupulouly regarded without some effectual power in the government to restrain or correct the infractions of them. The power must either be a direct negative on the state laws, or an authority in the federal courts to overrule such as might be in manifest contravention of the articles of Union. There is no third course I can imagine. The latter appears by the convention preferable to the former, and, I presume, will be most agreeable to the states."

The enforcement of national supremacy also justified the power of Congress to create inferior federal courts. Hamilton could see "substantial reasons" against using the state courts for the same purpose. Even "the most discerning cannot foresee how far the prevalency of a local spirit may be found to disqualify the local tribunals for the jurisdiction of national causes; whilst every man may discover, that courts constituted like those of some of the states would be improper channels of the judicial authority of the Union. State judges, holding their offices during pleasure, or from year to year, will be too little independent to be relied upon for an inflexible execution of the national laws."

Notwithstanding all the foregoing, Hamilton sought to soothe the opposition by asserting that it was still a "federal" government for which the Constitution provided:

> The definition of a confederate republic seems simply to be "an assemblage of societies," or an association of two or more states into one state. The extent, modifications, and objects of the federal authority are mere matters of discretion. So long as the separate organization of the members be not abolished; so long as it exists, by a constitutional necessity, for local purposes; though it be in perfect subordination to the general authority of the union, it would still be, in fact and in theory, an association of states, or a confederacy. The proposed Constitution, so far from implying an abolition of the state governments, makes them constituent parts of the national sovereignty, by allowing them a direct representation in the Senate, and leaves in their possession certain exclusive and very important portions of sovereign power. This fully corresponds, in every rational import of the terms, with the idea of a federal government.

ESSAYS BY MADISON

Madison's contribution to the *Federalist Papers* was also predicated upon the inadequacy of the Articles. "It has been shown in the course of these papers, that the existing Confederation is founded on principles which are fallacious; that we must consequently change this first foundation, and with it the superstructure resting upon it." This "first foundation," of course, was that the Articles provided for a confederation of sovereign states, and Madison therefore undertook to answer the criticism based on the abandonment of this principle. Adversaries of the Constitution, Madison knew, had wanted the convention not merely to adhere to a republican form. They wanted a *"federal* form, which regards the Union as a *Confederacy* of sovereign states. Instead, the delegates "framed a *national* government, which regards the Union as a consolidation of the states."

Madison's answer, which did not deny the national character of the new government in its most important aspects, sought to de-emphasize this characteristic by calling attention to features he saw as federal. His treatment of the matter is worth setting forth in some detail.

In order to ascertain the real character of the government, Madison considered it in five separate relations. The first of these was to the foundation on which it was to be established. "On examining the first relation, it appears, on one hand, that the Constitution is to be founded on the assent and ratification of the people of America, given by deputies elected for the special purpose; but on the other, that this assent and ratification is to be given by the people, not as individuals composing one entire nation, but as composing the distinct and independent states to which they respectively belong." The people themselves, as the "supreme authority in each state," will assent to and ratify the Constitution. "The act, therefore, establishing the Constitution, will not be a *national,* but a *federal* act. . . . Were the people regarded in this transaction as forming one nation, the will of the majority of the whole people of the United States would bind the minority. . . . Each state, in ratifying the Constitution, is considered as a sovereign body, independent of all others, and only to be bound by its own voluntary act. In this relation, then, the new Constitution will, if established, be a *federal,* and not a *national* Constitution."

The second relation was to the sources from which the new government would receive its force. "The House of Representatives will derive its powers from the people of America. . . . So far the government is *national,* not *federal.* The Senate, on the other hand, will derive its powers from the states, as political and coequal societies. . . . So far the government is *federal,* not *national.* The executive power will be derived from a very compound source. . . . From this aspect of the government, it appears to be of a mixed character, presenting at least as many *federal* as *national* features."

The third relation was the operation of the powers of the government:

> The difference between a federal and national government, as it relates to the *operation of the government,* is supposed to consist in this, that in the former the powers operate on the political bodies composing the confederacy, in their political capacities; in the latter, on the individual citizens composing the nation, in their individual capacities. On trying the Constitution by this criterion, it falls under the *national,* not the *federal* character . . . the operation of the government on the people, in their individual capacities, in its ordinary and most essential proceedings, may, on the whole, designate it, in this relation, a *national* government.

The fourth relation was the extent of the powers of the new government. "But if the government be national with regard to the *operation* of its powers, it changes its aspect again when we contemplate it in relation to the *extent* of its powers. . . . In this relation . . . the proposed government cannot be deemed a *national* one; since its jurisdiction extends to certain enumerated objects only, and leaves to the several states a residuary and inviolable sovereignty over all other subjects." When controversies developed concerning the "boundary between the two jurisdictions, the tribunal which is ultimately to decide, is to be established under the general government. . . . Some such tribunal is clearly essential to prevent an appeal to the sword and a dissolution of the compact; and . . . it ought to be established under the general rather than under the local governments. . . ."

The fifth relation Madison dealt with was to the authority by which future changes in the government were to be introduced. "If we try the Constitution by its last relation to the authority by which amendments are to be made, we find it neither wholly *national* nor wholly *federal*. Were it wholly national, the supreme and ultimate authority would reside in the *majority* of the people of the Union. . . . Were it wholly federal, on the other hand, the concurrence of each state in the Union would be essential to every alteration that would be binding on all. . . . In requiring more than a majority, and particularly in computing the proportion by states, not by citizens, it departs from the national and advances toward the federal character; in rendering the concurrence of less than the whole number of states sufficient, it loses again the federal and partakes of the national character." Madison's conclusion was that, as proposed, the "Constitution, therefore, is, in strictness, neither a national nor a federal Constitution, but a composition of both."

Madison devoted four essays—numbers 41 through 45—to discussing the sum or quantity of powers vested in the general government, including restraints imposed on the states. He reduced the powers into different classes as they related to the following objects: "1. Security against foreign danger; 2. Regulation of the intercourse with foreign nations; 3. Maintenance of harmony and proper intercourse among the states; 4. Certain miscellaneous objects of general utility; 5. Restraints of the states from certain injurious acts; [and] 6. Provisions for giving due efficacy to all these powers."

His defense of the first five classes was vigorous, but the discussion most relevant here was developed in connection with the sixth class.

The first provision examined by Madison was the "necessary and proper" clause. "Few parts of the Constitution have been assailed with more intemperance than this; yet on a fair investigation, no part can appear more completely invulnerable. Without the *substance* of this power, the whole Constitution would be a dead letter."

Madison said there were four other possible methods which the Constitution might have taken on this subject, and proceeded to show why each was inferior to the course actually taken. First, the convention "might have copied the second Article of the existing Confederation, which would have prohibited the exercise of any power not *expressly* delegated." If the convention had done this, Madison wrote, "it is evident that the new Congress would be continually exposed, as their predecessors have been, to the alternative of construing the term 'expressly' with so much rigor as to disarm the government of all real authority whatever, or with so much latitude as to destroy altogether the force of the restriction." Second, "they might have attempted a positive enumeration of the powers comprehended under the general terms 'necessary and proper.'" Had the convention done this, "the attempt would have involved a complete digest of laws on every subject to which the Constitution relates." Third, "they might have attempted a negative enumeration of them, by specifying the powers excepted from the general definition." Then "the task would have been no less chimerical; and would have been liable to this further objection, that every defect in the enumeration would have been equivalent to a positive grant of authority." Finally, "they might have been altogether silent on the subject, leaving those necessary and proper powers to construction and inference." This course having been followed, "there can be no doubt that all the particular powers requisite as means of executing the general powers would have resulted to the government, by unavoidable implication. No axiom is more clearly established in law, or in reason, than that wherever the end is required, the means are authorized; wherever a general power to do a thing is given, every particular power necessary for doing it is included. Had this last method, therefore, been pursued by the convention, every objection now urged against their plan would remain in all its plausibility." Madison was here in full agreement with Hamilton, but he then added one cogent reason for the inclusion of the clause. This was that if the Constitution were silent on the subject, "the real inconveniency would be incurred of not removing a pretext which may be seized on critical occasions for drawing into question the essential powers of the Union."

The second provision for giving efficacy to all the powers of the national government was the "supremacy" clause. Without this clause, Madison said, the Constitution "would have been evidently and radically defective. To be fully sensible of this, we need only suppose for a moment that the supremacy of the state constitutions had been left complete by a saving clause in their favor . . . as these constitutions invest the state legislatures with absolute sovereignty . . . the new Congress would have been reduced to the same impotent condition with their predecessors." The world, in short, said Madison, "would have seen, for the first time, a system of government founded on an inversion of the fundamental principles of all government; it would have seen the authority of the whole society everywhere subordinate to the authority of the parts; it would have seen a monster, in which the head was under the direction of the members." After all, it was one of the fallacies of the Articles that they "inconsiderately endeavored to accomplish impossibilities; to reconcile a partial sovereignty in the Union, with complete sovereignty in the states; to subvert a mathematical axiom, by taking away a part, and letting the whole remain."

In spite of the scope and supremacy of national power, however, Madison, like Hamilton, recognized the concept of a division of powers. "In the first place," Madison wrote, "it is to be remembered that the general government is not to be charged with the whole power of making and administering laws. Its jurisdiction is limited to certain enumerated objects, which concern all the members of the republic, but which are not to be attained by the separate provisions of any. The subordinate governments, which can extend their care to all these other objects which can be separately provided for, will retain their due authority and activity. Were it proposed by the plan of the Convention to abolish the governments of the particular states, its adversaries would have some ground for their objection; though it would not be difficult to show that if they were abolished the general government would be compelled, by the principle of self-preservation, to reinstate them in their proper jurisdiction."

Again, in defending the power of the convention to write a new Constitution rather than merely to amend the Articles, Madison wrote:

> Will it be said that the *fundamental principles* of the Confederation were not within the purview of the convention, and ought not to have been varied? I ask, What are these principles? Do they require that, in the establishment of the Constitution, the states should be regarded as distinct and independent sovereigns? They are so regarded by the Constitution proposed. . . . Do these principles, in fine, require that the powers of the general government should be limited, and that, beyond this limit, the states should be left in possession of their sovereignty and independence? We have seen that in the new government, as in the old, the general powers are limited; and that the states, in all unenumerated cases, are left in the enjoyment of their sovereign and independent jurisdiction.

Madison attacked the question whether the whole mass of the powers of the national government "will be dangerous to the portion of authority left in the several states." His answer first was that it was not likely to happen.

"Several important considerations . . . discountenance the supposition that the operation of the federal government will by degrees prove fatal to the state governments." One such consideration was the dependence of the federal government on the states. "The state governments may be regarded as constituent and essential parts of the federal government; whilst the latter is nowise essential to the operation or organization of the former. Without the intervention of the state legislatures, the President of the United States cannot be elected at all . . . The Senate will be elected absolutely and exclusively by the state legislatures." Another consideration was the powers vested respectively in the national and state governments, and here Madison used language which seemed to support a strict construction approach to national powers:

> The powers delegated by the proposed Constitution to the federal government are few and defined. Those which are to remain in the state governments are numerous and indefinite. The former will be exercised principally on external objects, as war, peace, negotiation, and foreign commerce; with which last the power of taxation will, for the most part, be connected. The powers reserved to the several states will extend to all the objects which, in the ordinary course of affairs, concern the lives, liberties, and properties of

the people, and the internal order, improvement, and prosperity of the state. . . . If the new Constitution be examined with accuracy and candor, it will be found that the change which it proposes consists much less in the addition of new powers to the Union, than in the invigoration of its original powers.

Another consideration conducive to the protection of state powers was that there was no doubt that "the first and most natural attachment of the people will be to the governments of their respective states." This partiality for local government, said Madison, would be shared by the state's representatives in Congress.

The prepossessions which the members themselves will carry into the federal government, will generally be favorable to the states; whilst it will rarely happen, that the members of the state governments will carry into the public councils a bias in favor of the general government. A local spirit will infallibly prevail much more in the members of Congress, than a national spirit will prevail in the legislatures of the particular states. . . . For the same reason that the members of the state legislatures will be unlikely to attach themselves sufficiently to national objects, the members of the federal legislature will be likely to attach themselves too much to local objects. . . . Measures will too often be decided according to their probable effect, not on the national prosperity and happiness, but on the prejudices, interests, and pursuits of the government and people of the individual states.

Madison said he did not mean to insinuate "that the new federal government will not embrace a more enlarged plan of policy than the existing government may have pursued; much less, that its views will be as confined as those of the state legislatures; but only that it will partake sufficiently of the spirit of both, to be disinclined to invade the rights of the individual states, or the prerogatives of their governments."

And in Congress, equal state representation in the Senate was a potent political protection. The "equal vote allowed to each state," said Madison, "is at once a constitutional recognition of the portion of sovereignty remaining in the individual states, and an instrument for preserving residual sovereignty. So far the equality ought to be no less acceptable to the large than to the small states; since they are not less solicitous to guard, by every possible expedient, against an improper consolidation of the states into one simple republic."

The importance of this protective device was proved by the exception to the amending power that no state should be deprived of its equal representation in the Senate. "The exception in favor of the equality of suffrage in the Senate was probably meant as a palladium to the residuary sovereignty of the states, implied and secured by that principle of representation in one branch of the legislature; and was probably insisted on by the states particularly attached to that equality." As a matter of fact, Madison continued, this political power was so potent that it necessitated an oath of allegiance to the Constitution. Madison saw no need for officials of the United States to take a like oath. "The members of the federal government will have no agency in carrying the state constitutions into effect. The members and officers of the state governments, on the contrary, will have an essential agency in giving effect to the federal Constitution."

But, notwithstanding the foregoing considerations, did not the possibility remain of national usurpation of state power? In his discussion of the "necessary and proper" clause, Madison wrote: "If it be asked what is to be the consequence, in case the Congress shall misconstrue this part of the Constitution, and exercise powers not warranted by its true meaning, I answer, the same as if they should misconstrue or enlarge any other power vested in them. . . ." His answer was essentially the same as Hamilton's. "In the first instance, the success of the usurpation will depend on the executive and judiciary departments, which are to expound and give effect to the legislative acts; and in the last resort a remedy must be obtained from the people, who can, by the election of more faithful representatives, annul the acts of the usurpers."

No power existed in the states as such to prevent such an exercise of power from becoming operative as a matter of law, for the reason that under the "proposed Constitution, the federal acts will take effect without the necessary intervention of the individual states. They will depend merely on the majority of votes in the federal legislature." As a matter of politics, however, the states might prevent any effective enforcement of a federal act considered to be a usurpation of state power:

> The disquietude of the people; their repugnance and, perhaps, their refusal to cooperate with the officers of the Union; the frowns of the executive magistracy of the state; the embarrassments created by legislative devices, which would often be added on such occasions, would oppose, in any state, difficulties not to be despised; would form, in a large state, very serious impediments; and where the sentiments of several adjoining states happened to be in unison, would present obstructions which the federal government would hardly be willing to encounter.

But whatever solace particular sentences might have given, or been intended to give, to the devotees of state sovereignty, on net balance Madison's essays give small reason for comfort. Relatively speaking, federal law was more important than state law and would inevitably be of an expansive nature. Defending two-year terms for Representatives rather than annual elections as in the states, Madison wrote:

> In a single state, the requisite knowledge relates to the existing laws, which are uniform throughout the state, and with which all the citizens are more or less conversant; and to the general affairs of the state, which lie within a small compass, are not very diversified, and occupy much of the attention and conversation of every class of people. The great theatre of the United States presents a very different scene . . . the public affairs of the Union are spread throughout a very extensive region . . . the business of federal legislation must continue so far to exceed, both in novelty and difficulty, the legislative business of a single state, as to justify the longer period of service assigned to those who are to transact it.

If this resulted in federal encroachment in areas previously reserved to the states, Madison reminded his readers that

> The federal and state governments are in fact but different agents and trustees of the people, constituted with different powers, and designed for different purposes. The adversaries of the Constitution seem to have lost sight of the people altogether in their reasonings on this subject; and to have viewed these different establishments, not only as mutual rivals and enemies, but as uncontrolled by any common superior in their efforts to usurp the authorities of each other . . . the ultimate authority, wherever the derivative may be found, resides in the people alone, and that it will not depend merely on the comparative ambitions or address of the different governments, whether either, or which of them, will be able to enlarge its sphere of jurisdiction at the expense of the other. Truth, no less than decency, requires that the event in every case should be supposed to depend on the sentiments and sanction of their common constituents.

Madison was explicit that state sovereignty was an expendable value.

> But if the Union, as has been shown, be essential to the security of the people of America against foreign danger; if it be essential to their security against contentions and wars among the different states; if it be essential to guard them against those violent and oppressive factions which embitter the blessings of liberty . . . if, in a word, the Union be essential to the happiness of the people of America, is it not preposterous, to urge as an objection to a government, without which the objects of the Union cannot be obtained, that such a

government may derogate from the importance of the governments of the individual states?

Did men spill blood in the Revolution, Madison asked, "not that the people of America should enjoy peace, liberty, and safety, but that the government of the individual states, that particular municipal establishments, might enjoy a certain extent of power, and be arrayed with certain dignities and attributes of sovereignty?" The supreme object to be pursued was "the real welfare of the great body of the people . . . and . . . no form of government whatever has any other value than as it may be fitted for the attainment of this object. Were the plan of the Convention adverse to the public happiness, my voice would be, Reject and plan. Were the Union itself inconsistent with the public happiness, it would be, Abolish the Union. In like manner, as far as the sovereignty of the states cannot be reconciled to the happiness of the people, the voice of every good citizen must be, Let the former be sacrificed to the latter."

XXVIII

Early Ratifications

AT THE beginning, the Constitution had smooth sailing. To Delaware went the honor of being first to ratify, its convention adopting the Constitution unanimously on December 7, 1787. Five days later Pennsylvania's convention ratified by a two-to-one majority. New Jersey followed on December 18 with a unanimous ratification. On January 2, 1788, Georgia's convention also gave unanimous acceptance. On January 9 Connecticut ratified by a convention majority of three to one. In little more than a month, five states—a majority of the nine necessary to put the Constitution into operation—had ratified. They had done so, moreover, without formally recording any objections or proposing any amendments to the Constitution. In three of the states—Delaware, New Jersey, and Georgia—there was apparently no debate in the conventions, and the ratifications were unanimous. (Only fragments of the convention debates in Connecticut have been preserved; these will be noted later.) The sole opposition of any strength was recorded in Pennsylvania.

The Pennsylvania legislature, on September 29, 1787, enacted a resolution designating the first Tuesday in November for the election of delegates to a state convention. Nineteen members of the legislature, all opposed to the Constitution, sought to prevent this action by absenting themselves and thereby destroying a quorum. Two of the members were taken forcibly from their lodgings, dragged to the statehouse, and there detained against their wills in order to reconstitute the necessary quorum. After adjournment, the minority promptly published an address to the people in which they protested against the indignity visited upon them and proceeded to attack the Constitution. Among the grounds were that the delegates to the convention had no authority "to annihilate the present Confederation and form a constitution entirely new"; that under the Constitution the state government would be annihilated or "dwindle into a mere corporation"; and that the judiciary of the United States was "so constructed as to absorb and destroy the judiciaries of the several states."

The elections of November 6 were a resounding victory for the Federalists. When the convention met on November 21, the result could already be foreseen. The lines were sharply drawn numerically. The majority never received more than forty-six votes on any motion during the convention, the minority never less than twenty-three, and no vote varied more than one or two from this division. The Anti-federalists were determined, however, to articulate their opposition, which they did through their principal spokesmen, John Whitehill, William Findley, and John Smilie. The Federalist leaders were James Wilson and Thomas McKean, chief judge of the supreme court of Pennsylvania.

On Saturday, November 24, McKean moved the adoption of the Constitution and Wilson, "as the only member of this respectable body who had the honor of a seat in the late federal convention," led off with an opening speech in support. After reviewing the situation of the states, Wilson said, "In this dilemma, a federal republic naturally presented itself to our observation, as a species of government which secured all the internal advantages of a republic, at the same time that it maintained the external dignity and force of a monarchy." In the creation of this federal republic, Wilson stated that "perhaps the most important obstacle to the proceedings of the federal convention, arose in drawing the line between the national and the individual governments of the states. On this point a general principle readily occurred, that whatever object was confined in its nature and operation to a particular state, ought to be subject to the separate government of the states; but whatever in its nature and operation extended beyond a particular state, ought to be comprehended within the federal jurisdiction. The great difficulty, therefore, was the application of this general principle, for it was found impracticable to enumerate and distinguish the various objects to which it extended; and as the mathematics only are capable of demonstration, it ought not to be thought extraordinary that the convention could not develop a subject involved in such endless perplexity."

Notwithstanding the impossibility of exact enumeration, Wilson said the general principle was clear that in proposing a federal republic the convention had had "not only to consider the situation, circumstances, and interests of one, two, or three states, but of the collective body; and as it is essential to society, that the welfare of the whole should be preferred to the accommodation of a part, they followed the same rule in promoting the national advantages of the Union, in preference to the separate advantages of the states." Wilson then offered a term, "federal liberty," which, he said, "consists in the aggregate of the civil liberty which is surrendered by each state to the national government; and the same principles that operate in the establishment of a single society, with respect to the rights reserved or resigned by the individuals that compose it, will justly apply in the case of a confederation of distinct and independent states."

The first two days of the next week were occupied with discussion of procedural matters. On Wednesday, November 28, the opponents of the Constitution began their attack. Smilie opened with a criticism based on the absence of a "full and explicit declaration of rights," asserting: "So loosely, so inaccurately are the powers which are enumerated in this Constitution defined, that it will be impossible, without a test of that kind, to ascertain the limits of authoriy, and to declare when government has degenerated into oppression. In that event the contest will arise between the people and the rulers. 'You have exceeded the powers of your office, you have oppressed us,' will be the language of the suffering citizens. The answer of the government will be short —'We have not exceeded our power; you have no test by which you can prove it.' "

Whitehill joined Smilie in the attack.

But let us attend to the language of the system before us. 'We the people of the United States,' is a sentence that evidently shows the old foundation of the union is destroyed, the principle of confederation excluded, and a new and unwieldy system of consolidated empire is set up, upon the ruins of the present compact between the states. Can this be denied? No, Sir. It is artfully, indeed, but it is incontrovertibly designed to abolish the independence and sovereignty of the states individually. [Whitehill spent considerable time criticizing the latitude of the powers of Congress.] That government possesses all the powers of raising and maintaining armies, of regulating and commanding the militia, and of laying imposts and taxes of every kind, must be supreme, and will (whether in twenty or in one year, it signifies little to the event) naturally absorb every subordinate jurisdiction. . . . But, besides the powers enumerated, we find in this Constitution an authority is given to make all laws that are necessary to carry it effectually into operation, and what laws are necessary is a consideration left for Congress to decide. . . . The giving such extensive and undefined power is a radical wrong that cannot be justified by any subsequent merit in the exercise. . . . Then, Sir, can it longer be doubted that this is a system of consolidation?

In answer to this assault, Wilson said that it seemed "rather unnatural that a government should be expressly calculated to produce the destruction of other governments upon which its own existence must entirely depend. . . . Is it not evident, Sir, when we particularly examine the structure of the proposed system, that the operation of the federal legislature necessarily presupposes the existence of the legislatures of the several states? . . . Thus," Wilson continued, "by a clear deduction, it is evident that the existence and efficiency of the general government presupposes the existence and full operation of the separate governments." It seemed unnecessary, Wilson said, to dwell on the subject longer, "for, when gentlemen assert that it was the intention of the federal convention to destroy the sovereignty of the states, they must conceive themselves better qualified to judge of the intention of that body than its own members, of whom not one, I believe, entertained so improper an idea."

Smilie made a rebuttal to Wilson. He knew, he said, that the Constitution did not set out to "directly abolish the governments of the several states." Indeed, no one had said or thought "that the words of this instrument expressly announce that the sovereignty of the several states, their independence, jurisdiction, and power, are at once absorbed and annihilated by the general government. To this position and to this alone, the arguments of the honorable gentlemen effectually reply, and there they must undoubtedly hold as long as the forms of state government remain, at least, till a change takes place in the federal constitution. It is, however," Smilie continued, "upon other principles that the final destruction of the individual governments is asserted to be a necessary consequence of their association under this general form —for, Sir, it is the silent but certain operation of the powers, and not the cautious, but artful tenor of the expressions contained in this system, that can excite terror, or generate oppression. The flattery of language was indeed necessary to disguise the baneful purpose."

The "Preamble" to the Constitution was enough to disclose its purpose to Smilie. When "it is declared that 'We the people of the United States do ordain and establish this constitution,' is not the very foundation a proof of a consolidated government, by the manifest subversion of the principle that constitutes a union of states, which are sovereign and independent, except in the specific objects of confederation? These words have a plain and positive meaning, which could not be misunderstood by those who employed them; and therefore, Sir, it is fair and reasonable to infer, that it was in contemplation of the framers of this

system, to absorb and abolish the efficient sovereignty and independent powers of the several states, in order to invigorate and aggrandize
the general government." Smilie had reached the close of his peroration. "The plan before us, then, explicitly proposes the formation of a
new constitution upon the original authority of the people, and not an
association of states upon the authority of their respective governments." At this, he supported Whitehill's argument on the dangerous
amplitude of national powers.

The rejoinder to Smilie was made by Judge McKean. "This system
proposes a union of thirteen sovereign and independent states, in order
to give dignity and energy to the transaction of their common concerns;
it would be idle therefore to countenance the idea that any other powers
were delegated to the general government than those specified in the
Constitution itself. . . . Sir, there is not a power given in the article before us that is not in its expression, clear, plain, and accurate, and
in its nature proper and absolutely necessary to the great objects of
the Union."

Referring to the taxation power, McKean asked: "What is there,
however, that should render it a more dangerous trust in the hands of
the general than of a particular government; for, is it not as much in
the power of the state legislatures at this day to do all this mischief, as
it will be hereafter in the power of Congress? . . . For my part, Sir, I
can perceive that the power is absolutely necessary to support the
sovereignty and preserve the peace of the Union, and therefore, I will
not idly argue against its use, from the possible abuse."

Referring to the powers of the national government generally, he
added, "Nor am I, Sir, impressed with the opinion which has given
so much pain to the worthy gentlemen in the opposition, that the powers
are so vaguely expressed, so indefinite and extensive in their nature,
that they may hereafter be stretched to every act of legislation, and
construed to imply something beyond what is here specified."

After all, McKean reminded his peers, "the people will, from time
to time, have it in their power to remove those persons who have promoted any measure that tends to injure and oppress them. In short,
Sir, it seems that the honorable members are so afraid the Congress
will do some mischief, that they are determined to deny them the power
to do any good."

On Friday, November 30, Whitehill pursued the point in another
speech. "I have said, and with increasing confidence I repeat, that
the proposed constitution must eventually annihilate the independent

sovereignty of the several states. . . . For, Sir, the first article comprises the grants of powers so superlative in their nature, and so unlimited in their extent, that without the aid of any other branch of the system, a foundation rests upon this article alone, for the extension of the federal jurisdiction to the most extravagant degree of arbitrary sway. It will avail little to detect and deplore the encroachments of a government clothed in the plenitude of these powers."

Here Whitehill turned to implied powers. "It is not alone, however, the operative forces of the powers expressly given to Congress that accomplish their independence of the states, but we find an efficient auxiliary in the clause that authorizes that body 'to make all laws which shall be necessary and proper,' etc." In conclusion, he said: "That it was the design of the late federal convention to absorb and abolish the individual sovereignty of the states, I seek no other evidence but this system."

The debate was equally lively the next day, Saturday, December 1. Benjamin Rush started it by saying, in effect, that he was glad to be getting rid of state sovereignty. "On the subject of the new government tending to abridge the states of their respective sovereignty," he observed that "this passion for separate sovereignty had destroyed the Grecian Union. This plurality of sovereignty is in politics what plurality of gods is in religion—it is the idolatry, the heathenism of government." He then proceeded to summarize the advantages of the Constitution in what was described as "an animated speech."

Findley immediately took the floor and noted that while Rush was the only one who had responded to the charge of consolidation, the substance was that he had "insinuated that he saw and rejoiced at the eventual annihilation of the state sovereignties."

Then Findley "delivered an eloquent and powerful speech, to prove that the proposed plan of government amounted to a consolidation, and not a confederation of the states." He argued that the proposed constitution established a general government and destroyed the individual governments:

First. In the "Preamble," it is said, "We the People," and not "We the States," which therefore is a compact between individuals entering into society, and not between separate states enjoying independent power, and delegating a portion of that power for their common benefit. Second. That in the Legislature each member has a vote, whereas in a confederation, as we have hitherto practiced it, and from the very nature of the thing, a state can have only one voice, and therefore all the delegates of any state can only give one vote.

Third. The powers given to the federal body for imposing internal taxation
will necessarily destroy the state sovereignties, for there cannot exist two
independent sovereign taxing powers in the same community, and the strongest will of course annihilate the weaker. Fourth. The power given to regulate
and judge of elections is a proof of a consolidation, for there cannot be two
powers employed at the same time in regulating the same elections, and if
they were a confederated body, the individual states would judge of the elections, and the general Congress would judge of the credentials which proved
the elections of its members. Fifth. The judiciary power, which is coextensive with the legislative, is another evidence of a consolidation. Sixth.
The manner in which the wages of the members is paid, makes another
proof. And lastly, the oath of allegiance directed to be taken establishes it
incontrovertibly; for would it not be absurd, that the members of the legislative and executive branches of a sovereign state should take a test of allegiance
to another sovereign or independent body?

Wilson then came back by juxtaposing the doctrine of state sovereignty with the doctrine of popular sovereignty. "Upon what principle
is it contended that the sovereign power resides in the state governments? The honorable gentleman has said truly that there can be no
subordinate sovereignty. Now if there cannot, my position is, that the
sovereignty resides in the people. They have not parted with it; they
have only dispensed such portions of power as were conceived necessary for the public welfare. This Constitution stands upon this broad
principle.

"I know very well, Sir," Wilson continued, "that the people have
hitherto been shut out of the federal government, but it is not meant
that they should any longer be dispossessed of their rights. . . . When
the principle is once settled that the people are the source of authority,
the consequence is that they may take from the subordinate governments power with which they have hitherto trusted them, and place
those powers in the general government, if it is thought that there they
will be productive of more good. They can distribute one portion of
power to the more contracted circle called state governments; they
can also furnish another proportion to the government of the United
States. Who will undertake to say as a state officer that the people
may not give to the general government what powers and for what
purposes they please? How comes it, Sir, that these state governments
dictate to their superiors—to the majesty of the people? . . . As this
government is formed, there are two sources from which the representation is drawn, though they both ultimately flow from the people.
States now exist and others will come into existence; it was thought

proper that they should be represented in the general government. But gentlemen will please to remember, this Constitution was not framed merely for the states; it was framed for the people also."

On Tuesday, December 4, Wilson took the floor again for a lengthy speech in which he answered the criticisms of the opposition and extolled the virtues of the Constitution. Referring to Findley, Wilson said:

> His position is, that the supreme power resides in the states, as governments, and mine is, that it resides in the people, as the fountain of government. . . . I agree with the members in opposition, that there cannot be two sovereign powers on the same subject. I consider the people of the United States as forming one great community, and I consider the people of the different states as forming communities on a lesser scale. From this great division of the people into distinct communities it will be found necessary that different proportions of legislative powers should be given to the governments, according to the nature, number, and magnitude of their objects. . . . State sovereignty, as it is called, is far from being able to support its weight. Nothing less than the authority of the people could either support it or give it efficacy.

Wilson proceeded to explain his position, saying "that in this country the supreme absolute, and uncontrollable power resides in the people at large; that they have vested certain proportions of this power in the state governments, but that the fee simple continues, resides, and remains with the body of the people. . . . Because this recognition is in the proposed constitution, an exception is taken to the whole of it, for we are told it is a violation of the present confederation—a confederation of sovereign states. . . . I am astonished to hear the ill-founded doctrine, that states alone ought to be represented in the federal government; these must possess sovereign authority forsooth, and the people be forgot! No," he concluded, "let us *reascend* to first principles."

In this same speech Wilson undertook to respond to the charge that the Constitution provided for a consolidation. "It is repeated with confidence, 'that this is not a *federal* government, but a complete one, with legislative, executive and judicial powers; it is a *consolidating* government. I have already mentioned the misuse of the term; I wish the gentleman would indulge us with his definition of the word.

"If, when he says it is a consolidation, he means so far as relates to the general objects of the Union—so far it was intended to be a consolidation, and on such a consolidation, perhaps, our very existence, as a nation, depends. If, on the other hand . . . he (Mr. Findley) means that it will absorb the governments of the individual states, so far is this position from being admitted, that it is unanswerably controverted. The existence of the state governments is one of the most prominent features of this system. With regard to these purposes which are allowed to be for the general welfare of the union, I think it no objection to this plan, that we are told it is a complete government. I think it no objection, that it is alleged the government will possess legislative, executive, and judicial powers."

Wilson also used this speech to discuss the division of power between nation and states. "Sir, I think there is another subject with regard to which this Constitution deserves approbation. I mean the *accuracy* with which the *line is drawn* between the powers of the *general government,* and that of the *particular* state governments. We have heard some general observations on this subject, from the gentlemen who conduct the opposition. They have asserted that these powers are unlimited and undefined. These words are as easily pronounced as limited and defined. They have already been answered by my honorable colleague (Mr. McKean) ; therefore, I shall not enter into an explanation; but it is not pretended, that the line is drawn with mathematical precision; the inaccuracy of language must, to a certain degree, prevent the accomplishment of such a desire. Whoever views the matter in a true light, will see that the powers are as minutely enumerated and defined as was possible, and will also discover that the general clause, against which so much exception is taken, is nothing more than what was necessary to render effectual the particular powers that are granted."

On Wednesday, December 5, Findley made a long speech in which he discussed "the amount of sovereignty it was safe for the states to give up; how much the Constitution would take from them; [he] ended with an appeal for a *federal* in preference to a *consolidated* government."

Two days later Wilson defended the judicial power of the United States under the Constitution. In the course of this address he discussed the clause extending the judicial power to "controversies to which the United States shall be a party." He said he understood it was "something very incongruous that, because the United States are a party, it should be urged as an objection, that their judges ought not to decide, when the univesal practice of all nations have and unavoidably must admit of this power. But, say the gentlemen, the sovereignty of the states is destroyed, if they should be engaged in a controversy with the United States, because a suitor in a court must acknowledge the jurisdiction of the court, and it is not the custom of sovereigns to suffer their names to be made use of in this manner. The answer is plain and easy: The government of each state ought to be subordinate to the government of the United States."

On Monday, December 10, McKean returned and answered the charge that the Constitution was a consolidation and not a confederation. "To this I answer, the name is immaterial—the thing unites the several states, and makes them like one in particular instances and for particular purposes, which is what is ardently desired by most of the sensible men in this country. I care not whether it is called a consolidation, confederation, or national government, or by what other name, if it is a good government, and calculated to promote the blessings of liberty, tranquillity, and happiness."

Wilson's final speech of the convention refuted the theory—subsequently advanced up until the time of the Civil War and even into our own time—that the Constitution is a compact or contract between the states.

> We were told some days ago . . . that the convention, no doubt, thought they were forming a compact or contract of the greatest importance. Sir, I confess I was much surprised at so late a stage of the debate to hear such principles maintained. It was matter of surprise to see the great leading principle of this system still so very much misunderstood. "The convention, no doubt, thought they were forming a contract!"
>
> I cannot answer for what every member thought; but I believe it cannot be said that they thought they were making a contract, because I cannot discover the least trace of a compact in that system. There can be no compact unless there are more parties than one. It is a new doctrine that one can make a compact with himself. "The convention were forming compacts!" With whom? I know no bargains were made there. I am unable to conceive who the parties could be. The state governments make a bargain with one another; that is the doctrine that is endeavored to be established, by gentlemen in opposition; their state sovereignties wish to be represented! But far other were the ideas of this convention, and far other are those conveyed in the system itself.
>
> This, Mr. President, is not a government founded upon compact; it is founded upon the power of the people. They express in their name and their authority, *"We the people do ordain and establish,"* etc , from their ratification, and their ratification alone it is to take its constitutional authenticity; without that it is no more than *tabula rasa*. I know very well all the commonplace rant of state sovereignties, and that government is founded in original

compact. . . . I have already shown that this system is not a compact or contract; the system itself tells you what it is; it is an ordinance and establishment of the people.

Wilson closed his speech with an eloquent evocation of the blessings of nationhood which would flow from the adoption of the Constitution:

I stated on a former occasion one important advantage; by adopting this system we become a nation; at present we are not one. Can we perform a single national act? Can we do anything to procure us dignity, or to preserve peace and tranquillity? Can we relieve the distress of our citizens? Can we provide for their welfare or happiness? The powers of our government are mere sound. . . . This system, Sir, will at least make us a nation, and put it in the power of the Union to act as such. We will be considered as such by every nation of the world. We will regain the confidence of our own citizens, and command the respect of others. As we shall become a nation, I trust that we shall also form a national character; and that this character will be adapted to the principles and genius of our system of government. . . . What a happy exchange for the disjointed contentious state sovereignties!

The next day, Wednesday, December 12, Whitehill for the minority offered fifteen proposed amendments to the Constitution, together with a motion that the convention adjourn so that the people might consider the proposals before the Constitution was ratified. Most of the proposed amendments were in the nature of a bill of personal rights. Reservations of state taxing power, conduct of elections, and control over the militia were the subjects of separate amendments. Another provided for the supremacy of state constitutions over national treaties, and still another redefined and reduced the jurisdiction of the United States courts.

The fifteenth and final amendment was: "That the sovereignty, freedom and independence of the several states shall be retained, and every power, jurisdiction, and right which is not by this Constitution expressly delegated to the United States in Congress assembled." This, of course, was Article II of the Articles of Confederation all over again. The majority did not deign to argue against Whitehill. His motion was defeated, 46 to 23, and the Constitution was then approved by precisely the same vote. On December 18 the minority published an address and reasons for dissent, in which they set forth for public consideration the bases of their opposition to the Constitution, one of which was that it would destroy the sovereignty of the states.

Although Pennsylvania had thus ratified, and although each succeeding state convention saw still another approval added, the agitation of the Anti-federalists in Pennsylvania against the Constitution continued throughout most of the next year and finally culminated in a convention at Harrisburg in September 1788. This convention proposed twelve amendments for adoption. The first of these proposed amendments read: "That Congress shall not exercise any powers whatsoever, but such as are expressly given to that body by the Constitution of the United States; nor shall any authority, power or jurisdiction, be assumed or exercised by the executive or judiciary departments of the Union under color or pretense of construction or fiction. But all the rights of sovereignty, which are not by the said Constitution expressly and plainly vested in the Congress, shall be deemed to remain with, and shall be exercised, by the several states in Union according to their respective constitutions." Other proposals would have curtailed Congress' power over taxation, elections, and the militia, and prohibited inferior federal courts.

In Connecticut, meanwhile, the legislature on October 16 had unanimously authorized a convention, which met on January 4, 1788, and which included among its members Oliver Ellsworth, Roger Sherman, and William Samuel Johnson. Only portions of the proceedings have been preserved, but they afford some insight into an understanding of the convention.

On January 4 Ellsworth, in an opening speech, contrasted the weakness of the Articles with the strength of the Constitution. "A more energetic system is necessary. The present is merely advisory. It has no coercive power. Without this, government is ineffectual, or rather is no government at all. But it is said, 'Such a power is not necessary. States will not do wrong. They need only be told their duty, and they will do it.' I ask, Sir, what warrant is there for this assertion? Do not states do wrong?"

After reviewing the inadequacy of other confederations, Ellsworth continued, "Enough has been said to show that a power in the general government to enforce the decrees of the Union is absolutely necessary. The Constitution before us is a complete system of legislative, judicial, and executive power. It was designed to supply the defects of the former system; and I believe, upon a full discussion, it will be found calculated to answer the purposes for which it was designed."

On January 7 Ellsworth defended the principle of national supremacy enforced through legal coercion of individuals. "How contrary, then, to republican principles, how humiliating, is our present situation! A single state can rise up, and put a veto upon the most important public measures. We have seen this actually take place. A single state has controlled the general voice of the Union; a minority, a very small minority, has governed us. So far is this from being consistent with republican principles, that it is, in effect, the worst species of monarchy.

"Hence we see how necessary for the Union is a coercive principle. No man pretends the contrary: we all see and feel this necessity. The only question is, Shall it be a coercion of law, or a coercion of arms? There is no other possible alternative. Where will those who oppose a coercion of law come out? Where will they end? A necessary consequence of their principles is a war of the states one against the other. I am for coercion by law—that coercion which acts only upon delinquent individuals. This Constitution does not attempt to coerce sovereign bodies, states, in their political capacity. No coercion is applicable to such bodies, but that of an armed force. If we should attempt to execute the laws of the Union by sending an armed force against a delinquent state, it would involve the good and bad, the innocent and guilty, in the same calamity. But this legal coercion singles out the guilty individual, and punishes him for breaking the laws of the Union. All men will see the reasonableness of this; they will acquiesce and say, 'Let the guilty suffer.' "

Governor Huntingdon defended the Constitution on the same day. "It is an established truth," he said, "that no nation can exist without a coercive power—a power to enforce the execution of its political regulations. . . . The great power of preserving liberty is, to lodge the supreme power so as to be well supported, and not abused." Huntingdon was convinced that Congress "must have a controlling power with respect to national concerns. There is, at present, an extreme want of power in the national government; and it is my opinion that this Constitution does not give too much. . . . The state governments I think, will not be endangered by the powers vested by this Constitution in the general government. While I have attended in Congress, I have observed that the members were quite as strenuous advocates for the rights of their respective states, as for those of the Union. I doubt not but that this will continue to be the case; and hence I infer that the general government will not have the disposition to encroach upon the states."

A third speaker on January 7 was Richard Law, who also denied any danger to the states. Men who had such fears ought to "consider that this general government rests upon the state governments for its support. It is like a vast and magnificent bridge, built upon thirteen strong and stately pillars. Now, the rulers, who occupy the bridge, cannot be so beside themselves as to knock away the pillars which support the whole fabric."

And Oliver Wolcott, using the same analogy, emphasized the political checks on the exercise of national power. "The Constitution," Wolcott said, "effectually secures the states in their several rights. It must secure them for its own sake; for they are the pillars which uphold the general system. The Senate, a constituent branch of the general legislature, without whose assent no public act can be made, are appointed by the states, and will secure the rights of the several states. The other branch of the Legislature, the Representatives, are to be elected by the people at large. They will therefore be the guardians of the rights of the great body of the citizens. So well guarded is this Constitution throughout, that it seems impossible that the rights either of the states or of the people should be destroyed."

On January 9, five days after assembling, the Connecticut convention ratified the Constitution, 128 to 48. No amendments were proposed.

XXIX

Ratification in Massachusetts

THE MASSACHUSETTS legislature on October 25, 1787, authorized a convention, which assembled in Boston on January 9, 1788. It was the largest of any of the state conventions, with 364 delegates. There is no doubt that at the outset a majority was opposed to the Constitution. In general, the commercial interests on the seaboard supported the Constitution, whereas the agricultural elements of the inland opposed it. About twenty of the delegates actually had participated in Shays' Rebellion. Many of the towns instructed their delegates to vote against ratification. Thus Harvard in Worcester County so instructed its delegate, on the ground that "the proposed Constitution will, if adopted, effectually destroy the sovereignty of the states, and establish a national government that, in all probability, will soon bring the good people of the United States under despotism."

Although the Anti-federalists held the initial majority, the Federalists were decidedly superior in their leadership. King, Gorham, and Strong, who had been delegates to the federal convention, attended, along with other state leaders: Governor John Hancock, popular with the common people; Theodore Sedgwick, speaker of the house in the state legislature and subsequently Congressman, Senator, and judge of the state supreme court; Theophilus Parsons, a leader of the Massachusetts bar and later chief judge of the state supreme court; Fisher Ames, a rising political figure, subsequently to become a brilliant Federalist leader in Congress; and William Heath, revolutionary war general. The Anti-federalist leaders were men who were obscure at the time and have come to be known to history for no reason than that they attended this convention: William Widgery, Samuel Thompson, Samuel Nason, John Taylor, and Phanuel Bishop.

The superior talent of the Federalist leadership was reflected in the high degree of political skill by which they ultimately secured ratification. The choice of Hancock as president of the convention was suggested and carried by the Federalists who thus hoped to obtain, and did assure themselves of, his influence in support of the Constitution. The Federalists also engineered a meeting of Boston tradesmen and mechanics two days before the convention and secured the adoption of a resolution approving ratification. This was done to influence not only Hancock but more especially Samuel Adams, the Revolutionary hero who, although now past his prime, was still both leader of and servant to the Boston masses.

Adams had expressed his view of the Constitution in a letter to Richard Henry Lee in December 1787. "I stumble at the threshold," he wrote. "I meet with a national government, instead of a federal union of sovereign states." So successful were the Federalists in neutralizing Adams' private opposition that he never once in the convention spoke against the Constitution and actually rendered service to their cause. Whereas the Federalists in Pennsylvania, being in the heavy majority, had run roughshod over the opposition, the situation in Massachusetts called for a different tactic. The Anti-federalists, being of greater strength there, were throughout treated with high respect and great tact, while the Federalists sought, through persuasion and political maneuver, to convert their minority to a majority. They even invited Elbridge Gerry, who had been defeated as a delegate, to sit on the floor with the convention and be available for questions.

Being in the minority, the Federalists had to prevent an early vote on ratification. They did this by moving that the convention consider the Constitution section by section, this to be followed by debate on the general question of ratification. For almost three weeks, therefore, the convention considered, in desultory fashion, the provisions of the Constitution.

The state's traditional devotion to annual elections occasioned some debate over the length of terms of Representatives and Senators. Ames said, "The Senators will represent the sovereignty of the states. The Representatives are to represent the people. The offices ought to bear some proportion in point of importance. This will be impossible if they are chosen for one year only." Gore argued in similar fashion: "The Senate represents the sovereignty of the states; the House of Representatives the people of the United States. The former have a longer term in their office; it is then necessary that that body which represents the people should have a permanence in their office, to resist any operations of the Senate, which might be injurious to the people."

Rufus King distinguished between the relative importance of state and national legislation. "If one year is necessary for a representative to be useful in the state legislature, where the objects of his deliberations are local, and within his constant observation, two years do not appear too long, where the objects of deliberation are not confined to one state, but extend to thirteen states; where the complicated interests of united America are mingled with those of foreign nations; and where the great duties of national sovereignty will require his constant attention . . . as in each of these colonies, when under the British government, the duties of the representatives were merely local, the great duties of sovereignty being vested in their king, so, since the revolution, their duties have continued local, many of the authorities of sovereignty being vested in Congress. It is now proposed to increase the powers of Congress; this will increase the duties of the Representatives, and they must have a reasonable time to obtain the information necessary to a right discharge of their office."

Congress' power over elections led to sharp dispute in which the oratorical skill of the Federalists was clearly demonstrated. Bishop opposed the provision, observing that "by the fourth section, Congress would be enabled to control the elections of representatives. It has been said . . . that this power was given in order that refractory states may be made to do their duty. But if so, Sir," Bishop asked, "why was it not so mentioned? If that was the intention . . . why the clause did not run thus: 'The times, places, and manner of holding elections for Senators and Representatives, shall be prescribed in each state by the legislature thereof; but,' *if any state shall refuse or* neglect to do so, 'Congress may,' etc. This . . . would admit of no prevarication . . . if the states shall refuse to do their duty, then let the power be given to Congress to oblige them to do it. But if they do their duty, Congress ought not to have the power to control elections."

Strong followed Bishop to point out the necessity for Section 4. "The power . . . to regulate the elections of our federal representatives must be lodged somewhere. I know of but two bodies wherein it can be lodged —the legislatures of the several states, and the general Congress. If the legislative bodies of the states, who must be supposed to know at what time, and in what place and manner, the elections can best be held, should so appoint them, it cannot be supposed that Congress, by the power granted by this section, will alter them; but if the legislature of a state should refuse to make such regulations, the consequence will be, that the representatives will not be chosen, and the general government will be dissolved. In such case, can gentlemen say that a power to remedy the evil is not necessary to be lodged some-where? And where can it be lodged but in Congress?" Bishop was unconvinced, however, saying that "the great difficulty with him was, that the power given by the fourth section was unlimited; and he did not yet see that any advantage would arise from its being so."

Cabot spoke in support of the power. "I confess that I prize the fourth section as highly as any in the Constitution; because I consider the *democratic* branch of the national government, the branch chosen im-mediately for the people, as intended to be a *check* on the *federal* branch, which latter is not an immediate representation of the people of America, and is not chosen by them, but is a representation of the sovereignty of the individual states, and its members delegated by the several state legislatures."

Cabot continued, observing that if state legislatures "are suffered to regulate conclusively the elections of the democratic branch, they may, by such an interference, first weaken, and at last destroy, that check; they may at first diminish, and finally annihilate, that control of the general government, which the people ought always to have through their immediate representatives."

Widgery, in opposition, insisted that "we had a right to be jealous of our rulers, who ought never to have a power which they could abuse." As for the fourth section, it "ought to have gone further; it ought to have had the provision in it mentioned by Mr. Bishop; there would then be a mutual check." White said that if "we give up this section . . . there is nothing left." Turner stated that he did not wish to give Congress "a power which they can abuse." He wished to know "whether such a power is not contained in this section? I think it is," he said. —"Pardon me, Sir, if I say I feel the want of an energetic government, and the dangers to which this dear country is reduced, as much as any citizen of the United States; but I cannot prevail on myself to adopt a government which wears the face of power, without examining it. Relinquishing a *hair's breadth* in a constitution, is a great deal; for by small degrees has liberty, in all nations, been wrested from the hands of the people. I know great powers are necessary to be given to Congress, but I wish they may be well guarded."

In connection with the matter of representation and tenure, the Fed-eralists answered the charge of consolidation. Judge Dana, replying to a critic, said that "if the Constitution under consideration was in fact what its opposers had often called it, a consolidation of the states, he should readily agree with that gentleman that the representation of the people was much too small; but this was a charge brought against it without any foundation in truth. So far from it, that it must be apparent to every one, that the federal government springs out of, and can alone be brought into existence by, the state governments. Demolish the latter." Judge Dana said, "and there is an end to the former."

Ames replied at greater length.

It is necessary to premise that no argument against the new plan has made a deeper impression than this, that it will produce a consolidation of the states. This is an effect which all good men will deprecate. For it is obvious, that if the state powers are to be destroyed, the representation is too small. . . . The state governments are essential parts of the system, and the defense of this article is drawn from its tendency to their preservation. The *Senators* represent the *sovereignty of the states;* in the other house, individuals are represented. . . . Senators are in the quality of ambassadors of the states, and it will not be denied that some permanency in this office is necessary to a discharge of their duty. Now, if they were chosen yearly, how could they perform their trust? If they would be brought by that means more immediately under the influence of the people, then they will represent the state legislatures less, and become the representatives of individuals. This belongs to the other house. This would totally obliterate the federal features of the Constitution.

What would become of the state governments, and on whom would devolve the duty of defending them against the encroachments of the federal government? A consolidation of the states would ensue, which, it is conceded, would subvert the new Constitution, and against which this very article, so much condemned, is our best security. Too much provision cannot be made against a consolidation. The state governments represent the wishes, and feelings, and local interests, of the people. They are the safeguard and ornament of the Constitution; they will protract the period of our liberties; they will afford a shelter against the abuse of power, and will be the natural avengers of our violated rights.

Article I, Section 8, setting forth the powers of Congress, touched off spirited debate. King was first with a defense of the section. "We now come, Sir, to the consideration of the powers with which that government shall be clothed. The introduction to this Constitution is in these words: 'We, the people,' etc. The language of the Confederation is, 'We, the states,' etc. The latter is a mere federal government of states. These, therefore, that assemble under it, have no power to make laws to apply to the individuals of the states confederated; and the attempts to make laws for collective societies necessarily leave a discretion to comply with them or not. In no instance has there been so frequent deviation from first principles, as in the neglect or refusal to comply with the requisitions of general governments for the collection of moneys.

"Now, Sir," King asked, "what faith is to be put in requisitions on the states? . . . Sir, experience proves, as well as anything can be proved, that no dependence can be placed on such requisitions. What method, then, can be devised to compel the delinquent states to pay their quotas? Sir, I know of none. Laws, to be effective, therefore, must not be laid on states, but upon individuals. Sir, it has been objected to the proposed Constitution, that the power is too great, and by this Constitution is to be sacred. But if the want of power is the *defect in the old Confederation,* there is a fitness and propriety in adopting what is here proposed, which gives the necessary power wanted. . . . Sir, I would ask, whether any government can exist, or give security to the people, which is not possessed of this power." Dawes followed with a strong argument that the national power proposed was essential for the protection and development of agriculture, commerce, and manufactures.

Bodman then spoke in opposition. He said "that the power given to Congress to lay and collect duties, taxes, etc., as contained in the section under consideration, was certainly unlimited, and therefore dangerous." He wished to know "whether it was necessary to give Congress power to do harm, in order to enable them to do good. It has been said that the *sovereignty of the states* remains with them; but if Congress has the power to lay taxes, and in cases of negligence or non-compliance, can send a power to collect them, he thought that the idea of sovereignty was destroyed."

Judge Sumner, in defense, said that in order to know "whether such powers are necessary, we ought . . . to inquire what the design of uniting under one government is. It is that the national dignity may be supported, its safety preserved, and necessary debts paid. Is it not necessary, then, to afford the means by which alone those objects can be attained? . . . But some gentlemen object further, and say the delegation of these great powers *will destroy the state legislatures*; but I trust this never can take place, for the general government depends on the state legislatures for its very existence. The President is to be chosen by electors under the regulation of the state legislature; the Senate is to be chosen by the state legislatures; and the representative body by the people, under like regulations of the legislative body in the different states . . . nothing is clearer than that the existence of the legislatures, in the different states, is essential to the *very being* of the general government."

Symmes then took up the attack, demanding to know "why an unlimited power in the affair of taxation is so soon required. . . . Here, Sir, however kindly Congress may be pleased to deal with us is a very good and valid conveyance of all the property in the United States —to certain uses indeed, but those uses capable of any construction the trustees may think proper to make. . . . The paragraph in question is an absolute decree of the people. The Congress *shall* have power. It does not say that they shall *exercise* it; but our necessities say they *must*, and the experience of ages say that they *will*."

Continuing, Symmes expressed his disapproval of the power to collect. "It is a power . . . to burden us with a standing army of ravenous collectors." Then, calling attention to the qualifying clause "to pay the debts and provide for the common defense and general welfare," he said:

> These words, Sir, I confess, are an ornament to the page, and very musical words; but they are too general to be understood as any kind of limitation on the power of Congress, and not very easy to be understood at all. When Congress have the purse, they are not confined to rigid economy; and the word *debts* here is not confined to debts already contracted; or, indeed, if it were, the term "general welfare" might be applied to any expenditure whatever. . . . This clause, sir, contains the very sinews of the Constitution. And I hope that the universality of it may be singular, but it may easily be seen, that it tends to produce, in time, as universal powers in every other respect.

Thompson, speaking again in opposition, stated: "Sir, the question is, whether Congress shall have power. Some say that, if this section was left out, the whole would fall to the ground. I think so too, as it is all of a piece. We are now fixing a national consolidation. This section, I look upon it, is big with mischiefs. . . . Gentlemen say this section is clear as the sun, and that all power is retained which is not given. But where is the bill of rights which shall check the power of this Congress; which shall say, *Thus far shall ye come, and no farther?*

"The safety of the people," Thompson said, "depends on a bill of rights. If we build on a sandy foundation, is it likely we shall stand? I apply to the feelings of the convention. There are some parts of this Constitution which I cannot digest; and, sir, shall we swallow a large bone for the sake of a little meat? Some say, 'Swallow the whole now, and pick out the bone afterwards.' But I say, 'Let us pick off the meat, and throw the bone away'. . . . if this Constitution is got down, we shall alter the system entirely and have no checks upon Congress."

Bowdoin defended the section without equivocation. "There have been many objections offered against the Constitution; and of these the one most strongly urged has been, the great power vested in Congress . . . the investiture of such power, so far from being an objection, is a most cogent reason for accepting the Constitution. . . . If we consider the objects of the power, they are numerous and important; and as human foresight cannot extend to many of them, and all of them are in the womb of futurity, the quantum of the power *cannot* be estimated . . . as it must be applied to a vast variety of objects, and to cases and exigencies beyond the ken of human prescience, the power must be very great; and which *cannot* be limited without endangering the public safety." Bowdoin concluded on this note: "A possibility of abuse, as it may be affirmed of any delegated power whatever, is by itself no sufficient reason for withholding the delegation. If it were a sufficient one, no power could be delegated; nor could government of any sort subsist."

Bowdoin was supported by Parsons, who said that the Constitution would create "a government to be administered for the common good by the servants of the people, vested with delegated powers by popular elections at stated periods." The people, Parsons said, would "divest themselves of nothing; the government and powers which the Congress can administer, are the mere result of a compact made by the people with each other, for the common defense and general welfare."

Continuing his discourse, Parsons discussed the checks against any usurpation of power by the national government. "But there is another check, founded in the nature of the Union, superior to all the parchment checks that can be invented. If there should be a usurpation, it will not be on the farmer and merchant, employed and attentive only to their several occupations; it will be upon thirteen legislatures, completely organized, possessed of the confidence of the people, and having the means, as well as inclination, successfully to oppose it." Parsons was sure that "none but madmen would attempt a usurpation" under these conditions. "But, Sir, the people themselves have it in their power effectually to resist usurpation, without being driven to an appeal to arms. An act of usurpation is not obligatory; it is not law; and any man may be justified in his resistance. Let him be considered as a criminal by the general government, yet only his own fellow-citizens can convict him; they are his jury, and if they pronounce him innocent, not all the powers of Congress can hurt him; and innocent they will certainly pronounce him, if the supposed law he resisted was an act of usurpation."

At this point the Anti-federalists, evidently perceiving that the Federalists were getting much the better of the debate, sought to hasten action lest they lose their majority. Nason therefore moved to reconsider the former vote to discuss the Constitution by paragraphs, and to discuss the subject at large. This motion "met with a warm opposition." Adams aided the Federalist cause by speaking against the motion, and it was defeated.

The discussion was resumed. Dench said "it had been observed, and he was not convinced that the observation was wrong, that the grant of the powers in this section would produce a consolidation of the states, and the moment it begins, a dissolution of the state governments commences." He gathered "from the words, 'We, the People,' in the first clause" that the Constitution represented "an actual consolidation of the states."

Brooks, in answer, said that Dench's idea was "ill founded—or rather a loose idea. In the first place," Brooks said, "the Congress, under this Constitution, cannot be organized without repeated acts of the legislatures of the several states; and, therefore, if the creating power is dissolved, the body to be created cannot exist. In the second place, . . . it is impossible the general government can exist, unless the governments of the several states are forever existing. . . . It was, therefore," Brooks said, "impossible that the state governments should be annihilated by the general government . . . and . . . as the United States guarantee to *each state* a republican form of government, the state governments were as effectually secured as though this Constitution should never be in force."

Singletary, however, "thought we were giving up all power, and that the states will be like towns in this state." Going back to the days of 1775, he said that "if any body had proposed such a constitution as this in that day, it would have been thrown away at once. It would not have been looked at. We contended with Great Britain, some said for a three-penny duty on tea; but it was not that; it was because they claimed a right to tax us and bind us in all cases whatever. And does not this Constitution do the same? Does it not take away all we have—all our property? Does it not lay all taxes, duties, imposts, and excises? And what more have we to give?" he asked. "These lawyers and men of learning, and moneyed men, that talk so finely, and gloss over matters so smoothly, to make us poor illiterate people swallow down the pill, expect to get into Congress themselves; they expect to be the managers of this Constitution, and get all the power and all the money into their own hands, and then they will swallow up all us little folks, like the great Leviathan, Mr. President; yes, just as the whale swallowed up Jonah. This is what I am afraid of; but I won't say any more at present."

Then a delegate named Smith took the floor and delivered what has come to be one of the better-known defenses of the Constitution given in any of the state conventions. "Mr. President," he said, "I am a plain man, and get my living by the plough. I am not used to speak in public, but I beg your leave to say a few words to my brother plough jog- gers in this house. I have lived in a part of the country where I have known the worth of good government by the want of it." Then he de- scribed, in words eloquent for their simplicity, the anarchy and the excesses of Shays' Rebellion.

> Now, Mr. President, when I saw this Constitution, I found that it was a cure for these disorders. It was just such a thing as we wanted. I got a copy of it, and read it over and over. I had been a member of the convention to form our own state constitution, and had learnt something of the checks and balances of power, and I found them all here. I did not go to any lawyer, to ask his opinion; we have no lawyer in our town, and we do well enough without. I formed my own opinion, and was pleased with this Constitution. My honor- able old daddy there [pointing to Mr. Singletary] won't think that I expect to be a Congressman, and swallow up the liberties of the people. I never had any post, nor do I want one. But I don't think the worse of the Constitution be- cause lawyers, and men of learning, and moneyed men, are fond of it. I don't suspect that they want to get into Congress and abuse their power. . . . There is a time to sow and a time to reap; we sowed our seed when we sent men to the federal convention; now is the harvest, now is the time to reap the fruit of our labor; and if we won't do it now, I am afraid we shall never have an- other opportunity.

The discussion on the remainder of the Constitution is not reported at length and is not very revealing. The recorders said: "We do not think it essential to go into a minute detail of the conversation; as, in the speeches on the grand question, the field is again gone over. We can only say that, with the utmost attention, every objection, however trifling, was answered, and that the unremitted endeavors of gentle- men who advocated the Constitution to convince those who were in error, were not without effect."

The convention had now been in session for about three weeks, and although the Federalists had gained support it seemed certain that the Constitution could not be ratified without some apparent concession to its opponents. Federalist political skill was equal to the occasion: the opposition would be mollified by bringing .forward amendments covering the most serious objections. These amendments would be approved as recommendations to Congress, to be introduced and urged by the Massachusetts delegation. Meanwhile, ratification would not be conditional upon their eventual adoption into the Constitution.

The true finesse of the Federalists is demonstrated by their persuading Hancock to introduce the amendments as president of the convention, and to support ratification on that basis. This they accomplished by promising Bowdoin's withdrawal as a rival to Hancock's re-election as governor, and also by dangling before Hancock the prospect of the presidency or vice-presidency of the new government. Although president of the convention, Hancock had not appeared on the floor, the reason given being that he had the gout, which King said would be cured "as soon as the majority is exhibited on either side." So the maneuver was executed. Hancock took his seat on January 30. On January 31 Parsons moved that the convention "do assent to, and ratify, this Constitution." Heath then read a preparatory statement suggesting what was to come. In the afternoon, Hancock took the floor to play his role, introducing the series of amendments and managing to convey the impression, without actually saying so, that this was his own idea and that they were his handiwork. The amendments had in fact been prepared by King, Parsons, and Sedgwick. Hancock's proposal met with the approval of Adams, who sought to convey the idea, again without actually saying so, that ratification should be conditional upon the adoption of the amendments in Congress and by the states. The amendments were referred to a committee and discussion meanwhile continued.

Seeing that the Federalist strategy was undermining their strength, the more avid of the Anti-federalists now were forced to oppose the amendments they had been urging. They sought to make their position less anomalous by pleading lack of power.

Taylor said he "liked the idea of amendments; but, he said, he did not see any constitutional door open for the introduction of them by the convention. He read the several authorities which provided for the meeting of conventions, but did not see in any of them any power given to propose amendments. We are, he said, therefore treading on unsafe ground to propose them; we must take the whole, or reject the whole."

Widgery said "he did not see the probability that these amendments would be made, if we had authority to propose them. He considered, he said, that the convention did not meet for the purpose of recommending amendments, but to adopt or reject the Constitution."

And Thompson declared that the convention had no right to make amendments. "It was not, he said, the business we were sent for. He was glad . . . that gentlemen were now convinced it was not a perfect system, and that it wanted amendments. This, he said, was different from the language they had formerly held. However, as to the amendments, he could not say amen to them, but they might be voted for by some men—he did not say Judases."

Others were more openly intransigent. Nason took the position that, even with the amendments, he was still opposed to the Constitution because it destroyed the sovereignty of the states.

> When, Sir, we dissolved the political bands which connected us with Great Britain, we were in a state of nature. We then formed and adopted the Confederation, which must be considered as a sacred instrument. This confederates us under one head, as sovereign and independent states. Now, Sir, if we give Congress power to dissolve the Confederation, to what can we trust? If a nation consent thus to treat their most solemn compacts, who will ever trust them? Let us, Sir, begin with this Constitution, and see what it is. And first, "We, the people of the United States, do," etc. If this, Sir, does not go to an annihilation of the state governments, and to a perfect consolidation of the whole Union, I do not know what does. What! Shall we consent to this? Can ten, twenty, or a hundred persons in this state, who have taken the oath of allegiance to it, dispense with this oath? Gentlemen may talk as they please of dispensing, in certain cases, with oaths; but . . . with me they are sacred things. We are under oath; we have sworn that Massachusetts is a sovereign and independent state. How, then, can we vote for this Constitution, that destroys that sovereignty?

The success of the Federalist strategy in winning votes for ratification cannot be doubted. Barrell said that he feared the Constitution was "pregnant with baneful effects, although I may not live to feel them," and that under it Congress "will be vested with more extensive powers than ever Great Britain exercised over us." Some, but not all, of his objections, he said, "have been removed, in the course of the debates, by the ingenious reasonings of the speakers." He added that delegates could tell from his remarks that he did not feel the Constitution was "the most perfect system" he could wish for, yet he was "possessed with an assurance that the proposed amendments will take place. . . . I dread the fatal effects of anarchy. . . . I am convinced the Confederation is essentially deficient, and that it will be more difficult to amend that than to reform this." He thought the Constitution, despite its imperfections, was "excellent, compared with that, and that this is the best constitution we can now obtain." He said he would have preferred an adjournment to enable him to consult with his constituents. "But, sir, if I cannot be indulged on this desirable object, I am almost tempted to risk their displeasure, and adopt it without their consent."

Turner said: "I have been averse to the reception of this Constitution, while it was considered merely in its original form; but since the honorable convention have pleased to agree to the recommendation of certain amendments, I acknowledge my mind is reconciled." And Symmes, who had previously spoken against the Constitution, now declared: "Upon the whole, Mr. President, approving the amendments, and firmly believing that they will be adopted, I recall my former opposition, such as it was, to this Constitution, and shall—especially as the amendments are a standing instruction to our delegates until they are obtained—give it my unreserved assent."

The Federalists steadily pressed their case, reiterating their belief in the intrinsic merit of the Constitution and expressing their willingness to ratify even without amendments. They also took pains to make it clear that there was no intention that ratification should be conditional upon the eventual incorporation of the amendments into the Constitution. Dalton said: "I am willing to accept this Constitution as it is; and I am in favor of the motion of proposing amendments, only as it is of a conciliating nature, and not as a concession that amendments are necessary."

Jarvis remarked that if the amendments "were made conditional to our receiving the proposed Constitution, it has appeared to me that a conditional amendment must operate as a total rejection. . . . It has been insinuated, Sir, that these amendments have been artfully introduced to lead to a decision which would not otherwise be had. . . . The propositions are annexed, it is true, to the ratification; but the assent is complete and absolute without them. It is not possible that it can be understood otherwise by a single member in this honorable body."

And Ames asserted that only one question seemed troublesome: "the amendments are not a part of the Constitution, and there is nothing better than a probability to trust to, that they will ever be adopted.

. . . Very few among us now deny that a federal government is necessary to save us from ruin; that the Confederation is not that government; and that the proposed Constitution, connected with the amendments, is worthy of being adopted. The question recurs, 'Will the amendments prevail, and become part of the system?' In order to obtain
such a system as the Constitution and the amendments, there are but
three ways of proceedings—to reject the whole, and begin anew; to
adopt this plan upon condition that the amendments be inserted into
it; or to adopt his excellency's proposition." Ames concluded with a
peroration that rang with metaphors, including the familiar pillars.
"The Union is essential to our being as a nation. The pillars that prop
it are crumbling to powder. The Union is the vital sap that nourishes
the tree. . . . If we reject the Constitution . . . we girdle the tree, its leaves
will wither, its branches drop off, and the mouldering trunk will be
torn down by the tempest." Many of the delegates, Ames noted, were
satisfied with a confederation of states. "But when the inundation
comes, shall we stand on dry land? The state government is a beauti-
ful structure. It is situated, however, upon the naked beach. The Union
is the dike to fence out the flood."

On February 5 the opposition realized that the Federalist strategy
was likely to result in unconditional ratification. Desperate, they sought
to stave off defeat by moving to adjourn the convention to a future
day. But it was too late. The motion was defeated. Next day the Rev-
erend Stillman concluded the arguments. Contrasting the national with
the state governments, he said that "in the former, the objects of government will be great, numerous, and extensive; in the latter, comparatively small and limited." Next he asked:

> Who are Congress, then? They are ourselves; the men of our own choice, in
> whom we can confide; whose interest is inseparably connected with our own.
> Why is it, then, that gentlemen speak of Congress as some foreign body, as
> a set of men who will seek every opportunity to enslave us? Such insinuations
> are repugnant to the spirit of the Constitution. . . . Viewing the Constitution
> in this light, I stand ready to give my vote for it, without any amendments at
> all. Yet, if the amendments proposed by your excellency will tend to concilia-
> tion, I readily admit them, not as a condition of acceptance, but as a matter
> of recommendation only; knowing that blessed are the peacemakers. I am
> ready, sir, to submit my life, my liberty, my property, and, as far as my
> note will go, the interest of my constituents, to this general government.

Hancock then arose and addressed the convention. He said: "That
a general system of government is indispensably necessary to save our

country from ruin, is agreed upon all sides. . . . I give my assent to the Constitution, in full confidence that the amendments proposed will soon become a part of the system." The ratification resolution, Hancock continued, revealed the nature of the compact and the ratifying authority. "The convention, having impartially discussed and fully considered the Constitution for the United States of America . . . and acknowledging with grateful hearts the goodness of the supreme ruler of the universe in affording the people of the United States, in the course of his Providence, an opportunity, deliberately and peaceably, without fraud or surprise, of entering into an explicit and solemn compact with each other . . . do, in the name and in behalf of the people of the commonwealth of Massachusetts, assent to and ratify the said Constitution for the United States of America."

The resolution also made clear that the amendments were merely recommendations. "And, as it is the opinion of this convention, that certain amendments and alterations in the said Constitution would remove the fear and quiet the apprehensions of many of the good people of the commonwealth, and more effectually guard against an undue administration of the federal government, the convention do therefore recommend that the following alterations and provisions be introduced into the said Constitution." The state's representatives in Congress were enjoined, "agreeably to the fifth article of the said Constitution, to exert all their influence, and use all reasonable and legal methods, to obtain a ratification of the said alterations and provisions."

The vote was close—187 to 168. A change of ten votes would have defeated ratification. But the Federalists had won, and the beaten opponents accepted the result without bitterness or rancor.

Three of the nine amendments that expedited ratification have special relevance. The very first one was an echo from Article II of the Confederation: "That it be explicitly declared, that all powers not expressly delegated by the aforesaid Constitution are reserved to the several states, to be by them exercised." Amendment No. 3 was that Congress should not exercise its power over elections under Article I, Section 4, "but in cases where a state shall neglect or refuse to make the regulations therein mentioned, or shall make regulations subversive of the rights of the people to a free and equal representation in Congress." The fourth amendment was that Congress should not lay direct taxes, "but when the moneys arising from the impost and excise are insufficient for the public exigencies," and not even then, until Congress had first tried to raise the money through state requisitions.

These were the amendments which would have cured what were for the opponents of the Constitution its major defects. The fact that they were recommended as additions to the Constitution is a measure of what that document, without such amendments, meant both to its supporters and its opponents.

Ratification in Massachusetts was of pivotal importance to the Constitution's ultimate acceptance elsewhere. For one thing, the result in Massachusetts was being anxiously awaited in those states whose conventions had not yet met or acted. The New York legislature, in fact, had not yet even decided to call a convention. Because of the high prestige which Massachusetts held among the states, a rejection by her convention of the Constitution might well have been fatal to its adoption. Secondly, the Constitution was still in very real danger so long as the issue before the remaining conventions was the choice between bare acceptance and rejection. The technique evolved in Massachusetts of offering recommended amendments had shown the way whereby the Federalists could undermine opposition and achieve unconditional ratification of the Constitution as it came out of the convention. In a letter to Randoph in April 1788, Madison wrote: "A conditional ratification or a second convention appears to me utterly irreconcilable with the dictates of prudence and safety. Recommendatory alterations are the only ground for a coalition among the real Federalists." Before Massachusetts, not one of the ratifying conventions had recommended amendments; after Massachusetts, all the remaining conventions except Maryland did so.

XXX

Ratification in Maryland, South Carolina, and New Hampshire

ALTHOUGH six state conventions had now ratified, the result was still in doubt. The New Hampshire convention had adjourned without taking any action, thereby encouraging the opposition in South Carolina and Virginia, which were soon to decide. Because of the proximity between the latter two states, it was recognized that the action taken by Maryland would have a great effect on Virginia, and both Virginia Federalists—notably Washington and Madison—and Anti-federalists— Richard Henry Lee and Patrick Henry—exerted their influence in Maryland. By tradition, the state was national-minded. It had been the last to ratify the Articles, holding out until the wealth of the western lands should be devoted to the entire union. It had consistently supported the efforts to augment Congress' powers under the Articles, and the call for the Philadelphia convention had gone forth from Annapolis. Sentiment was heavily in favor of the Constitution.

The state's delegation to the federal convention was asked to appear before the legislature in November 1787, but only Luther Martin's report has been preserved. Published as his *Genuine Information,* it has already been discussed. The legislature authorized a convention to meet the following April.

In the interim, debate and discussion took place throughout the state and in the newspapers. The ablest Federalist tract published during this period was Alexander Contee Hanson's "Remarks on the Proposed Plan of a Federal Government." The candidates for delegates to the convention ran on the basis of their support or opposition to the Constitution, and when the convention of seventy-six members assembled at Annapolis on Monday, April 21, there were only twelve opponents of ratification present. The most prominent of the Federalists were Hanson and McHenry; the Anti-federalist leaders were Martin, Mercer, and Samuel Chase.

Before the convention assembled, the Federalists in caucus had agreed that ample time and opportunity had been afforded for discussion of the merits and demerits of the Constitution, that the main question had already been decided in the county elections of delegates, and that the convention's purpose therefore was merely to register the people's choice formally. Confident of their strength, their strategy thus was to expedite matters as much as possible, to ratify quickly and decisively, and adjourn. The action would give the maximum encouragement to the remaining conventions. On Wednesday, therefore, the convention resolved not to discuss the particular parts of the Constitution but to read it twice, "after which the subject may be fully debated and considered," and then the question of ratification should be put. The Federalists stepped up matters further by refusing to engage in the debate.

On Thursday afternoon William Paca arrived late and, after taking his seat, announced that he wished to offer amendments, saying that "although he did not expect amendments to be made the condition of ratification, he wished them to accompany it, as standing instructions to our representatives in Congress." Having just arrived, he asked the convention's indulgence until the next day. The convention did not expressly agree to receive the amendments, but it did then adjourn.

The next morning, much to Paca's surprise and indignation, numerous Federalists objected to the introduction of the amendments, on the ground "that they were elected and instructed, by the people they represented, to ratify the proposed Constitution, and that as speedily as possible, and to do no other act." The result was that Paca was not even permitted to read his amendments.

Discussion was then resumed in one-sided fashion. The Anti-federalists continued to make their objections, which were steadfastly ignored by the Federalists. The records state that the "advocates of the government, although repeatedly called on, and earnestly requested, to answer the objections, if not just, remained inflexibly silent." The discussion itself has not been preserved. Finally, on Saturday afternoon, April 26, the Federalists called for the question, and the Constitution was ratified by a vote of 63 to 11. The ratification was "in the name and on the behalf of the people of this state."

Paca then again asked permission to lay his amendments before the convention. He said that without them his constituents would "firmly oppose" the Constitution, "even with arms," he believed. The Federalists were now willing to mollify the opposition. Although they "did not deem the proposed amendments necessary to perfect the Constitution," they did agree to the appointment of a committee to consider them. Generously they gave the opposition four of the thirteen members of the committee and resolved that they would consider no amendments except those which might be reported to them by the committee. Working over the weekend, the committee agreed on thirteen amendments but rejected fifteen others. The first of the accepted amendments was, "The Congress shall exercise no power but what is expressly delegated by this Constitution." Its purpose was explained by Paca in this way: "By this amendment, the general powers given to Congress by the first and last paragraphs of the eighth section of Article I, and the second paragraph of the sixth Article, would be in a great measure restrained; those dangerous expressions, by which the bills of rights, and constitutions, of the several states, may be repealed by the laws of Congress, in some degree moderated; and the exercise of constructive powers wholly prevented." The provisions referred to, of course, were the taxing power, the necessary and proper clause, and the supremacy clause.

Included in the amendments which were rejected by a majority of the Committee were the following: that Congress should have no power over elections unless a state should neglect to make or execute the necessary regulations; that the collection of any direct tax imposed by Congress should be suspended until the states should have an opportunity to pay the sums involved; that no treaty should be effectual to repeal or abrogate any part of any state constitution or bill of rights; that Congress could exercise its power to regulate commerce only by a two-thirds vote.

The majority of the committee was willing to report to the convention only the thirteen proposed amendments which had been approved by the majority. But the minority insisted that the first three of the rejected amendments also be included. As a result the committee made no report at all to the convention. Paca presented the minority's views, and after hearing him courteously, the convention, by vote of 47 to 27, adjourned without taking action on the amendments. On May 6 Paca and the minority published their address to the people, setting forth the above events. A reply by the majority was prepared by Hanson but never published.

In South Carolina the principal recorded opposition to the Constitution took place in the legislature which was considering the call of a convention. On January 16, 1788, Charles Pinckney summarized for the legislature the origin and development of the new scheme of government and described its principal defects. He said that the Confederation had been "nothing more than a federal union; or, strictly speaking, a league founded in paternal and persuasive principles, with nothing permanent and coercive in its construction, where the members might, or might not, comply with their federal engagements, as they thought proper. . . . It was sufficient to remark that the convention saw and felt the necessity of establishing a government upon different principles, which, instead of requiring the intervention of thirteen different legislatures between the demand and the compliance, should operate upon the people in the first instance."

Pinckney minimized the likelihood that the new government would be too vigorous in its operation. "In a Union extensive as this is, composed of so many state governments, and inhabited by a people characterized, as our citizens are, by an impatience under any act which even looks like an infringement of their rights, an invasion of them by the federal head appeared to him the most remote of all our public dangers. So far from supposing a change of this sort at all probable, he confessed his apprehensions were of a different kind: he rather feared that it was impossible, while the state systems continue—and continue they must—to construct any government upon republican principles sufficiently energetic to extend its influence through all its parts."

He also thought, in this same connection, that it would be "impossible so far to divest the majority of the federal representatives of their state views and policy, as to induce them always to act upon truly national principles."

Pinckney's remarks on the national judiciary were striking. The judiciary was, he declared,

at once the most important and intricate part of the system. That a supreme federal jurisdiction was indispensable, cannot be denied. It is equally true that, in order to insure the administration of justice, it was necessary to give it all the powers, original as well as appellate, the Constitution has enumated . . . from the extensiveness of its powers, it may be easily seen that, under a wise management, this department might be made the keystone of the arch, the means of connecting and binding the whole together, of preserving uniformity in all the judicial proceedings of the Union . . . its duty would be not only to decide all national questions which should arise within the Union, but to control and keep the state judicials within their proper limits whenever they shall attempt to interfere with its power.

Opposition to the Constitution was expressed by Rawlins Lowndes. Reading the supremacy clause, he asked whether there was, "in the history of the known world" an "instance of the rulers of a republic being allowed to go so far?" He criticized the commerce power in this fashion: "Congress [of the Confederation] laboring under many difficulties, asked to regulate commerce for twenty-one years, when the power reverted into the hands of those who originally gave it; but this infallible new Constitution eased us of any more trouble, for it was to regulate commerce *ad infinitum*; and thus called upon us to pledge ourselves and posterity, forever, in support of their measures." Lowndes defended the Articles and the men who had written them, saying that "their prudence and wisdom particularly appeared in the care which they had taken sacredly to guarantee the sovereignty of each state. The treaty of peace expressly agreed to acknowledge us as free, sovereign, and independent states, which privileges we lived at present in the exercise of. But this new Constitution at once swept those privileges away, being sovereign over all; so that this state would dwindle into a mere skeleton of what it was; its legislative powers would be pared down to little more than those now vested in the corporation; and he should value the honor of a seat in the legislature in no higher estimation than a seat in the city council. It has been said," Lowndes observed, "that this new government was to be considered as an experiment. . . . So far from having any expectation of success from such experiments, he sincerely believed that, when this new Constitution should be adopted, the sun of the southern states would set, never to rise again."

Lowndes was answered by General Pinckney. The Declaration of Independence, Pinckney said, "which, for importance of matter and elegance of composition, stands unrivalled, sufficiently confutes the honorable gentleman's doctrine of the individual sovereignty and independence of the several states." The Declaration, he said, does not even enumerate "the several states. . . . The separate independence and individual sovereignty of the several states were never thought of by the enlightened band of patriots who framed this Declaration; the several states are not even mentioned by name in any part of it—as if it was intended to impress this maxim on America, that our freedom and independence arose from our Union, and that without it we could neither be free nor independent. Let us, then, consider all attempts to weaken this Union, by maintaining that each state is separately and individually independent, as a species of political heresy, which can never benefit us, but may bring on the most serious distresses."

Lowndes then "thanked those gentlemen on the other side of the question for the candid, fair manner in which they had answered his arguments. Popularity was what he never courted; but on this point he spoke merely to point out those dangers to which his fellow-citizens were exposed—dangers which were so evident that, when he ceased to exist, he wished for no other epitaph, than to have inscribed on his tomb, 'Here lies the man that opposed the Constitution, because it was ruinous to the liberty of America.'"

The legislature then unanimously authorized a convention which should meet on May 12. By a single vote, Charleston was chosen over Columbia as the place of meeting. The convention which assembled in response to this call numberd 236. It included the two Pinckneys and John Rutledge of the state's delegation to the federal convention; Thomas Pinckney, the governor; Christopher Gadsden, the state's most venerable statesman; and David Ramsey, the historian whose tract in support of the Constitution has been discussed earlier. The leading Anti-federalists were General Sumter and Edanum Burke. Unfortunately, only fragments of the debates have been preserved. On May 21 the Anti-federalists sought to adjourn the convention until October 20, but the motion was defeated, 135 to 89. On May 23 the Constitution was ratified by a comfortable two-to-one majority, 149 to 73.

The convention then, as a concession to the minority, resolved in favor of four amendments which the state's delegates in the new Congress should seek to effectuate. The first of these was that control over elections "should be forever inseparably annexed to the sovereignty of the several states," and that Congress should have no power over elections "except in cases where the legislatures of the states shall refuse or neglect to perform and fulfill the same according to the tenor of the said Constitution." The second was "that no section or paragraph of the said Constitution warrants a construction that the states do not retain every power not expressly relinquished by them and vested in the general government of the Union." The third was that Congress should lay no direct taxes except where duties and imposts proved to be insufficient and not even then until Congress should first have made requisitions on the states.

The steady advance toward ratification had achieved its first check in New Hampshire. At the convention of 113 delegates assembled at Exeter on February 13, 1788, a heavy majority had been opposed to the Constitution and many delegates were under instructions from their towns to vote against it. As usual, however, superior ability and political skill had been on the side of the Federalists, in the person of John Langdon, delegate to the Federal Convention; John Sullivan, the governor; Samuel Livermore, chief justice of the superior court; and John Taylor Gilman, member of the old Congress and later governor four times. The opposition had been led by Joshua Atherton, Charles Barrett, Abel Parker, William Hooper, and Matthias Stone.

Adapting their strategy to the circumstances, the Federalists had sought to postpone a vote until such time as they could win. The debate proceeded for about a week; unfortunately no record was preserved. During this period the persuasive oratorical skill of the Federalists had won many converts, but it was still apparent that if a vote were taken, the Constitution would be defeated. They had therefore moved to recess the convention until June 18, when it should reconvene at Concord. Langdon's motion had been opposed by Atherton, but it had carried by the narrow margin of 56 to 51.

Having thus averted outright defeat, the Federalists diligently used the interim period to educate the people and to change local instructions to the delegates. When the convention reassembled, Federalists were in a much stronger position. During the recess Maryland and South Carolina had ratified, bringing the total of ratifications to eight. The Virginia convention had been in session since June 2, and the New York convention had assembled on June 17. This situation enabled the Federalists to argue that, by quick action, New Hampshire could achieve the distinction of being the ninth convention to ratify, thereby putting the Constitution into operation. They followed up this appeal on June 20 with a motion by Landgon, following the example set in Massachusetts, offering a series of recommended amendments to accompany the ratification. The amendments, in fact, were almost identical with those proposed in Massachusetts and therefore will not be rehearsed here.

Atherton for the opposition sought to frustrate the Federalists' strategy by moving that the Constitution be ratified but that it should not be operative in New Hampshire until the amendments should be incorporated. This motion, of course, was equivalent to a rejection of the Constitution as it stood. Livermore countered for the Federalists by moving that the Atherton motion be postponed to make way for a substitute motion that in case the Constitution should be ratified, the amendments should be recommended to Congress. This motion carried by a small majority.

It was now clear that the Constitution would be ratified. The Antifederalists' turn to postpone the vote had now come, but Atherton's motion that the convention adjourn to some future day failed to carry. Then Livermore, seconded by Langdon, moved that the main question be put. By a vote of 57 to 47 the convention ratified the Constitution. Once again Federalist political expertise had turned defeat into victory. The vote was taken at one o'clock on Saturday, June 20, and not knowing whether the Virginia convention had yet acted, the New Hampshire convention protected its claim to the honor of being the ninth ratifier by recording the hour as well as the day of the vote.

XXXI

Ratification in Virginia

ALTHOUGH New Hampshire's action assured ratification the accession of Virginia and New York to the Constitution was still essential to its success. Failure of either state to ratify would have meant a geographically fragmented nation, as well as the loss of the particular strength and resources each state had to offer. This was especially true of Virginia, for she was at this time and for a generation afterward the foremost of the states in population, wealth, and political influence.

The Virginia legislature, on October 25, 1787, authorized a convention to assemble on the first Monday of June 1788. In the interim both friends and foes of the Constitution exerted every effort to influence the voters in the election of delegates. Washington was especially active in this his home state. In the convention of 170 members which assembled on June 2, 1788, the strength of the Federalists and Anti-federalists was very nearly equal. With the exception of Washington, Jefferson (who was serving as minister to France), and Richard Henry Lee, nearly all of Virginia's most prominent citizens were chosen.

Madison was the leader of the Federalist forces, assisted principally by Randolph, John Marshall, and George Nicholas. At the head of the opposition was Patrick Henry, who had declined appointment as a delegate to the federal convention with the statement that he "smelled a rat." He was now backed by George Mason, William Grayson, and James Monroe.

At times the Virginia convention gave the appearance of being a personal debate between Henry and Madison. It therefore affords a striking study in contrasts. Henry was a flamboyant and emotional orator, while Madison relied on quiet and rational persuasion. The convention unanimously chose Pendleton, chancellor of the state, as its president. Although the delegates voted to discuss the Constitution part by part in sequence, in fact the discussion frequently ranged over the whole plan without restriction. The Virginia convention debates are recorded more fully than those of any other state.

The principal objection levied against the Constitution throughout the convention was that it created a national and consolidated government instead of a confederation, and that the powers granted were so extensive and limitless as to inevitably reduce the states to insignificance and destroy the liberties of the people.

Henry lost no time in plunging into the attack. On June 4 he stated:

> I would make this inquiry of those worthy characters who composed a part of the late federal convention. I am sure they were fully impressed with the necessity of forming a great consolidated government, instead of a confederation. That this is a consolidated government is demonstrably clear; and the danger of such a government is, to my mind, very striking. I have the highest veneration for those gentlemen; but, Sir, give me leave to demand, "What right had they to say, *We, the people?*" My political curiosity, exclusive of my anxious solicitude for the public welfare, leads me to ask, "Who authorized them to speak the language of, *We, the people,* instead of, *We, the states?*" States are the characteristics and the soul of a confederation. If the states be not the agents of this compact, it must be one great, consolidated, national government, of the people of all the states. . . . The federal convention ought to have amended the old system; for this purpose they were solely delegated; the object of their mission extended to no other consideration.

Randolph, who had refused to sign the Constitution as a delegate to the federal convention, now arose and announced that he had decided, in the interest of union, to support it. In response to Henry, he said, "The gentleman then proceeds, and inquires why we assumed the language of 'We, the people.' I ask, Why not? The government is for the people; and the misfortune was, that the people had no agency in the government before." He then asked, "What harm is there in consulting the people on the construction of a government by which they are to be bound? Is it unfair? Is it unjust? If the government is to be binding on the people, are not the people the proper persons to examine its merits or defects? I take this to be one of the least and most trivial objections that will be made to the Constitution; it carries the answer with itself."

Mason joined in to support Henry:

> Mr. Chairman, whether the Constitution be good or bad, the present clause clearly discovers that it is a national government, and no longer a confederation. I mean that clause which gives the first hint of the general government laying direct taxes. The assumption of this power of laying direct taxes does, of itself, entirely change the Confederation of the states into one consolidated

government. This power, being at discretion, unconfined, and without any kind of control, must carry everything before it. The very idea of converting what was formerly a confederation to a consolidated government is totally subversive of every principle which has hitherto governed us. This power is calculated to annihilate totally the state governments. Will the people of this great community submit to be individually taxed by two different and distinct powers? Will they suffer themselves to be doubly harassed? These two concurrent powers cannot exist long together; the one will destroy the other; the general government being paramount to, and in every respect more powerful than the state governments, the latter must give way to the former.

After questioning the inadequacy of representation in the lower house, Mason said his principal objection was that the Confederation had been converted into one "consolidated government, which, from my best judgment of it (and which perhaps will be shown, in the course of this discussion, to be really well founded), is one of the worst curses that can possibly befall a nation." Mason wondered how one such government could hope to operate over such a vast nation. "I hope that a government may be framed which may suit us, by drawing a line between the general and state governments, and prevent that dangerous clashing of interest and power, which must, as it now stands, terminate in the destruction of one or the other. When we come to the judiciary, we shall be more convinced that this government will terminate in the annihilation of the state governments: the question then will be, whether a consolidated government can preserve the freedom and secure the rights of the people."

The next day—Thursday, June 5—the convention met as a committee of the whole, with George Wythe in the chair. Pendleton, now on the floor, arose to reply to Henry's challenge of the previous day:

But an objection is made to the form: the expression, "We, the people," is thought improper. Permit me to ask the gentleman who made this objection, who but the people can delegate powers? Who but the people have a right to form government? The expression is a common one, and a favorite one with me. The representatives of the people, by their authority, is a mode wholly inessential. If the objection be, that the Union ought to be not of the people, but of the state governments, then I think the choice of the former very happy and proper. What have the state governments to do with it? Were they to determine, the people would not, in that case, be the judges upon what terms it was adopted.

Then, replying to Mason, Pendleton continued. "But it is represented to be a consolidated government, annihilating that of the states—a consolidated government, which so extensive a territory as the United States cannot admit of, without terminating in despotism. If this be such a government, I will confess, with my worthy friend [Mason], that it is inadmissible over such a territory as this country. Let us consider whether it be such a government or not. I should understand a consolidated government to be that which should have the sole and exclusive power, legislative, executive, and judicial, without any limitation. Is this such a government? Or can it be changed to such a one? It only extends to the general purposes of the Union. It does not intermeddle with the local, particular affairs of the states."

Proceeding, Pendleton said that state governments must be preserved: the existence of the federal government depends on them. "The Senate derives its existence immediately from the state legislatures; and the Representatives and President are elected under their direction and control; they also preserve order among the citizens of their respective states, and without order and peace no society can possibly exist. Unless, therefore, there be state legislatures to continue the existence of Congress, and preserve order and peace among the inhabitants, this general government, which gentlemen suppose will annihilate the state governments, must itself be destroyed. When, therefore, the federal government is, in so many respects, so absolutely dependent on the state governments, I wonder how any gentleman reflecting on the subject, could have conceived an idea of a possibility of the former destroying the latter."

Henry's response was to reiterate and elaborate on his original premise. "I rose yesterday to ask a question which arose in my own mind. When I asked that question, I thought the meaning of my interrogation was obvious. The fate of this question and of America may depend on this. Have they said, 'We, the states?' Have they made a proposal of a compact between states? If they had, this would be a confederation. It is otherwise most clearly a consolidated government. The question turns, Sir, on that poor little thing—the expression, 'We, the *people,*' instead of the '*states,*' of America. I need not take much pains to show that the principles of this system are extremely pernicious, impolitic, and dangerous."

"Here," said Henry, "is a resolution as radical as that which separated us from Great Britain. It is radical in this transition; our rights and privileges are endangered, and the sovereignty of the states will be relinquished: and cannot we plainly see that this is actually the case?"

Here he proceeded to demonstrate that the Constitution called for a "consolidated" government:

Suppose the people of Virginia should wish to alter their government; can a majority of them do it? No; because they are connected with other men, or, in other words, consolidated with other states. When the people of Virginia, at a future day, shall wish to alter their government, though they should be unanimous in this desire, yet they may be prevented therefrom by a despicable minority at the extremity of the United States. The founders of your own Constitution made your government changeable: but the power of changing it is gone from you. Whither is it gone? It is placed in the same hands that hold the rights of twelve other states; and those who hold those rights have right and power to keep them. It is not the particular government of Virginia: one of the leading features of that government is, that a majority can alter it, when necessary for the public good. This government is not a Virginian, but an American government. Is it not, therefore, a consolidated government?

During this lengthy discourse, Henry also condemned the "unlimited and unbounded power of taxation," which, together with other powers of Congress which had been taken from the states, "will reduce the power of the latter to nothing."

The next day Madison rose to reply to Henry's animadversions. Did the Constitution indeed, Madison asked, create "consolidated" government? He proceeded rationally to examine the parts:

I conceive myself that it is of a mixed nature; it is in a manner unprecedented; we cannot find one express example in the experience of the world. It stands by itself. In some respects it is a government of a federal nature; in others, it is of a consolidated nature. Even if we attend to the manner in which the Constitution is investigated, ratified, and made the act of the people of America, I can say, notwithstanding what the honorable gentleman has alleged, that this government is not completely consolidated, nor is it entirely federal. Who are parties to it? The people—but not the people as composing one great body; but the people as composing thirteen sovereignties. Were it, as the gentleman asserts, a consolidated government, the assent of a majority of the people would be sufficient for its establishment; and, as a majority have adopted it already, the remaining states would be bound by the act of the majority, even if they unanimously reprobated it. Were it such a government as is suggested, it would be now binding on the people of this state, without having had the privilege of deliberating upon it.

But, said Madison, no states can be bound by the Constitution except by their own consent. If all thirteen states ratify, the government will have been established "by the people at large." Madison went on, that if "Virginia was separated from all the states, her power and authority would extend to all cases: in like manner, were all powers vested in the general government, it would be a consolidated government; but the powers of the federal government are enumerated; it can only operate in certain cases; it has legislative powers on defined and limited objects, beyond which it cannot extend its jurisdiction."

Madison did not agree that "its consolidated nature," together with direct taxation, would cause the government to "destroy all subordinate authority." This might come about if the general government were totally independent. "But, Sir, on whom does this general government depend? It derives its authority from these [state] governments, and from the same sources from which their authority is derived. The members of the federal government are taken from the same men from whom those of the state legislatures are taken. If we consider the mode in which the federal representatives will be chosen, we shall be convinced that the general will never destroy the individual governments; and this conviction must be strengthened by an attention to the construction of the Senate."

On Saturday, June 7, Francis Corbin joined in the Federalist reply to Henry. "The introductory expression of 'We, the people,' has been thought improper by the honorable gentleman. I expected no such objection as this. Ought not the people, Sir, to judge of that government whereby they are to be ruled?" Corbin noted that the "powers of the general government are only of a general nature, and their object is to protect, defend, and strengthen the United States; but the internal administration of government is left to the state legislatures, who exclusively retain such powers as will give the states the advantages of small republics, without the danger commonly attendant on the weakness of such governments.

"There are controversies even about the name of this government," Corbin said. "It is denominated by some a federal, by others a consolidated government. The definition given of it by my honorable friend [Madison] is, in my opinion, accurate. Let me, however, call it by another name—a representative federal republic, as contradistinguished from a confederacy."

Henry's attack on the taxing power was answered by both Randolph and Madison. Randolph begged "the friends of the Union to consider the necessity of this power: without it we may abandon the government altogether: it is the soul of the government; no substitute will answer in its stead. The history of other confederacies will instruct us that the general government must operate on the individuals of the community, or else be totally insufficient. Not ancient confederacies only, but certain modern ones, will point out to us the horrid situation in which these states must be involved, unless the general government be vested with this power." And Madison observed: "If a government depends on other governments for its revenues—if it must depend on the voluntary contributions of its members—its existence must be precarious. . . . If the general government is to depend on the voluntary contribution of the states for its support, dismemberment of the United States may be the consequence. In cases of imminent danger, the states more immediately exposed to it only would exert themselves; those remote from it would be too supine to interest themselves warmly in the fate of those whose distresses they did not immediately perceive. The general government ought, therefore, to be empowered to defend the whole Union."

Henry renewed his attack on the taxing power with vigor. Seizing upon figures of speech used by Randolph and Madison, he declared: "The power of direct taxation was called by the honorable gentleman the *soul* of the government: another gentleman called it the *lungs* of the government. . . . Must I give my soul, my lungs, to Congress?" He pursued the metaphor:

> I tell you, they shall not have the soul of Virginia. They tell us that one collector may collect the federal and state taxes. The general government being paramount to the state legislatures, if the sheriff is to collect for both—his right hand for Congress, his left for the state—his right hand being paramount over the left, his collections will go to Congress. We shall have the rest. Deficiencies in collections will always operate against the states. Congress, being the paramount, supreme power, must not be disappointed. Thus Congress will have an unlimited, unbounded command over the soul of this commonwealth. After satisfying their uncontrolled demands, what can be left for the states? Not a sufficiency even to defray the expense of their internal administration. They must therefore glide imperceptibly and gradually out of existence. This, sir, must naturally terminate in a consolidation. If this will do for other people, it never will do for me.

Then, adverting to an argument of Madison based on implication, Henry poured forth all the dread which a strict constructionist feels for such an approach. "If they can use implication for us, they can also use implication against us. We are giving power; they are getting power; judge, then, on which side the implication will be used! When we once put it in their option to assume constructive power, danger will follow. Trial by jury, and liberty of the press, are also on this foundation of implication. If they encroach on these rights, and you give your implication for a plea, you are cast; for they will be justified by the last part of it, which gives them full power 'to make all laws which shall be necessary and proper to carry their power into execution.' Implication is dangerous, because it is unbounded: if it be admitted at all, and no limits be prescribed, it admits of the utmost extension.

"They say that every thing that is not given is retained. The reverse of the proposition is true by implication. They do not carry their implication so far when they speak of the general welfare—no implication when the sweeping clause comes. Implication is only necessary when the existence of privileges is in dispute. The existence of powers is sufficiently established. If we trust our dearest rights to implication, we shall be in a very unhappy situation." Thus ended the first week's debate.

On Monday, June 9, Henry again took the initiative, this time directing his remarks to Madison's analysis of the previous Friday. "We are told," he began, "that this government, collectively taken, is without an example; that it is national in this part, and federal in that part, etc. We may be amused, if we please, by a treatise of political anatomy. In the brain it is national; the stamina are federal; some limbs are federal, others national. The Senators are voted for by the state legislatures; so far it is federal. Individuals choose the members of the first branch; here it is national. It is federal in conferring general powers, but national in retaining them. It is not to be supported by the states; the pockets of individuals are to be searched for its maintenance. What signifies it to me that you have the most curious anatomical description of it in its creation? To all the common purposes of legislation, it is a great consolidation of government."

Henry then drew a graphic picture of the debased role the states would play under the Constitution. "You are not to have the right to legislate in any but trivial cases; you are not to touch private contracts; you are not to have the right of having arms in your own defense; you cannot be trusted with dealing out justice between man and man. What shall the states have to do?" Would they be reduced, Henry asked, to caring for the poor, making and repairing highways, and erecting bridges? "Abolish the state legislatures at once. What purposes should they be continued for? Our legislature will indeed be a ludicrous spectacle—one hundred and eighty men marching in solemn, farcical procession, exhibiting a mournful proof of the lost liberty of their country, without the power of restoring it. But, Sir, we have the consolation that it is a mixed government; that is, it may work sorely on your neck, but you will have some comfort by saying, that it was a federal government in its origin."

Henry now asked how the Constitution could be said to provide a federal government:

> Is it not a consolidated government for almost every purpose? Is the government of Virginia a state government after this government is adopted? I grant that it is a republican government, but for what purposes? For such trivial domestic considerations as render it unworthy the name of a legislature. I shall take leave of this political anatomy, by observing that it is the most extraordinary that ever entered into the imagination of man. If our political diseases demand a cure, this is an unheard of medicine.

Lee of Westmoreland rebuked Henry for his lack of national spirit and his appeals to localism. "Am I to be told," Lee asked, "when I come to deliberate on the interest of Virginia, that it obstructs the interest of the county of Westmoreland? Is this obstruction a sufficient reason to neglect the collective interests of Virginia? Were it of a local nature, it would be right to prefer it; but, being of a general nature, the local interest must give way. I trust, then, that gentlemen will consider that the object of their deliberations is of a general nature."

He continued to chide Henry. "The people of America, Sir, are one people. I love the people of the north, not because they have adopted the Constitution, but because I fought with them as my countrymen, and because I consider them as such. Does it follow from hence that I have forgotten my attachment to my native state? In all local matters I shall be a Virginian: in those of a general nature, I shall not forget that I am an American."

The next day Monroe addressed himself to the dangers of the powers which the Constitution granted. He set out to "draw the line between the powers necessary to be given to the federal, and those which ought to be left to the state governments. To the former I would give control over the national affairs; to the latter I would leave the care of local interests."

He was especially critical of the taxing power. "What is the extent of the power of laying and collecting direct taxes? Does it not give to the United States all the resources of the individual states? Does it not give an absolute control over the resources of all the states? If you give the resources of the several states to the general government, in what situation are the states left? I therefore think the general government will preponderate." He also leveled an attack on the necessary and proper clause, saying, "There is a general power given to them to make all laws that will enable them to carry their powers into effect. There are no limits pointed out. They are not restrained or controlled from making any law, however oppressive in its operation, which they may think necessary to carry their powers into effect. . . . I conceive that such general powers are very dangerous. Our great unalienable rights ought to be secured from being destroyed by such unlimited powers, either by a bill of rights, or by an express provision in the body of the Constitution."

Monroe considered that conflict between the national and state governments was inevitable. The "communion of powers, legislative and judicial," forbids harmony. "I have never yet heard or read, in the history of mankind, of a concurrent exercise of power by two parties, without producing a struggle between them." In this conflict he argued that under the Constitution the states would be the losers. "Besides its possession of all the resources of the country, there are other circumstances that will enable it to triumph in the conflict with the states. Gentlemen of influence and character, men of distinguished talents, of eminent virtue, and great endowments, will compose the general government. In what a situation will the different states be, when all the talents and abilities of the country will be against them?"

John Marshall then addressed the convention for the first time, arguing that the powers granted were necessary and amply safeguarded. Nicholas then undertook to answer part of Monroe's argument that the "sweeping clause" harbored great dangers. "The committee will perceive that the Constitution had enumerated all the powers which the general government should have, but did not say how they were to be exercised. It therefore, in this clause, tells how they shall be exercised. Does this give any new power? I say not. Suppose it had been inserted, at the end of every power, that they should have power to make laws to carry that power into execution; would this have increased their powers? If, therefore, it could not have increased their powers, if placed at the end of each power, it cannot increase them at the end of all. This clause only enables them to carry into execution the powers given to them, but gives them no additional power."

On Wednesday, Madison answered Monroe's argument that the national government would overwhelm the states by asserting that in fact it would probably be just the other way around. "Will not the people (whose predominant interest will ultimately prevail) feel great attachment to the state legislatures? They have the care of all local interests —those familiar domestic objects, for which men have the strongest predilection. The general government, on the contrary, has the preservation of the aggregate interest of the Union—objects which, being less familiar, and more remote from men's notice, have a less powerful influence on their minds. Do we not see great and natural attachments arising from local considerations? This will be the case in a much stronger degree in the state governments than in the general government. The people will be attached to their state legislatures from a thousand causes; and into whatever scale the people at large will throw themselves, that scale will preponderate."

He therefore believed "that the state governments, and not the general government, will preponderate." The states had more extensive means of influence so "powerful and prevailing" as to produce "such attention to local considerations as will be inconsistent with the advancement of the interest of the Union." Madison sought to minimize the extent of national powers by stating that they "relate to external objects, and are but few," whereas "the powers in the states relate to those great objects which immediately concern the prosperity of the people."

Summarizing his position, Madison said that "the powers vested in the proposed government are not so much an augmentation of powers in the general government, as a change rendered necessary for the purpose of giving efficacy to those which were vested in it before."

Mason immediately took issue with Madison on the latter point. The Constitution, Mason said, does indeed give "great and important powers" to the general government. Turning to the Sixth Article, Mason read the supremacy clause and asked:

> Now, Sir, if the laws and Constitution of the general government, as expressly said, be paramount to those of any state, are not those rights which we were afraid to trust our own citizens annulled and given up to the general government? The bill of rights is a part of our own Constitution. The judges are obliged to take notice of the laws of the general government; consequently, the rights secured by our bill of rights are given up. If they are not given up, where are they secured? By implication! Let gentlemen show that they are secured in a plain, direct, unequivocal manner. It is not in their power.

To Mason, amendments were essential to secure individual rights, in unambiguous language. "We wish to give the government sufficient energy, on real republican principles," he said, "but we wish to withhold such powers as are not absolutely necessary in themselves, but are extremely dangerous." The most dangerous corruption of all was that of the people's own representatives. "We ask such amendments as will point out what powers are reserved to the state governments, and clearly discriminate between them and those which are given to the general government, so as to prevent future disputes and clashing of interests. Grant us amendments like these, and we will cheerfully, with our hands and hearts, unite with those who advocate it, and we will do every thing we can to support and carry it into execution. But in its present form we never can accede to it."

Grayson then spoke in opposition, especially against the taxing power. States who surrender to the central government their power of taxation "have nothing more to give," Grayson said. "Is it not a political absurdity," he asked, "to suppose that there can be two concurrent legislatures, each possessing the supreme power of direct taxation? If two powers come in contact, must not the one prevail over the other? Must it not strike every man's mind, that two unlimited, coequal, coordinate authorities, over the same objects, cannot exist together?"

Grayson also disputed Madison's claim that in the contest for power the states would preponderate. After the states have lost "their most important rights," Grayson said, what influence could they exert? "Will not the diminution of their power and influence be an augmentation of those of the general government? Will not the officers of the general government receive higher compensation for their services than those of the state governments? Will not the most influential men be employed by Congress? I think the state governments will be condemned and despised as soon as they give up the power of direct taxation; and a state, says Montesquieu, should lose her existence sooner than her importance."

Pendleton replied to Grayson on both points. Even if states relinquished their powers of taxation, they would have their own representatives in Congress. "Why should we fear so much greater dangers from our representatives there," Pendleton asked, "than from those we have here? Why make so great a distinction between our representatives here, and in the federal government, where every branch is formed on the same principle—preserving throughout the representative, responsible character?"

On the second point, Pendleton said he did not see how state government would be destroyed. The two governments operated in different ways in separate spheres. It was not reasonable to think that states would be reduced to maintaining roads and bridges:

I think that they are still possessed of the highest powers. Our dearest rights —life, liberty, and property—as Virginians, are still in the hands of our state legislature. If they prove too feeble to protect us, we resort to the aid of the general government for security. The true distinction is, that the two governments are established for different purposes, and act on different objects; so that, notwithstanding what the worthy gentleman said, I believe I am still correct, and insist that, if each power is confined within its proper bounds, and to its proper objects, an interference can never happen. Being for two different purposes, as long as they are limited to the different objects, they can no more clash than two parallel lines can meet. Both lay taxes, but for different purposes. The same officers may be used by both governments, which will prevent a number of inconveniences. If an invasion, or insurrection, or other misfortune, should make it necessary for the general government to interpose, this will be for the general purposes of the Union, and for the manifest interest of the states.

Henry now came to Grayson's support and also answered Madison. Madison's opinion and his own were "diametrically opposite," said Henry:

Bring forth the federal allurements, and compare them with the poor, contemptible things that the state legislatures can bring forth. On the part of the state legislatures, there are justices of the peace and militia officers; and even these justices and officers are bound by oath in favor of the Constitution. A constable is the only man who is not obliged to swear paramount allegiance to this beloved Congress. On the other hand, there are rich, fat, federal emoluments. Your rich, snug, fine, fat federal officers—the number of collectors of taxes and excises—will outnumber any thing from the states.

The "influence of this government will be such," Henry continued, "that you never can get amendments; for if you propose alterations, you will affront them. Let the honorable gentleman consider all these things, and say, whether the state governments will last as long as the federal government." Turning to answer Pendleton, Henry said that even when the Constitution drew a line between the two governments, there was no check to prevent encroachment of one upon the other.

On Saturday, June 14, Mason objected to Congress' power over the militia, saying that "unless there be some restrictions on the power . . . we may very easily see that it will produce dreadful oppressions." Using "various pretences, Congress," said Mason, "may neglect to provide for arming and disciplining the militia; and the state governments cannot do it, for Congress has an exclusive right to arm them, etc. Here is a line of division drawn between them—the state and general governments. The power over the militia is divided between them. The national government has an exclusive right to provide for arming, organizing, and disciplining the militia, and for governing such part of them as may be employed in the service of the United States." Congress could prescribe ways for the states to appoint officers and maintain militia, said Mason, but only if Congress *chose* to. "Should the national government wish to render the militia useless, they may neglect them, and let them perish, in order to have a pretense of establishing a standing army." Introduction of a standing army, indeed, was what Mason ultimately feared.

Madison replied that if the general government had "full power to call forth the militia," in emergencies, there would be no need for a standing army. "If you limit their power over the militia, you give them a pretext for substituting a standing army. If you put it in the power of the state governments to refuse the militia, by requiring their consent, you destroy the general government, and sacrifice particular states. The same principles and motives which produce disobedience to requisitions, will produce refusal in this case."

Nicholas took issue with Mason's proposed amendment that militia not be allowed to leave the state without "consent of the state legislature." How could Congress protect the Union if the general defense were dependent upon "the particular caprice of the members of the state governments?" Nicholas concluded by saying that if "the general government be obliged to apply to the states, a part will be thereby rendered superior to the whole."

Now that the Federalists had defended both the taxing and militia powers, Henry triumphantly affected to see all this as proof of his charge of a national, consolidated government. Henry asserted "it is now confessed that this is a national government. There is not a single federal feature in it. It has been alleged, within these walls, during the debates, to be national and federal, as it suited the arguments of gentlemen.

"But now, when we have heard the definition of it, it is purely national. The honorable member was pleased to say that the sword and purse included everything of consequence. And shall we trust them out of our hands without checks and barriers? The sword and purse are essentially necessary for the government. Every essential requisite must be in Congress. Where are the purse and sword of Virginia? They must go to Congress. What is become of your country? The Virginian government is but a name. It clearly results, from his last argument, that we are to be consolidated."

Now Henry referred to a statement that the means "must be commensurate to the end. How does this apply? All things in common are left with this government. There being an infinitude in the government, there must be an infinitude of means to carry it on." Here, certainly, Henry said, "the creature has destroyed and soared above the creator. For if its powers be infinite, what rights have the people remaining? By that very argument, despotism has made way in all countries where the people unfortunately have been enslaved by it. We are told, the sword and purse are necessary for the national defense. The junction of these, without limitation, in the same hands, is, by logical and mathematical conclusions, the description of despotism."

The third week of debate began with Henry once more complaining of Congress' power to raise armies and call out the militia. Mason joined in the attack, saying, "The objection was, that too much power was given to Congress—power that would finally destroy the state governments more effectually by insidious, underhanded means, than such as could be openly practised. This, said he, is the opinion of many worthy men, not only in this convention, but in all parts of America."

Mason felt strongly that "state governments ought to have the control of the militia, except when they were absolutely necessary for general purposes." Otherwise, he said, it "must finally produce, most infallibly, the annihilation of the state governments."

Henry then charged that since Congress was granted power to call out the militia, "it appeared to him, most decidedly, that the power of suppressing insurrections was exclusively given to Congress. If it remained in the states, it was by implication."

Corbin now replied to Mason. For Mason to say it would be humiliating for state governments not to control the general government was like complaining "that one county could not control the state at large."

And Marshall then answered Henry. "The state governments," said Marshall, "did not derive their powers from the general government; but each government derived its powers from the people, and each was to act according to the powers given it. Would any gentleman deny this?" Marshall wanted to know if powers not specifically bestowed were still implied:

Could any man say so? Could any man say that this power was not retained by the states, as they had not given it away? For, says he, does not a power remain till it is given away? The state legislatures had power to command and govern their militia before, and have it still, undeniably, unless there be something in this Constitution that takes it away. . . . The truth is that when power is given to the general legislature, if it was in the state legislature before, both shall exercise it; unless there be an incompatibility in the exercise by one to that by the other, or negative words precluding the state governments from it. But there are no negative words here. It rests, therefore, with the states. To me it appears, then, unquestionable that the state governments can call forth the militia, in case the Constitution should be adopted, in the same manner as they could have done before its adoption.

Henry, however, argued that Marshall's interpretation was not the correct one. The "nations of the earth," Henry said, all interpret the concession of power to mean that "when power was given, it was given exclusively." It was obvious, he said, that "the powers given to Congress were exclusively given. . . . The rights which the states had must be founded on the restrictions on Congress. . . . If the doctrine which had been so often circulated, that rights not given were retained, was true, why [were] there . . . negative clauses to restrain Congress[?]" For, Henry said, "if Congress had no power but that given to them, why restrict them by negative words? Is not the clear implication this—that, if these restrictions were not inserted, they could have performed what they prohibit?"

Henry then levied his argument on the necessary and proper clause. "By this they have a right to pass any law that may facilitate the execution of their acts. . . . Is there any act, however atrocious, which they cannot do by virtue of this clause?" he asked. "The sweeping clause will fully enable them to do what they please. What could the most extravagant and boundless imagination ask, but power to do every thing?"

Madison, in his reasonable way, undertook to answer Henry on this point:

If that latitude of construction which he contends for were to take place with respect to the sweeping clause, there would be room for those horrors. But it gives no supplementary power. It only enables them to execute the delegated powers. If the delegation of their powers be safe, no possible inconvenience can arise from this clause. It is at most but explanatory. For when any power is given, its delegation necessarily involves authority to make laws to execute it. Were it possible to delineate on paper all those particular cases and circumstances in which legislation by the general legislature would be necessary, and leave to the states all the other powers, I imagine no gentleman would object to it. But this is not within the limits of human capacity. The particular powers which are found necessary to be given are therefore delegated generally, and particular and minute specification is left to the legislature.

Mason, however, refused to accept Madison's explanation. He could see nothing in the Constitution "which secures to the states the powers which are said to be retained. . . . Will powers remain to the states which are not expressly guarded and reserved?" he asked. Then he referred to the Articles:

There was a clause in the Confederation reserving to the states respectively every power, jurisdiction, and right, not expressly delegated to the United States. This clause has never been complained of, but approved by all. Why not, then, have a similar clause in this Constitution, in which it is the more indispensably necessary than in the Confederation, because of the great augmentation of power vested in the former? In my humble apprehension, unless there be some such clear and finite expression, this clause now under consideration will go to any thing our rulers may think proper. Unless there be some express declaration that every thing not given is retained, it will be carried to any power Congress may please.

Henry reiterated his view of the construction which would obtain: "that all rights not expressly and unequivocally reserved to the people are impliedly and incidentally relinquished to rulers, as necessarily inseparable from the delegated powers." According to the Articles, therefore, "every right was retained by the states, respectively, which was not given up to the government of the United States. But there is no such thing here. You, therefore, by a natural and unavoidable implication, give up your rights to the general government."

Grayson also "thought it questionable whether rights not given up were reserved." A majority of the states, he observed, had expressly reserved "certain important rights by bills or rights, and . . . in the Confederation there was a clause declaring expressly that every power and right not given up was retained by the states. It was the general sense of America that such a clause was necessary; otherwise, why did they introduce a clause which was totally unnecessary?" The power of legislation, Grayson felt, was so extensive "that he doubted whether, when it was once given up, *anything* was retained."

On Wednesday, June 18, the treaty power came under fire. Henry asked "what condition this country would be in if two-thirds of a quorum should be empowered to make a treaty: they might relinquish and alienate territorial rights, and our most valuable commercial advantages. In short, if anything should be left us, it would be because the President and Senators were pleased to admit it. The power of making treaties," he said, "by this Constitution, ill-guarded as it is, extended farther than it did in any country in the world. Treaties were to have more force here than in any part of Christendom; for he defied any gentleman to show any things so extensive in any strong, energetic government in Europe. Treaties rest, says he, on the laws and usages of nations. To say that they are municipal" was to Henry "a doctrine totally novel. . . . To make them paramount to the Constitution and laws of the states, is unprecedented."

Earlier on June 13, Randolph had said of this power: "But it has been said that there is no restriction with respect to making treaties. The various contingencies which may form the object of treaties, are, in the nature of things, incapable of definition. The government ought to have power to provide for every contingency."

Now Nicholas answered Henry. It was not true, he said, that Congress could make a treaty "relinquishing our rights, and inflicting punishments." Article VI provides "that this Constitution, and the laws of the United States which shall be made in pursuance thereof, and all the treaties made, or which shall be made, under the authority of the United States, shall be the supreme law of the land. They can, by this, make no treaty which shall be repugnant to the spirit of the Constitution, or inconsistent with the delegated powers. The treaties they make must be under the authority of the United States, to be within their province."

Mason, however, insisted that he could find "nothing in that Constitution to hinder a dismemberment of the empire." As it stood, he thought the "President and Senate can make any treaty whatsoever. He wanted "an express and explicit declaration, in that paper, that the power which can make other treaties cannot, without the consent of the national Parliament—the national Legislature—dismember the empire. The Senate alone ought not to have this power; much less ought a few states to have it. No treaty to dismember the empire ought to be made without the consent of three-fourths of the legislature in all is branches."

The convention then took up Article III dealing with the judiciary. The attack here was of the same nature. Alluding to Section 1, Mason asked what would be left to the state courts. Congress could create any number of inferior courts, he said, "of whatever nature they please." Under Section 2 there would be no limit to the jurisdiction of these inferior courts.

If there be any limits, they must be contained in one of the clauses of this section; and I believe, on a dispassionate discussion, it will be found that there is none of any check. All the laws of the United States are paramount to the laws and constitution of any single state. "The judicial power shall extend to all cases in law and equity arising under this Constitution." What objects will not this expression extend to? Such laws may be formed as will go to every object of private property. When we consider the nature of these courts, we must conclude that their effect and operation will be utterly to destroy the state governments; for they will be the judges how far their laws will operate. They are to modify their own courts, and you can make no state law to counteract them.

Mason believed, "religiously and conscientiously," although he could not be "absolutely certain," that the principle of inferior courts was intended to "destroy the state governments." Without wishing to censure any man, he observed that there were many supporters of "one great, national, consolidated government." This "extensive judicial authority will be agreeable" to such men, but Mason hoped there were "many in this convention of a different opinion, and who see their political happiness resting on their state governments."

On Friday Madison answered with a statement which clearly foreshadowed judicial review. "It may be a misfortune," he said, "that, in organizing any government, the explication of its authority should be left to any of its coordinate branches. There is no example in any country where it is otherwise. There is a new policy in submitting it to the judiciary of the United States." He recognized the coextensiveness of judicial and legislative powers. "With respect to the laws of the Union, it is so necessary and expedient that the judicial power should correspond with the legislative, that it has not been objected to."

Then, in direct response to Mason, he continued:

It was objected, that this jurisdiction would extend to all cases, and annihilate the state courts. At this moment of time, it might happen that there are many disputes between citizens of different states. But in the ordinary state of things, I believe that any gentleman will think that the far greater number of causes—ninety-nine out of a hundred—will remain with the state judiciaries. All controversies directly between citizen and citizen will still remain with the local courts. The number of cases within the jurisdiction of these courts is very small when compared to those in which the local tribunals will have cognizance.

Marshall too defended the judiciary as a necessary check on Congress in another anticipation of judicial review. "Has the government of the

United States power to make laws on every subject? Does he understand it so? Can they make laws affecting the mode of transferring property, or contracts, or claims, between citizens of the same state? Can they go beyond the delegated powers? If they were to make a law not warranted by any of the powers enumerated, it would be considered by the judges as an infringement of the Constitution which they are to guard. They would not consider such a law as coming under their jurisdiction. They would declare it void. It will annihilate the state courts, says the honorable gentleman [Mason]. Does not every gentlemen here know that the causes in our courts are more numerous than they can decide, according to their present construction?" The dockets of state courts, said Marshall, are impossibly clogged. "If some of these suits be carried to other courts, will it be wrong? They will still have business enough."

On Saturday, June 21, however, Grayson was still unsatisfied. He thought the jurisdiction of states would be as much infringed upon by inferior national tribunals as by the central government's power of direct taxation, "there being no superintending central power to keep in order these two contending jurisdictions. This is an objection which is unanswerable in its nature." Referring to the Supreme Court, he said it had "more power than any court under heaven. One set of judges ought not to have this power—and judges, particularly, who have temptation always before their eyes." Continuing his criticism, he said:

> My next objection to the federal judiciary is, that it is not expressed in a definite manner. The jurisdiction of all cases arising under the Constitution and the laws of the Union is of stupendous magnitude. It is impossible for human nature to trace its extent. It is so vaguely and indefinitely expressed, that its latitude cannot be ascertained. . . . This high court has not a very extensive original jurisdiction. It is not material. But its appellate jurisdiction is of immense magnitude; and what has it in view, unless to subvert the state governments?

Randolph supported the judicial power. A federal judiciary, he said, is "a constituent part" of the government. The chief goal of the federal courts is self-defense:

> Has not the Constitution said that the states shall not use such and such powers, and given exclusive powers to Congress? If the state judiciaries could make decisions conformable to the laws of their states, in derogation to the general government, I humbly apprehend that the federal government would soon be encroached upon. If a particular state should be at liberty,

through its judiciary, to prevent or impede the operation of the general government, the latter must soon be undermined. It is, then, necessary that its jurisdiction should "extend to all cases in law and equity arising under this Constitution and the laws of the United States."

Randolph admitted that there were defects in the federal judiciary, "among which may be objected too great an extension of jurisdiction." Even though the jurisdiction may reach too far, its ends are proper. "It is ambiguous in some parts, and unnecessarily extensive in others. It extends to all cases in law and equity arising under the Constitution." Randolph wished to know what was meant "by the words *arising under the Constitution*? What do they relate to? I conceive this to be very ambiguous. If my interpretation be right, the word *arising* will be carried so far that it will be made use of to aid and extend the federal jurisdiction."

On Monday of the fourth and final week Henry again took the initiative, singling out for criticism the Constitution's ambiguities. "The whole history of human nature cannot produce a government like that before you. The manner in which the judiciary and other branches of the government are formed, seems to me calculated to lay prostrate the states, and the liberties of the people. But, Sir, another circumstance ought totally to reject that plan, in my opinion; which is, that it cannot be understood, in many parts, even by the supporters of it. A constitution, sir, ought to be, like a beacon, held up to the public eye, so as to be understood by every man." It was clear, however, that both sides had had their say.

On Tuesday, June 24, the committee of the whole having dissolved Wythe "proposed that the committee should ratify the Constitution, and that whatsoever amendments might be deemed necessary should be recommended to the consideration of the Congress which should first assemble under the Constitution, to be acted upon according to the mode prescribed therein." Henry then offered a counter proposal: to "refer a declaration of rights, with certain amendments to the most exceptionable parts of the Constitution, to the other states in the Confederacy, for their consideration, previous to its ratification." The issue was thus squarely posed between unconditional ratification with recommended amendments and conditional ratification with amendments a prerequisite. On Wednesday, by a vote of only 88 to 80, the convention voted that amendments should be recommendatory. Then, on the main question of ratification, the convention approved the Constitution, 89 to 79. The news from New Hampshire had not yet arrived, and for all the convention knew, its ratification was the ninth.

With the ratification the convention approved a declaration or bill of rights of twenty sections, and twenty amendments which the state's representatives in the new Congress were to seek to obtain. Of the recommended amendments, the following are most pertinent here:

1st. That each state in the Union shall respectively retain every power, jurisdiction, and right, which is not by this Constitution delegated to the Congress of the United States, or to the departments of the federal government. . . .

3d. When the Congress shall lay direct taxes or excises, they shall immediately inform the executive power of each state, of the quota of such state, according to the census herein directed, which is proposed to be thereby raised; and if the legislature of any state shall pass a law which shall be effectual for raising such quota at the time required by Congress, the taxes and excises laid by Congress shall not be collected in such state. . . .

7th. That no commercial treaty shall be ratified without the concurrence of two-thirds of the whole number of the members of the Senate; . . .

8th. That no navigation law, or law regulating commerce, shall be passed without the consent of two thirds of the members present, in both houses. . . .

11th. That each state respectively shall have the power to provide for organizing, arming, and disciplining its own militia, whensoever Congress shall omit or neglect to provide for the same. . . .

16th. That Congress shall not alter, modify, or interfere in the times, places, or manner of holding elections for senators and representatives, or either of them, except when the legislature of any state shall neglect, refuse, or be disabled, by invasion or rebellion, to prescribe the same. . . .

17th. That those clauses which declare that Congress shall not exercise certain powers, be not interpreted, in any manner whatsoever, to extend the powers of Congress; but that they be construed either as making exceptions to the specified powers where this shall be the case, or otherwise, as inserted merely for greater caution.

XXXII

Ratification in New York

THE CONSTITUTION'S most hostile reception occurred in New York. In no other state was the vote in the convention so close. Nowhere else were the Federalists forced to make so many concessions in order to achieve ratification. The educational and propaganda campaigns on both sides had begun as soon as the federal convention finished its work. When the New York legislature convened on January 9, 1788, the opposition in the lower house sought to include in the resolution calling a convention a statement that the delegates to Philadelphia had exceeded their powers. This initial obstacle was avoided by the bare margin of 27 to 25. In the Senate a vote to postpone action lost by a vote of 10 to 9, and the concurrence with the lower house in calling a convention carried by only 11 to 8.

The spring elections for delegates gave the Anti-federalists roughly a two-thirds majority of the sixty-five members of the convention which assembled on June 17, 1788. Leaders of the opposition were Governor Clinton, Melancton Smith, Lansing, Yates, and Williams. The Federalist champion was, of course, Hamilton, assisted by Robert Livingston, chancellor of the state, and John Jay. The oratorical contest was principally between Smith and Hamilton. After the unanimous election of Clinton as president and the usual preliminaries, the convention went into committee of the whole and began its debates on June 19.

Livingston opened for the Federalists, stating that not only were Americans possessed of a common language and religion, "they acknowledge the same great principle of government—a principle, if not unknown, at least little understood in the old world—that all power is derived from the people." Americans, he said, "consider the state and the general governments as different deposits of that power. In this view, it is of little moment to them whether that portion of it which they must, for their own happiness, lodge in their rulers, be invested in the state governments only, or shared between them and the councils of the Union. The rights they reserve are not diminished, and probably their liberty acquires an additional security from the division."

The Confederation erred in principle, by operating "upon states in their political capacity, and not upon individuals." The powers "of forming laws . . . of deciding upon these laws, and carrying them into effect," Livingston said, "could never be trusted to the individual states, whose interests might, in many instances, clash with that of the Union." He concluded that "if we could not longer retain the old principle of the Confederacy, and were compelled to change its form, we were driven to the necessity of creating a new constitution."

The next day Smith rose for his first speech in opposition. "The defects of the old Confederation needed as little proof as the necessity of a union. But there was no proof in all this that the proposed Constitution was a good one. Defective as the old Confederation is, he said, no one could deny but it was possible we might have a worse government. But the question was not whether the present Confederation be a bad one, but whether the proposed Constitution be a good one." Interpreting Livingston's remarks for his own convenience, Smith said he was "pleased that, thus early in debate, the honorable gentleman had himself shown that the intent of the Constitution was not a confederacy, but a reduction of all the states into a consolidated government. He hoped the gentleman would be complaisant enough to exchange names with those who disliked the Constitution, as it appeared from his own concessions, that they were Federalists, and those who advocated it were Anti-federalists." Then, giving his own reason for being opposed to the Constitution, Smith declared "that the great interests and liberties of the people could only be secured by the state governments. He admitted that, if the new government was only confined to great national objects, it would be less exceptionable; but it extended to every thing dear to human nature. That this was the case, would be proved without any long chain of reasoning; for that power which had both the purse and the sword had the government of the whole country, and might extend its powers to any and to every object."

Now Hamilton himself entered the lists. "We contend that the radical vice in the old Confederation is," he began, "that the laws of the Union apply only to states in their corporate capacity." Hamilton illustrated the weakness by reference to requisitions. "In this examination, not being furnished with those lights which directed the deliberations of the general government, and incapable of embracing the general interests of the Union, the states have almost uniformly weighed the requisitions by their own local interests, and have only executed them so far as answered their particular convenience or advantage." The Congress had been subject, therefore, to thirteen different wills. "Sir, if we have national objects to pursue, we must have national revenues. If you make requisitions, and they are not complied with, what is to be done? It has been observed, to coerce the states is one of the maddest projects that was ever devised. . . . Then we are brought to this dilemma —either a federal standing army is to enforce the requisitions, or the federal treasury is left without supplies, and the government without support. What, Sir, is the cure for this great evil? Nothing, but to enable the national laws to operate on individuals, in the same manner as those of the states do."

The next day Smith resumed his attack. "A few years ago, we fought for liberty; we framed a general government on free principles; we placed the state legislatures, in whom the people have a full and a fair representation, between Congress and the people." At that time, Smith admitted, we were "too cautious, and too much restricted the powers of the general government. But now it is proposed to go into the contrary, and a more dangerous, extreme—to remove all barriers, to give the new government free access to our pockets, and ample command of our persons, and that without providing for a genuine and fair representation of the people. Smith was apprehensive of the future:

> No one can say what the progress of the change of sentiment may be in twenty-five years. The same men who now cry up the necessity of an energetic government, to induce a compliance with this system, may, in much less time, reprobate this in as severe terms as they now do the Confederation, and may as strongly urge the necessity of going as far beyond this as this is beyond the Confederation. Men of this class are increasing: they have influence, talents, and industry. It is time to form a barrier against them. And while we are willing to establish a government adequate to the purposes of the Union, let us be careful to establish it on the broad basis of equal liberty.

Hamilton then sought to demonstrate that the Constitution provided ample checks on any possible abuse of national powers. "The people," he said, "have an obvious and powerful protection in their state governments." These "bodies of perpetual observation" can form and conduct "plans of regular opposition" if national powers become threatening. "Can we suppose the people's love of liberty will not, under the incitement of their legislative leaders, be roused into resistance, and the madness of tyranny be extinguished at a blow? Sir, the danger is too distant; it is beyond all rational calculations. . . . Where this prin-

ciple [popular elections] is adhered to; where, in the organization of
the government, the legislative, executive, and judicial branches are
rendered distinct; where, again, the legislature is divided into separate houses, and the operations of each are controlled by various checks
and balances, and, above all, by the vigilance and weight of the state
governments—to talk of tyranny, and the subversion of our liberties,
is to speak the language of enthusiasm.

"This balance between the national and state governments . . . forms
a double security to the people. If one encroaches on their rights, they
will find a powerful protection in the other. Indeed, they will both
be prevented from overpassing their constitutional limits, by a certain
rivalship, which will ever subsist between them. I am persuaded that
a firm Union is as necessary to perpetuate our liberties as it is to make
us respectable; and experience will probably prove that the national
government will be as natural a guardian of our freedom as the state
legislatures themselves."

But Smith was still unconvinced. Despite Hamilton's offer to list and
explain the checks that states could exert on the general government,
Smith himself could see no possibility of checking a government of
independent powers. He lamented that no constitutional checks were
provided—"such checks as would not leave the exercise of government
to the operation of causes which, in their nature, are variable and
uncertain."

At this Hamilton sought to explain how state interests and state
power could indeed operate as checks:

Sir, in my experience of public affairs, I have constantly remarked, in the
conduct of members of Congress, a strong and uniform attachment to the
interests of their own state. These interests have, on many occasions, been
adhered to with an undue and illiberal pertinacity, and have too often been
preferred to the welfare of the Union. This attachment has given birth to an
unaccommodating spirit of party, which has frequently embarrassed the best
measures. It is by no means, however, an object of surprise. The early connections we have formed, the habits and prejudices in which we have been
bred, fix our affections so strongly, that no future objects of association can
easily eradicate them. This, together with the entire and immediate dependence the representative feels on his constituent, will generally incline him
to prefer the particular before the public good. . . . Sir, the most powerful
obstacle to the members of Congress betraying the interest of their constituents, is the state legislatures themselves, who will be standing bodies of
observation, possessing the confidence of the people, jealous of federal encroachments, and armed with every power to check the first essays of treach-

ery. They will institute regular modes of inquiry. The complicated domestic attachments, which subsist between the state legislators and their electors, will ever make them vigilant guardians of the people's rights. Possessed of the means and the disposition of resistance, the spirit of opposition will be easily communicated to the people, and, under the conduct of an organized body of leaders, will act with weight and system. Thus it appears that the very structure of the Confederacy affords the surest preventives from error, and the most powerful checks to misconduct.

Thus ended the first week.

The next week Lansing criticized the failure of the Constitution to recognize, comparably to the Articles, any state power of recall over its Senators. The makers of the Constitution, he thought, intended to make "the lower house the proper, peculiar representative of the interests of the people," whereas the Senate was to represent "the sovereignty of the states." If this is indeed the Senate's role, Lansing said, "certainly the members of this body ought to be peculiarly under the control, and in strict subordination to the state who delegated them. In proportion to their want of dependence, they will lose their respect for the power from whom they receive their existence, and, consequently, will disregard the great object for which they are instituted. . . . No inconvenience can follow from placing the powers of the Senate on such a foundation as to make them feel their dependence. It is only a check calculated to make them more attentive to the objects for which they were appointed. . . . It is the only thing which can give the states a control over the Senate."

Chancellor Livingston replied to Lansing that the Senators "are also the representatives of the United States, and are not to consult the interest of any one state alone, but that of the Union. This could never be done, if there was a power of recall; for sometimes it happens that small sacrifices are absolutely indispensable for the good and safety of the confederacy; but, if a Senator should presume to consent to these sacrifices, he would be immediately recalled." Lansing believed that states would tend to pursue their own interests, even to "the hazard of the Union. . . . The general government may find it necessary to do many things which some states might never be willing to consent to. . . . There are a thousand things which an honest man might be obliged to do, from a conviction that it would be for the general good, which would give great dissatisfaction to his constituents."

Lansing insisted upon distinguishing between the House and the Senate. "Does not one represent the individuals, the people of a state, and the other its collective sovereignty?"

So Livingston amplified his reply. Recall power for the states would tend "to bind the Senators too strongly to the interests of their respective states." "Whenever the interests of a state clash with those of the Union," a Senator would be obliged "to sacrifice the great objects of his appointment to local attachments. He will be subjected to all the caprices, the parties, the narrow views, and illiberal politics, of the state governments, and become a slave to the ambitions and factions at home."

All of this, Livingston said, was inferred from a principle he had already explained: that "the state legislatures will be ever more or less incapable of comprehending the interests of the Union. They cannot perceive the propriety, or feel the necessity, of certain great expedients in politics, which may seem, in their immediate operation, to injure the private interests of the members."

Hamilton joined in the opposition to Lansing's advocacy of a state power of recall. Hamilton proceeded from the principle that "the small good ought never to oppose the great one. When you assemble from your several counties in the Legislature, were every member to be guided only by the apparent interest of his county, government would be impracticable. There must be a perpetual accommodation and sacrifice of local advantage to general expediency; but the spirit of a mere popular assembly would rarely be actuated by this important principle. It is therefore absolutely necessary that the Senate should be so formed as to be unbiased by false conceptions of the real interests or undue attachment to the apparent good of their several states." His opposition, Hamilton said, failed to consider the "natural strength and resources of state governments, which will ever give them an important superiority over the general government. If we compare the nature of their different powers, or the means of popular influence which each possesses, we shall find the advantage entirely on the side of the states."

The real danger, in fact, to Hamilton was just the opposite: "The probable evil is, that the general government will be too dependent on the state legislatures, too much governed by their prejudices, and too obsequious to their humors; that the states, with every power in their hands, will make encroachments on the national authority, till the Union is weakened and dissolved."

But Lansing thought the realities pointed to the other conclusion. "The states, having no constitutional control, would soon be found unnecessary and useless, and would be gradually extinguished." He asked if the states were "arrayed in all the powers of sovereignty. Could they maintain armies? Had they the unlimited power of taxation? There was no comparison, he said, between the powers of the two governments. The circumstances the gentleman had enumerated, which seemed to be in favor of the states, only proved that the people would be under some advantages to discern the encroachments of Congress and to take the alarm; but what would this signify? The gentleman did not mean that his principles should encourage rebellion: what other resources had they?" All the people could do, he said, was "to wait patiently till the long terms of their Senators were expired, and then elect other men. All the boasted advantages enjoyed by the states were finally reduced to this. The gentleman had spoken of an enmity which would subsist between the general and state governments: what, then would be the situation of both? His wish . . . was to prevent any enmity, by giving the states a constitutional and peaceable mode of checking maladministration, by recalling their senators, and not driving them into hostilities, in order to obtain redress."

Debate continued, nevertheless, on the recall. Smith supported Lansing. It was "reasonable and proper" that Senators should be under the control of state legislatures, Smith said. "When a state sends an agent commissioned to transact any business, or perform any service, it certainly ought to have a power to recall." Replying directly to Hamilton, Smith dismissed the charge that "if the Senator is rendered too dependent on his constituents, he will sacrifice the interests of the Union to the policy of his state. Sir, the Senate has been generally held up, by all parties, as a safeguard to the rights of the several states. In this view, the closest connection between them has been considered as necessary. But now, it seems, we speak in a different language; we now look upon the least attachment to their states as dangerous; we are now separating them and rendering them entirely independent, that we may root out the last vestige of state sovereignty."

Hamilton then distinguished states rights from states interests. "It has been remarked, that there is an inconsistency in our admitting that the equal vote in the Senate was given to secure the rights of the states, and at the same time holding up the idea that their interests should be sacrificed to those of the Union." There is a distinction involved, Hamilton said:

The rights of a state are defined by the Constitution, and cannot be invaded without a violation of it; but the interests of a state have no connection with the Constitution, and may be, in a thousand instances, constitutionally sacrificed. A uniform tax is perfectly constitutional; and yet it may operate oppres-

sively upon certain members of the Union. The gentlemen are afraid that
the state governments will be abolished. But, Sir, their existence does not
depend upon the laws of the United States. Congress can no more abolish the
state governments, than they can dissolve the Union. The whole Constitution
is repugnant to it, and yet the gentlemen would introduce an additional useless provision against it. It is proper that the influence of the states should
prevail to a certain extent. But shall the individual states be the judges how
far? Shall an unlimited power be left them to determine in their own favor?
The gentlemen go into the extreme. . . . As far as my observation has extended, factions in Congress have arisen from attachment to state prejudices.
We are attempting, by this Constitution, to abolish factions, and to unite
all parties for the general welfare. That a man should have the power, in private life, of recalling his agent, is proper; because, in the business in which
he is engaged, he has no other object but to gain the approbation of his principal. Is this the case with the Senator? Is he simply the agent of the state?
No. He is an agent for the Union, and he is bound to perform services necessary to the good of the whole, though his state should condemn them.

On Tuesday, June 24, the momentous word arrived from New Hampshire—by express rider, as previously arranged by Hamilton—that her
convention had ratified, thereby putting the Constitution in operation.
The next day Livingston pointedly observed that "it would not, perhaps,
be altogether impertinent to remind the committee, that, since the intelligence of yesterday, it had become evident that the circumstances
of the country were greatly altered, and the ground of the present debate changed." Smith, however, said that "it had not altered his feelings or wishes on the subject." And Lansing commented: "It is true,
we have received information that the ninth state has ratified the Constitution; but I contend that no such event ought to influence our deliberations." Despite such brave resolves, the news of New Hampshire's action clearly dealt the opposition a blow. Refusal to ratify now
meant that New York would be left out of the new nation.

On Thursday, Williams spoke against the range and depth of congressional power. "In the Preamble, the intent of the Constitution, among
other things, is declared to be, 'to provide for the common defense, and
promote the general welfare'; and in the clause under consideration,
the power is in express words given to Congress 'to provide for the
common defense and general welfare.' And in the last paragraph of
the same section, there is an express authority to make all laws
which shall be necessary and proper for the carrying into execution
this power. It is therefore evident that the legislature, under this Constitution, may pass any law which they may think proper. It is true,

the ninth section restrains their power with respect to certain objects. But these restrictions are very limited, some of them improper, some unimportant, and others not easily understood." Referring specifically to the necessary and proper power, Williams said, "It is perhaps utterly impossible fully to define this power," since one could not conceive a case that was not included under it. And on the taxing power, he said that every "source of revenue is therefore committed to the hands of the general legislature. Not only these terms are very comprehensive, and extend to a vast number of objects, but the power to lay and collect has great latitude: it will lead to the passing of a vast number of laws, which may affect the personal rights of the citizens of the states, and put their lives in jeopardy." Williams concluded: "He that hath the purse will have the sword; and they that have both have every thing; so that Congress will have every source from which money can be drawn."

On Friday, Smith addressed himself to the powers of Congress. All of the central government's powers, he said, "should be precisely defined, that the people may be able to know whether it moves in the circle of the Constitution. It is the more necessary in governments like the one under examination, because Congress here is to be considered as only a part of a complex system. The state governments are necessary for certain local purposes; the general government for national purposes. The latter ought to rest on the former, not only in its form, but in its operations. It is therefore of the highest importance that the line of jurisdiction should be accurately drawn."

Referring specifically to the taxing power, Smith declared that the clause bestowed "unlimited powers" on Congress.

> Another clause declares that Congress shall have power to make all laws necessary to carry the Constitution into effect. Nothing, therefore, is left to construction; but the powers are most express. How far the state legislatures will be able to command a revenue, every man, on viewing the subject, can determine. If he contemplates the ordinary operation of causes, he will be convinced that the powers of the Confederacy will swallow up those of the members. I do not suppose that this effect will be brought about suddenly. As long as the people feel universally and strongly attached to the state governments, Congress will not be able to accomplish it. If they act prudently, their powers will operate and be increased by degrees. . . . If the Constitution is accepted as it stands, I am convinced that in seven years as much will be said against the state governments as is now said in favor of the proposed system.

In Smith's judgment, the powers granted the national government were altogether too great. "We shall be unwise," he said, "to make a new experiment, in so important a matter, without some known and sure grounds to go upon. The state constitutions should be the guardians of our domestic rights and interests, and should be both the support and the check of the federal government." Until he came to the convention, Smith said, he had never heard the idea that Congress should have "unlimited" powers. "The general government once called on the states to invest them with the command of funds adequate to the exigencies of the Union; but they did not ask to command all the resources of the states. They did not wish to have a control over all the property of the people. If we now give them this control, we may as well give up the state governments with it. I have no notion of setting the two powers at variance; nor would I give a farthing for a government which could not command a farthing. On the whole, it appears to me probable, that, unless some certain specific source of revenue is reserved to the states, their governments, with their independency, will be totally annihilated."

Williams now added to his remarks of the previous day. "Sir, I yesterday expressed my fears that this clause would tend to annihilate the state governments. I also observed, that the powers granted by it were indefinite, since the Congress are authorized to provide for the common defense and general welfare, and to pass all laws necessary for the attainment of those important objects. The legislature is the highest power in a government. Whatever they judge necessary for the proper administration of the powers lodged in them, they may execute without any check or impediment. Now, if the Congress should judge it a proper provision, for the common defense and general welfare, that the state governments should be essentially destroyed, what, in the name of common sense, will prevent them? Are they not constitutionally authorized to pass such laws? Are not the terms, 'common defense and general welfare,' indefinite, undefinable terms? What checks have the state governments against such encroachments? Why, they appoint the Senators once in six years."

Williams also feared the consequences of interpretation:

Ingenious men may assign ingenious reasons for opposite constructions of the same clause. They may heap refinement upon refinement, and subtlety upon subtlety, until they construe away every republican principle, every right sacred and dear to man. . . . I would wish that little or no latitude might be left to the sophistical constructions of men who may be interested in betraying the rights of the people. . . . If we adopt this Constitution, it is impossible, absolutely impossible, to know what we give up, and what we retain.

Hamilton then examined the question of national and state power. "The question, then, of the division of powers between the general and state governments, is a question of convenience: it becomes a prudential inquiry, what powers are proper to be reserved to the latter; and this immediately involves another inquiry into the proper objects of the two governments. This is the criterion by which we shall determine the just distribution of powers.

"The great leading objects of the federal government, in which revenue is concerned, are to maintain domestic peace, and provide for the common defense. In these are comprehended the regulation of commerce—that is, the whole system of foreign intercourse—the support of armies and navies, and of the civil administration. It is useless to go into detail. Every one knows that the objects of the general government are numerous, extensive, and important. Every one must acknowledge the necessity of giving powers, in all respects, and in every degree, equal to these objects. This principle assented to, let us inquire what are the objects of the state governments. Have they to provide against foreign invasion? Have they to maintain fleets and armies? Have they any concern in the regulation of commerce, the procuring alliances, or forming treaties of peace? No. Their objects are merely civil and domestic—to support the legislative establishment, and to provide for the administration of the laws."

Then he asked: "Now, Sir, where ought the great resources to be lodged? Every rational man will give an immediate answer. To what extent shall these resources be possessed? Reason says, as far as possible exigencies can require; that is, without limitation. A constitution cannot set bounds to a nation's wants; it ought not, therefore, to set bounds to its resources."

Hamilton still maintained that national power posed no undue threat to the states. "If the state governments were to be abolished, the question would wear a different face; but this idea is inadmissible. They are absolutely necessary to the system. Their existence must form a leading principle in the most perfect constitution we could form.

I insist that it never can be the interest or desire of the national legislature to destroy the state governments. It can derive no advantage from such an event; but, on the contrary, would lose an indispensable support, a necessary aid in executing the laws, and conveying the influence of government to the doors of the people. The Union is dependent on the will of the state governments for its chief magistrate, and for its Senate. The blow aimed at the members must give a fatal wound to the head; and the destruction of the states must be at once a political suicide. Can the national government be guilty of this madness?

The next day Lansing emphatically disagreed on the latter point. If the states retained "no other check upon Congress than the power of appointing Senators, they will certainly be overcome. . . . Neither our civil nor militia officers will afford many advantages of opposition against the national government: if they have any powers, it will ever be difficult to concentrate them, or give them a uniform direction. Their inflence will hardly be felt, while the greater number of lucrative and honorable places, in the gift of the United States, will establish an influence which will prevail in every part of the continent."

Lansing then accused Hamilton of having argued at the Constitutional Convention "with much decision and great plausibility that the state governments ought to be subverted, at least so far as to leave them only corporate rights, and that, even in that situation, they would endanger the existence of the general government." The records state that "This produced a warm personal altercation between those gentlemen, which engrossed the remainder of the day." So ended the second week.

On the following Tuesday, Smith again discussed the question of the national powers. It "must be inferred," he said, "from general reasoning" that "if the objects of the general government were without limitation, there could be no bounds set to their powers; that they had a right to seek those objects by all necessary laws, and by controlling every subordinate power. The means should be adequate to the end: the less should give way to the greater. General principles, therefore, clearly led to the conclusion, that the general government must have the most complete control over every power which could create the least obstacle to its operations."

Smith proceeded to "an examination of the particular provisions of the Constitution, and compared them together, to prove that his remarks were not conclusions from general principles alone, but warranted by the language of the Constitution. He conceived, therefore, that the national government would have powers, on this plan, not only to lay all species of taxes, but to control and set aside every thing which should impede the collection of them. They would have power to abrogate the laws of the states, and to prevent the operation of their taxes; and all courts, before whom any disputes on these points should come, whether federal or not, would be bound by oath to give judgment according to the laws of the Union."

Jay answered Smith. "He began with a description of the general characteristics of a government proper for the United States. It had, he said, been justly laid down, that a government which was to accomplish national purposes should command the national resources. Here a question had been raised. Would it be proper that the state governments shoud limit the powers of the general government, relative to its supplies? Would it be right or politic that the sovereign power of a nation should depend for support on the mere will of the several members of that nation . . . that the interest of a part should take place of that of the whole, or that the partial views of one of the members should interfere with and defeat the views of all?" Jay concluded that, "after the most mature reflection, he could see no possible impropriety in the general government having access to all the resources of the country."

On Wednesday, July 5, the final recorded blast against the Constitution was made by a delegate named Tredwell who had not spoken before. He first stated his disagreement with the rule of construction advanced by the Federalists: that powers not delegated to the national government were reserved to the states. "Sir, I introduce these observations to combat certain principles which have been daily and confidently advanced by the favorers of the present Constitution, and which appear to me totally indefensible. The first and grand leading, or rather misleading, principle in this debate, and on which the advocates for this system of unrestricted powers must chiefly depend for its support, is that, in forming a constitution, whatever powers are not expressly granted or given the government, are reserved to the people, or that rulers cannot exercise any powers but those expressly given to them by the Constitution." Tredwell said that "the public bodies in the United States have uniformly acted upon a direct and contrary principle, not only in forming the state constitutions and the old Confederation, but also in forming this very Constitution, for we do not find in every state constitution express resolutions made in favor of the people; and it is clear that the late convention at Philadelphia, whatever might have been the sentiments of some of its members, did not adopt the principle, for they have made certain reservations and restrictions, which, upon that principle, would have been totally useless and unnecessary."

Tredwell then summarized his fears that the Constitution provided for a consolidated government under which state sovereignty would no longer exist:

> In this Constitution, Sir, we have departed widely from the principles and political faith of '76, when the spirit of liberty ran high, and danger put a curb on ambition. Here we find no security for the rights of individuals, no security for the existence of our state governments; here is no bill of rights, no proper restriction of power; our lives, our property, and our consciences, are left wholly at the mercy of the legislature, and the powers of the judiciary may be extended to any degree short of almighty. . . . We are told that this is a federal government. I think, sir, there is as much propriety in the name, as in that which its advocates assume, and no more; it is, in my idea, as complete a consolidation as the government of this state, in which legislative powers, to a certain extent, are exercised by the several towns and corporations. The sole difference between a state government under this Constitution, and a corporation under a state government, is, that a state being more extensive than a town, its power are likewise proportionably extended, but neither of them enjoys the least share of sovereignty; for, let me ask, what is a state government? What sovereignty, what power is left to it, when the control of every source of revenue, and the total command of the militia, are given to the general government? That power which can command both the property and the persons of the community, is the sovereign, and the sole sovereign.

It was just as absurd to think of "two distinct sovereigns in the same country," he said, "as that two distinct separate circles can be bounded exactly by the same circumference.

"This, Sir, is demonstration; and from it I draw one corollary, which, I think, clearly follows, although it is in favor of the Constitution, to wit—that at least that clause in which Congress guarantees to the several states a republican *form* of government, speaks honestly; that is, that no more is intended by it than is expressed; and I think it is clear that, whilst the mere form is secured, the substance—to wit, the whole power and sovereignty of our state governments, and with them the liberties of the country—is swallowed up by the general government; for it is well worth observing, that, while our state governments are held up to us as the great and sufficient security of our rights and privileges, it is carefully provided that they shall be disarmed of all power, and made totally dependent on the bounty of Congress for their support, and consequently for their existence—so that we have scarce a single right secured under either.

"This government is founded in sin, and reared up in iniquity; the foundations are laid in a most sinful breach of public faith; and I fear, if it goes into operation, we shall be justly punished with the total extinction of our civil liberties."

At this point the recorded discussion ends. The next day, July 6, word arrived that the Virginia convention had unconditionally ratified. This news had a powerful effect upon many of the Anti-federalists, including Smith, for the only remaining states were North Carolina and Rhode Island. The pressure was intensified by the circulation of a threat, inspired by Hamilton, that if New York did not ratify, New York City would secede from the state and join the Union. Indeed, from this moment on the question seems to have become whether or not the ratification should be conditional or unconditional. On July 10 Lansing introduced a series of amendments. Some were explanatory, some were recommendatory, and some were conditions precedent to ratification. These were referred to a committee, which deadlocked over the word "conditional" and dissolved without reporting.

The next day Jay moved to ratify the Constitution together with certain explanations and such recommended amendments as the convention might deem "useful or expedient." This motion led to protracted debate. On July 15 Smith moved to amend Jay's motion so that the ratification would be "upon condition" that Congress would not exercise certain powers within New York until a second convention could be called to propose amendments to the Constitution. The next day, July 16, a motion to adjourn was defeated, as was also a motion by Duane to postpone Smith's amendment in favor of Jay's original motion. Debate resumed on Smith's amendment.

On Saturday, July 19, Lansing moved to postpone all pending motions in order again to consider a conditional ratification, and this motion carried. Very much alarmed, Hamilton wrote quickly to Madison, who had now returned to New York as a member of Congress. Madison replied immediately, and within the week Hamilton read Madison's letter to the convention. "My opinion is," Madison wrote, "that a reservation of a right to withdraw, if amendments be not decided on under the form of the Constitution within a certain time, is a conditional ratification; that it does not make New York a member of the new Union, and, consequently, that she could not be received on that plan. The Constitution requires an adoption in toto and forever. It has been so adopted by the other states. An adoption for a limited time would be as defective as an adoption of some of the articles only. In short, any condition whatever must vitiate the ratification. The idea of reserving a right to withdraw was started at Richmond, and considered as a conditional ratification, which was itself abandoned as worse than a rejection."

Madison's letter had the desired effect. On July 23 Smith supported an amendment which changed the words "upon condition" in the ratification to "in full confidence." The same day the convention defeated a motion by Lansing that "there should be reserved to the state of New York a right to withdraw herself from the Union after a certain number of years, unless the amendments proposed should previously be submitted to a general convention." The convention then for two days considered the many amendments which should be recommended. As a further price for ratification, it was agreed that a circular letter should be prepared for transmittal to the other state legislatures, urging a second general convention to propose amendments.

The concessions made in order to win ratification were therefore fourfold. First, the form of ratification began with twenty-three declarations of understanding or explanations of the Constitution, mainly dealing with matters of individual liberty. The following are germane here:

> That the powers of government may be reassumed by the people, whenever it shall become necessary to their happiness; that every power, jurisdiction, and right, which is not by the said Constitution clearly delegated to the Congress of the United States, or the departments of the government thereof, remains to the people of the several states, or to their respective state governments to whom they may have granted the same; and that those clauses in the said Constitution, which declare, that Congress shall not have or exercise certain powers, do not imply that Congress is entitled to any powers not given by the said Constitution; but such clauses are to be construed either as exceptions to certain specified powers, or as inserted merely for greater caution. . . .
>
> That the jurisdiction of the Supreme Court of the United States, or of any other court to be instituted by the Congress, is not in any case to be increased, enlarged, or extended by any fiction, collusion, or mere suggestion;—and that no treaty is to be construed so to operate as to alter the constitution of any state.

Then followed the second concession to the opposition. The ratification was declared to be "In full confidence nevertheless that until a convention shall be called and convened for proposing amendments to the said Constitution," the following things should not take place: the state militia should not be continued out of the state longer than six weeks without the consent of the state legislature; Congress should not exercise its power to make or alter election regulations in New York unless the state should refuse or neglect to make such regulations; and Congress should lay no direct taxes within the state without first making a requisition upon the state which the New York legislature should have an opportunity to satisfy.

The third concession was a series of thirty-two recommended amendments which the state's representatives in Congress were enjoined to promote. One would have curbed Congress' taxing power by requiring resort to the requisition system first; one would have conditioned Congress' power over elections upon the neglect or refusal of the states to provide the necessary regulations; others would have required two-thirds majorities for the exercise of congressional power to raise armies, declare war, and borrow money; one would have confined inferior federal courts to admiralty and maritime cases, leaving original jurisdiction in all other cases to the state courts.

The final concession was the circular letter to the various state legislatures. This letter, which urged the other states to join in a move to call a second convention to propose amendments to the Constitution, said in part: "Several articles in it appear so exceptionable to a majority of us, that nothing but the fullest confidence of obtaining a revision of them by a general convention, and an invincible reluctance to separating from our sister states, could have prevailed upon a sufficient number to ratify it, without stipulating for previous amendments."

The depth and intensity of the opposition to the Constitution in New York is revealed by the fact that, with all the foregoing concessions and with the knowledge that New Hampshire and Virginia had ratified, the convention approved the Constitution by a vote of only 30 to 27. On the crucial vote, Smith voted to ratify.

XXXIII

Final Ratifications

THE LEGISLATURE of North Carolina in December 1787 authorized an election to be held in March 1788 for delegates to a state convention to consider the Constitution. On July 21, 1788, 228 delegates assembled at Hillsboro. The outstanding Federalist leaders were James Iredell, later appointed to the Supreme Court by Washington; William R. Davie and Richard Dobbs Spaight, who had been delegates to the federal convention; Samuel Johnston, the governor; and Archibald Maclaine, a prominent lawyer. The opposition was firmly controlled by Willie Jones, who had declined an appointment as delegate to the federal convention and who now participated but little in the debates; David Caldwell, Timothy Bloodworth, and Samuel Spencer were his principal supporters.

As elsewhere, although the Federalists were superior in intellect and ability, they were in the minority, outnumbered by the Anti-federalists by slightly more than two to one. After the preliminaries were over, Jones on Wednesday, July 23, alarmed the Federalists by moving that the question be immediately put. The Federalists' only hope lay in delay, and after spirited remarks by Iredell and others, the convention agreed to sit as a committee of the whole and discuss the provisions of the Constitution in order. The situation was just opposite from that in Maryland. Being confident of their majority, the North Carolina Anti-federalists frequently refused to enter into the debates, although solicited to do so. More than once the Federalists raised arguments for the opposition simply to establish rebuttal.

The debates opened on Thursday with an objection by Caldwell to the Preamble. "Mr. Chairman, if they mean by 'We, the people' the people at large, I conceive the expression is improper. Were not they who framed this Constitution the representatives of the legislatures of the different states? In my opinion, they had no power, from the people at large, to use their name, or to act for them. They were not delegated for that purpose." Maclaine replied that the "sanction of the state legislatures was in some degree necessary. It was to be submitted by the legislatures to the people; so that, when it is adopted, it is the act of the people. When it is the act of the people, their name is certainly proper."

Davie then rehearsed the inadequacies of the Articles and suggested how they would be cured by the Constitution. "The Confederation derived its sole support from the state legislatures," he said. "This rendered it weak and ineffectual. It was therefore necessary that the foundations of this government should be laid on the broad basis of the people. Yet the state governments are the pillars upon which this government is extended over such an immense territory, and are essential to its existence. The House of Representatives are immediately elected by the people. The Senators represent the sovereignty of the states; they are directly chosen by the state legislatures, and no legislative act can be done without their concurrence." Here Davie alluded to the fact that the Articles did not legislate directly on individuals and that powers of the old confederated government could not be executed. "It was therefore absolutely necessary that the influence of the magistrate should be introduced, and that the laws should be carried home to individuals themselves. . . . Every member saw that the existing system would ever be ineffectual, unless its laws operated on individuals, as military coercion was neither eligible nor practicable. . . . These considerations determined the convention to depart from that solecism in politics—the principle of legislation for states in their political capacities. . . . Founded on the state governments solely, as I have said before, it would be tottering and inefficient. It became, therefore, necessary to bottom it on the people themselves, by giving them an immediate interest and agency in the government."

Caldwell said he still "wished to know why the gentlemen who were delegated by the states, styled themselves 'We, the people.' He said that he only wished for information." Iredell answered that "it would be easy to satisfy the gentleman; that the style, 'We, the people,' was not to be applied to the members themselves, but was to be the style of the Constitution, when it should be ratified in their respective states."

Taylor brought Caldwell's point out in the open. The "very wording of this Constitution," Taylor said, "seems to carry with it an assumed power. 'We, the people,' is surely an assumed power. Have they said, 'We, the delegates of the people'? It seems to me that, when they met in convention, they assumed more power than was given them. . . . Matters may be carried still farther. This is a consolidation of all the states. Had it said, 'We, the states,' there would have been a federal intention in it. But, Sir, it is clear that a consolidation is intended.

"Will any gentleman say that a consolidated government will answer this country? . . . I am astonished that the servants of the legislature of North Carolina should go to Philadelphia, and, instead of speaking of the 'state' of North Carolina, should speak of the 'people.' I wish to stop power as soon as possible; for they may carry their assumption of power to a more dangerous length. I wish to know where they found the power of saying 'We, the people,' and of consolidating the states."

Maclaine now replied. "Mr. Chairman, I confess myself astonished to hear objections to the Preamble. They say that the delegates to the federal convention assumed powers which were not granted them; that they ought not to have used the words 'We, the people.' That they were not the delegates of the people, is universally acknowledged. The Constitution is only a mere proposal. . . . If the people approve of it, it becomes their act. Is not this merely a dispute about words, without any meaning what ever? . . . It is no more than blank till it be adopted by the people. When that is done here, is it not the people of the state of North Carolina that do it, joined with the people of the other states who have adopted it? The expression is, then, right."

Congress' power over elections, as elsewhere, sparked debate. Spencer said that the clause seemed to be "reprehensible," because it struck at the state legislatures "and seems to take away that power of elections which reason dictates they ought to have among themselves. It apparently looks forward to a consolidation of the government of the United States, when the state legislatures may entirely decay away.

"This is one of the grounds," Spencer continued, "which have induced me to make objections to the new form of government. It appears to me that the state governments are not sufficiently secured, and that they may be swallowed up by the great mass of powers given to Congress. If that be the case, such power should not be given; for, from all the notions which we have concerning our happiness and well-being, the state governments are the basis of our happiness, security, and prosperity. . . . This supersedes the necessity of continuing the state legislatures. This is such an article as I can give no sanction to, because it strikes at the foundation of the governments on which depend the happiness of the states and the general government."

Iredell answered Spencer's charge of consolidation. "I heartily agree with the gentleman, that, if any thing in this Constitution tended to the annihilation of the state government, instead of exciting the admiration of any man, it ought to excite the resentment and execration. No such wicked intention ought to be suffered. . . . The very existence of the general government depends on that of the state governments. The state legislatures are to choose the Senators. Without a Senate there can be no Congress. The state legislatures are also to direct the manner of choosing the President. Unless, therefore, there are state legislatures to direct that manner, no President can be chosen. The same observation may be made as to the House of Representatives, since, as they are to be chosen by the electors of the most numerous branch of each state legislature, if there are no state legislatures, there are no persons to choose the House of Representatives. Thus it is evident that the very existence of the general government depends on that of the state legislatures, and of course, that their continuance cannot be endangered by it."

Spencer attacked the clause again, this time on the ground of its generality. He said that "the words in this place were exceedingly vague. . . . In a matter of so great moment, words ought not to be so vague and indeterminate. . . . This clause provides that a Congress may at any time alter such regulations, except as to the places of choosing Senators. These words are so vague and uncertain, that it must ultimately destroy the whole liberty of the United States. It strikes at the very existence of the states, and supersedes the necessity of having them at all. I would therefore wish to have it amended in such a manner as that the Congress should not interfere but when the states refused or neglected to regulate elections." McDowell echoed Spencer, saying that the clause pointed "forward to the time when there will be no state legislatures—to the consolidation of all the states. The states will be kept up as boards of elections."

Bloodworth, adverting to Congress' power again, said it was "easy for [his opponents] to mention that this control should only be exerted when the state would neglect, or refuse, or be unable in case of invasion, to regulate elections. If so, why did they not mention it expressly." Spencer reiterated his earlier point. "It is well known that men in power are apt to abuse it, and extend it if possible. From the ambiguity of this expression, they may put such construction upon it as may suit them." And Galloway asked: "What have the state governments left for them, if the general government is to be possessed of such extensive powers, without control or limitation, without any responsibility to the states? . . . where the great principles of liberty are endangered, no general, indeterminate, vague expression ought to be suffered."

On Congress' power of taxation, Spencer said he conceived the power "to be too extensive, as it embraces all possible powers of taxation, and gives up to Congress every possible article of taxation that can ever happen . . . would give them powers to support the government, but would not agree to annihilate the state governments is an article which is most essential to their existence." And Goudy said this was "a dispute whether Congress shall have great, enormous powers. . . . This clause, with the clause of elections, will totally destroy our liberties. The subject of our consideration therefore is, whether it be proper to give any man, or set of men, an unlimited power over our purse, without any kind of control. The purse-strings are given up by this clause. The sword is also given up by this system. Is there no danger in giving up both? . . . That the Constitution has a tendency to destroy the state governments, must be clear to every man of common understanding."

The treaty power also came under attack. Parker asserted that the "President and seven Senators, as nearly as I can remember, can make a treaty which will be of great advantage to the northern states, and equal injury to the southern states. They might give up the rivers and territory of the southern states. Yet, in the Preamble of the Constitution, they say all the people have done it. I should be glad to know what power there is of calling the President and Senate to account." The power was defended by Davie. "The honorable gentleman has spoken of a consolidation in this government. That is a very strange inconsistency, when he points out, at the same time, the necessity of lodging the power of making treaties with the Representatives, where the idea of a consolidation can alone exist; and when he objects to placing it in the Senate, where the federal principle is completely preserved. As the Senate represents the sovereignty of the states, whatever might affect the states in their political capacity ought to be left to them. This is the certain means of preventing a consolidation. How extremely absurd is it to call that disposition of power a consolidation of the states, which must to all eternity prevent it!"

Iredell also answered complaints of "consolidation." The "great caution of giving the states an equality of suffrage in making treaties," he said, "was for the express purpose of taking care of that sovereignty, and attending to their interests, as political bodies, in foreign negotiations. . . . It seems to be forgotten that the Senate is placed there for a very valuable purpose—as a guard against any attempt of consolidation. The members of the convention were as much averse to consolidation as any gentleman on this floor; but without this institution (I mean the Senate, where the suffrages of the states are equal), the danger would be greater. There ought to be some power given to the Senate to counteract the influence of the people by their biennial representation in the other house, in order to preserve completely the sovereignty of the states."

The grants of jurisdiction to the United States courts were vigorously assailed by Spencer. He objected to them because he felt they would be oppressive in their operation.

> I would wish that the federal court should not interfere, or have anything to do with controversies to the decision of which the state judiciaries might be fully competent, nor with such controversies as must carry the people a great way from home. With respect to the jurisdiction of cases arising under the Constitution, when we reflect on the very extensive objects of the plan of government, the manner in which they may arise, and the multiplicity of laws that may be made with respect to them, the objection against it will appear to be well founded. If we consider nothing but the articles of taxation, duties, and excises, and the laws that might be made with respect to these, the cases will be almost infinite. . . . I know it is said that what is not given up to the United States will be retained by the individual states. I know it ought to be so, and should be so understood; but, sir, it is not declared to be so.

The Confederation, Spencer pointed out, "expressly declared that all rights and powers, of any kind whatever, of the several states, which are not given up to the United States, are expressly and absolutely retained, to be enjoyed by the states. . . . Oppression may therefore take place by degrees; but if there were express terms and bounds laid down, when these were passed by, the people would take notice of them, and oppression would not be carried on to such a length. I look upon it, therefore, that there ought to be something to confine the power of this government within its proper boundaries." Spencer's basic fear was that the states would be swallowed up. "For the reasons I before gave," he said, "I think that the jurisdiction of the federal court, with respect to all cases in law and equity, and the laws of Congress, and the appeals in all cases between citizens of different states, etc., is inadmissible."

Maclaine answered on the point of enumerated and reserved powers.

"The powers of Congress are limited and enumerated. We say we have given them those powers, but we do not say we have given them more. We retain all those rights which we have not given away to the general government. . . . If they can assume powers not enumerated, there was no occasion for enumerating any powers. . . . It is as plain a thing as possibly can be, that Congress can have no power but what we expressly give them.

"There is an express clause which, however disingenuously it has been perverted from its true meaning, clearly demonstrates that they are confined to those powers which are given them. This clause enables them to 'make all laws which shall be necessary and proper for carrying into execution the foregoing powers, and all other powers vested by this Constitution in the government of the United States, or any department or officers thereof.' This clause specifies that they shall make laws to carry into execution all the powers vested by this Constitution; consequently, they can make no laws to execute any other power. This clause gives no new power, but declares that those already given are to be executed by proper laws. I hope this will satisfy the gentlemen."

But Spencer was unconvinced; he insisted that powers to be retained by the states should be "expressly declared" and "not left to mere construction and opinion. I am authorized to say it was heretofore thought necessary. The Confederation says, expressly, that all that was not given up to the United States was retained by the respective states. If such a clause had been inserted in this Constitution, it would have superseded the necessity of a bill of rights. But that not being the case, it was necessary that a bill of rights, or something of that kind should be a part of the Constitution. . . . The states do not act in their political capacities, but the government is proposed for individuals. The very caption of the Constitution shows that this is the case. The expression, 'We, the people of the United States,' shows that this government is intended for individuals; there ought, therefore, to be a bill of rights."

Spencer was ready "to acknowledge that the Congress ought to have the power of executing its laws. Heretofore, because all the laws of the Confederation were binding on the states in their political capacities, courts had nothing to do with them; but now the thing is entirely different. The laws of Congress will be binding on individuals, and those things which concern individuals will be brought properly before the courts. In the next place, all the officers are to take an oath to carry into execution this general government, and are bound to support every act of the government, of whatever nature it may be."

Maclaine replied to Spencer's complaint that the Constitution was an act not of the states but of the people. "I hope, Sir," said Maclaine, "that all power is in the people, and not in the state governments. If he will not deny the authority of the people to delegate power to agents, and to devise such a government as a majority of them thinks will promote their happiness, he will withdraw his objection. The people, Sir, are the only proper authority to form a government. They, Sir, have formed their state governments, and can alter them at pleasure. Their transcendent power is competent to form this or any other government which they think promotive of their happiness.

"But the gentleman contends that there ought to be a bill of rights, or something of that kind—something declaring expressly, that all power not expressly given to the Constitution ought to be retained by the states, and he produces the Confederation as an authority for its necessity. When the Confederation was made, we were by no means so well acquainted with the principles of government as we are now. . . . We know now that it is agreed upon by most writers, and men of judgment and reflection, that all power is in the people, and immediately derived from them. The gentleman surely must know that, if there be certain rights which never can, nor ought to be, given up, these rights cannot be said to be given away, merely because we have omitted to say that we have not given them up."

Iredell said a few words on the Supreme Court: "The propriety of having a Supreme Court in every government must be obvious to every man of reflection. There can be no other way of securing the administration of justice uniformly in the several states. There might be, otherwise, as many different adjudications on the same subject as there are states."

And Davie defended the federal judiciary at some length. "I believe, however, that before we take into consideration these important clauses, it will be necessary to consider in what manner laws can be executed by any government. If there be any other, it is unknown to me. The first mode is coercion by military force, and the second is coercion through the judiciary. With respect to coercion by force, I shall suppose that it is so extremely repugnant to the principles of justice and the feelings of a free people, that no man will support it. It must, in the end, terminate in the destruction of the liberty of the people. I take it, therefore, that there is no rational way of enforcing the laws but by the instrumentality of the judiciary. From these premises we are left only to consider how far the jurisdiction of the judiciary ought to extend. It appears to me that the judiciary ought to be competent to the decision of any question arising out of the Constitution itself. On a review of the principles of all free governments, it seems to me also necessary that the judicial power should be coextensive with the legislative."

Davie continued:

> It is necessary in all governments, but particularly in a federal government, that its judiciary should be competent to the decision of all questions arising out of the constitution. . . . Every member who has read the Constitution with attention must observe that there are certain fundamental principles in it, both of a positive and negative nature, which, being intended for the general advantage of the community, ought not to be violated by any future legislation of the particular states. Every member will agree that the positive regulations ought to be carried into execution, and that the negative restrictions ought not to be disregarded or violated. Without a judiciary, the injunctions of the Constitution may be disobeyed, and the positive regulations neglected or contravened. . . . Gentlemen must have observed the contracted and narrowminded regulations of the individual states, and their predominant disposition to advance the interests of their own citizens to the prejudice of others. Will not these evils be continued if there be no restraint? The people of the United States have one common interest; they are all members of the same community, and ought to have justice administered to them equally in every part of the continent, in the same manner, with the same despatch, and on the same principles. It is therefore absolutely necessary that the judiciary of the Union should have jurisdiction in all cases arising in law and equity under the Constitution. Surely there should be somewhere a constitutional authority for carrying into execution constitutional provisions; otherwise, as I have already said, they would be a dead letter. . . I think he must be of opinion, upon reflection, that the jurisdiction of the federal judiciary could not have been constructed otherwise with safety or propriety. It is necessary that the Constitution should be carried into effect, that the laws should be executed, justice equally done to all the community, and treaties observed. These ends can only be accomplished by a general, paramount judiciary.

When the convention reached the supremacy clause, it was defended by Iredell. The clause, he said, did not bestow too much power; "in fact, it only provides for the execution of those powers which are already given in the foregoing articles." After quoting the clause, Iredell asked: "What is the meaning of this, but that, as we have given power, we will support the execution of it? We should act like children, to give power and deny the legality of executing it. It is saying no more than that, when we adopt the government, we will maintain and obey it; in the same manner as if the Constitution of this state had said that, when a law is passed in conformity to it, we must obey that law. Would this be objected to? Then, when the Congress passes a law consistent with the Constitution, it is to be binding on the people.

"The question, then, under this clause, will always be, whether Congress has exceeded its authority. If it has not exceeded it, we must obey, otherwise not. This Constitution, when adopted, will become a part of our state constitution; and the latter must yield to the former only in those cases where power is given by it. It is not to yield to it in any other case whatever. . . . It appears to me merely a general clause, the amount of which is that, when they pass an act, if it be in the execution of a power given by the Constitution, it shall be binding on the people, otherwise not. As to the sufficiency or extent of the power, that is another consideration, and has been discussed before."

But Bloodworth said the supremacy clause "appears to . . . sweep off all the constitutions of the states. It is a total repeal of every act and constitution of the states. The judges are sworn to uphold it. It will produce an abolition of the state governments. Its sovereignty absolutely annihilates them. . . . This clause will be the destruction of every law which will come in competition with the laws of the United States. Those laws and regulations which have been, or shall be, made in this state, must be destroyed by it, if they come in competition with the powers of Congress."

Maclaine replied to Bloodworth. "But what is the sovereignty, and who is Congress? One branch, the people at large; and the other branch, the states by their representatives. Do people fear the delegation of power to themselves—to their own representatives?

"But he objects that the laws of the Union are to be the supreme laws of the land. Is it not proper that their laws should be the laws of the land, and paramount to those of any particular state—or is it proper that the laws of any particular state should control the laws of the United States? Shall a part control the whole? To permit the local laws of any state to control the laws of the Union, would be to give the general government no powers at all. If the judges are not to be bound by it, the powers of Congress will be nugatory. This is self-evident and plain. . . . Every gentleman must see the necessity for the laws of the Union to be paramount to those of the separate states, and that the powers given by this Constitution must be executed. What, shall we ratify a government and then say it shall not operate? This would be the same as not to ratify."

When the discussion of the Constitution clause by clause had been completed, Governor Johnston moved that the convention ratify the Constitution and recommend amendments. The procedure at this point is not clear, but apparently no vote was ever taken on Johnston's motion. Instead, a resolution offered by Jones was carried, under which the convention did not reject but simply refused to ratify the Constitution at the present time, Jones believing that North Carolina could enter the new nation whenever she wished to do so. Jones's resolution also called for a declaration of rights and a series of amendments. Iredell moved to substitute for Jones's proposal an unconditional ratification with six recommended amendments, but this was voted down, 184 to 84. The convention then voted, by an identical division, to support Jones's plan.

Several of the amendments approved by the convention have application for this study. The first declared "That each state in the Union shall respectively retain every power, jurisdiction, and right, which is not by this Constitution delegated to the Congress of the United States, or to the departments of the federal government." The eighteenth provided: "That those clauses which declare that Congress shall not exercise certain powers be not interpreted in any manner whatsoever to extend the power of Congress; but that they be construed either as making exceptions to the specified powers, where this shall be the case, or otherwise as inserted merely for greater caution." Others included the usual limitations on Congress' powers with respect to elections, taxes, the militia, and navigation laws. Two proposed amendments dealt with treaties, one providing "That no commercial treaty shall be ratified without the concurrence of two-thirds of the whole number of the members of the Senate," and the other that no treaty shall be valid "which is contradictory to the Constitution of the United States."

Although the convention refused to ratify the Constitution, there is reason to believe that the Anti-federalists did not intend to keep North Carolina permanently out of the Union. The motivation seems rather to have been, by withholding approval, to encourage the adoption of amendments. Actually, the delegates took care to protect the future position of the state. As its closing action, the convention adopted a resolution offered by Jones which stated: "Whereas this convention has thought proper neither to ratify nor reject the Constitution," it was recommended to the legislature that, should Congress lay an impost on goods imported into the ratifying states, the legislature should lay a similar impost, for the use of Congress, on goods imported into North Carolina. After this action, the convention adjourned on August 4.

Fifteen months later, a second convention of 294 delegates met at Fayetteville from November 16 to November 23, 1789. At least 120 delegates from the first convention were present. Iredell was absent from the Federalist ranks, but Johnston and Davie were present, augmented by Hugh Williamson. Of the opposition, Jones was missing, but Spencer, Bloodworth, Lenoir, and Caldwell were there.

This time, however, the story was vastly different. The dominant Anti-federalist party of 1788 had now dwindled to an insignificant minority. The new government under the Constitution was in operation, and it had become apparent that North Carolina had no future as an independent state. Further, the new Congress had already submitted twelve amendments to the Constitution to the states for ratification.

The debates in the second convention were not recorded, but proceedings must have been brief in any case. On November 17 Hugh Williamson moved for ratification. On November 18, 19, and 20 the Constitution and the amendments proposed by Congress were considered in committee of the whole. The Constitution was then ratified by a vote of 194 to 77, this being a greater majority than the Anti-federalist majority of the previous year. Then, as a concession to the opposition, the convention recommended eight further amendments.

There remained to ratify only one of the original thirteen states. Rhode Island, among all the states, had been most reluctant to increase the powers of Congress under the Articles. There, devotion to state sovereignty and, consequently, to anti-federalism reached their peak. Only Rhode Island had refused to send delegates to the federal convention. This had prompted a group of merchants in Providence to send a letter to the convention apologizing for the action of the state and expressing their individual agreement with the movement for a stronger government.

When the Constitution was received in Rhode Island, the assembly refused to call a convention and instead submitted the Constitution directly to the freemen voters to be voted on in town meetings. The Federalist minority protested against this action by staying away from the polls, with the result that the vote in March 1788 showed 2,708 against the Constitution, and only 237 for it. Six times thereafter over a period of almost two years the Rhode Island assembly refused to call a state convention to consider the Constitution. Unfortunately, in Rhode Island the Federalists were not only in the minority, they also lacked the leadership of skilled and able men which had turned the tide in other states.

External pressures finally brought Rhode Island into line. In 1789, shortly after the new government was formed, Congress passed an impost law. Goods from North Carolina and Rhode Island were excepted from the impost, but only until January 15, 1790. By this expiration date, North Carolina had ratified and Rhode Island stood alone. In the middle of January, therefore, the assembly by a very close vote—34 to 29 in the house and 5 to 4 in the senate—finally authorized the election of delegates to a convention. The result of the election was a decided victory for the Anti-federalists.

The convention of seventy delegates met in South Kingstown on March 1, 1790. None of the discussion has been preserved. A committee appointed for the purpose recommended a bill of rights of eighteen sections, and twenty-one amendments. the convention on March 6 adjourned until May 24 so that the bill of rights and amendments might be considered by the freemen at the annual elections on April 21. These elections again resulted in complete victory for the Anti-federalists.

But pressure from outside the state continued. On April 28, in the United States Senate, a committee was appointed "to consider what provisions will be proper for Congress in the present session respecting the state of Rhode Island." On May 11, on this committee's recommendation, a resolution was introduced that "all commercial intercourse between the United States and Rhode Island" should be prohibited after July 1. The resolution also authorized the President to "demand" of Rhode Island payment of a share of the revolutionary debt.

In the face of these threats, the Rhode Island convention reassembled on May 24. Again, no records of the proceedings were preserved. On May 29, 1790, the convention ratified the Constitution by a bare majority. The vote was 34 to 32.

The ratification was preceded by a declaration of eighteen rights, the third of which stated:

> That the rights of the states respectively, to nominate and appoint all state officers, and every other power, jurisdiction, and right, which is not by the said constitution clearly delegated to the Congress of the United States or to the departments of government thereof, remain to the people of the several

states, or their respective state governments to whom they may have granted the same; and that those clauses in the said constitution which declare that Congress shall not have or exercise certain powers, do not imply that Congress is entitled to any powers not given by the said Constitution, but such clauses are to be construed as exceptions to certain specified powers, or as inserted merely for greater caution.

Under "these impressions, and declaring that the rights aforesaid cannot be abridged or violated, and that the explanations aforesaid are consistent with the said constitution, and in confidence that the amendments hereafter mentioned will receive an early and mature consideration, and conformably to Article V of said constitution, speedily become a part thereof," that the convention ratified the Constitution "in the name, and in the behalf of the people, of the state of Rhode Island."

Then followed twenty-one recommended amendments. The first came verbatim from Article II of the Articles of Confederation: "The United States shall guarantee to each state its sovereignty, freedom, and independence, and every power, jurisdiction, and right, which is not by this Constitution expressly delegated to the United States." The second would have made Congress' power over elections contingent upon a state's neglect or refusal to act. Three and five would have limited the judicial power of the United States. The eighth would have required resort to the requisition system prior to the imposition of direct taxes. The ninth would have required the consent of three-fourths of the state legislatures for any direct taxes. Thirteen and fourteen would have required a two-thirds vote in Congress to borrow money and declare war. Eighteen would have given the state legislatures power of recall over Senators.

XXXIV

The People
Approve Nationhood

SPEAKING in the House of Representatives in 1796, James Madison said that, in spite of how much one might venerate "the body of men who formed our Constitution, the sense of that body could never be regarded as the oracular guide in expounding the Constitution. As the instrument came from them it was nothing more than the draft of a plan, nothing but a dead letter, until life and validity were breathed into it by the voice of the people, speaking through their several state conventions. If we were to look, therefore, for the meaning of the instrument beyond the face of the instrument, we must look for it, not in the general convention, which proposed, but in the state conventions, which accepted and ratified the Constitution."

Madison's statement has been largely disregarded. The debates in the federal convention and the discussions in the *Federalist Papers* have been accorded far more weight in constitutional interpretation than have the debates in the state conventions. And yet on the subject of state sovereignty as affected by the Constitution the debates of the state conventions are the most important source for a clear and explicit understanding of the people of the time.

Literally dozens of specific criticisms were made against the Constitution by the opponents of ratification. Most of these coalesce into two broad and fundamental grounds of objection. One was the absence of a Bill of Rights; if the power of the new national government was to be exercised directly upon individuals, then, it was argued, limitations upon that power should be expressly set forth so as to protect certain individual liberties from destruction or infringement. Second was the belief that the Constitution would inevitably result in the complete destruction of state sovereignty and the reduction of state power to insignificance. It is in terms of this second seminal ground of opposition to the Constitution that the state convention debates have been set forth here in relevant extracts.

One outstanding fact is that state sovereignty received a much more vigorous, solid defense in the state conventions than in the federal convention. Indeed, one cannot fail to be impressed by the narrow margin of victory for the forces of ratification in several of the state conventions. The vote in Massachusetts was 187 to 168, in New Hampshire 57 to 47, in Virginia 89 to 79, in New York 30 to 27, and in Rhode Island 34 to 32. A change of twenty-six votes in these five states—ten in Massachusetts, six in New Hampshire and Virginia, and two in New York and Rhode Island—and the Constitution would have been defeated. In spite of these close divisions on ratification, there was remarkably broad agreement between Anti-federalists and Federalists on how the Constitution would affect state sovereignty.

The Anti-federalists frequently made the blanket charge that the Constitution would result in a "consolidated" government. Probably no more than a few of the men who used the term actually believed that the states would be literally obliterated as geographical and political entities. But the Federalists would invariably reply to the charge of "consolidation" by pointing to the many ways in which the structure of the national government assumed and was predicated on the continued, vital existence of the states. This answer was not, of course, responsive to what most of the Anti-federalists had in mind: that the powers of the national government would be so great as to reduce the states to a position of complete and impotent subordination. The belief and fear which underlay the charge of "consolidation" was not that the Constitution would abolish the states as such, but that it would destroy their sovereignty.

When the general charge was reduced to particulars, there was usually little disagreement as to the potential scope and extent of the Constitution's grants of power to the national government. When the Anti-federalists charged that a national power was unlimited, the Federalists did not usually deny that this was true as a matter of law, but they argued that, for various reasons, the power in practice would not be carried to its ultimate. Thus, Congress' power to control the time, place, and manner of elections of Representatives and Senators was opposed as being so broad as to permit Congress to practically exclude the states from any control in this area. The answer of the Federalists was not to deny the charge but to assert that Congress probably would not exercise the power at all unless it became necessary to protect its own existence, that is, unless the states failed or refused to provide for elections.

Again, to the charge that Congress' taxing power was virtually unlimited and could be used to undermine the taxing power and therefore the political strength of the states, the answer was that the states would enjoy a concurrent power of taxation. And when it was asserted that the absence of limitations would enable Congress to take any or all sources of revenue for federal taxation, the answer was not a denial that this was constitutionally possible but simply that it was necessary for Congress to have the power so as to provide for all possible emergencies, and that it should not be assumed that the power would be abused. The same general pattern is observable in connection with the objections to Congress' military powers and the treaty power as avenues for the invasion of the area of state power.

As to the "necessary and proper" power, the difference between Federalists and Anti-federalists was more semantic than real. This "sweeping clause," according to the opposition, would further expand the powers of the national government to an undefinable extent and thus assimilate all those things which had been, or ought to be, considered as within the province of the states. The Federalists argued, in effect, that the clause was mere tautology, that everything expressly authorized by the clause was impliedly authorized by the express grants. It is important to note that both views recognize the departure from the requirement of the Articles that only expressly granted powers could be exercised. Both views therefore repudiate a strict construction approach to national power.

On other particulars vitally important to the question of state sovereignty as opposed to national supremacy, opponents and supporters of the Constitution were in agreement. The Anti-federalists complained that the supremacy clause would reduce all the state constitutions and state laws to a position inferior to the U.S. Constitution, national laws, and treaties. The Federalists replied that that was exactly what the clause was intended to do, and that this function was essential. The Anti-federalists asserted that the Constitution in its most important provisions was ambiguous and general. The Federalists answered that it was as plain and clear as the subject matter permitted.

The Anti-federalists charged that this generality and ambiguity opened the way to a loose construction, expanding national power at the expense of state power; that the Constitution would invariably favor national power, since the national government had the power to construe its own powers. The Federalists replied that it should not be assumed that the Constitution would be construed improperly or unfairly. It was true that the power of interpretation was in the national government, but it was necessarily so in order to assure its supremacy.

The Anti-federalists charged that the judicial power of the United States courts was so great as to overwhelm the state judiciaries and further consolidate all power in the national government. It was necessary, the Federalists replied, that the judicial power of the United States should be coextensive with the legislative power in order to assure national supremacy. It should not be assumed the federal courts would exercise powers beyond their proper extent, and in any case, there would still be plenty of litigation to keep the state courts busy.

The Anti-federalists complained again and again of the lack of a clearcut dividing line between national and state power to prevent encroachments on the states. The Federalists replied that, under the proper rule of construction, the national government would have only those powers expressly delegated to it or fairly implied therefrom, and that all other powers would be reserved to the states. The Anti-federalists countered that the Constitution required no such rule of construction, and there was no assurance it would be followed after ratification. In any event, it was no real answer to the objection, for such a rule of construction imposed no limitation on the extent to which a delegated power could be carried by interpretation nor on what national powers could be derived by implication.

The Federalists maintained that the broad dividing line was between matters of national and matters of local importance, but they offered no formula for distinguishing the two. They also asserted that the federal judiciary would have the power to invalidate acts of Congress which transcended its powers, but this again raised the objection that the national government was construing its own powers and, further, it was no limitation of the expansion of judicial power. Finally, the Federalists sought to minimize the importance of the objection by invoking the doctrine of popular sovereignty. Both national and state governments were the recipients of power granted by the people, so what real difference did it make which government exercised the power? The people were supreme in either case.

When the Anti-federalists thus lamented the lack of *constitutional* limitations on the powers of the national government to keep it from overwhelming the state governments, the main answer of the Federalists was to point to those features of the Constitution which afforded *political* limitation on the *exercise* of the national powers. The bi-cameral Congress in which each house, representing a different constituency, had to approve all laws, was one such political check. Repeatedly the Senate was characterized as the agency created for the express purpose of representing the states as entities in the national government, thereby affording them a means of protecting their sovereignty. The executive power of veto was another check.

Repeatedly, too, the Federalists asserted that members of Congress, being elected in the states, would be attached to state and local interests. The desire for re-election would ever make them responsive to state and local attitudes and opinions. The existence of the state legislatures as watchful guardians and articulate organs of protest was another political fact of life. The real danger, the Federalists claimed, was not that the rights and powers of the states would not be respected; it was that national powers would be vitiated and national interests ignored.

It is no coincidence that those aspects of the Constitution which were attacked most strenuously in the conventions were the favorite subjects of the recommended amendments. Four states—Delaware, New Jersey, Georgia, and Connecticut—ratified without proposing amendments. In two states—Pennsylvania and Maryland—attempts to recommend amendments were defeated. Amendments were recommended by the conventions in Massachusetts, South Carolina, New Hampshire, Virginia, New York, North Carolina, and Rhode Island.

Of these seven states, six conventions recommended an amendment which would reserve to the states all powers not delegated to the United States. Four of these referred to powers not "expressly" delegated. In New York one of the "understandings" on which ratification was based was that all powers not "clearly" delegated were reserved. All seven conventions recommended an amendment making Congress' power over elections conditional on state refusal or neglect to act. All seven conventions wanted an amendment limiting Congress' power to lay direct taxes by requiring prior resort to state requisitions. Six conventions recommended limitations of various kinds on the judicial power of the United States. Five conventions recommended amendments imposing various limitations on the military powers of Congress. The commerce power, the borrowing power, and the treaty power were subjects of recommended amendments in two states each. One state wanted an amendment providing for state recall of Senators.

Two important conclusions may be drawn from the recommendation of these amendments. First, they were in no sense conditions upon the ratification of the Constitution in any state. Efforts were made in the conventions to make adoption of the amendments a condition precedent to the taking effect of the ratification, but this was recognized as equivalent to a rejection of the Constitution as it stood, and such efforts were defeated. This issue was well understood and fully articulated by both sides. The records leave no room for doubt that the Constitution was ratified unconditionally in every state and that the amendments were recommendations only.

Second, the fact that amendments limiting national power in favor of state power were considered to be necessary or desirable clearly demonstrates the understanding in the conventions that, without the amendments, there would be no such limitations. The conclusion, although superficially self-evident, is amply supported by the debates. The mere recommendation of amendments was in no sense conceived to be a diminution of the national powers but rather a recognition and measure of the scope of those powers in the Constitution as it was drafted and ratified. Any limitation on the national powers granted in the original Constitution could be determined only by reference to the amendments which were actually adopted after the Constitution was ratified. It may not be amiss to note that the Tenth Amendment is the only one of the amendments adopted immediately after ratification which dealt with the question of national and state power. In the Tenth Amendment Congress consciously and intentionally omitted the word "expressly" in referring to the powers delegated to the United States, for the very purpose of permitting the use of implied powers and thus preventing a repetition of the experience under the Articles.

What was the understanding in the conventions as to the finality of the choice which was being made? All evidence supports the conclusion that ratification was considered to be permanent and irrevocable. It was explicitly so recognized in the *Letters of a Federal Farmer* and the *Letters of Agrippa* by the Anti-federalists Richard Henry Lee and James Winthrop, and also by James Madison in his letter to the New York convention. The New York convention at the end rejected a motion by Lansing which would have reserved the right of New York to withdraw from the Union unless amendments were submitted to a general convention. Indeed, the whole idea of amendments is inconsistent with the idea that a state could withdraw from the Union at will.

It should also be noted that no ratification resolution contains such a reservation. One of New York's "understandings" was that "the powers of government may be reassumed by the people, whensoever it shall become necessary to their happiness," and a like statement was made by the Rhode Island convention. Virginia was more explicit. That state's convention declared that "the powers granted under the Constitution being derived from the people of the United States may be resumed by them whensoever the same shall be perverted to their injury or oppression." No state convention declared any such power of resumption by a state or even by the people of a state.

One final point of agreement remains to be noted. The Antifederalists opposed the Constitution because it destroyed the kind of government which they cherished, namely, a confederation of sovereign states. The Federalists did not deny that this was so; rather, they defended the necessity and desirability of the change. The Constitution was characterized by many delegates as an ordinance of the American people. But not a single delegate in a single state convention maintained that the Constitution was a compact between sovereign states. On this point the understanding was unanimous.

Part Five:
A Perspective on State Sovereignty

UNDER Article II of the Articles of Confederation, each state retained its sovereignty and independence and every power, jurisdiction, and right which was not expressly delegated to the United States. This precluded the existence of any implied powers. The powers which were expressly delegated to Congress were limited, but even for these there was no power of enforcement. The central government, with rare exceptions, operated not on individuals but through the states, and its authority was effective only as far as, and no farther than, the states were willing to accept it. The states remained free to ignore the central government with impunity, which they did, in spite of their pledged word in Article XIII that they would abide by the determination of Congress on all matters delegated to it. Under the Articles there existed in America a compact of sovereign states with a mutual agent. And history records that it was a failure.

Throughout the states there were men of prominence who were determined, for reasons sufficient to themselves, to eradicate this system. Being individuals of surpassing political skill and ability, and aided by the course of events under the Articles, these men brought about the calling of the Constitutional Convention of 1787 and dominated its membership. The fundamental purpose of the convention was to change the system. The Founding Fathers decided at the outset that no mere federation would suffice. Instead, they created a national government which would operate directly on individuals, gave it vastly increased sweeping powers, and created a national executive and a national judiciary for their enforcement. Severe limitations were placed on the powers of the states, and the supremacy of the central government over the states was clearly and expressly set forth. With deliberate intent and great care, the Founders remedied the defects of the system under the Articles. And because it was recognized that the Constitution was fatal to the sovereignty of the states, they by-passed the state governments and went directly to the people for rati-fication of the great transition. There was no misunderstanding as to the effect that the Constitution would have upon state sovereignty, for in the campaign for ratification one of the principal bases of opposition to the Constitution was that it would destroy the sovereignty of the states.

Even after 180 years, the nationalism of the Founding Fathers is startling. That they were able in the 1780's to replace the Articles with the Constitution must be recognized as one of the great political achievements in history. Years later Chief Justice Marshall was to refer to the adoption of the Constitution as a "great revolution." And so it was, a constitutional revolution achieved by men with a vision of a great nation and endowed with the political ability to create legiti-mately the document and the government which made the nation pos-sible.

Study of the contemporary sources reveals that among both the sup-porters and opponents of the Constitution there was no doubt, disagree-ment, or misunderstanding on the following particulars. Ratification of the Constitution was final and irrevocable, and no right of seces-sion from the United States was contemplated. The power to determine constitutional meaning and applicability lay with the instrumentalities of the national government. In making such determinations there was no expectation that any strict construction in favor of state power would be followed. Although national powers were enumerated, state power was not expected to be a constitutional limitation on the scope or extent of any enumerated national power. While there was no inten-tion to create a national government of unlimited power, it is clear that the limitations were not to be imposed by considerations of state sovereignty. Rather, they were to be ascertained by reference to spe-cific prohibitions designed to protect individual liberty. The demand for a Bill of Rights was created by failure of the Constitution to ex-pressly put certain personal freedoms beyond national power.

It is obvious, however, from even a cursory view of American consti-tutional history since 1789, that the ratification of the Constitution did not settle these matters permanently, or even for very long. As noted at the very outset of this book, the Constitution had only just been adopted when the argument was advanced that since the states were sovereign under the Articles, they were still sovereign except to the extent that sovereignty had been expressly surrendered in the Constitution. Therefore national powers should be strictly and narrowly construed. It was argued then that the Tenth Amendment supported the strict construction approach—and the same argument is still advanced today.

Later a more vigorous position was taken. The admission made during the ratification campaign that the Constitution was fatal to state sovereignty was conveniently forgotten, and men affected to discover that it was an idle thing which had been done after all: the system of government under the Constitution was still what it had been under the Articles of Confederation—a compact of sovereign states. From this premise there flowed logically the doctrines of state interposition and nullification articulated by John C. Calhoun, the brilliant pre-Civil War high priest of state sovereignty. Finally, there came the most radical assertion of all. Since the Union was merely a compact of sovereign states, it followed that there was no such thing as a permanent and indivisible nation. Therefore, by the same process through which it ratified the Constitution and entered the Union in the first place—i.e., an exercise of popular sovereignty—a state could likewise secede from the United States.

It may be stated flatly that none of these doctrines—strict construction of the Constitution, interposition or nullification, and secession—can find support from the contemporary sources on the drafting and ratification of the Constitution. Beyond a few scattered passages taken out of context, the evidence of 1787-1788 is overwhelming against each of these subsequent theories. And yet it is undeniable that these doctrines have had an enormous impact upon American history. They have been compelling issues over which men have argued, fought, and died. How could it happen that doctrines so demonstrably untenable could have attained such vitality?

It is true that Elliot's *Debates* were not published until 1836 and Madison's *Notes* not until 1840. From this circumstance of publication, it might be suggested that state sovereignty doctrines flourished because their documentary refutation remained undisclosed for fifty years after ratification. But this explanation is both superficial and erroneous. It is erroneous because the philosophical and political advocates of the state sovereignty doctrines were participants in, or at least contemporaries of, the drafting and ratification of the Constitution and hence were fully aware of the understanding at the time. One need go no further than Madison and Jefferson who, less than ten years after the Constitution became operative, were authors of the Virginia and Kentucky Resolutions setting forth a compact theory of the Constitution. In Madison's case, considering the extent of his nationalism in 1787, this is one of the most complete turnabouts in history.

But any explanation is superficial which fails to take into account the fact that men of affairs almost invariably espouse those philosophies, forms, and policies of government under which they feel that cherished values, interests, and goals—public and private—will be best advanced and protected. As the first part of this book suggests, the nationalists who were defeated in 1776 did not accept the result as irremediable. Similarly, the opponents of strong central government in 1787, while they accepted ratification of the Constitution as final, did not accept as inevitable in practice the fulfillment of that national power of which the Constitution was the promise. What they did was completely natural. They engaged in political action to restrain and limit the use of national power, and they advanced interpretations of the Constitution which would protect the power of the states against national aggrandizement.

In their political struggle, advocates of the state sovereignty doctrines found their principal source of strength and support in the circumstance to which Madison and Hamilton had repeatedly called attention. This was the political fact that the people as a general rule would feel closer to their state and local governments and more remote from the national government. Since members of Congress were to be elected by local constituencies, it was maintained that the men elected to these offices would carry with them into national office a tendency or predisposition to favor state over national power. And survival in office would frequently demand giving precedence to parochial and provincial over national and general interests.

Time has demonstrated the acuteness of Madison's and Hamilton's perception. Throughout our history, far more often than not, Congress has been very sensitive to state interests and to areas and subjects of state power. Such political considerations have frequently resulted in the non-use of national powers. This has been true even to the point of reducing some national powers to dormancy. Congress' power to control the manner of election of Representatives and Senators has never been utilized to any great extent, and even the modest exercise of this power proposed in recent years has been bitterly attacked as an invasion of states rights. To give another example, Congress' powers under the "full faith and credit" clause remain to this day virtually untapped.

In their constitutional struggle, the defenders of state sovereignty were immensely aided by the very characteristic of the Constitution against which they had vigorously protested in the ratification campaign: its generality and ambiguity. All hands in 1787-1788 recognized that the Constitution's generalities opened the way to indefinite augmentation of national power through latitudinal construction. Indeed, the main defense of the Constitution's generality was that it would permit whatever national action the future exigencies of an unknown future might demand. But, by definition, ambiguity means the capability of supporting more than one meaning or interpretation. If the Constitution could support an interpretation that favored national power, it could also support a construction that favored state power. And so began the perennial debate between "liberal" and "strict" construction through which contests between national and state power have been waged ever since, each side claiming that its interpretation of the Constitution is the "true" one.

Adherents of the state sovereignty doctrines soon found another ally in their struggle—again through one of the features of the Constitution against which they had levied severe strictures. This ally was the federal judiciary, and especially the United States Supreme Court. The establishment of judicial review—the power to interpret the Constitution with finality and to invalidate acts contrary to that interpretation—provided the advocates of state sovereignty with the device through which their views could be given legal efficacy. Although judicial review was established by a relatively nationalist-minded Marshall Court, it was put to far different uses in the century following Marshall's death.

It is true that the Supreme Court never yielded to state sovereignty doctrines in their advanced forms—nullification, interposition, and secession. But the Court did, on many occasions and as recently as 1936, accept the doctrine of strict construction of the Constitution against national power and in favor of state power. What came to be known as "dual sovereignty" was, in essence, no more than a judgment that the existence of state power was in and of itself a limitation on the scope of national power. The doctrine that national powers were enumerated, and that those not enumerated were reserved to the states, served as sufficient reason for a narrow interpretation of the enumerated powers. State autonomy was elevated to state sovereignty by judicial construction. And if there were also decisions which applied the contrary construction, it only served to underscore the power of the Court and the importance of having a majority on the side one preferred.

The facility with which men could find in the amorphous language of the Constitution approval and sanction of their own political and economic philosophies prompted John Adams, at an early date in our history, to declare that "I have always called our Constitution a game at leap frog." American constitutional history from John Adams' day to mid-twentieth-century America amply demonstrates the truth of his observation. The listing of great nationalist decisions by the Supreme Court could be paralleled by a similar catalog of decisions favoring states rights.

And yet there is reason to believe that the final leap may have been taken, so far as constitutional law is concerned. The compact theory of the Constitution and the state sovereignty doctrines which flowed from it were abandoned after the Civil War and may today be considered extinct, despite recent abortive attempts to revive them in various interposition resolutions adopted by southern legislatures. And the strict construction approach to the Constitution may well have received the final and lethal blow in the Supreme Court's recognition in 1941 that the Tenth Amendment merely declares a relationship and hence does not substantively limit national power.

Modern society increasingly makes the exercise of national power imperative, and the allegiance of the people to the national government increases commensurately with their expectations and demands. Strict construction thus loses the support of public opinion. It is inconceivable to imagine ever again Supreme Court decisions comparable to those of 1935 and 1936. Even the polemics of southern Senators in the field of civil rights have for many years lacked real conviction that national power is inadequate to the purpose. In the future, the distribution of power between nation and state will continue to be a political and a legislative question, as it always has been. But it is doubtful if ever again it will be a constitutional and a judicial question as it has been in the past. Future debates over the respective roles and functions of nation and states will increasingly turn on questions of policy rather than power.

This book has been an inquiry into the dialectics of original intent on the question of the relationship and the distribution of power between the national government and the states under the Constitution. The contemporary understanding of the men who drafted the Constitution and the men who supported and opposed its ratification has been set forth in the preceding parts of the study. The validity of the conclusions seems clear beyond doubt. In one sense, of course, any inquiry into original intent is futile, for it is true that, in the final analysis, the actions of men, including their interpretations of the Constitution, are determined more by the demands and desiderata of the present than by the understandings of the past. It is also true that the intent and understanding of 1787-1788 were almost immediately challenged, and have subsequently been denied, confused, submerged, and even lost at times throughout our history.

The fact that original intent lacks the power to control later action does not, however, render inquiries into original intent irrelevant. Throughout our history, justification has always been sought for conflicting constitutional interpretations in terms of original intent. Men prefer to defend their positions not only on grounds of the expediency of the moment but also in terms of historic legitimacy. So long as there is constitutional debate, it seems inevitable that original intent will be a part of the rhetoric. Knowledge on the subject is therefore necessary for forensic purposes at least.

The author feels, however, that there is a larger and more fundamental value to be derived from this study. It is trite to observe that the national government today exercises greater and more pervasive powers than ever before in our history. Of course, there never has been and never can be a permanently fixed number of public functions or subjects of power, with clearly established and mutually exclusive lists of what is national and what is state or local. In a complex and interdependent industrial society, it is a commonplace that what was local yesterday has today assumed dimensions and effects which transcend state boundary lines. Much of the increased activity of the national government in this century has resulted from the fact that modern society generates problems which are beyond the capacity of individual states to control The trend seems likely to accelerate rather than to abate.

On the other hand, it becomes increasingly evident that convenience and practicality frequently require the involvement and assistance of state and local governments in the administration of nationally determined programs. Furthermore, while many erstwhile local matters have become national, our dynamic society is constantly generating new problems which can be best handled, initially at least, on a local basis. Indeed, the demands on state and local government frequently exceed the resources available to meet them. It seems unlikely that these political units will atrophy for want of important business. If they have the will to do so, state and local authorities can assure themselves of a vital role in the governing of America.

The same Americans who accept the necessity of an increased centralization of authority in order to cope with the problems of today's world often have feelings of misgiving and disquietude. Although events and circumstances make increased national activity imperative, many persons are apprehensive that we are departing from the original grand design of the Constitution, that although the increased exercise of national power can be justified on grounds of expediency, it nevertheless lacks historic legitimacy.

Speaking in the Constitutional Convention, James Madison said:

> The great objection made against an abolition of the state governments was that the general government could not extend its care to all the minute objects which fall under the cognizance of the local jurisdictions. The objection as stated lay not against the probable abuse of the general power but against the imperfect use that could be made of it throughout so great an extent of country, and over so great a variety of objects. As far as its operation would be practicable, it could not in this view be improper; as far as it could be impracticable, the conveniency of the general government itself would concur with that of the people in the maintenance of subordinate governments. Were it practicable for the general government to extend its care to every requisite object without the cooperation of the state government, the people would not be less free as members of one great republic than as members of thirteen small ones.

The states have never since 1787 been in any danger of being abolished. The historic contest has been waged over questions of the respective sovereignty and power of nation and state. After 170 years we seem finally to have settled on the approach originally advanced by Madison.

The state sovereignty of the Articles was extinguished and replaced by the state autonomy of the Constitution. Although the *existence* of state power is not a *constitutional* limitation upon the *scope* of national power, the responsible *exercise* of state power can operate, in many areas, as a *political* limitation on the *use* of national power. Remembering that the Constitution was grounded on the Virginia plan of which James Madison was the author, the words of the "father of the Constitution" in his letter to Washington on the eve of the convention have modern relevance: "Conceiving that an individual independence of the states is utterly irreconcilable with their aggregate sovereignty, and that a consolidation of the whole into one simple republic would be as inexpedient as it is unattainable, I have sought for some middle ground, which may at once support a due supremacy of the national authority, and not exclude the local authorities wherever they can be subordinately useful."

There has been no departure from our ancient moorings. The Constitution was "intended to endure for ages to come, and consequently, to be adapted to the various crises of human affairs." The grand design has not been abandoned. It is continually being fulfilled.

BIBLIOGRAPHICAL NOTE

A STUDY of any period in American constitutional history may profitably begin with the general treatises. Valuable primarily for their factual material rather than for interpretation are the nineteenth-century standard works of George Bancroft, *History of the Formation of the Constitution of the United States*, 2 vols. (New York, 1882), and George Ticknor Curtis, *History of the Origin, Formation and Adoption of the Constitution*, 2 vols. (New York, 1854-1858). The modern treatises which I found most helpful are Andrew C. McLaughlin, *A Constitutional History of the United States* (New York, 1935); Homer C. Hockett, *The Constitutional History of the United States*, 2 vols. (New York, 1939); and A. H. Kelly and W. A. Harbison, *The American Constitution* (New York, 1948). Much of the factual data throughout this book is drawn from these five sources, which, like many other works cited herein, embrace the Revolutionary and Confederation periods, the convention, and the ratification campaigns.

The portion of Chapter One dealing with the drafting of the Articles of Confederation, including the quotations, has been taken largely from E. C. Burnett, *Letters of the Members of the Continental Congress*, 8 vols. (Washington, 1921-1936), and *The Continental Congress* (New York, 1941). The summary of the career of Thomas Burke is based on accounts in the *Dictionary of American Biography* and *The Encyclopedia Americana*. Unfortunately, there is no published biographical study of this interesting man. Merrill Jensen, *The Articles of Confederation* (Madison, 1940), the best detailed account of the drafting of the Articles, is basic for interpretation. The Confederation period itself is best covered in Andrew C. McLaughlin, *The Confederation and the Constitution* (New York, 1905); Allan Nevins, *The American States During and After the Revolution* (New York, 1924); and Merrill Jensen, *The New Nation* (New York, 1950). Articles which were especially helpful in the preparation of Part One are Claude H. Van Tyne, "Sovereignty in the American Revolution: An Historical Study," *American Historical Review*, XII (1907); Edward S. Corwin, "The Progress of Constitutional Theory Between the Declaration of Independence and the

Meeting of the Philadelphia Convention," *American Historical Review,* XXX (1925); and Merrill Jensen, "The Idea of a National Government during the American Revolution," *Political Science Quarterly,* LVIII (1943). An excellent discussion of the national sovereignty point of view may be found in Irving Brant, *"E pluribus,"* Chap. XVIII in *James Madison: Virginia Revolutionist* (Indianapolis, 1941). (The Appendix, "American Nationhood during the Revolution," is a collection of quotations from writings by Madison's contemporaries.)

Passages from the letters of Washington, Madison, and Hamilton are taken from J. C. Fitzpatrick, ed., *The Writings of George Washington,* 39 vols. (Washington, 1931-1944); Gaillard Hunt, ed., *The Writings of James Madison,* 9 vols. (New York, 1910); Harold C. Syrett and Jacob E. Cooke, eds., *The Papers of Alexander Hamilton,* 7 vols. to date (New York, 1961-).

The biographical data in Part Two are taken largely from the *Dictionary of American Biography* and Fred T. Wilson, *Our Constitution and Its Makers* (New York, 1937). Washington's role is discussed by Max Farrand in "George Washington in the Federal Convention," *Yale Review,* XVI (1907). Biographies of several of the delegates from which quotations in Part Two have been taken are Richard Barry, *Mr. Rutledge of South Carolina* (New York, 1942); Gertrude S. Wood, *William Paterson of New Jersey* (Fair Lawn, N.J., 1933); Sister Mary V. Geiger, *Daniel Carroll: A Framer of the Constitution* (Washington, 1943); and C. R. King, *The Life and Correspondence of Rufus King,* 6 vols. (New York, 1894-1900). An excellent biography is Irving Brant, *James Madison,* 6 vols. (Indianapolis, 1941-1961). (Especially valuable for the subject of my study were the volumes in Brant's work entitled *The Nationalist, 1780-1787* and *Father of the Constitution, 1787-1800.*) Other biographies which were helpful are Roger S. Boardman, *Roger Sherman; Signer and Statesman* (Philadelphia, 1938); William G. Brown, *The Life of Oliver Ellsworth* (New York, 1905); George C. Groce, *William Samuel Johnson: A Maker of the Constitution* (New York, 1937); John C. Miller, *Alexander Hamilton: Portrait in Paradox* (New York, 1959); and Charles P. Smith, *James Wilson: Founding Father* (Chapel Hill, 1956). An excellent analysis is Clinton Rossiter, *Alexander Hamilton and the Constitution* (New York, 1964). The data on the composition of the convention at the beginning of Part Three is drawn from Wilson's *Our Constitution and its Makers* and from Clinton Rossiter, *1787: The Grand Convention* (New York, 1966). An illuminating discussion of the motives and purposes of the framers is Stanley Elkins and Eric Mc-

Kitrick, "The Founding Fathers: Young Men of the Revolution," *Political Science Quarterly*, LXXVI (1961).

The most complete notes of the convention debates were kept by James Madison. Fragmentary notes were kept by Robert Yates, Rufus King, James McHenry, William Pierce, William Paterson, Alexander Hamilton, Charles Pinckney, and George Mason. The definitive compilation of the materials is Max Farrand, *The Records of the Federal Convention*, rev. ed., 4 vols. (New Haven, 1937). Vols. I and II contain the convention notes, Vol. III consists of correspondence concerning the convention, and Vol. IV contains corrections and additions, together with comprehensive indices of the debates by subject matter, specific article and section numbers, and delegates. In Parts Two and Three, unless otherwise indicated, all quotations are taken from these volumes, and all quotations from the debates are from Madison's notes. Volume and page number footnotes are omitted because of the ease with which any quotation can be located through the appropriate index.

Other documentary materials which have been of assistance are *Documentary History of the Constitution of the United States of America*, 5 vols. (Washington, 1894-1905); *Documents Illustrative of the Formation of the Union of the American States*, House Doc. 398, 69th Cong. 1st Sess. (1927); Arthur T. Prescott, *Drafting the Federal Constitution* (University, La., 1941); and W. U. Solberg, ed., *The Federal Convention and the Formation of the Union of the American States* (New York, 1958).

The convention itself has inspired a voluminous literature. The best accounts, in my judgment, are Max Farrand, *The Framing of the Constitution* (New Haven, 1913); Robert L. Schuyler, *The Constitution of the United States* (New York, 1923); Charles Warren, *The Making of the Constitution* (Cambridge, 1928); and Carl Van Doren, *The Great Rehearsal* (New York, 1948). The most recent, and perhaps the best and most readable account to date, is Clinton Rossiter's *1787: The Grand Convention*. An especially perceptive and lively article is John P. Roche's "The Founding Fathers: A Reform Caucus In Action," *American Political Science Review*, LV (1961).

In Part Four the literature opposing and supporting the Constitution, and all quotations therefrom, are taken from P. L. Ford, ed., *Pamphlets on the Constitution of the United States* (Brooklyn, 1888), and *Essays on the Constitution of the United States* (Brooklyn, 1892). There are so many editions of *The Federalist Papers* available that it seems practical to indicate only the papers from which the quotations are taken. Of the papers written by Hamilton, I have drawn on Nos. 15, 16, 17, 20, 21, 22, 23, 26, 28, 31, 32, 33, 34, 78, 80, and 81. Of the papers written by Madison, I have drawn on Nos. 14, 37, 39, 40, 41, 42, 43, 44, 45, 46, 53, 54, and 62.

Only fragmentary records exist of the debates in the various state ratification conventions. These are collected in Jonathan Eliot, ed., *The Debates in the Several State Conventions on the Adoption of the Federal Constitution*, 2nd ed., 5 vols. (Philadelphia, 1876). Studies of the ratification in particular states which I have used are Frank G. Bates, *Rhode Island and the Formation of the Union* (New York, 1898); H. B. Grigsby, *The History of the Virginia Federal Convention* (Richmond, 1890-1891); Samuel B. Harding, *The Contest over the Ratification of the Federal Constitution in the State of Massachusetts* (New York, 1896); J. B. McMaster and F. D. Stone, *Pennsylvania and the Federal Constitution, 1787-1788* (Philadelphia, 1942); C. E. Miner, *The Ratification of the Federal Constitution by the State of New York* (New York, 1921); B. C. Steiner, "Maryland's Adoption of the Federal Constitution," *American Historical Review*, V (1900); and Louise Trenholme, *The Ratification of the Federal Constitution in North Carolina* (New York, 1932). Linda G. DePauw, *The Eleventh Pillar: New York State and the Federal Constitution* (Ithaca, 1966), was published after my manuscript was completed. The ratification process is the subject of Robert A. Rutland, *The Ordeal of the Constitution* (Norman, Okla., 1966). The basis of the opposition to the Constitution is ably discussed in Jackson T. Main, *The Antifederalists* (Chapel Hill, 1961) and Cecelia Kenyon, "Men of Little Faith: The Anti-federalists on the Nature of Representative Government," *William and Mary Quarterly*, XII (1955).

The above sources are certainly not exhaustive but are only those from which I derived the most assistance. Readers who wish a more extensive bibliography will find an excellent one in Rossiter, *1787: The Grand Convention*.

INDEX

A NOTE ON THE AUTHOR

William P. Murphy was born and grew up in Memphis. He received his B.A. degree from Southwestern College, his LL.B. from the University of Virginia, and his J.S.D. from Yale. He was forced to leave the University of Mississippi Law School in 1962 because of his defense of Supreme Court decisions and his attitude on the state sovereignty question. He is now Professor of Law at the University of Missouri, where he teaches constitutional law and labor law.